THE FILMS OF

Carbondale and Edwardsville

William J. Palmer

THE EIGHTIES

A Social History

Southern Illinois University Press

Printed in the United States of America

Edited by Teresa White

Designed by David Ford

Production supervised by Natalia Nadraga

96 95 94 93   4 3 2 1

Library of Congress Cataloging-in-Publication Data
Palmer, William J., 1943–
    The films of the eighties : a social history / William J. Palmer.
       p.   cm.
    Includes bibliographical references and index.
    1. Motion pictures—Social aspects—United States.   I. Title.
PN1995.9.S6P33   1993
302.23′43′097309048—dc20   92-33720
ISBN 0-8093-1837-7   CIP

The paper used in this publication meets the minimum requirements of
American National Standard for Information Sciences—Permanence of
Paper for Printed Library Materials, ANSI Z39.48-1984. ∞

This book is dedicated to Maryann

Contents

Illustrations   viii

Preface   ix

1   The Holograph of History   1

2   The Vietnam War as Film Text   16

3   The "Coming Home" Films   61

4   The Terrorism Film Texts   114

5   The Nuclear War Film Texts   179

6   From the "Evil Empire" to *Glasnost*   206

7   The Feminist Farm Crisis and Other Neoconservative Feminist Texts   246

8   The Yuppie Texts   280

9   Film in the Holograph of New History   308

Notes   313

Index   325

Illustrations

FOLLOWING PAGE 164

Casualties of War

Braddock: Missing in Action III

Mike Shelton editorial cartoon

Brazil

Colors

Robocop

No Way Out

Russkies

Steel Magnolias

Gorillas in the Mist

Bright Lights, Big City

Troop Beverly Hills

The 'burbs

Baby Boom

Preface

IT IS FITTING that *The Films of the Eighties: A Social History* should be a sequel to a book with the identical title about the seventies. Sequels—from *Superman* to *Star Wars* to *Rocky* and *Rambo* to *Indiana Jones* and *Beverly Hills Cop* to *Halloween* and *Friday the 13th* to *Mad Max* and *Lethal Weapon*—ruled the film offerings of the eighties. The films of the eighties, however, were simply mirroring the fact that the decade itself, in its social history, was a sequel. Call it *The Fifties II*. Billy Joel's popular song of 1989, "We Didn't Start the Fire," a flashcard social history of America from the fifties to the eighties, sums up this reduplication of history.

In both the fifties and the eighties, eight years of the American presidency were occupied by a smiling, grandfatherly figure who communicated very little very well while vigorously doing nothing as the country looked on in smiling acceptance. Both decades politically embraced the ascendancy of style over substance. The striking similarity of the Eisenhower and Reagan administrations and their attendant personality cults notwithstanding, those two decades bear the burdens of quite similar social histories as well.

Both had the previous decade's war to remember and get over. Except for brush-fire wars of short duration, compared with World War II and Vietnam, both decades enjoyed peace attended by cold war manuevering against Russia. Both were acutely nuclear holocaust conscious: the fifties in the first glow of the atomic age, and the eighties in the final realization that the fate of the earth (to purloin Jonathan Schell's title) rested in, first, the "freezing" and, then, the "disarming" of the nuclear arsenals of the world's major powers. Over the course of both decades, America and Russia continuously confronted one another. Eisenhower's fifties had Joseph McCarthy and the U-2 spy plane incident, while Reagan indulged early in his "evil empire" rhetorical saber rattling. Ironically in the eighties, as America and Russia confronted each other and jockeyed for position, Japan moved in and claimed the spoils of victory.

In the domestic arena, America in the fifties saw new beginnings of political consciousness focused upon the issues of sexual (in the aftermath of the World War II "Rosie the Riveter" women's liberation) and racial (in the dawnings of the civil rights movement) equality, while in the eighties feminism reached its maturity and the first necessity to combat a "new racism" arose. The fifties decade began a change in the American land-scape as Levittown signaled the exodus from urban enclosure and the creation of a suburban middle ground embracing the values of small-town America. The split-level yuppie housing developments of the eighties realized the dark side of that suburban dream as all of the problems of the cities (homelessness, drugs, disease, crime, racism) seemed to be moving outward and infecting small-town America. The major issues of American social history of both decades were strikingly similar and were explored and disseminated to a mass audience through the movies.

In fact, one notable trend of both the films of the seventies and of the eighties was their nostalgic attraction to fifties and sixties events, issues, and social mores. James Greenberg describes how in the Reaganite-yuppie eighties, "Hollywood went for the Fifties where kids only wanted the right to drink and drive, not burn their draft cards."[1] Eighties America, Reagan's America, appeared, superficially, to be a safe place, especially in terms of economic stability. Like America in the fifties, eighties America was a "sure-thing society." Taking its cue from Reaganomics, Hollywood opted for the safety of sequels, the belief that if something worked once it will surely continue to work. The decade of the eighties often seemed under the influence of a "Sequel-Librium" that tranquilized it out of most of its impulses toward risk taking, innovation, and imagination. James Woods, one of the untranquilized film actors of the eighties, said near mid-decade, "that's what Sylvester Stallone does, makes the same movie over and over for all that money. I can't do that."[2] But the eighties did do that to the tune of the highest grosses and biggest salaries ever. Nonethe-less, even in many of these sequels, the social issues of the eighties decade were being examined. The mirroring of society is one of the things that films do best.

If, however, *The Films of the Eighties: A Social History* is a sequel to its seventies predecessor, it is also a progress. One of the advantages of writing a sequel is that the scene setting, characterizing, and defining are already on-line, and the sequel can move on directly to more complex theoretical issues. Whereas *The Films of the Seventies: A Social History* defined the basic terms of the relationship between social history and films, this sequel goes further in defining a New Historicist theoretical model for viewing that relationship. This New Historicist "holograph of history" is defined out of the theoretical pronouncements of Michel Foucault, Hayden White, and Dominick LaCapra.

Despite this theoretical progress in the definition of the part film plays in history, *The Films of the Eighties: A Social History* is still very much a sequel, due mainly to the factual carry-over in the issues of the seventies and eighties decades. Some of the major social issues of the eighties, which dictate the chapters of this book, are either carry-overs from, or similar to, the issues and chapters in *The Films of the Seventies: A Social History*. For example, where the Vietnam War was central to the relationship between film and social history in the seventies, it remained so throughout the eighties. Or whereas a prominent chapter in its predecessor defined the major villain of seventies film as a corporate entity, in this eighties film history the ubiquitous villain is the political terrorist.

One of the central polemic concerns of *The Films of the Seventies: A Social History* was that despite the long-standing and consistent charges of the film industry's traditional exploitation of historical fact and realism, Hollywood (a generic term for the film industry) is usually quite reactive and timely in its handling of social history. Since the New Historicists have presented their arguments that historical "fact" is much more complex than conventional historians have portrayed it, and historical "reality" is extremely difficult to re-create and may not even exist, those charges against Hollywood's exploitation of history have been rendered even more moot. Because of the nature of the movie business, not out of any altruistic or socially responsible motives, movies have always shown and explored either directly or metaphorically what was on the mind of the ticket-buying public. *The Films of the Eighties: A Social History* continues that analysis of how film does indeed react to the issues of social history. It examines how, as one layer in a complex multidimensional holograph of history, film history enters into the major debates and issues. Further, it defines the forms, the texts, that the discourse of film takes within that larger discourse of history.

In most instances, film is a reactive analytic text that explores what happened after the historical fact, but in some instances film takes up direct simultaneous participation in the texts of social history and even predicts the directions that social history will ultimately take. If anyone ever had any doubts about the premise that "life imitates art" (in this case, the movies), all one needs to consider is the eighties ending of *The Natural* (which was not Bernard Malamud's book's ending) and the ending of the first game of the 1988 World Series when Kirk Gibson, hobbling on one leg, hit a two-run homer on a 3-and-2 count with two outs in the ninth to win the game.

This book deals with more serious issues—terrorism, détente, nuclear holocaust, racism, yuppieness—than baseball, but at its core is that same point: that Hollywood creates a discourse in clearly defined texts that not only comment perceptively upon contemporary social history but actually participate in it. Thus it is also most fitting that the central figure of eighties social history, Ronald Reagan, was a former film actor who repeatedly employed film images and references to advance his historical goals. In his farewell speech to the Republican National Convention in 1988, for example, the president reprised his most famous film role as he exhorted his successor, Vice-President George Bush, to "go out there and win one for the Gipper." No other president since John F. Kennedy was more conscious of the power of visual imagery than Ronald Reagan. He was a master at using what Hollywood has always known: that the American people are most comfortable in believing and understanding events that they can see. Film images verify and reveal history, and eighties society was acutely aware of that eye-mind relationship. "Film," Graeme Turner writes, "is a social practice for its makers and its audience; in its narratives and meanings we can locate evidence of the ways in which our culture makes sense of itself."[3]

The Films of the Eighties: A Social History, as did its predecessor, unfolds in terms of a constant binary focus. Social history, the major issues, and film history, the representation of those issues in motion pictures, constantly interact as a binary discourse. These two types of texts, historical event and film representation, participate in an interactive relationship. Historical event generates film representation, which accelerates the progress of the original historical event. What results is proof of both film's aesthetic relevance and social history's widening dissemination.

The Films of the Eighties: A Social History's binary discourse of the interaction of social history and film criticism divides into two sections: international issues and domestic issues. The sequel identity of the book both in terms of eighties social history's echoing of the fifties and of the book's continuation of the exploration of issues first opened in its predecessor is most evident in its first section where international issues that impacted upon American society are examined. The Vietnam War, terrorism, the nuclear threat, détente, are all issues that had a profound impact upon the formation of American social history during the decade. Some of these international issues were carry-over issues from both the fifties and the seventies. They either grew in significance in the eighties as the society tried to resolve them (such was the case with Vietnam and détente) or were resurrected from previous decades out of a state of dormancy by the pressure of eighties events (as was the case with the nuclear threat).

The second, domestic, section is much less a sequel, much more eighties distinctive. Issues such as the farm crisis, the new racism, and the yuppie phenomenon exhibit the tenacious contemporaneity of Hollywood in its taking of the pulse of American society. These sections are more specifically located in the American social landscape. Yet the whole book consistently focuses, whether the issue at hand is an international or a domestic one, upon the film representations of those issues as they participated in American culture. Film in the eighties not only bore witness to cultural change but in many instances (such as attitudes toward Vietnam veterans and America/Russia understanding) actually participated in those changes.

In the film industry, from the early seventies on, businessmen have been in control. The period from 1975 (immediately following the success of *Jaws*) to the present has been a cycle in which the creative has been consistently overshadowed by the commercial. This materialist emphasis, stimulated after 1980 by the ascendance of Reaganomics, overshadowed older standards of critical taste and social consciousness. As Steve Randall, senior vice-president of Tri-Star Pictures, makes abundantly clear: "The 12-to-24 audience sells two-thirds of the movie tickets. It's a fact of life, and if we ever forget it, we'll be out of business."[4]

In the eighties, the producer, rather than the director or star actor, took over the media spotlight. Coverage of a major new film focused less upon the film's subject matter and more upon the trials of bringing that film to the screen. It all began in 1978 when Francis Coppola publicized the making of *Apocalypse Now* as a war almost equal to the Vietnam War, which was the subject of the film. Throughout the eighties, sagas of agonizing struggles to bring films to the screen accumulated. While the *Heaven's Gate* and *The Cotton Club* sagas failed miserably, other sagas—*Platoon*, *Born on the Fourth of July*—succeeded in stimulating audience interest.

The eighties, then, was a decade of commercial performance, the yuppie decade in which status was judged almost exclusively in material terms. Though the "Best Sellers" list mentality has ruled the publishing industry for more than half a century, book critics have never taken it very seriously. Strangely, however, in the eighties, the media film criticism fraternity became immediately enchanted by the dance of the box-office numbers. As one critic, Jack Mathews, cynically put it: "In Hollywood, truth is measured in box-office receipts" (*USA Today*, 19 October 1984).

Despite this bottom-line mentality, the aesthetic community within the film industry continued to find viable ways to locate, represent, comment upon, actually influence, and participate in the social history of its time. Over the course of the decade, major sociohistorical issues accumulated referential bodies of films that formed coherent "texts." Other issues—such as the farm crisis or the attempt to understand what happened to a soldier in-country Vietnam—drew pockets of concentrated focus at circumscribed points in the decade.

The eighties in film history actually began with a British invasion. Epic inspirational films—first *Chariots of Fire* (1981) and then *Gandhi* (1982)—won the first two Academy Awards, while other literary films like *The French Lieutenant's Woman* (1981), *Educating Rita* (1983), *A Passage to India* (1984) and *A Room with a View* (1985) seemed to signal an impulse toward the BBC/PBS "Masterpiece Theatre" mode of austere socially distanced moviemaking. With the British successes came curiosity toward, and acceptance of, other foreign films such as *Diva* (1982) and foreign directors such as Louis Malle who made *Atlantic City* (1980) and *Alamo Bay* (1985) in America. But that British sophistication trend and English producer David Puttnam's sojourn in Hollywood did not last long. Actually, the years 1980–81 were a false start. The literariness of the British *French Lieutenant's Woman* and the American *Ragtime* (1981), the success of

Chariots of Fire, and the promise of existential films such as Michael Mann's *Thief* (1981) and Richard Rush's *Stunt Man* (1980) never amounted to a trend in film history's participation in social history.

The first real formation of sociohistorical "texts" in eighties film history, the first gatherings of film texts around contemporary life texts, began between 1982 and 1984. In 1983–84 films like *Testament* and *Silkwood*, prodded, perhaps, by Israel's air strike against an Iraqi nuclear reactor in 1981, again signaled the dangers of the long-standing nuclear threat to the planet. These films actually predicted disastrous events such as the gas leak in Bhopal, India, that killed thirty-four hundred people in 1984 and the Chernobyl nuclear plant explosion in 1986. Simultaneously, however, these films lobbied for the nuclear disarmament that would become a major political issue of the decade.

Nineteen eighty-four was the Year of the Family Farm in film history. While thousands of real families were fighting to save real family farms, films like *Places in the Heart*, *Country*, and *The River* dramatized their struggle and lobbied Congress and the Reagan government for farm aid in the public way that political films always have. The lead actresses in all three of these farm films were nominated for the Best Actress Academy Award that year.

Nineteen eighty-seven was the Year of Vietnam at the movies. *Platoon*, released in December of 1986, was the first of five major films all focusing upon the Vietnam experience. It was a year of self-examination and reconciliation to the history of the previous decade. It was an honest public admission of defeat in that twenty-year-old war for which in the first half of the eighties the Reagan administration was still claiming victory.

Nineteen eighty-eight, in comic retreat from the horrors of Vietnam, became the Year of the Baby in American film. This second generation baby boom was predictable in the light of all those post–World War II baby boomers turning forty and their children starting to have babies, thus creating large numbers of proud parents and grandparents.

But if these clusters of sociohistorically conscious films marked certain periods of the eighties decade, there were also other sociohistorical issues that, year after year, consistently influenced themes and genres of film "texts." Terrorism—from the Iran Hostage Crisis at the beginning of the eighties to Israel's invasion of Lebanon in 1982 to the truck bombings in Beirut in 1983 to the kidnappings, plane hijackings, and the *Achille Lauro* in the Middle East in 1984 to the bombing of a passenger jet over Scotland in 1988—was the real war being fought, and it became the most prominent political concern and plot device of the decade's dramatic films. Similarly, America's relationship to Russia and the cold war maneuverings of détente spawned another cluster of films of sociohistoric signification. Of the domestic issues of the decade, eighties film history developed an ongoing fascination for the intricacies and ironies of the yuppie lifestyle.

"Popular culture and official history share two vital aspects," Thomas Myers writes, "the tendency to ignore the deeper, disquieting elements within the mythic history they write; and the likelihood of finding an enthusiastic mass audience for the finished texts."[5] What the films of the eighties managed was to step beyond "popular culture" and to challenge "official history."

The texts of those films' social history not only exposed but probed those "deeper, disquieting elements" of the main issues of the eighties and took mass audiences beneath the story lines of "official history." This book collects and examines the major sociohistorical texts that emerged from the film history of the eighties decade. It begins with a New Historicist model for the participation of film in the writing of a fuller history. It then proceeds to examine the individual historical texts that film wrote during the eighties. This book examines what Edward Pechter calls "the cultural production of texts"[6] and what Dominick LaCapra designates "the critical reading of texts (including items usually referred to as documents) in a manner that may itself affect both the conception of former 'reality' and activity in the present."[7]

Essential to any study of these "texts" written by films over the course of the decade is the analysis of the rhetorics that these different "texts" employ. LaCapra comments upon this rhetorical necessity:

> One prominent feature of this discussion and institutional context in the modern period has been a marked split between (and within) elite and popular cultures accompanied by the emergence of a commodified "mass culture" or "culture industry" that has alienated certain cultural elites and threatened to appropriate both older and newer forms of popular culture.[8]

In dealing with the rhetorics of its film texts as they deal with their historical texts, *The Films of the Eighties: A Social History* works to discover and thus minimize the problems of communication that inevitably arise between the demands of the historical text and the criticism function of the film text. The goal is to achieve the paradigm that LaCapra recommends, the integration of history and criticism through the study of film texts.

The Holograph of History

IF HISTORIANS of our generation were willing to participate actively in the general intellectual and artistic life of our time,"
Hayden White writes, "the worth of history would not have to be defended
in the timid and ambivalent ways that are now used."[1] One conservative
historian answers White with scorn by characterizing all attempts to
vitalize dry-as-dust history via the inclusion of new methodologies of
interpretation borrowed principally from literary criticism, philosophy,
and linguistics as "McHistory,"[2] all "special sauce, lettuce, cheese, pickle
on a sesame seed bun."[3]

What the conservative view of history often fails to consider is the
ambient mobility of "facts" themselves, their variant textuality dependent
upon who is reporting them and how, the complexity of the context out of
which those "facts" are generated. Michael Herr in *Dispatches* defines this
ephemerality of historical "facts" and texts: "It was late '67 now," he writes,
"even the most detailed maps didn't reveal much anymore; reading them
was like trying to read the faces of the Vietnamese, and that was like trying
to read the wind. We knew that the uses of most information were flexible,
different pieces of ground told different stories to different people."[4]

Of all the humanities disciplines, history has resisted adaptation to the
electronic/computer age the most tenaciously. It has resisted analysis of its
own motives and style the most adamantly. It has resisted Einstienian
relativity as an answer to the perplexing nineteenth-century historical
questions concerning the nature and graspability of "reality" the most
agressively. In the mid-twentieth century, the main target of charges of
"McHistory" was "revisionist history," which dared to superimpose Marxist theory over the study of the "facts." "Revisionist history," however, is a
comparatively forthright establishing of a dialectic between the "facts"
and a "reinterpretation" of the facts based largely upon economic motives.
But what happens when there are more than two views of the facts?

The primary target of the charge of "McHistory" in the late twentieth
century is the New Historicism, which focuses upon an interdisciplinary,
liberal, contextualized, postmodernist view of history. The New Historicism views history as a holograph. Drawing upon postmodernist critical
theories generated in literary and philosophical studies, theories that
emphasize the multiplicity of levels of interpretation of texts and the

1

hidden emplotments (language patterns) of both style and contextuality, the New Historicism's history holograph is layered in texts, subtexts, and stylistic emplotments. This history holograph is simultaneously a metahistory in that it is consistently examining its own motives and methods. Social historian Todd Gitlin defines this postmodernist view as "indifferent to consistency and continuity. . . . It self-consciously splices genres, attitudes, styles. . . . it pulls the rug out from under itself."[5] Such a "holograph of history" is composed of descending textual levels, levels of self-reflexivity, contextuality, and intertextuality. The New Historicism has challenged the belief of the Realist Historicism of the nineteenth century that the antiquarian goal of history was to distill documents down into clear one-dimensional facts. Conversely the New Historicism argues for a postmodernist recognition of the holographic truth of history. The New Historicism views itself as a computer-generated enhancement that can give new dimension and flexibility to previously static, one-dimensional views of history.

The New Historicism

Hayden White is but one of the New Historicists intent upon this holographic enhancement of historical discourse. His interdisciplinarily generated holograph stresses the inclusion of new subject matters as the texts of historical discourse. He identifies history as still anchored in the nineteenth century when the overriding motive was "to tell a story," but only one story. For White, these static historians are unable "to identify themselves with action painters, kinetic sculptors, existentialist novelists, imagist poets, or *nouvelle vague* cinematographers" of the twentieth century, and thus there "have been no significant attempts at surrealistic, expressionistic, or existentialist historiography in this century (except by novelists and poets themselves)."[6] White's argument implies that because of the conservatism of the historical establishment, the function of conveying historical truth to the mass culture of the twentieth century has been usurped by more carnivalesque interpreters such as plastic artists, writers, filmmakers.

White argues that "we require a history that will educate us to discontinuity more than ever before; for discontinuity, disruption, and chaos is our lot."[7] History can no longer build narratives out of the chronological alignment of events because the postmodernist world, itself computer-motivated toward holographic modes of conceptualization, can no longer accept one-dimensional linear definitions of its operation. History needs to adapt to a holographic model, redefine itself as layers of texts accumulating one atop another upon the base of an event or a document to create a mobile, light-sensitive, multidimensional image of its subject. As White notes, historicism ought to amend its goal of trying to organize the events of modern life into a single coherent narrative pursuant to a single meaning: "it will be lived better if it has no single meaning but many different ones."[8]

Late-twentieth-century historicism needs to define itself as a discourse of critical interpretation as well as antiquarian preservation, as a discourse of relativist contextualizing as well as mononarrative backgrounding, as a discourse of culture-generated stylistic and thematic subtexts as well as factual reconstructions. This type of a "metahistory," always aware of itself as text and of the interrelation between its texts, subtexts, contexts, intertexts, can elevate the past into the participatory position of being a layer in the holograph of present history.

Dominick LaCapra also lobbies polemically on the necessity and potential for a new approach to history. In *History and Criticism*, LaCapra states (in concert with White) that "I continue to believe that historians have much to learn from disciplines such as literary criticism and philosophy where the debates over the nature of interpretation have been particularly lively."[9] LaCapra is much more adamant than White in asserting that historians need to focus more upon interpretation: "Literary criticism and philosophy are in many ways the 'heavy sectors' of self-reflexive and self-critical theory at the present time. And it is perhaps by inquiring into these neighboring fields, where theoretical developments bearing upon the reading of texts have emerged in their strongest forms, that intellectual historians can acquire the conceptual means to come to terms with problems in their own field."[10] Thus, as does White, LaCapra argues that history can no longer be a single authoritative voice presenting exhaustive documentation as evidence of factuality. Dialogical history, conversely, would be the analysis and interpretation of a number of voices (or "texts") as a means of arriving at a pattern or rhythm of circumambient truth. In documentary history, "the basis of research is 'hard' fact derived from the critical sifting of sources." Thus documentary historicism can only revise the historical record by unearthing new documents that contain "hitherto unknown information," while the New Historicism is capable of "seeing the phenomenon differently or transforming our understanding of it through reinterpretation."[11]

Whereas these polemicists of the New Historicism stress the necessity to reinterpret past histories, the more important application of the New Historicism is to the holographic interpretation of contemporary history. Concepts of textuality are central to the methods of the New Historicism. LaCapra predicts that "all forms of historiography might benefit from modes of critical reading premised on the conviction that documents are texts that supplement or rework 'reality.' "[12] Whether those texts be classified materials or letters and diaries or presidential papers or public speeches or trial evidence or business files or novels or audio tapes or films, the interpretation of their own textuality qualifies them as layers in the holograph. Popular film is an excellent example of a LaCaprian text that can both "supplement or rework 'reality'" while also serving as a source open to textual, holographic interpretation which can "divulge facts about 'reality.'"

The documentary historian's conception of textuality has too often been an exploitative one that "often encouraged narrowly documentary readings in which the text becomes little more than a sign of the times or a straightforward expression of one larger phenomenon or another. At the limit, this indiscriminate approach to reading and interpretation becomes a detour around texts and an excuse for not really reading them at all. It simultaneously avoids the claims texts make on us readers."[13] This charge that historians use texts rather than reading them is a harsh but necessary one. The New Historicism wishes to elevate the documents of history from the subservient position of tools in the construction of a monologic, omnisciently narrated story to the contributary position of free voices in the dialogic holograph of history.

Instead of simply serving as the mortar of history, texts are, for the New Historicists, the tropes that mirror the nature of twentieth-century history itself. Texts are history and history defines itself in its texts. Neither can afford to remain static or one-dimensional. LaCapra echoes White in arguing that postmodernist historians, unlike the historians of the past who sought "to find order in seeming chaos,"[14] have realized that the "dream of a 'total history' corroborating the historian's own desire for mastery of a documentary repertoire and furnishing the reader with a vicarious sense of—or perhaps project for—control in a world out of joint has of course been a lodestar of historiography" but "its intellectual and practical limitations are only recently becoming evident in the historical profession."[15]

Because of the chaotic nature of the postmodern world, historians have been "confronted with phenomena that pose resistances to their shaping imagination."[16] Thus the historian is doomed by the nature of late-twentieth-century life to deny order in favor of the representation of chaos. History needs to take its cue from surrealism in painting or the existentialist novel or postmodernist film, all of which eschew or overcome plot ("story") to represent confusion, the multiplicity of interpretation, emptiness as opposed to order and resolution.

In lieu of order and resolution, White's theory of tropes and deep stylistic emplotments offers a methodology for the interpretation of the historical texts that LaCapra defines. By White's definition, "tropics is the process by which all discourse *constitutes* the objects which it pretends only to describe realistically and to analyze objectively."[17] A tropological theory of discourse is a mobile way of navigating the confusion, disruption, and chaos of postmodernist tensions and seeming oppositions. White writes: "The tropological theory of discourse gives us understanding of the existential continuity between error and truth, ignorance and under-standing, or to put it another way, imagination and thought. For too long the relationship between these pairs has been conceived as an opposition. The tropological theory of discourse helps us to understand how speech mediates between these supposed oppositions."[18] In a sense, White is defining a new theory of taxonomy based upon style and structure rather than upon subject matter or subdiscipline approach or genre.

For White, historical discourse especially should aim toward "the assim-ilation of history to a higher kind of intellectual inquiry which, because it is founded upon the *similarities* between art and science, rather than their differences, can be properly designated as neither."[19] This assimilation to a new form of historical discourse is necessary because in "the world in which we daily live, anyone who studies the past as an end in itself must appear to be either an antiquarian, fleeing from the problems of the present into a purely personal past, or a kind of cultural necrophile, that is, one who finds in the dead and dying a value he can never find in the living."[20]

How does the late-twentieth-century historian, infected with a one-dimensional, linear, nineteenth-century mode of static narrative dis-course, cure this antiquarian cultural necrophilia? White prescribes

> a willingness on the part of the contemporary historian to come to terms with the techniques of analysis and representation which *modern* science and *modern* art have offered for understanding the operations of consciousness and social process. In short, the historian can claim a voice in the contempo-rary cultural dialogue only insofar as he takes seriously the kinds of questions that the art and the science of *his own time* demand that he ask of the materials he has chosen to study.[21]

Where White points to the techniques of science and art as the salvation of historical discourse, LaCapra is more specific when he writes that intellec-tual history "shares with disciplines such as literary criticism and the history of philosophy, however, an initial focus upon complex written texts and a need to formulate as a problem what is often taken, deceptively, as a solution: the relationship between texts and their various pertinent contexts."[22]

This relation of history to its texts and those texts to their historical contexts is a constantly shifting one, changing in each new light as a holographic image does. The texts of history must be read both horizon-tally and vertically. Not only do they serve as the sources for linear narratives, but they also offer depths of potential interpretation and contextual connection. Social history, formulated out of political events and propaganda, economic conditions, lifestyle trends, media influences, and aesthetic representations, is especially complex in its horizontal and vertical textuality. In his "analysis of the deep structure of the historical imagination," White defines history as "a verbal structure in the form of a narrative prose discourse,"[23] a definition that could be just as easily applied to a novel or a biography or a piece of music or a film. The "historical imagination," for White, attempts "to explain the past by 'finding,' 'identifying,' or 'uncovering' the 'stories' that lie buried in chronicles." The problem is, however, that after "a given set of events has been motifically encoded"[24] by the historian, he is satisfied and fails to interpret the meaning or meanings of those events, not to mention their contextual relationship to other events. Thus the historian is intent merely on creating a text without any self-reflexive sense that under interpretation that text may comprise a number of other corollary texts. "Providing the *meaning* of a story by identifying the *kind of story* that has been told is called explanation by emplotment," and this sort of explanation is central to the concept of metahistorical analysis.[25]

Modern social history fits White's definition of the contextualist position: "the informing presupposition of Contextualism is that events can be explained by being set within the 'context' of their occurence." Thus historical facts can only be interpreted by the examination of their relationship "to other events occurring in their circumambient historical space." What contextualist history strives for is to define the "'trends' or general physiognomies of periods and epochs."[26]

In the late twentieth century, this pursuit of the trends within the layers of the holograph of history is the tool of the social historian. The study of film as sociohistorical document fits this model of contextualized history in that films frequently carry on social and mass cultural debates upon the trends of contemporary history. The importance of film history lies not in the images or themes of individual films but in the emplotted metaphors and motifs shared by groups of films that together portray, approach, and often even comment upon a specific historical event or sociohistorical trend. In the twentieth century in America (which epoch coincides with the life span of film art), history and film have formed an active dialogic relationship. History has provided situations, themes, characters, and interpretive possibilities that Hollywood has been more than eager to exploit. Conversely Hollywood has courted social credibility and even political power by supporting projects that portray, interpret, and, in some cases, even push debate upon major "trends" or "threads" of sociocultural history. The holographic model opens the way for the layering of a mass media history over a social history to generate a cultural history of the temper of a society in a particular time and place (in this case the eighties in America).

History as Film Text: Film as Historical Text

Like the documents out of which the conventional histories are constituted, the supposed "facts" or events of history are also "texts" that "rework" reality. Both Hayden White and Dominick LaCapra stress the duty of history to study "mechanisms of diffusion" whereby "texts and other artifacts are circulated and used in society."[27] In these mechanisms of diffusion, historical events, which are inevitably susceptible to interpretation as texts, are expropriated, interpreted, and "reworked" by mass culture mechanisms (books, the print media, television, films) to the point that new levels of the text become holographically overlaid atop the original text. LaCapra sees the focus upon these "mechanisms of diffusion" as central to a definition of late-twentieth-century "sociocultural history" that is "motivated by a justifiable revolt against an abstracted history of ideas" and "has sometimes proceeded under the banner of a populism ('history from the bottom up')"[28] that in its very language describes history as holograph. Under the mechanisms of diffusion, historical texts both reveal new dimensions of their own textuality and participate in the generation of new intertexts of historical interpretation.

Film director and cinematographer Haskell Wexler senses how the mechanisms of diffusion not only exploit history but enlarge the historical textuality:

> In past times, the monks had the pens and the paper and were literate and they wrote down, "this is what happened." This became "history." In a sense, we as filmmakers are contemporary historians. The system—basically the networks—writes history. They tell you what's important, what exists. As filmmakers we have the opportunity to write our view of the world and what will ultimately be called history.[29]

In the second half of the twentieth century, film art has become deeply involved in the holograph of history. It draws its subject matters from history, but it has become much less concerned with epic documentation as in the sweeping war movies of the fifties, sixties, and seventies—such as *A Bridge Too Far* (1977) or *The Longest Day* (1962)—and more concerned with interpreting history. Films in the seventies and eighties often portray the events of history as swirling around characters, burying characters in complexities, utterly confusing characters, often leaving characters suspended in a nihilistic void in which history either has no meaning or has too many meanings to comprehend. Film diffuses the social history of the eighties by defining those "trends" or "threads"—such as Vietnam guilt or yuppie cynicism—that hold the time together and then places historical events within the contexts of that time as a means of interpreting.

The usual naysayers upon the possibility of Hollywood film having the capacity to deal with social history are still around and as vocal as they have been in every decade of film history. Director Richard Lester charges that "the films of the '70s and '80s seem to have come from one studio. Ostrich Films Ltd. You can always finance films that have their heads stuck in the sand."[30] Hollywood has always been criticized as escapist, nostalgic, sentimental, historically inaccurate, and socially unresponsive. Hollywood's tendency to duck social, political, and historical issues in deference to a box-office censorship that stresses caution has been a film criticism cliché for seventy years. Actor Peter Boyle supports the Hollywood-as-ostrich cliché when he declares "that during the time of Reagan, the movies that have been made have almost no political content at all."[31]

The problem with this Hollywood-as-ostrich cliché is that it simply is not true. In the eighties, Hollywood offered a series of warnings against the tragedy of nuclear war, proposed scenarios for America-Russia détente, laid bare the human realities of the American farm crisis, explored the fanaticism of the terrorist mind, and chronicled the yuppie phenomenon in American life. No film historian has his finger more firmly on the pulse of the film industry than James Monaco, and when he compares the social consciousness of the films of the eighties with those of the sixties the present shakes out pretty well:

> I don't dislike movies now, they're just "normalized," and with a lack of that sharp and heady generational, political tension that fired not just music but most culture and politics until the day the music died, more than 15 years ago.
>
> In a curious way, the generation of the '60s succeeded too well. Movies (and television) are overflowing now with the stuff lacking in films then. Issues? If he's paid attention to his movies-of-the-week, there isn't a kid over eight who doesn't know all about AIDS, the homeless, the bomb, the inexorable pollution of the environment, abortion, the destruction of the ozone, and sex of all sorts.[32]

For Monaco, the films of the eighties may not have that taut political tension of the sixties, yet they are anything but ostrichlike.

A foreign observer, David Puttnam, who in 1986 became head of Columbia Studios in a noble experiment that failed, agrees with Monaco that film is the diffuser of social history: "Whether we like it or not, filmmakers are in the propaganda business. . . . film sets the social agenda—more so, in my view, than television. Attitudes are altered by film, particularly kid's attitudes. Therefore, filmmakers better jolly well grow up and accept the fact that whether they like it or not, their job carries enormous responsibility."[33] Puttnam goes further than Monaco when he asserts that film does not just diffuse the events, the facts, the threads of social history, but rather actually "sets the social agenda."

Two other foreign voices, those of directors Terence Davies and Alan Parker, strongly agree with the power of Hollywood film to deal with social history. Davies remembers seeing the Hollywood musical *Singin' in the Rain* (1952) when he was a child: "When you grew up in a Liverpool slum and you saw these films, that's what you thought America was like. Everyone was rich, everyone was beautiful. There was no want, no poverty;

it was always summer. That's very potent. It's as potent as religion."[34] Davies's example is an artificial, sound-stage view of America, but his point speaks to the power of film to present America. American films define the temper of American society in the time of their time. There is no better example of this manipulation of message by means of the meticulous choice of strategies of discourse than Alan Parker's *Mississippi Burning* (1988).

In Reagan-era America, Parker set out to deliver a potent message about racism and white supremacist violence. He chose, however, not to present that film's message from a black point of view. His was a choice quite similar to that made earlier by Sir Richard Attenborough in *Cry Freedom* (1987), which views the evils of South African apartheid mainly through the eyes of a white journalist. Parker, in *Mississippi Burning*, chose to couch the event, the political message, the eighties condemnation of Reagan administration softness on racism, within the discourse of the Hollywood buddy movie genre: "Nobody is suggesting that the film's ideological/historical project is as blatantly revisionist as this," Gavin Smith protests, "but it's [*Mississippi Burning*] a classic case of a film not being what it should be . . . Hollywood modes of discourse infiltrate the good political instincts of writers and directors. To make a film about racism, Hollywood uses the buddy movie genre."[35] In defending himself against naysayers like Gavin Smith, Parker is quite clear about the historical and political textuality of *Mississippi Burning*: "I wouldn't pretend that *Mississippi Burning* is the definitive story of the civil rights movement the way that *Platoon* or *Apocalypse Now* were meant to be definitive stories about the Vietnam War."[36] Parker goes on to explain that the original script of *Mississippi Burning* "didn't quite have the political backbone that I wanted. . . . I think the subtext of the film is there now. . . . Without giving them an overtly political film, it is political, because the politics are underneath every line."[37]

What Parker is saying about his film is interesting in a localized way, but what he is saying about the sociohistorical agenda of American film in general is much more important. American movies are always made in terms of those modes of discourse that will attract the widest possible audience, yet those films still are able to subtextualize those surface modes of discourse with potent sociohistorical messages. Text and subtext constantly complement each other in American films, and Alan Parker is perfectly aware of their sociohistorical diffusing power: "All of our European influences have been American films because American society has been sold to the rest of the world with the greatest propaganda machine any nation ever invented—the Hollywood movie."[38] American films, no matter how trivial or serious, are always about America, and no one recognizes this more clearly than these foreign commentators.

History as film text, then, is a holograph within a holograph that tends to shift shape on different textual levels. On a primary text level, history may indeed be simply an event that provides a backdrop for a film's human action. Also, on a primary text level, history may embody an idea that gives a general definition to the vision of the film and points in a general way toward the other levels of textuality of the film—its subtexts and/or metatexts (self-reflexive discourses). If history is a holograph, then so is film because film is also composed of different layers of textuality. The surface texts of most films are constructed out of a limited number of conventional mass modes of discourse (plots), whereas the subtexts of films consist of a variety of sociohistorical discourse contexts (themes) such as politics, social consciousness, revisionist history, moral messaging and existential themes. The diffusion of history as film text, then, might be holographed visually in this manner:

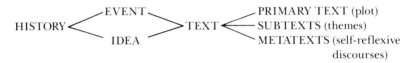

HISTORY < EVENT / IDEA > TEXT < PRIMARY TEXT (plot) / SUBTEXTS (themes) / METATEXTS (self-reflexive discourses)

What this declares is that in contemporary society history has become a text for interpreting and often substantiating present action.

In the eighties, history is being used to substantiate both the most important and the most trivial aspects of American culture. While the history of the Vietnam War constantly comments upon Reagan-era foreign policy in Central America and the Middle East, a hair conditioner bottle's label declares that "herbal history traces the use of Chamomile to bring out highlights." The fates of nations and the fates of hair follicles are both dependent upon historical texts. Only by defining this issue of textuality can the holographic nature of history itself and history as film text come clear. Like History, film is diverse, not restricted (as is most print) to the monologic. Film can capture the simultaniety of the events of history, the multiplicity of history's meanings. Film, better than any other medium, is capable of reacting to that need to exist within the confusion of postmodernist life.

The confluence of social history and film history in a holographic textuality, then, is a culmination of the New Historicist push for the integration of criticism into the methodology of the study of history. The study of that confluence of social history and film history defines the function of film as a mass culture diffuser as well as interpreter. Film distributes the holographic possibilities of history to the masses, offers a variety of interpretations of history that help to foster understanding of the nature of our past and our contemporary world. In that sense, then, as prime diffusers of a New Historicism, films do not simply portray history or diffuse historical information, they actually interpret history in the same way that literary criticism interprets novels and, in some cases, such as the powerful effect on mass consciousness of the Vietnam war films of

1978–79 or the equally powerful effect of *The Day After* (1983), they actually participate in the making of history by motivating the mass mind of society to its own historical interpretation.

But no social historian of film can ever lose sight of the fact that film not only diffuses and interprets history but also uses and abuses history. Every mass medium is capable of both interpretation and distortion. Every mass medium is capable of obliterating history in a chaos of interpretations. That is why the holographic model works so well. A holograph is a unity composed out of layers of diversity. The holograph of history notes the multiplicity of the "facts" and "events," attempts definition and interpretation of the multiple texts that accrue in layers, and finally attempts self-reflexive analysis of those different texts as a means of arriving at a metatext or metahistory. This metahistory places both the "facts" and the various "texts of the facts" within a larger historical system of interpretation.

But if, in the eighties, under the expansiveness of the New Historicism, history became a more complex film text, film much more often found itself participating at the center of historical event. In a number of cases, film actually became historical text rather than vice versa. Perhaps the best example of this phenomenon of a mass medium itself actually becoming news is the made-for-TV movie *The Day After*. The impact of that single "media event" so catalyzed public opinion that it influenced the Reagan government to pursue more serious nuclear arms control negotiations with Russia. In 1983, three films—*Places in the Heart, Country, The River*—made news in their sharp criticism of the government's abandonment of the family farmer and actually helped to lobby the Congress into "bail-out" legislation for beleagured American farmers. Martin Scorcese's *Last Temptation of Christ* (1988) precipitated protests in the streets, while other films such as *Mississippi Burning, The Color Purple* (1985), *Colors* (1988) and the prolife documentary *The Silent Scream* (1985) generated vehement social debates. Typically, the media discussion of films is restricted to the "Arts and Liesure" pages of the newspaper, but in the eighties, films frequently gained the status of hard news or editorial metaphor. At times, film even took on a prophetic function. In 1988, three films appeared—Costa-Gavras's *Betrayed*, Oliver Stone's *Talk Radio*, Parker's *Mississippi Burning*—that warned of an upsurge in white supremacist organization and action. Later that same year, eerily, one David Duke, a former grand dragon of the Ku Klux Klan, running on a transparently white supremacist platform, was elected to the Louisiana legislature.

This relationship between history and film is also unique in the eighties because of the sociopolitical stability of that decade, its overpowering Reaganness comparable to the Ikeness of the fifties. *The Films of the Seventies: A Social History* dealt with an era of social and film history that really began in the mid-sixties and actually lapped over into a few early eighties films. That precursor to this book denied the validity of arbitrarily organizing a film history on a principle as artificial as a decade in time. Curiously, however, *The Films of the Eighties: A Social History* validates exactly the opposite situation in both social and film history. While the concept of the seventies in that earlier study encompassed approximately seventeen years, the eighties really do begin in 1980 with the ascendance of the Reagan administration and continue of a piece throughout that decade. The victory of the Reagan agenda changed everything in America and by as early as 1982 had also changed the very nature of Hollywood films. Marc Cooper, in an essay about the decline of drug use in eighties films, writes: "There is a different moral tenor now, a general conservatism in the culture, and that's why movies have shifted to the right in the last eight or nine years."[39]

Both the social history and the film history of the eighties take the form of complexly layered holographs. Reagan-era conservative politics constitute one full layer that overlays all of the others. The legacies of the past, particularly Vietnam and the resurrection of fifties issues such as détente with Russia and the nuclear threat, form another layer of the holograph. The new form of war, terrorism, the new racism, the new feminism, all form a constantly shifting social layer of the holograph.

As a by-product of Reagan-era political conservatism, a growing cynicism toward America's moral stature in the world community that began with Watergate and grew in the huckstering of the Reagan foreign policy culminated in the embarrassment of Iran-*contra*. This cynicism of the eighties toward government and politicians was mirrored by the cynicism that began to appear in films. This cynicism took shape in a national fixation upon materialism as exemplified in the yuppie phenomenon. That cynicism also took the form of regional jealousy such as the discontent of Middle America with the concentration of eighties wealth on the high-tech coasts. It was as if everyone in America knew that Reagonomics was a damn-the-deficit game and they all decided to play and not pay. That national cynicism formed yet another important layer in the holograph of both social and film history.

In the 1978 film *Coming Home*, a character complains, "they tore down my past and built a shopping center." Perhaps that irony best characterizes this subtext of cynicism that moves throughout both eighties social and film history. America in the eighties is caught in the throes of "grand mall." Whereas the generation of the sixties were shapers, the generation of the eighties are shoppers. Perhaps the one most prominent icon in the films of the eighties is the shopping mall.

Another layer in the holograph of not only American film but American social history is the consistent self-reflexive impulse, the metaconsciousness of both past history and past films. American society in the eighties consistently employed an intertextuality with the past as a means of understanding and dealing with the issues of its present. It resurrected issues from the fifties, the nuclear threat and détente, to deal with the new cold war of the eighties. It consistently alluded to the history of the sixties and the seventies, principally the Vietnam War, the civil rights movement, and Watergate, as cautionary metaphors for its international and domestic policies in the eighties. In film, this same self-reflexivity took the form of a consistent examination of eighties issues in terms of past history. A fascination for the Vietnam War, its meaning and aftermath, especially exemplified this eighties self-reflexiveness. The Vietnam War became the dominant metaphor for postmodernist confusion, paranoia, and alienation within both eighties society and film.

Perhaps the best example of this self-reflexive consciousness in both the social history and the film history of the eighties can be found in a cluster of futuristic films, all of which turn on the premise that in order for the future to exist and continue, the past must be understood and even revised. In *The Terminator* (1984), *Star Trek IV* (1986), *Back to the Future* (1985), and *Peggy Sue Got Married* (1986), time travelers consistently found the answers to the human and political puzzles of the future written in the critical act of reinterpreting and even reshaping past history. These films examined the self-reflexive need to reexamine our political consciousness toward the issue of nuclear war (*The Terminator*), our ecological consciousness of endangered species (*Star Trek IV*), and our human attitudes toward materialism (*Peggy Sue Got Married*, *Back to the Future*). This whole cluster of time-travel movies embody Hayden White's concepts of a "metahistory" that can go back and by means of critical reinterpretation change the meaning of history.

Themes like this concept of self-reflexivity form like crystals upon each of the layers of the film holograph. That film holograph in turn overlays the holograph of social history. Each of the layers of the holograph of social history is refracted through a corresponding layer of film history. Each chapter of this book will examine one of those refractions, will interpret that layer of social history in terms of its corresponding film history. The methodology for this New Historicist confluence of history and film criticism will characteristically begin with an analysis of the textuality of a social event or trend or theme that has generated filmic representations. Next, it will proceed to critical analysis of the visual/verbal representation of that social text in specific film texts.

This New Historicist methodology demands consideration of the choices the events of social history impose upon film history. In each era of film history, certain film genres tend to rise above others as more popular and appropriate forms for that particular time and place. In the seventies, for example, the subgenre of the disaster film found a short-lived popularity. Like the microcosmic community in *The Posiedon Adventure* (1972), the American people in the seventies were trying to make their way out of a national situation that had suddenly turned upside down. Like the be-leaguered firemen in *The Towering Inferno* (1974), the American people in the seventies were trying to put out fires that their leaders had started. The seventies was characterized by America's struggle to escape and survive Vietnam exacerbated by the international embarrassment of Watergate. Thus the sociohistorical climate itself chose the type of film that best represented that particular alignment of events.

In the eighties, the same sociohistorical selectivity, the same dynamic of the temper of the times choosing the type of metaphoric vehicles most appropriate for the representations of its themes, is evident. For example, in past eras of film history a critic concentrating upon films that displayed a sociohistorical consciousness rarely got the opportunity to analyze comedies. In the eighties, however, due mainly to the yuppie phenome-non, the satiric comedy is the most prominent vehicle for the representa-tion of the excesses of eighties materialism.

The eighties is also the most high-tech of decades, and its films, especially its special effects action films, embrace this eighties love affair with machines. Whereas in a 1976 film like *All The President's Men*, the opening shot was of typewriter keys striking paper, in the eighties, computer screens are much more likely to fill the movie screen. The films of the eighties seem to be consistently offering images of screens within screens. Often, as in *War Games* (1983) or *Winter Kills* (1979, 1983), computer screens become villains capable of destroying reputations or even destroying the world, but they are not the only machines that either threaten or seduce moviegoers. Violent killing machines like *The Termina-tor* (1984) and *Robocop* (1987) replace the depraved human villains of the past. More friendly, childlike machines like R2D2 and C3PO of the *Star Wars* series (1977, 1980, 1983), Number 5 of the *Short Circuit* series (1986, 1988), and even Steven Spielberg's *E.T.* (1982) and the versatile little family of junk machines of *Batteries Not Included* (1987) replace the heroic figures of the old Westerns and cop movies. The eighties is the flowering of the age of high-tech gadgetry and computer proliferation, thus the films of the decade mirror this increased interest in machines over people.

But the eighties is also a decade of strong political consciousness especially on an international stage. The intrusion of worldwide terrorism exported from Iran, Libya, South America, even Russia, within the always perceived as safe boundaries of the continental United States planted seeds of paranoia in American society. Whereas in the seventies political thrillers were domesticated and mostly based upon Watergate themes of paranoia, in the eighties political thrillers build their plots upon the themes of international terrorism, international economic collapse, cold war intrigue and espionage, international blackmail, and fanatical revolu-tion. Of all the genres, the political thriller has historically been the most attentive to the issues of social history because political thrillers generically deal with contemporary events and contemporary themes, thus consciously attempting to be timely in realistic ways. If in the films of the seventies "nothing was ever what it seemed to be,"[40] in the films of the eighties everything is simply out of control, and the world is struggling to stave off chaos. If in the seventies, political thrillers were most worried about corruption and cover-up within America's domestic government and corporate institutions, in the eighties those films are most worried about the chaos of the wide world from which America had always held itself aloof intruding upon our previously safe domestic life.

The holograph of the social history of the eighties in America finds its complex, multidimensional embodiment in both realistic and metaphoric terms in the films of the decade. Twenty years ago in 1970, Ian Jarvie described how

> there was something else that was vigorous and exciting about the American cinema, something deeply entwined in the relation it bore to its society: its ability to portray every aspect of American society with almost clinical accuracy: from the urban, rural and negro slums, through suburbia, to its highest social and political realms: American film men knew their society and put it on their screens.[41]

Jarvie's confidence in film as American text is as viable in 1990 as it was in 1970. The themes have changed. The genres have changed. The temper of the society has evolved from the complacency and optimism of the early sixties to the idealistic anger of the late sixties to the embarrassment and paranoia of the seventies to the accommodation to chaos of the eighties. But these social and/or aesthetic changes have only altered the color of the holograph, have not changed the basic layered structure of its textuality. Social history and film history continue to represent each other in a complex relationship built upon ascending layers of meaning. As has always been the case, social history remains the single most important generator of film texts. But in the eighties, films are actually generating texts of social history. Films dealing with the Vietnam War and postwar issues, for example, function as a New Historicist interpretation of a sociohistorical text neither interpreted nor understood in the previous decade. In the eighties, film history becomes the mass media vehicle for the representation and interpretation of the complex holograph of social history.

2

The Vietnam War as Film Text

N THE LATE seventies, the Vietnam War films, specifically *Coming Home*, *The Deer Hunter*, *Go Tell the Spartans*, and *Apocalypse Now*, served as barometers that measured the submerged public opinion toward that war and the soldiers who fought in that war. These movies indicated that beneath the surface of American society there was both a thoughtful sympathy for understanding the situations of the veterans who fought and survived that war and a historical curiosity as to how that war was fought and what that war meant.

In the eighties, however, the social interest in the Vietnam War lost its immediacy with increased assimilation of Vietnam veterans into American society. The curiosity about the war had been satisfied by the outpouring in the late seventies of both the films and the many excellent books (Michael Herr's *Dispatches*, Philip Caputo's *Rumor of War*, James Webb's *Fields of Fire*, Tim O'Brien's *Going After Cacciato*, Gustav Hasford's *Short Timers*, Donald Bodey's *FNG*, John Del Vecchio's *13th Valley*) about the war. Yet despite these accommodations of the Vietnam War as active issue, that war did not simply fade away. A number of particularly eighties events kept the Vietnam War alive, not as a social issue but as a metaissue, a cautionary metaphor from the seventies for other eighties issues. That unique set of events that kept both America and the eighties attuned to the lessons of the Vietnam War were the Russian invasion of Afghanistan in late 1979, the failure of the hostage rescue mission into Iran due to blowing sand (another failure of American technology), the increasing American presence in Central America, the loss of life, and the withdrawal of troops from Beirut. In all of these cases, the Vietnam War was repeatedly cited as a text for contemporary comparison, a precedent for American failure. Political voices used the Vietnam War to make points about the political choices open to the Reagan administration in Central America. Vietnam veterans used the war to gain political leverage and push a number of issues relevant to their reinstated voices. These issues kept alive the American social consciousness of the legacy and the continuing quest for meaning of the Vietnam War.

In the late seventies and burgeoning throughout the eighties, simultaneous to all of this mass culture attention (in the film, TV, and print media), the academic establishment discovered the Vietnam War. English

16

departments generally were the first to offer courses in the war because by 1979 an impressive body of literature had been published. Political science and history departments also began creating Vietnam War courses. National literature conferences regularly scheduled sessions on the teaching and the scholarship of the Vietnam War. By the late eighties, conferences dealing exclusively with the Vietnam War began to appear.[1]

Vietnam remained a fascination in movies, in books, in classrooms, and in the American social consciousness all through the eighties because it had become a metaphor for what America was afraid it was going to become in the economic and political cold war with Russia and Japan, a loser. Vietnam became a warning, a symbol of defeat and loss, but most of all, it became a text.[2] It became an extremely complex text that was constantly being interpreted, reinterpreted, and exploited all through the eighties. In fact, the Vietnam War became a whole series of texts. The textuality issue as a starting point in turn involves two other essential issues: (1) what and where that text is; (2) how to interpret that text. It is extremely difficult, however, to either interpret or teach the Vietnam War because the texts are either extinct or corrupt or too limited or too various.

The Vietnam War, at the time that it was going on, was composed of more than 2.5 million American TEXTS and an indeterminate number of Vietnamese TEXTS possessed by the soldiers who were fighting it. Add to those TEXTS the multimillions of SUBTEXTS created by the homebound, yet Vietnam War sensitive, American, Australian, New Zealand, Korean, Vietnamese, Cambodian, Laotian, French populations who were effected by what the primary TEXTS of the soldiers in Vietnam were expressing.

Beyond those two obvious types of Vietnam war texts, there were, at the time the war was going on, a number of OVERTEXTS such as those presented by:

1. The media
2. The military
3. The political administrations of
   a) America
   b) North Vietnam
   c) South Vietnam
4. The American antiwar movement

In almost every instance, these OVERTEXTS were self-serving and drastically edited.

All of these TEXTS, SUBTEXTS, and OVERTEXTS were in existence while the war was in session, but after the war, other texts surfaced generated by academic disciplines or social agendas. The period of 1977–79 was the real turning point in Vietnam War consciousness-raising stimulated mainly by mass culture. In that period of about sixteen months, the films *Coming Home*, *The Deer Hunter*, and *Apocalypse Now* generated mass interest in the Vietnam War.

These films served as the publicists of a Vietnam War consciousness that was abroad in the country yet dormant for various reasons (bitterness, shame, depression, decompression, inarticulateness). American society had avoided thinking about the war since the withdrawal of 1973. The American media, including Hollywood, had refused to consider the war retrospectively just as the movie industry (with the ludicrous exception of John Wayne's *Green Berets*) had refused to portray the war in films while the war was going on. The American academic establishment had not yet gotten around to teaching it. Thus some catalyst was needed to generate interest. When those three 1977–79 films made money and won Academy Awards, it served notice that American society was ready to talk about Vietnam, that the healing had begun.

The discipline texts, mainly in universities, were among the first to take up these discussions. These discipline texts, generated in the earliest attempts to teach and undertake scholarly research on the Vietnam War, can rightly be called TUNNELTEXTS. For example, the history tunneltext, whether it be military or political or social or economic history, through the collecting, arranging, and interpreting of "perceived" facts built time lines and strategies of what happened in Vietnam as a means of possibly understanding. Another tunneltext, the literary text, was an existential text focusing upon the individual in the war. Call it the "grunt" text. The racial text, one of the most prominent social tunneltexts, can be divided into four approaches: the white of the officers and politicians; the poor white of the grunts; the black/chicano; and, of course, the Vietnamese. This racial text is perhaps the least examined text of all. William Duiker is one of the major explorers of the Vietnamese side of the war and one of the few to escape the Amerocentrism that has dominated the teaching of that war in America since 1978–79.[3] Both ethnocentrism and Amerocentrism have dominated the vast majority of the Vietnam War films and have even, as in the case of *The Deer Hunter* and *Rambo II*, moved over the edge into racism against the Vietnamese. In those films, the Vietnamese are portrayed as either sadistic animals or faceless cannon fodder. In *The Deer Hunter*, the false ascribing of Russian roulette as the Vietnamese national pastime is especially demeaning. In *Rambo II*, the Vietnamese are like the Indians in American Westerns, targets to be shot down. The social text, which studies the class structures of the war, breaks down into two categories: the class structures within the military (officers vs. grunts or REMFs vs. combat soldiers) and the class structures within society in terms of draft eligibility (college students vs. the draftable poor).

The best critics, such as Thomas Myers in his book on the Vietnam War literature, film, history, and philosophy—titled *Walking Point: American Narratives of Vietnam* (New York: Oxford University Press, 1988)—or John

Del Vecchio in his novel, *The 13th Valley*, have found language constructs whereby they can combine a number of these tunneltexts to form a MEGATEXT that escapes troglodicity.

Finally, into the eighties, the Vietnam War became a tool, a strategy text, that could be used to teach other, more universal things. Let us call these strategy texts METATEXTS, texts about the creation of texts, self-reflexive texts. In academia, this metatext realization came about when teachers of Vietnam War courses began realizing that they could not hope to really teach the Vietnam War, to really answer the questions that all the students who signed up for those courses were asking: What was the war like? Why was it fought? What did it mean? Those questions may not be answerable, but they can be approached, observed, and *used*. This concept of "using" the war has, in the eighties, become a way of presenting students and the society at large with an anchor in their own life-texts, a sense of their own history and that of their parents, their generation, their society. This metatextual approach can become a way to make the mass public, which may not know anything about Central America but may have learned a great deal about Vietnam, listen.

Because there are too many texts, and because the Vietnam War was consciously deconstructing itself even as it was going on, the megatext and/or the metatext approaches are the most valid. All of the rest, especially the overtexts and the tunneltexts, can be viewed as narrowly self-serving. The primary texts of those who served in Vietnam, even when collected, as in the number of excellent oral histories now available,[4] often are less satisfying than fictionalized accounts of life in the war because, unfortunately, the voices recorded in books like Al Santoli's *Everything We Had* and the documentary film *Dear America: Letters Home from Vietnam* generally do not interpret the war.

But what does this textual model have to do with the Vietnam War films?

In the eighties, the Vietnam War continued to exist in the obsession of American film with it. All through the decade films of every genre employed Vietnam as text or subtext. For example, *Off Limits* (1988) is both a Vietnam War film and a buddy-chase thriller like *Lethal Weapon* (1987) or *To Live and Die in L.A.* (1986) or "Miami Vice" on TV. *Off Limits*, however, happens to be set in Saigon in 1968 rather than in San Francisco or L.A. or Miami, which changes the whole context of violence in the film. "In a war," as Samuel Popkin has stated, "the first and foremost issue is the containment of violence."[5] Dirty Harry operating in San Francisco is trying to contain violence. Harry has a gun and the bad guys have guns, but everybody else is unarmed. In *Off Limits*, literally everybody has a gun, good guys, bad guys, innocent bystanders and children. The violence has escalated to the point where the buddy-chase genre movie is no more than a text within a bigger text, a small war caught in the context of a larger war, a microcosm of the Vietnam War's macroviolence. *Off Limits* clearly demonstrates the futility of trying to contain violence in a war zone such as Saigon. Films like *Platoon* (1986), *Off Limits*, *Full Metal Jacket* (1987), or *Hamburger Hill* (1987) provide fuel for the American imagination because that is where the real text of the Vietnam War now resides.

Perhaps the best example of a Vietnam War megatext is Del Vecchio's *13th Valley*. It is both a realistic novel and an anatomy that presents historical, racial, sexual/psychological, economic, philosophical perspectives on the war from the voices of its different characters, each of whom represents one of those points of view. Del Vecchio's platoon in *The 13th Valley* is the most highly educated, articulate, introspective collection of black and white grunts imaginable. In other ways, especially the patrol and battle sequences, *The 13th Valley* is starkly realistic. In fact, that book mirrors the war in the same way that the movie *Platoon* does. Both are alive and real in their action sequences, yet both are artificial and pretentious in their subjective, metaphoric, intellectual discussions of the war. The Vietnam War is a text that just happens, like a spurt of automatic weapons fire. It is much harder to grasp when it is not happening, when it is being pondered and intellectualized. This distinction is one reason why the mass culture of American society can learn so much about the Vietnam War from films. Motion pictures are always happening, just as a book like Michael Herr's *Dispatches* is always happening, through style.

Finally, the Vietnam War films can be studied from a megatextual/ metatextual perspective simply by analyzing them for themselves, on their own visual/verbal terms. When assimilating a film in a theater or studying it in a classroom, the medium presents its own concept of "story" that is different from the concept of "story" presented in literature. *Platoon* is an example of an excellent film's failure in the attempt to present both a literary story and a postmodernist, holographic vision. Its medieval-morality-play, literary-allusion, clichéd-Christ-figure script is a real intrusion upon what the movie *Platoon* is really about. What it is about is the *feel* of the Vietnam War, the experience of it, its immediacy, not some abstract morality symbolism for modern man.

The Vietnam War Film History

The literary concept of story has found diverse form in a large and growing body of Vietnam War literature. Simultaneously a whole body of Vietnam War films have accumulated into a rather full subgenre. The history of the Vietnam War film is a clear one and the first phase of it has been defined before by a number of commentators, myself included in *The Films of the Seventies: A Social History*.[6] The history of the treatment of the Vietnam War in movies begins in 1976 with the film *Taxi Driver*, the first of the films, which include *Coming Home*, *Rolling Thunder*, *Who'll Stop the Rain*, and *Heroes*, to portray troubled Vietnam veterans bringing the violence and frustration of the war home to roost in American society.

Beginning in 1976, the Vietnam War film has progressed through three rather clearly delineated phases: (1) the epic phase, (2) the comic book phase, and (3) the symbolic nihilist phase. Folded or layered into these three phases are the three major themes that dominate the Vietnam War films: (1) life in the war itself (adaptation, survival, loss of innocence, change, morality); (2) the meaning of the war; (3) coming home from the war. Some themes are much more prominent in some phases of this time line than in others.

By far the most often explored of these three themes is the third, "coming home." Thus the Vietnam War films are both a text of the war as well as of the postwar reentry of the soldier into "the world" as he called it. The first epic phase (1976–79) was a traditional, story-oriented text, a war text aligned with the traditions of twentieth-century American literary and film war texts. In one sense, the films of the epic phase were all clichés. How different, for example, is the journey through the Vietnam War of Captain Willard (Martin Sheen) in *Apocalypse Now* from that of Henry Fleming in Stephen Crane's *Red Badge of Courage*? How different, for example, are the training-camp-to-combat films like *The Boys in Company C* from the dozens of movies beginning with *Sergeant York* to *To Hell and Back* to *The Sands of Iwo Jima* to *Darby's Rangers* to *The Devil's Brigade* to *The Dirty Dozen* to *The Big Red One* of the same type made about earlier wars. It is no coincidence that two of the earliest and most powerful books about the Vietnam War, Philip Caputo's *Rumor of War* and Gustav Hasford's *Short Timers*, both choose a conventional structure to present their versions of the evolution of the Vietnam War Everyman soldier.

Phase two of the Vietnam War film history, the comic book phase, is a text corrupted mainly by Reagan administration chauvinistic rhetoric. In speeches throughout the eighties, President Reagan valorized the idea that America did not really lose the Vietnam War and that the war can be refought and rewon in places such as Grenada, Central and South America, the Middle East. This valorization by an extremely popular president cleared the way to profitability for a whole series of "return to Vietnam and do it right this time" propagandist fantasies in the period 1980–86. John Rambo was the Sergeant Rock of this Reagan administration war comic. In 1986, as his comic book image, more often than not draped in the American flag, appeared on the covers of *Time* and *Newsweek* and in the pages of every newspaper and magazine in America, John Rambo, née Sylvester Stallone, was invited to the White House and treated as if he were a real Congressional Medal of Honor winner. Perhaps this comic book phase of the Vietnam War films is one of the best examples of the manner in which American film and orchestrated (propagandist) social history can complement one another.

Only the third phase, the symbolic nihilist phase of 1987–88, makes an honest attempt to portray the Vietnam War in ways that film as medium best deals with human experience, history, and idea. In general, these films eschew story and, while focused upon stereotypical characterization, attempt to capture the moments, the confusion and chaos of the war in the same way that the "illumination rounds" of Michael Herr's *Dispatches* did through his remarkable postmodernist style. These movies of the third phase do not generally attempt to impose order upon a primary text that had no order. In the case of *Platoon*, when such an attempt to impose the order of story is made, that attempt pales in the face of the consistently deconstructing text. When these third phase movies succeed, they capture the existential feel of disorder, confusion, utter meaninglessness. Thus, the 1987–88 phase of Vietnam War film history is its postmodernist phase, a series of films that consciously deconstruct the war that was consistently deconstructing itself even as it was going on.

The epic phase begins in 1976 with *Taxi Driver* and continues through 1978–79 when *Apocalypse Now* is released. It comprises those two films plus three other major films—*Coming Home, The Deer Hunter, Go Tell the Spartans*—and a number of minor films such as *Who'll Stop the Rain, Heroes, Rolling Thunder,* and *The Boys in Company C.* Only two of these movies, *Apocalypse Now* and *Go Tell the Spartans,* are actually fully set in Vietnam. The reason for calling this the epic phase is based upon the nature of the two most important films of the phase, *The Deer Hunter* and *Apocalypse Now.* Both are films of epic scope. *The Deer Hunter* reigned for twelve years as *the* epic treatment of the "coming home" theme, while its major competitor at the 1978 Academy Awards, *Coming Home,* was but a domestic, soap-opera treatment of that theme. In the final month of the eighties, however, *Born on the Fourth of July* proffered a challenge to *The Deer Hunter.* *Apocalypse Now* is still unsurpassed as *the* Vietnam War epic.

From 1980 to 1986 the Vietnam War entered its comic book phase. The two *Rambo* sequels and the POW rescue movies such as *Uncommon Valor* and Chuck Norris's three *Missing in Action* shoot-em-ups are the best examples of the exploitation of the war and of Vietnam veterans that was so rampant in American society and the American media. This comic book approach involves the creation of shallow stereotyped military or commando characters of the sort that appeared in comic books like *G.I. Joe* or *Men at War* or *Sergeant Rock.* These stereotyped characters take the form of either a single, larger-than-life fighting machine like Sergeant Rock or a commando team of specialists (usually a demolition expert, an inventive tactician/con man, and a strongman as in the TV series "Mission Impossible" or "The A Team") led by an officer/administrator. Ironically *Apocalypse Now,* generally considered *the* Vietnam War epic, was originally conceived, in its first script version by John Milius, as a sort of G.I. Joe comic book set in Vietnam.

In describing that first script of *Apocalypse Now*, Francis Coppola said:

> The script as I remember it, took a more comic-strip Vietnam War and moved it through a series of events that were also comic strip: a political comic strip. The events had points to them—I don't say comic strip to denigrate them. The film continued through comic strip episode and comic strip episode until it came to a comic strip resolution: Attila the Hun (i.e. Kurtz) with two bands of machine-gun bullets around him, taking the hero (Willard) by the hand, saying "Yes, yes, here! *I have the power in my loins!*" Willard converts to Kurtz' side; in the end, he's firing up at the helicopters that are coming to get him, crying out crazily. A movie comic strip. . . . That was the tone and the *resolution*. The first thing that happened after my involvement was the psychologization of Willard."[7]

Coppola's vision of the war was more expansive, psychological, and literary than was Milius's shallow, pop-culture, comic book approach. But since that time Hollywood writers, producers and directors have much more often opted for the comic book vision.

Jerrold Stahr, speaking at a conference on the Vietnam War at George Mason University in April 1988, noted that "even comic books on the war are doing a booming business. Marvel Comics has a comic book, if you haven't seen it, both of my sons subscribe to it, it's called *The Nam*, and it sells 500,000 a month which is the largest selling comic book in the country."[8] Professor Stahr may be sanguine about his sons getting their information about the Vietnam War from comic books, but Francis Coppola, Oliver Stone, and Stanley Kubrick, as well as the growing number of novelists of the Vietnam generation, have opted for exploring the Vietnam War in more complex, human, and unexploitive ways.

At that same conference, Larry Engelmann characterized the teaching and the general study of the Vietnam War as "McHistory." Comparing some of the pop-culture and pop-academic approaches to the Vietnam War with fast food preparation and merchandising, Engelmann represents the other extreme from Stahr in saying that the study of the Vietnam War should stick to only the most conventional, dry-as-dust pedogogical principles.[9] Neither the comic book approach of Stahr nor the hard facts approach of Engelmann give the best view of what the Vietnam War and its aftermath are all about. Both fail in "contextualizing" history. A *via media* needs to be found between comic book exploitation and hard fact impersonality to represent the Vietnam War as the complex political, social, psychological event that it was. Nevertheless, in the brief history of the Vietnam War film, the bulk have, like 500,000 people every month, subscribed to the comic book approach. That bulk of films is flattened by the comic book simplifying of the issues of the Vietnam War and the choice of noncredible action over human characterization. In *Rambo II* (1986) and *III* (1988) there is no concern whatsoever for John Rambo as a person, a returned, grieving, and alienated Vietnam veteran as in *First Blood*. The only concern is for John Rambo as a killing machine similar to the high-tech Russian helicopter he confronts in *Rambo III*.

Not all of the comic book characters of this second phase are action figures out of Marvel Comics, however. Richard Pryor plays a Vietnam POW as a black Bugs Bunny in the "coming home" film *Some Kind of Hero* (1981), and the sequel to *American Graffiti* (1973), *More American Graffiti* (1979), portrays the Vietnam generation as if they were the characters in Archie comic books. *The Stunt Man* (1980), however, is one film from this period worth noting. It is possibly the most artful and sophisticated of all the veteran-coming-home Vietnam films. In *The Stunt Man*, life and the Vietnam War are metaphorically represented as movie. An anonymous Vietnam veteran joins the crew of a movie company making a World War I movie, and suddenly his sense of never knowing what was going on, of what was real and what was just an illusion, comes flooding back to him as a strange sort of variation on a Vietnam War flashback. In portraying the issues of the Vietnam War as movie, *The Stunt Man* shares its central metaphor with Julian Smith who in *Looking Away: Hollywood and Vietnam* (New York: Charles Scribner's Sons, 1975) wrote:

> Vietnam was like a movie that had gotten out of hand: gigantic cost overruns, a shooting schedule run amuck, squabbles on the set, and back in the studio, the first *auteur* dying with most of the script in his head, the second quitting in disgust, and the last swearing it was finally in the can, but sneaking back to shoot some extra scenes. (103)

and with Michael Herr who in *Dispatches* (New York: Alfred A. Knopf, 1977) wrote:

> In any other war, they would have made movies about us too, *Dateline: Hell!*, *Dispatch from Dong Ha*, maybe even *A Scrambler to the Front*, about Tim Page, Sean Flynn and Rick Merron, three young photographers who used to ride in and out of combat on Hondas. . . . So we have all been compelled to make our own movies, as many movies as there are correspondents, and this is mine. (One day at the battalion aid station in Hue a Marine with minor shrapnel wounds in his legs was waiting to get on a helicopter, a long wait with all of the dead and badly wounded going out first, and a couple of sniper rounds snapped across the airstrip, forcing us to move behind some sandbagging. "I hate this movie," he said, and I thought, "Why not?") My movie, my friends, my colleagues. (189)

The Stunt Man's portrayal of the Vietnam War as movie subtly represents the situation of the Vietnam veteran in the American society of the eighties. In the film, elaborate dangerous illusion and aimless post-Vietnam War reality contest for a wandering Vietnam veteran's soul. In *The Stunt Man* that American dilemma is resolved comically, but on the set of *The Twilight Zone: The Movie* (1985), during the filming of scenes representing the Vietnam War, the black comedy of *The Stunt Man* turned into real tragedy with the deaths of actor Vic Morrow and two Vietnamese children.

This whole series of comic book passes at the issues and themes of the Vietnam War focused almost exclusively upon the theme of "coming home" and then somehow going back, either psychologically as in *Some Kind of Hero* or *The Stunt Man* or *Cease Fire* (1986) or *Firefox* (1985) or actually (though unbelievably) physically returning to rescue those who were originally left behind as in *The Deer Hunter, Uncommon Valor* (1983), *Rambo II*, and the *Missing in Action* (1984–87) films. This wishful-survivor-guilt fantasy best fit the comic book commando type and, culminating in *Rambo II* in 1986, was the essential plot of the majority of the films dealing with the legacy of Vietnam.

And then came 1987–88, the year of Vietnam at the movies, the second coming of 1977–78 when *Coming Home, The Deer Hunter,* and *Apocalypse Now* all appeared. In the short space of sixteen months, no less than six major Vietnam War films were released. Of these six, only *Platoon, Full Metal Jacket, Hamburger Hill,* and *Off Limits* are really about the Vietnam War. *Gardens of Stone* and *Good Morning, Vietnam* are not really about the war itself. Of the six, *Full Metal Jacket* is the most important because it does what *Platoon* makes a valiant attempt to do. It gives a full definition to the nihilism that all the soldiers in the Vietnam War films of this year feel. In John Del Vecchio's novel, *The 13th Valley,* the recurring grunt expression of the nature of the infantryman's situation in Vietnam is "It don't mean nothin'." *Full Metal Jacket* also underscores that phrase and then, in a series of striking images, presents a full, highly symbolic view of that nihilistic approach to life in the Vietnam War. Thus, because the recurring conclusion that each film in its own way draws is that "It don't mean nothin'," the third phase, the postmodernist phase, of the history of the Vietnam War film can be called the symbolic nihilist phase.

What is important about this symbolic nihilist third phase of Vietnam War films is that, except for *Gardens of Stone,* all of the films are set in Vietnam, in the war. The consensus that all of these films arrive at is that being in the Vietnam War occasioned an almost complete annihilation of a former, civilized, moral self just as the circumstances of the war itself had accomplished a complete annihilation of the participant's grasp of reality, morality, or sanity. As Conrad wrote about Africa in *Heart of Darkness,* Vietnam also was a world where everyone had been "kicked loose of the earth" and was operating with "no restraint." Symbolic nihilism is the representation or dramatization of an individual's or a group of individuals' gradual movement into a void in which all positive aspects of the self, all powers of self-determination and control of action and context are not simply temporarily lost but rather are so totally annihilated that the self no longer believes in any contexts, no longer hopes for any progress toward any of the ideals, moral designs, social relationships that it held before entering that void. In literary/filmic terms, each of the Vietnam War films of 1987–88 work on two levels of symbolic interpretation. Each is a film of the initiation of the protagonists into nothingness, the annihilation of the self. Simultaneously, however, each is also about what Vietnam did to America, how it annihilated the Kennedy idealism of the early sixties, took what had been the world's most powerful society's positive (even arrogant) sense of itself and humiliated that sense of itself into emptiness and complete moral breakdown.

In *Going After Cacciato*, Paul Berlin's father tells him, "You'll see some terrible stuff, I guess. That's how it goes. But try to look for the good things, too. They'll be there if you look." But for Chris Taylor in *Platoon*, for Joker in *Full Metal Jacket*, for the whole faceless platoon in *Hamburger Hill* and for the two utterly confused cops in *Off Limits*, there are no good things. They all realize, as did Sergeant Egan in *The 13th Valley*, that "it don't mean nothin'" is ultimately the only way that the nihilism of the Vietnam War can be encountered. Those books and these films form a literature of rejection. Their characters reject their former selves and realize that all that is left for them is to wander like ghosts within the void of those rejections.

Platoon

The release of Oliver Stone's *Platoon* in December of 1986 opened the year of Vietnam at the movies. When *Platoon* appeared, the professional movie critics were unanimous in their praise for it as film.[10] What was more interesting about *Platoon*'s critical reception, however, was the number of essays by nonprofessional critics generated in major newspapers and magazines. These commentaries on the film, written almost always by Vietnam veterans, are also generally positive toward the film while going a number of steps further than the professional film critics who had praised and analyzed the film as art, who had unanimously stressed the film's realism, its representation of what the life (and death) of an infantryman in the Vietnam War was really like. The nonprofessional critics analyze the aesthetic realism of the scenes, the characters, the themes of *Platoon* much more carefully than do many of the professional film critics. These nonprofessional critics make a clearer distinction between realism in art and the realism of life. It is a textual distinction that sets the inevitable differentation between combatant textuality and noncombatant textuality. For the Vietnam War, the credential of having "been there" overrides any other credential. Unfortunately, the combatant textuality tends to reach for personal emotional reasons for making critical judgments rather than artistic or historical or social reasons. However, some of these nonprofessional critics also examine the film from the perspective of social history.

They attempt to analyze why, more than fifteen years after the fact, a film on the Vietnam War could still frag the American cultural imagination.

Henry Allen, writing in the *Washington Post* (7 January 1987) before he had seen the movie, strikes a cautionary note about the ability of war movies to be realistic:

> Now we've got *Platoon*. A young man who was in grade school when I was in Vietnam tells me it's "authentic." *Time* magazine published a cover story about it and the headline said: "Vietnam As It Really Was."
>
> This is silly and decadent, this willful confusion of life and art. And it's dangerous. War is too wildly stupid, glorious, hideous, huge and human for us to think that art can tell us what it really is.

Allen's skepticism about *Platoon*'s authenticity was echoed by General William Westmoreland in a speech at Purdue University in January 1987 when he said, "I haven't seen this movie *Platoon*, but it is full of lies and I don't think anyone should go see it." As nonprofessional film critics, both Allen and Westmoreland raise both social and aesthetic issues. Allen, like a good postmodernist, intuitively deconstructs the attempted realism of the film, while Westmoreland simply denounces it because it violates the old rules of positively upholding the American myth of the moral soldier. Other nonprofessional film commentators, who did manage to see the film before they wrote about it, take a more positive approach to *Platoon* as both film and social history.

David Halberstam, writing in the *New York Times* (8 March 1987), argues:

> Of the serious postwar films that have preceded *Platoon*, none to me ever passed the test of being a true Vietnam War movie. . . .
>
> By contrast, *Platoon* is about Vietnam. It exists only, as they say, in-country. It has no other objective, no other agenda. To me it is both a great American movie and a great War movie. Its combat scenes are as good as any I have ever seen. . . . It is painfully realistic.

General Bernard E. Trainor of the Marine Corps, writing in that same issue of the *New York Times*, echoes Halberstam's evaluation:

> As a career Marine, I had seen my share of war, both on the silver screen and in real life. Needless to say, they are different, but *Platoon* does succeed in narrowing some of the differences. A filmgoer does not experience Vietnam by seeing *Platoon*, but he will see those who did. It is less a war movie than a movie of men at war. . . . A film can never replicate those experiences although this one makes an honest attempt to do so . . . what does come through in *Platoon*, to make it a notable war movie, is its authentic portrayal of infantrymen.

As *Platoon*'s title intimates, and as both Halberstam and Trainor stress, the film is not really about its young protagonist or the conflict between its two symbolic sergeants, it is about the whole platoon, this microcosm of America sentenced to the jungles of Vietnam.

Both the professional film critics intuitively and the nonprofessional Vietnam veteran film critics stress the manner in which *Platoon* attempts through art to realistically represent the *feel* of Vietnam. The dynamism, the fluidity, the nonlinear, almost vortextual, motion of that aesthetic realism is the film's major contribution. *Platoon* is a divided movie in terms of story and intention much as was Coppola's *Apocalypse Now*. David Halberstam writes of *Apocalypse Now* (*Washington Post*, 8 March 1987) that it "was two films, an occasionally brilliant Vietnam movie mixed together with Coppola's version of *Heart of Darkness*." A similar doubleness exists in two of the major Vietnam War films of 1987–88. *Full Metal Jacket* is without question two movies, one about Parris Island, one about in-country Vietnam. *Platoon*, like *Apocalypse Now*, does not really split as does *Full Metal Jacket* but rather is layered into a double structure, one conventional and linear, the other fluid and postmodernist. *Platoon* attempts to tell the linear story of a group of allegorical *Bildungsroman* characters. On a second plane, it offers, in unstructured bursts of imagery, language, emotion, and realistic detail (like automatic weapons fire or like what Michael Herr in *Dispatches* calls "illumination rounds") the feel of what it was like to be there in Vietnam in 1968.

Story and intention are the two sides of *Platoon*'s split personality. In terms of story, *Platoon* is a conventional, utterly predictable, flatly characterized, simplistic, clichéd narrative. Its story of a young man coming of age in a world peopled with, as Pauline Kael has noted (*New Yorker*, 12 January 1987), "medieval morality play" characters does not explain *Platoon*'s tremendous impact upon eighties audiences.[11]

In terms of representational narrative, the story told in *Platoon* is a cumbersome Manichean myth of Good and Evil, the Light side and the Dark side. It attempts the same sort of dialectical narrative tension that the symbolic myth of "the Force" in the *Star Wars* trilogy posited. Chris Taylor (Charlie Sheen) serves as the synthesis character in the Manichean dialectic of *Platoon*, as does Luke Skywalker serve as mediator between the Light side of "the Force" as represented by Obi Wan Kenobe/Yoda and the Dark side as embodied in Darth Vader. *Platoon*'s "medieval morality play" story also carries all sorts of mythic, literary baggage. As did Francis Coppola's *Apocalypse Now*, *Platoon* offers simultaneous representations of the Christ myth and the mad intensity of Ahab's quest for Moby Dick.[12] The Christ imagery, as unmistakeable in the slow-motion death of Elias (Willem Dafoe), and the Ahab parallel, as intoned in Chris Taylor's voice-over, are as obvious and pretentious as was Coppola's ponderous panning over the books in Kurtz's selective library in *Apocalypse Now*—Fraser's *Golden Bough*, Jessie Weston's *From Ritual to Romance*, T. S. Eliot's *Wasteland and Other Poems*—which constitutes a sort of pedantry that turns a movie theater into a lecture hall. *Platoon* is not about the story of Chris Taylor and Sergeants Elias and Barnes (Tom Berenger). It is not a film about growing up. It is not a film about Good and Evil. It is not a film about Life and Death. It is certainly not a film about Christ or Captain Ahab. It is a film about fear, about death in the lowercase, about anger, about pain, about love, about honesty and dishonesty, about stupidity and cowardice and courage, about drugs and booze and blacks and whites and rich and poor and hippies and rednecks, about smells and tastes and how the jungle feels and sounds, about snakes and bugs and rain and blood and fire, about screams and terrible silences, about darkness shattered by bright light, about calm erupting into frenzied flight, about tracer bullets and invisible trip wires, about helicopters and tunnels, about sexual depravity and mindless brutality and instinctual sympathy, about atrocity and survival, about children caught in war and warriors who are still children, about green and red and brown and black, about flesh and metal and wind and water, about how people feel in war, the Vietnam War. Story in *Platoon* is of little concern. Waste the story and concentrate on the imagery, the action, the words.

More than anything else, however, *Platoon* is about confusion.[13] That theme of confusion embraces a whole hierarchy of forms in the film. In *Platoon*'s rudimentary story structure, Chris Taylor suffers from a severe identity confusion. Even though Taylor's letters to his grandmother read in voice-over are generally sentimental, portentous, and unbelievable (Would he really write these kinds of details to a white-haired old lady back in the States?) every once in a while the words cut right to the heart of the young soldier's identity confusion.

Chris writes, "I don't even know what I'm doin'. . . . Nobody cares about the new guys. They don't even wanna know my name." Only moments later, Taylor's perception is confirmed as two battle-hardened veterans, Elias and O'Neil (John C. McGinley), argue about whose fireteam should go out on ambush. "Whaddaya want me to do?" O'Neil whines, "Send some of my guys out? You got the new meat, Elias." Only short screen minutes later, after a "cherry" or "FNG" who came in with Taylor is killed in his first night in the bush, Elias zips him into a body bag and, almost noncommittally, notes, "He'd still be alive if he had a few more days to learn somethin'." An individual's confusion about himself is really no different in Vietnam than it is anywhere else; it is just much more dangerous and demands resolution more quickly. The whole first section of *Platoon*'s structure is a "naming of parts" necessitated by the confusion about how to survive that plagues the mind of Chris Taylor. As David Denby (*New York*, 15 December 1986) notes, "Barnes doesn't tell Taylor what to do on his first patrol, yet considers him completely responsible for anything he does wrong." By extension, this detailed "naming of parts" is also necessary for the theater audience who must, simultaneously with Chris Taylor, learn the territory, the tricks of how to interpret the world of the film. Chris Taylor becomes the audience's surrogate for immersion into the life of the Vietnam War. But along with learning how the war works, the audience, through its identification with Chris Taylor, learns how an infantryman in Vietnam feels. *Platoon* is not a conventional existential film about identity confusion. In a war zone, there is not much time to be confused about oneself when there are so many other types of confusion to confront and resolve.

Besides this confusion of the new guy trying to survive in a hostile environment without any help, there are other, more complex types of confusion in *Platoon*. There is the moral confusion embodied in the morality play characters of Sergeants Elias and Barnes who are meant to represent the ambiguities of Good and Evil to Chris Taylor's Everyman. Because this morality play story is so melodramatic and pretentious, its too obvious artificiality disqualifies it from delivering the thematic and emotional impact that less stylized aspects of *Platoon* do indeed carry. Thus the themes of existential confusion and moral confusion are not developed either meaningfully or powerfully in *Platoon*. Two other types of confusion, however, class confusion and ultimate chaos, do take on the immediacy and thematic impact necessary to actually make the audience feel that the unique confusion of a grunt in Vietnam has been contextualized.

Platoon has a three-part dramatic structure that overlays its linear plot and bursts of imagistic realism. Each of the film's parts underscores the social theme of class confusion, and each of the three parts contains an apocalyptic scene(s) in which ultimate chaos reigns. The class confusion of the characters, especially Chris Taylor, builds toward the ultimate rejection of all identity, morality, class identification, and humanity in the midst of the utter nihilism of chaos. In *Platoon* the ultimate symbol of this nihilistic chaos is the firefight. In part one. a night ambush, the searching of a booby-trapped bunker complex and, finally, a village atrocity right off the CBS News, begins the gradual escalation of chaos. In each succeeding scene, the violence gets heavier, the corpses get bloodier, the humanity of the infantrymen gets raggeder. Scene by scene, Stone chronicles the wearing away of the existence, the morality, the social class, of his grunt characters. In part two, the morality play is resolved in the confrontation between Elias and Barnes in the jungle and the firefight crucifixion of Elias as his fellow grunts watch helplessly from on high. Part three of *Platoon* is composed almost exclusively of the ultimate firefight, the culmination in nihilistic chaos.

Part one of *Platoon* is an extended "naming of parts." It fulfills the purpose that the basic training sequences in most conventional World War II movies and in *Full Metal Jacket* serve. As the audience goes out on patrol with the platoon to which Chris Taylor has been assigned, it is oriented to the Vietnam War right along with Taylor. But this orientation is much more direct and graphic and real than any basic training simulation could ever be. *Platoon* is absolutely at its best when it is presenting even the tiniest visceral details of what life in the Vietnam War is all about. In the first dramatic firefight scene, Chris Taylor's first guard duty on a night ambush, the tiny detail of the condensation on his wristwatch is simultaneously real and symbolic. This is the first instance of time being blurred and meaningless, a subtheme that will recur throughout the film and contribute to the universal meaninglessness that is *Platoon*'s central theme. In this scene, Chris's sense of time breaks down, then his defenses break down, then the perimeter of the platoon breaks down, and the result is chaos as, suddenly, the firefight erupts. When the shooting stops, all that is left is the screams of the wounded, followed by the hopeless, scared— "Take the pain! Take the pain!"—orders of the survivors. Those frantic screams are the first indication of the utter unintelligibility of this war.

As punishment for his breakdown on ambush, Taylor is given the duty of pulling the shit cans out of the latrine. This duty too vibrates with symbolic irony as the young grunts realize that they are pulling everybody else in America's shit. This simultaneously realistic and symbolic "naming of parts" continues in the next scene in the Heads Bunker as Elias teaches Chris Taylor to shotgun dope. Though it seems just an exotic foray into drug lore, it too carries a symbolic irony. Taylor, in volunteering for Vietnam, has put a gun to his own head just as surely as he is accepting the double barrels of Elias's shotgun. Each visual detail upon which Stone's camera lingers in this opening "naming of parts" section carries this real/symbolic irony duality. Echoing Jake Gittes in *Chinatown* (1974), when a booby trap explodes killing one of his men, Barnes screams "nothing is ever what it seems."[14] The platoon's entry into the *Chinatown* world of the bunker complex, which Stone offers in a series of subjective point-of-view shots from a handheld camera, identifies the audience with the unsuspecting members of the platoon. Their immediate setting off of the booby trap on the box of NVA documents points to the film's building sense of confusion. You can name the parts, but you can never understand them. You are your own worst enemy.

Part one ends with the burning of a Vietnamese village by the enraged platoon. It is a scene that draws heavily upon the earlier Vietnam War literature. It is a scene out of Caputo's *Rumor of War*.[15] Taylor's portentous voice-over introduces the scene badly: "Barnes was the eye of our rage. Our Captain Ahab." It is hard to believe that he is really writing this sort of thing to his grandma. As soon as the platoon enters the village, the madness of the war confronts them in the blank mad eyes of a Vietnamese boy. In *Dispatches*, Michael Herr writes:

A little boy of about ten came up to a bunch of Marines from Charlie Company. He was laughing and moving his head from side to side in a funny way. The fierceness in his eyes should have told everyone what it was but it had never occurred to most of the grunts that a Vietnamese child could be driven mad too, and by the time they understood it the boy had begun to go for their eyes and tear at their fatigues, spooking everyone, putting everyone really uptight, until a black grunt grabbed him from behind and held his arm. "C'mon, pore lil' baby, 'fore one of these grunt mothers shoots you." (75)

The village burning scene begins with an instant replay of Herr's description. First, Taylor makes the mad boy dance with machine gun fire, then another young American, unable to stand the madness, beats the mad boy to death with the butt of his rifle. Ironically the Americans strike out at the madness of the war with their own form of madness as they kill, rape, and burn the village and its inhabitants, then walk away from the holocaust like missionaries, carrying the children of their victims.

This is a pivotal scene in *Platoon*. In earlier scenes, the chaos, the annihilation of normality and reason, was engineered by the enemy, but in this village scene it is the Americans who are accepting the chaos of the war, who are annihilating their own moral images of themselves. As Taylor breaks up the gang rape of a Vietnamese child, he screams, "She's a fuckin' human being, man. You're all animals." Philip Caputo, in a speech on the war (Purdue University, March 1988), defines a dialectical tension between "the outlaw and the missionary." For Caputo, young Americans in Vietnam were always torn between the idealistic view of themselves as moral crusaders, spreaders of the Kennedy doctrine, and the realistic view of themselves as outlaws, like Conrad's Kurtz.

The final scene of part one of *Platoon*, the burning of the village, captures this frightening duality. Earlier in the movie, when Chris was telling two other grunts about his past life and why he enlisted, he generated this reaction: "What we got here is a Crusader," one of his fellow grunts comments sarcastically. As the Americans snap in the village scene—"Let's do the whole fuckin' village," one proposes—Chris realizes that the "crusader," the "missionary," must always contend with the "outlaw" in Vietnam, or every act will result in madness, atrocity, and the total annihilation of all that is human. When he screams, "You're all animals! You just don't fuckin' get it," as he breaks up the gang rape, he is commenting directly upon the nihilism that has caught the Americans in its grip. Finally, all is settled in the least satisfactory manner. An order comes down from command to torch the village and the scene ends in caustic irony. As the grunts of the platoon set fire to the hootches and walk away carrying the Vietnamese children who, only moments before, they were brutalizing, orchestral music, all violins and oboes, the somber music of missionaries, rises. It is so out of place at the conclusion of this nihilistic scene of confusion and insanity that it draws absurd attention to itself. The scene has the same terrible impact that the brutally nihilistic sampan scene in *Apocalypse Now* had. These young Americans are not missionaries headed, with the children on their shoulders, to some Vietnamese version of Father Flanagan's Boys Town. They are a group of brutal, frightened, empty young killers who, only moments before, had lost all control and indulged themselves, as Kurtz did in Conrad's *Heart of Darkness*, in "the fascination of abomination."

Part two of *Platoon* is the least interesting part of the film. It is the morality play. All through part one, the "naming of parts," and part two, the "morality play," a subtext of class confusion parallels the larger, more deadly, confusion of the firefights. This class confusion takes dualistic forms just as the stereotyped character oppositions and the conventional moral oppositions (outlaw vs. missionary) do. All through *Platoon*, the white Taylor, the middle-class Taylor, the volunteer Taylor, the morally conscious humanist Taylor, is contrasted to the black, the poor and uneducated, the forced and unwilling, the bestial and violent members of the platoon. As the members of the platoon become identifiable, if not by names like the black King and the white Kong or the hippie Elias and the redneck Barnes or the college-boy Lieutenant. and the utterly paranoid O'Neil, then by their repeated presence on-screen, the audience realizes that they are not really characters but simply pawns being moved around on this big green gameboard because the war has made their existence meaningless. King (Keith David) says, "this shit is gettin' 'way outa hand." Taylor, writing home, confesses, "I don't know right from wrong anymore." In part two, the platoon returns to the bunker complex where earlier they were warned that "nothing is ever what it seems" and are ambushed by a large detachment of uniformed NVA. Again, the class confusion is superseded by the chaos of the firefight.

The symbolic, allegorical opposition between Sergeants Elias and Barnes dominates the morality play dramatics of part two of *Platoon*. Ultimately, these two, Light and Dark, Good and Evil, Life and Death, Christ and Satan, face off alone in the bush to orchestrate the dialectic clash of their contending philosophies. They confront each other. Elias smiles in conciliation. Barnes shoots him in cold blood. Nihilism murders reason. But who cares? Elias and Barnes are eminently predictable, given their flat characterizations and their painfully obvious symbolic functions. Only one aspect of the whole acting out of this morality playlet has any significant meaning for the central thematics of the film: Chris Taylor stands as witness to it.

Waiting in the LZ for the choppers to evacuate them from the firefight, the platoon learns that Barnes and Elias are still in the bush. Taylor goes back to help them. In doing so, he becomes a witness to American naïveté being shot down, to American betrayal by fellow Americans, to American opportunism, to American murderousness, to the ultimate nihilism that the Vietnam War has dropped over the American character like a bell jar.

The choppers arrive. In the chopper wind, Barnes tells Taylor that Elias is dead. The choppers rise off the hot LZ and suddenly, the whole film goes maudlin. The orchestral "Adagio for Strings" rises out of the gunfire like a dirge. Elias appears running and being shot repeatedly. In slowmotion to orchestral strings he stretches his arms out to the sky, to the choppers hovering overhead, in the classic death pose of the Christus. It is all a contrived, sentimental set piece, and in the context of what *Platoon* is about (Chris Taylor's confusion, America's confusion in Vietnam), it means nothing.

Part three of *Platoon* is what the film is really about. In this section, the confusion escalates out of control and Taylor's role as observer and witness changes to that of participant and focus of the film's symbolic nihilism. Back in the base camp after the death of Elias, the platoon talks of fragging Barnes. Drunk, taking long pulls from his bottle of Kentucky bourbon as if it were a moonshine jug, Barnes intrudes upon their guilty conspiring and, in one speech, defines the whole "reality vs. humanism" dialectic of the war. He synthesizes that dialectic into a mechanistic, dehumanized nihilism that offers no solution, no hope, only endurance, survival. What Stanley Kauffman (*New Republic*, 19 January 1987) says about Taylor's voice-over narration is exactly what Barnes is telling the platoon about the war. Kauffman writes, the "voice-over comments. . . . shunt the film momentarily into the shape of an object lesson, when the real point is that there is no lesson."

"I am reality," Barnes growls. "Here's the way it oughta be. Here's the way it is. Elias is full of shit. Elias was a Crusader. Now I got no fight with anyone does what he's told. But when he don't the machine breaks down. And when the machine breaks down, we break down, and I ain't gonna allow that." Barnes's speech echoes the earlier sarcastic characterization of Taylor as a "Crusader" and goes on to characterize the platoon as simply a machine with interchangeable human parts. Barnes's declaration, "I am reality," is a statement of the nihilism, the scarred, empty, dehumanized, brutal, survivalist, mad nihilism that they all must accept and embrace if they are to exist as cogs in the machine of the war. What Barnes is saying is that all must become like him if they are to survive. In affirmation of Barnes's speech, in the last major scene of the film, Chris Taylor, who earlier was a "Crusader," becomes exactly like Barnes. Taylor accepts and acts upon the nihilism of Barnes's speech, enters the utter nihilism of his own heart of darkness. Proving once again that the Americans are their own worst enemies, that the nihilism of the Vietnam War lies within the American psyche not in the war itself, Taylor murders Barnes in cold blood as Barnes had earlier murdered Elias.

This scene in which Taylor murders Barnes is only a symbolic resolution to the "morality play" symbolism of part two of the film. It may serve as a coda, but it is not what *Platoon* is really about. *Platoon* ultimately is not at all about Elias or Barnes or Americans killing each other in Vietnam. *Platoon* is about confusion, confusion on every level of human perception, confusion on every level of national intention, confusion swirling and popping and exploding and spurting and twisting and turning and rising and falling so fast that nothingness, total void, is the only resting place. Moral confusion, existential confusion, confusion of time, of place, of reality, of sanity, confusion of intention, confusion of direction, ultimately just the utter confusion of meaningless action is the fuel that fires the film. All that happens in *Platoon* leads to the ultimate symbol of nihilistic confusion, the Ur-firefight, chaos personified and extended.

By the time the final firefight begins, Chris Taylor has learned the Vietnam War, has become proficient in death-dealing. He has learned to read the bush and see the attacking NVA in the night as he could not in the opening night ambush scene. He can find his claymore switches right away as he could not in the opening night ambush scene. He knows by instinct exactly when to get out of his foxhole as he did not earlier. When the final firefight starts, Chris Taylor goes on automatic, gives himself over to the confusion of the moment, becomes one wih the chaotic, whirling action. He chooses to exist within the nullity of the moment. Insanely, he charges the enemy.

The firefight begins slowly with shadows darting in the jungle and frightened screams piercing the terrified silence. A basketball flare floats down on its fragile Cracker Jack box parachute throwing surreal light over the dark jungle. Chris has time to make a few rational decisions—to stay not run, to set off the mines, to get out of the foxhole—but immediately the firefight explodes into what Vietnam was really all about, chaos. Once the enemy gets inside the perimeter, the real Vietnam, the nihilist place where utter confusion reigns, asserts itself. Images, actions, rip by faster than automatic weapons fire. Oliver Stone empties clip after clip at the theater audience. Chris Taylor rushes face first into the firefight in a mad suicidal charge. The phones, the machines, do not work. The American commander drops napalm inside his own perimeter. All is confusion, a drawn-out nihilistic nightmare. For a few brief seconds a film actually captures the mad-minute pace of the Vietnam War. *Platoon*, quite simply, is a brilliant movie of how the Vietnam War was a straightforward process of things getting out of control.

The final scene of *Platoon* in which Taylor confronts and murders Barnes is anticlimactic. Like the aftermath of the final battle in *Go Tell the Spartans* (1978), Taylor's killing of Barnes, like the panorama of the dead, stripped corpses of Major Barker's (Burt Lancaster) platoon in *Go Tell the Spartans*, is simply a symbolic coda to this fable of the loss of American innocence in Vietnam. *Platoon* is a straightforward, slice-of-life parable of the descent of American optimism into the black hole of utter nihilism. In this coda scene, an American kills an American, stressing once again that in Vietnam America was its own worst enemy. Chris Taylor literally kills the self he has followed and become. He repeats Barnes's act of killing Elias. He becomes Barnes even as he kills Barnes. He refuses to accept any meaning in either Elias or Barnes. He kills meaning, opts for nothing.

Why does Chris Taylor kill Sergeant Barnes? Perhaps because "it don't mean nothin'." Perhaps because he sees murder as a moral act. Perhaps as an act of revenge for Elias. Perhaps as a mercy killing, because Barnes asks him (tells him?) to "do it" just as the dying sniper begs Joker to kill her in the climactic scene of *Full Metal Jacket*. Perhaps Chris Taylor kills Sergeant Barnes for all or none of these reasons, but what is important is that he kills him. In *Heart of Darkness*, Marlow draws back from Kurtz, never really descends into the nihilistic horror within which Kurtz has chosen to live, lies to Kurtz's intended. In *Apocalypse Now* and in *Platoon* Captain Willard and Chris Taylor both descend all the way down into the nothingness of Vietnam's special heart of darkness. In both films, that descent into nothingness involves the killing of a part of themselves, an American killing an American. In *Walking Point: American Narratives of Vietnam*, Thomas Myers writes:

> The prime historical message within the new literature of Vietnam resides finally in how terminally its heroes are transformed by the experience, in how complete seems the discrepancy between necessary personal explanation and inevitable violent agency. Most often, the protagonist is not merely affected or altered by the history he helps to write; he is spiritually and emotionally annihilated by it, reshaped internally so that his new state becomes a dark joke that only the initiated can share. (31–32)

In the final analysis, the classic American folk song "Oh! Susannah" that the platoon sang as it left base camp on Chris Taylor's first day in Vietnam echoes as a terribly ironic commentary upon the death of the American dream in this remote Southeast Asian outpost. The sentimental optimism of that classic folk love song has no place in the nihilistic cacophony of the Vietnam War.

Chris Taylor's final speech in voice-over as he is airlifted out of Vietnam is about emptiness—"I think now, looking back, we did not fight the enemy but ourselves, and the war was in us . . . but be that as it may, those of us who did make it have an obligation to build again, to teach to others what we know, and to try with what's left of our lives to find a goodness and meaning to this life." But the vets like Chris Taylor have not been able to find that meaning. The ultimate example of the war's nihilistic meaninglessness is the continuing confused mobility in the eighties of every text, be it film or novel or history or oral history or analytic study or classroom discussion, which attempts to find meaning in that war. The meaning of the Vietnam War is not, like the Viet Cong, merely elusive; in almost every extant text, it seems to be utterly nonexistent. What *Platoon* says—in accordance with Michael Herr in *Dispatches*:

Straight history, auto-revised history, history without handles, for all the books and articles and white papers, all the talk and the miles of film, something wasn't answered, it wasn't even asked. We were backgrounded, deep, but when the background started sliding forward not a single life was saved by the information. The thing had transmitted too much energy, it heated up too hot, hiding low under the fact-figure crossfire there was a secret history, and not a lot of people felt like running in there to bring it out. (51)

—is that history is not enough, not at all the right text for the representation of the Vietnam War. What *Platoon* says is that this war went way beyond history, dug down beneath the surface into the darkest caverns of the American soul as guarded by those poor troglodytes, those hopeless grunts in Vietnam. The grunt history, the history recorded in *Dispatches* and in *Platoon* is not the history of the books, the maps, the dates, the place names, the military operations, the logs, the company commanders' reports, the Pentagon Papers, but rather it is the history of the sounds and the smells, the sudden terrible fears and the smoldering rages, the sounds of artillery and mortar and screaming in the flames, the smell of napalm and rotting flesh and wet jungle in the morning and marijuana at night, the feel of rivers of sweat and hatred as dry as a desert, the history of a vast emptiness, the emptiness within yourself, the emptiness of the whole campaign, the emptiness of all American life. Ultimately, the real contextualized history of the Vietnam War is a perfect postmodernist text. Ultimately, the history of the Vietnam War is a holographic, multilayered history of nothingness, of an event that never had, ever actively denies, meaning.

Full Metal Jacket

Because of the rather surprising success, both critical and box-office, of *Platoon* (culminating in the Academy Award for Best Picture), five more films plus two weekly prime-time network TV shows ("Tour of Duty", "China Beach") followed in the next sixteen months. The other films of this Year of Vietnam at the movies, especially *Full Metal Jacket*, *Hamburger Hill*, and *Off Limits*, duplicate the symbolic nihilism of *Platoon*. Each examines the thesis of loss of innocence, dislocation from a real and moral world of normality, descent into a meaningless void, utter despair and the ultimate denial and jettisoning of the former self. Whereas *The Deer Hunter* and *Apocalypse Now* of the late seventies were exercises in romanticism, *Platoon* and *Full Metal Jacket* are strong attempts to pierce the hard armor of realism.

Stanley Kubrick especially is no neophyte in the exploration of nihilism. All through his career, from the mad zaniness of the world coming to an end in *Dr. Strangelove* to the slow, tortuous exploration of the emptiness of *Barry Lyndon* to the mad mouse in a maze cinematography of *The Shining*, Kubrick's stock in trade has been nihilism. It was inevitable that sooner or later his black comic vision of the world, his cinema of cynicism, would lead him to Vietnam. *Full Metal Jacket* fits into the Kubrick canon as tightly and precisely as a clip clicks into an M-16.

J. Hoberman, writing about the Vietnam War films of the eighties, makes an excellent distinction: "But if *Rambo: First Blood Part II*, *Missing in Action*, and the other Vietnam exorcisms of the early Eighties were obsessed with refighting the war, those of the late Eighties are concerned with re-presenting it."[16]

Hoberman is recognizing the decidedly postmodernist themes of these late eighties Vietnam War films and his concept of "re-presenting" holds especially true for *Platoon*, *Full Metal Jacket*, and *Hamburger Hill*. "Re-presentation" is the high-focusing, the ultraclarifying of the realities that are already known but have been deceptively or unclearly presented in the past. Matthew Modine, an incisive and extremely analytic actor who plays the lead role in Kubrick's *Full Metal Jacket*, agrees with Hoberman: "The reason that Stanley's stories are so shocking is because they're so truthful. He doesn't try to create some sympathy for somebody because it's a film, because he wants to win the audience over. It's not pleasant to see somebody killed. And it's not pleasant to die. Why try to make it some thing romantic when it's not?"[17]

This whole concept of "re-presenting" reality is what fuels the Vietnam War films of the third phase, 1987–88. Whereas *Platoon* is brilliant in its images and action yet terribly pretentious in its narrative intention, *Full Metal Jacket* is a much more focused, thematically coherent film.

The central theme of *Full Metal Jacket* is an examination of nihilism at its most elemental level. *Full Metal Jacket* is about the failure of words in a world that is utterly denatured, unsexed, defoliated, and dehumanized. Only one critic, Penelope Gilliatt, initially recognized this theme of the failure of language in the Vietnam War as it appears in *Full Metal Jacket*. She writes:

> The title . . . describes the encasement around a bullet-head that doesn't disintegrate when it enters the body. It is held to be a more humane way of killing: a death-given piece of the counterfeit language that Kubrick sees as a symptom of our growing and perilous willingness to entertain the sham. It is not just that our military jargon endows the manic with apparent levelheadedness, it is that pseudoscientific euphemisms congratulate clever-ness when we urgently need intelligence. . . . *Full Metal Jacket* shows that specious wording is as much the stuff of war now as it is of faith healing.[18]

The "counterfeit language," "military jargon," the "euphemisms," and "specious wording" are the main focus of *Full Metal Jacket*.

Kubrick agrees that Vietnam was always a war of words:

> Vietnam was probably the first war that was run—certainly during the Kennedy era—as an advertising agency might run it. . . . It was managed

with cost-effective estimates and phony statistics and kill ratios and self-deceiving predictions about how victory was the light at the end of the tunnel. The Americans in Vietnam were encouraged to lie about the progress they were making. If a couple of shots were fired on patrol, it was good to say that you killed two gooks and if you said two, somebody would make it eight.[19]

Full Metal Jacket has no real plot. It simply consists of disposable characters and motion. The motion, the dialogue, the images of *Full Metal Jacket* are about words in the same way that some aspects of *Platoon* are about confusion.

Private Joker (Matthew Modine) is not at all like Chris Taylor in *Platoon*. Joker is not confused. He is a writer, a word-man, who is painfully aware of how words can be exploited for all sorts of devious purposes. Joker is smarter, more streetwise, much more sympathetic and aware than Chris Taylor who, in the comparison, comes off a rather spoiled, bumbling, slow-on-the-uptake rube. Joker is a much more cerebral, verbal character, quick to move and speak, whereas Chris Taylor is more a passive observer, a *tabula rasa* waiting to be written on.

Like *Platoon*, the narrative of *Full Metal Jacket* is in parts, but the separation of those parts is much more dramatic. Whereas *Platoon* lands the audience in Vietnam in its opening frame and spends its whole time in-country single-mindedly unfolding a young soldier's initiation and psychological hardening, *Full Metal Jacket* at first seems to be two totally distinct films. No Vietnam War film, except a feeble stereotypical section of *The Boys in Company C* (1978), has attempted, as Philip Caputo in *A Rumor of War* and Gustav Hasford in *The Short Timers* (from which *Full Metal Jacket* is adapted) did so brilliantly, to portray the training experience of Vietnam-bound American soldiers. The first half of *Full Metal Jacket*, set at the Marine boot camp at Parris Island, portrays that experience with a vengeance. The second half also differs in setting from all the other Vietnam War films. It takes place in a city, not in a jungle. It offers stark images of the urban warfare of the battle for Hue during the Tet Offensive of 1968 that are reminiscent of the combat footage and film versions of World War II in Europe or the eighties TV news footage of downtown Beirut. This second act of *Full Metal Jacket* is divided into two extended scenes. The first shows Joker "in the rear with the gear" as a *Stars and Stripes* journalist in a supposedly secure headquarters company. This scene examines the war as presented by the overtext words of the media. The second scene of this second half is, as was the last part of *Platoon*, a single extended urban firefight that is Kubrick's symbolic crystallization of the futility of America's machines, firepower, and, especially, the words invented to deal with the ballet of death that is the Vietnam War.

Seemingly there is little connection between the Parris Island and the in-country Vietnam halves of *Full Metal Jacket*. In the second half, except for Joker and a minor character named Cowboy, the characters are new and as disposable as the characters in the Parris Island half of the film. Yet despite this vast difference in setting and characters between the two halves, in terms of theme they complement each other and form a complex unity for the film.[20] Sergeant Hartman (Lee Ermey), the DI, dominates the first half, and with good reason. Hartman is the teacher in this "eight week college for the phony tough and the crazy brave." This whole first half is made up of Hartman's screaming monologues couched in the magical, mystical, obscene language of the Marine Corps. He assaults the recruits, applies relentless psychological pressure, with words that slam into them like automatic weapons fire. He humiliates them and makes them grovel with his mocking words. He strikes fear into their hearts with his violent words. He changes them forever with his war of words.

Hartman and his words in act 1 of *Full Metal Jacket* is the equivalent of the war in act 2. Both Hartman and the war are always there, always a threat, unrelenting, murderous, hateful, impersonal, utterly psychologically destructive. In one important speech in act 2, Hartman's analogic equivalency to the enemy in the war is clearly drawn. Crazy Earl (Kieron Jacobus), sitting next to a dead Viet Cong, says:

> I love the little Commie bastards. I really do. These enemy grunts are *as hard as slant-eyed drill instructors*. These are great days we're livin' bros. We are jolly green giants walkin' the earth with guns. These people we wasted here today are the finest human beings we will ever know. After we rotate back to the world, we're gonna miss not havin' anyone around *who's worth shootin'*. (my italics)

In this speech, the analogy between Hartman, the hardest of drill instructors, someone who Gomer Pyle (Vincent D'Onofrio) certainly believes is "worth shootin'," and the Vietnamese enemy is explicitly drawn.

What happens at Parris Island to those raw Marine recruits is meant to be compared with what happens to these supposed combat veterans in Hue in act 2 of the film. Just as the recruits at Parris Island have no idea how to answer Hartman's unanswerable questions, on patrol in Hue the grunts have no idea where they are. Eightball (Dorian Harewood), the point man, turns the map this way and that, even upside down, studies it as if it were some ancient hieroglyph as Cowboy looks helplessly on holding a useless compass in his hand. Just as Hartman gloats over the fact that the recruits are helpless lost souls whose asses he owns, so also are the grunts in Hue lost, abandoned to their own devices with little sense of direction, owned by a single VC sniper whose power and eloquent accuracy with bullets is directly analogous to Hartman's power and oppressive accuracy with words. In order to free himself from the prison house of language that Hartman has pounded together around him, Gomer Pyle must kill the DI; in order to gain their freedom from the sniper, the platoon must kill her. In both cases, previously innocent young men, Gomer Pyle and Joker, must become killers because of their circumstances. Gomer Pyle, as he sits in the stark white latrine loading his rifle and waiting for Hartman, then kills Hartmen, then blows his own tortured and twisted psyche into a terrible red pattern all over the white porcelain walls, has undergone the most nihilistic of metamorphoses. He has been transformed by Hartman's words from a stupid innocent farm boy into a pariah into an utterly psychotic mad killer into a grinning suicide. Hartman annihilates all that is human in Gomer Pyle and Gomer Pyle chooses to annihilate both Hartman and himself. In the sniper scene at the end of *Full Metal Jacket*, the red of Pyle's twisted brains splattered all over the latrine walls becomes the red glare of the burning city that filters through the holes in the walls of the burned-out building, the backdrop against which the tableau of the sniper takes place. The sniper also chooses death, begs the platoon "Shoot me. Shoot me. Shoot me." And ultimately Joker obliges.

Joker's killing of the sniper at the end of *Full Metal Jacket* calls up the killing of the mistakenly wounded Vietnamese girl on the sampan by Captain Willard (Martin Sheen) in *Apocalypse Now*. Both scenes are capitulations to the utter nihilism of the war. The ironic absurdity of it all is, perhaps, best expressed by Willard as, in voice-over, he says, "We blow them in half with a machine gun, then we give them a bandaid." Joker, who all through *Full Metal Jacket* has ridiculed the language of the war, words like "confirmed kill," in the sniper scene as he looks down at the dying girl who is begging him to kill her, realizes that he is about to make a truly confirmed kill. The nihilism of Joker's "damned if I do and damned if I don't" situation involves the irony of cold-blooded murder being a moral act, a mercy killing, contradictions in terms, oxymoronic manipulations of words. The point of Joker's decision to kill the sniper and his final voice-over to the tune of the Mickey Mouse Club song is that self-justification, morality, the overcoming of guilt, are all simply a word game, a nihilistic manipulation of language, that which makes humans separate from animals.

Both act 1 and act 2 of *Full Metal Jacket* end with acts of symbolic nihilism, a suicide and a murder. Acts 1 and 2 are connected, because, in both, the theme of words as the weapons of the war's nihilism is the central focus. Sergeant Hartman must be a powerful, dominant character in act 1 because he must be equal to the power and dominance of the war in act 2. His language must be so powerful, hard core, brutal and nihilistic of the recruits' identity, manhood, and humanity that it equals the same powerful nihilism of combat in act 2.

Sergeant Hartman's ritualized language is one-part obscenity, one-part sexual humiliation, one-part personal threats, one-part war threats, one-part loaded Socratic discourse, and a sixth-part religious incantation. All of Hartman's speeches are orations of one form or another: the tirade, the sermon, the lecture. As was the opening section of *Platoon*, all of the Parris Island section of *Full Metal Jacket* is an exhaustive "naming of parts." For Kubrick, however, the verbal naming is emphasized, whereas for Oliver Stone the visual naming was emphasized. In Kubrick's movie, it is the words that draw attention to themselves, not the action or the story. Hartman's ritualized annihilation of his recruits' humanity in pursuance of turning them into "Marines," uses obscenity for punctuation and emphasis. As one Vietnam veteran once said, "if the word 'fuck' was suddenly thrown out of the English language, the U.S. Army wouldn't even be able to park a truck." Hartman's ritualized language also repeatedly attacks the recruits' gender, their masculinity, their sexual identity. They are mocked as "girls," "ladies," and "pussies." Their rifles become a substitute for their sexuality. Hartman makes them give their rifles girls' names, marries them to their rifles, makes them sleep with their rifles. Marching them in the barracks in their BVDs, Hartman makes them put one hand on their genitals while the other shoulders their rifles, and leads them in the doggerel chant:

> This is my rifle.
> This is my gun.
> This is for fighting.
> This is for fun.

Third, Hartman's ritualized language is laced with personal threats and physical abuse (punches, slaps, kicks) that includes racial and personal insults. Fourth, Hartman's language constantly calls up war threats, images of what will happen if and when this sorry class of recruits ever makes it into combat. The Jody songs that the recruits sing as they drill are an aspect of Hartman's ritualized language that has been passed down from generation to generation and war to war. Fifth, Hartman consistently barks questions at his recruits, but this Socratic discourse usually is used as a trap to generate new opportunities for Hartman to berate and intimidate. Last, Hartman's ritualized language at times takes on quite clearly delineated religious emphasis. For Hartman, war is a religion, the Marine Corps, his "beloved Corps," a church, and Marines an elect. Battle is a Black Mass and a Marine who does honor to the Corps achieves immortality. Hartman's religious imagery is eccentric but prominent. "Do you believe in the Virgin Mary?" he screams at Joker. "Give your heart to Jesus but your ass belongs to me" unequivocally parallels the biblical "give Caesar that which is due to Caesar and God that which is due to God" episode. At another point, Hartman notes that "God has a hard-on for Marines" because Marine killers keep "heaven full of new souls." Finally, Hartman presents his boots with the ultimate prize, the revelation that the Marine Corps bestows immortality. "The Marine Corps lives forever," Hartman assures them, "therefore you live forever." He ought to tell that to the corpses of Eightball, Doc, and Cowboy at the end and see if they still believe him.

This marvelously complex ritualized language asserts relentless psychological pressure upon the recruits. It tears them down and rebuilds them in the image of its own words. That, then, is why Sergeant Hartman, the Ur-DI, must be such a powerful character in act 1. His nihilistic language must simulate the nihilistic war he is preparing these recruits to enter. Hartman's elaborate ritualized language repertoire is an overtext of the American military mentality that took us into Vietnam and kept us there for so long as a means of finding manhood, purging ourselves against the past, and getting religion.

Joker counters Hartman's orations and obscene incantations with a comical impression of America's mythical twentieth-century warrior, John Wayne. Just as Hartman barks the formulaic chants of the ritualized Marine Corps language, Joker mimics the words and voice of the one mythic figure whose image hangs over both World War II and the Vietnam War. Joker's confrontation with Sergeant Hartman is occasioned by his John Wayne imitation. Later, in act 2 in a confrontation with Animal Mother (Adam Baldwin), Joker uses his John Wayne imitation to laugh off the threat of violence. Gustav Hasford's use of John Wayne in his novel, *The Short Timers*, and Kubrick's repeated use of Joker's John Wayne imitation throughout *Full Metal Jacket* is no coincidence. Almost every literary work generated by the Vietnam War refers to the John Wayne syndrome that makes young men enlist to go off and fight American wars. Philip Caputo tells the story in *A Rumor of War* of how he once intentionally exposed himself to possible enemy sniper fire because "I was John Wayne in *The Sands of Iwo Jima* (1949)."[21] Michael Herr in *Dispatches* writes about the range of reasons that Americans had for being in Vietnam "from the lowest John Wayne wetdream to the most aggravated soldier-poet fantasy" (27).[22] Thomas Myers in *Walking Point: American Narratives of Vietnam* argues that "the power of popular myth is located within the very narrowness and consistency of its narrative renderings. . . . Can there be any question, for instance, that American historical memory of World War II is largely mythic, one in which Roosevelt, Hitler and Churchill contend with John Wayne, Audie Murphy and Dana Andrews as historical actors" (6).[23] Joker perceives that Hartman is a parody of a movie DI, so he counters Hartman's parody with one of his own. Gustav Hasford's narrator in *The Short Timers* signals their parodic duel when he says that a Parris Island DI does not subscribe to "that I'm-only-rough-on-'em-because-I-love-'em crap civilians have seen in Jack Webb's Hollywood movie *The D.I.* or in Mr. John Wayne's *The Sands of Iwo Jima*" (7).[24]

The second half of *Full Metal Jacket*, which takes place in-country Vietnam, is divided into two sections. The first section shows Joker as a member of the media. The second section shows Joker in combat at the Battle of Hue. In both, John Wayne raises his mocking voice. In one of Joker's *Stars and Stripes* press meetings, the theme of language is everywhere. The words of the war are being mercilessly parodied. "If we move the Vietnamese they are 'evacuees,'" says the media officer, "but if they come to us to be evacuated they are 'refugees.'" For this officer, "'search and destroy' becomes 'sweep and clear.'" This whole section of the film satirizes the manner in which the military attempted to manipulate the media coverage of the Vietnam War by the manipulation of words. Joker is literally fighting a war of words, and his John Wayne imitation is the only relief he has.

In the second section of act 2 of *Full Metal Jacket*, Joker and the rest of the platoon move slowly behind the tanks into Hue. The setting could be San Diego or L.A., any city with palm trees, after a nuclear war. Kubrick shot this whole section in an abandoned gas works in London, but what it looks like more than anything else is Beirut circa 1984–90. During the battle, once again Vietnam, the war, is compared to a movie. To the rock-'n'-roll gibberish of "Bop Bop a Oooo Mau Mau" a TV camera crew pans along a line of bombarding tanks and exhausted grunts sitting in the corner of a low wall. As the camera pans, each grunt, starting with Joker, adds a new line of dialogue to *Vietnam the Movie*:

JOKER: Hey, you John Wayne? Is this me?

COWBOY: Hey, start the cameras. This is *Vietnam the Movie*.

EIGHTBALL: Hey, Joker can be John Wayne and I'll be a horse.

DONLON: T.A.C. Rock can be a rock.

T.A.C. ROCK: Yea, I'll be Ann Margret.

RAFTERMAN: Animal Mother can be a rabid buffalo.

PAYBACK: I'll be General Custer.

SNOWBALL: Who'll be the Indians?

ANIMAL MOTHER: Hey, we'll let the gooks be the Indians.

Vietnam the Movie starts with the mythic deception of John Wayne that causes all kinds of confusion in the identities of young men. "Is this me?" Joker asks, as if John Wayne could answer his existential question. But, as *Vietnam the Movie* is written line by line, we realize that these Marines are not heroically taking *The Sands of Iwo Jima* but are being stupidly massacred like Custer and his troops at the Little Big Horn. *Vietnam the Movie* is no longer John Wayne forties romanticization of men in war, but sixties ultrarealism ala Sam Peckinpah's vision of slow-motion death in *The Wild Bunch* (1969).[25] In the sniper scene that follows, whenever one of the platoon gets hit—first Eightball (Dorian Hareward), then Doc, then Cowboy—the film goes to Peckinpah's slow-motion at the moment of the bullet's impact as the limbs are torn and the blood spurts. It is an ultraviolent, ultrarealistic vision of death that John Wayne's forties patriotic romanticism does not allow.

The whole concept of *Vietnam the Movie* again harks back to Michael Herr's sense of being in his own movie in *Dispatches*. His metaphor (and Hasford's and Kubrick's) of Vietnam as some weird metamovie being projected in the minds of its soldier participants has held up into the eighties. For the Marines of *Full Metal Jacket* the reality of death in Vietnam must somehow be distanced. As only the movies can do, the reality of war must somehow be romanticized. Joker's John Wayne imitation, the recurring tendency of all of the Vietnam literature to metaphorically represent the war as some wild improvisational movie run amok, is the method of distancing necessary to counter the screaming nihilism of the war as represented in the language of Sergeant Hartman. Yet movies are not real, and that is what both *Platoon* and *Full Metal Jacket* set out to prove. The symbolic nihilism of the Vietnam War is a reality that neither of these films can accommodate by means of metaphor, a reality that cannot be hidden behind word manipulation no matter how elaborate. Just as the grunts in *Full Metal Jacket* attempt to distance the reality of the war and romanticize their own roles by pretending that it is a movie, so too does the American military attempt to distance and romanticize the war by means of the manipulation of language. *Full Metal Jacket* is perhaps at its most nihilistic when it is denying the power of words to convey reality. Words fail in *Full Metal Jacket*. Ritualized language no longer works when it comes right down to fighting and dying in Vietnam.

In two crucial scenes, the falsity of the Marine Corps' (and by extension the American military-industrial complex's) words and the confusion (remember the central theme of *Platoon*?) of the grunts over the words they are to believe and live by is clearly presented in highly ironic dialogue exchanges. Outside of the city of Hue, as Joker is viewing a mass grave of Vietnamese civilians, he is accosted by a gung-ho officer:

COLONEL: Marine, what is that button on your body armor?

JOKER: A peace symbol, sir.

COLONEL: What is that you've got written on your helmet?

JOKER: Born to kill, sir.

COLONEL: You write 'Born to kill' on your helmet and wear a peace button. What is that supposed to be, some kind of sick joke?

JOKER: No, sir.

COLONEL: What is it supposed to mean?

JOKER: I don't know, sir. . . .

COLONEL: Now answer my question. . . .

JOKER: I think I was trying to suggest something about the duality of man, sir. The Jungian thing, sir.

COLONEL: Whose side are you on, son?

JOKER: Our side, sir.

COLONEL: Don't you love your country?

JOKER: Yes, sir.

COLONEL: Then how about getting with the program. Why don't you jump on the team and come on in for the big win.

JOKER: Yes, sir.

COLONEL: Son, all I've ever asked of my Marines is to obey my orders as if they were the word of God. We are here to help the Vietnamese because inside any gook there's an American trying to get out. It's a hardball world, son. We've got to try to keep our heads until this peace craze blows over.

Joker wears his contradictory words, the symbolic nihilism of language, on his sleeve. The Colonel repeats a whole litany of military overtext clichés having to do with love of country, taking sides, getting with the program, jumping on the team, coming in for the big win, all of which, faithful to their sports metaphor clichéness, refuse to acknowledge the reality and confusion of the war. The Colonel's words portray the war as some meta-football game being played to pass the time, "until this peace craze blows over." Joker's words, however, shout of duality. Birth and death, peace and war, all of the contending and confusing impulses of the Vietnam War are represented in the symbolic nihilism of the words that Joker wears. Yet this word-Colonel goes one step further just as Hartman had gone one step further with his words. This word-Colonel talks of God. What this whole passage finally argues is that this sacrilegious use of words leads men into war. What this whole dialogue exchange demonstrates is the patent ridiculousness of the word manipulation of the military in Vietnam. How can anyone who actually says and believes that "inside every gook there's an American trying to get out" be taken seriously? Another scene, however, more poignantly shows the grunts discovering the reality of this war of word manipulation.

As the platoon looks at their dead Lieutenant who is about to be choppered away, the camera pans over their faces as they say their final good-bye:

RAFTERMAN: Well, at least they died for a good cause.

ANIMAL MOTHER: What cause was that?

RAFTERMAN: Freedom.

ANIMAL MOTHER: Flush out your head, new guy. You think we waste gooks for "freedom"? This is a slaughter. If I'm gonna get my balls blown off for a word, my word is "poontang."

What Animal Mother is saying is that wars are started and based on words, that in wars men die for words, and if that is the case, they ought at least to be able to die for their own words. The ultimate symbolic nihilism of *Full Metal Jacket* is the words that cause and sustain wars. The final ironic words of the film, the ritualized language of the Mickey Mouse Club chant, poke fun at the whole military war of words that has been satirized all through the film from Hartman at Parris Island to the commanding officer of *Stars and Stripes* to the word-Colonel in Hue. It is the ridiculous attempt to manipulate words as a means of masking reality that has turned the Vietnam War into a Mickey Mouse venture.

Other critics have noted this nihilistic temper not only in *Full Metal Jacket* but in all of the Vietnam War films of 1987–88. Penelope Gilliatt, who of all the critics has written most perceptively on *Full Metal Jacket*, states the nihilism of the film:

> *Full Metal Jacket* shows us that total dehumanizing is possible with stage-by-stage perversion. . . . The film's Vietnam is a world of no compass points: A young black American turns a map round in vain and finally says, "I think we should change direction." Yes, but where to? The war is a war of no declaration, no conclusion, no truthfully named enemy. Its muddled bloodshed yields no gains. . . . The war, the unwinnable war. No victors, only victims.[26]

The world of the Vietnam War is an utterly negative one and the final acts of the protagonists of both *Platoon* and *Full Metal Jacket* are the most negative of human acts, murders. Chris Taylor kills Sergeant Barnes and Joker kills the sniper as acts of bearing ultimate witness to the nihilism of the war. These are not mercy killings. They are annihilations of one already destroyed life (Barnes's, the sniper's) and of the innocence of another life (Chris's, Joker's). These final acts show Chris Taylor and Joker bearing witness to the annihilation of all that they thought themselves to be.

Hamburger Hill

Of all the Vietnam War films of 1987–88, *Hamburger Hill* is the most oppressively nihilistic. J. Hoberman agrees:

> A sense of abandonment amid brutally absurd conflict is central to the grunt-ensemble films; bereft of even the most minimal ideological support, our teenage warriors nevertheless perform their duty. (This sort of excruciatingly pointless heroism is most strongly articulated in *Hamburger Hill* where the central battle for the control of Dong Op Bia seems to have no intrinsic meaning, strategic or otherwise.)[27]

In her essay on *Hamburger Hill*, Pauline Kael decides that "almost inevitably the hill comes to represent Vietnam." Thus the nihilism that she sees in the film, "The men keep going up the hill, and being driven back by enemy fire. . . . At times the task assigned them seems hopeless—Sisyphean,"[28] represents not just the factual events of this film but, meta-phorically, the whole war effort. Kael's identification of Camus's *Myth of Sisyphus* as the source of the film's nihilistic imagery and Hoberman's focus upon the sense of abandonment that echoes in almost every verbal exchange among the grunt ensemble company of the film both point to the manner in which *Hamburger Hill* repeatedly assaults the viewer with the nothingness of life in the war as well as the corollary reality that life in the war utterly destroys the possibilities of returning to any sort of normal life in "the world." In Vietnam, there is nowhere to hide. After Vietnam, there is nowhere to go. The grunt in *Hamburger Hill*, therefore, is caught between two types of nothingness and can only choose action, going up that hill one more time—some choice!

Hamburger Hill is different from *Platoon* and *Full Metal Jacket* in that it is fact-based. The real battle of *Hamburger Hill* was part of Operation Apache Snow that began on 10 May 1969 at the base of Dong Ap Bia, Hill 937. In the next ten days, the grunts of the 101st Airborne assaulted that hill, sustaining 70 percent casualties, eleven times before taking it. They were supported by 272 Air Force sorties that dropped a million pounds of bombs, including 150,000 pounds of napalm.[29] Soon after, that expensive hill was abandoned and the war moved on. In its factual base and its brutal repetition of the uphill assaults, the film becomes almost documentary-like. Unlike *Platoon*, which artificially attempts to create myth out of the war, *Hamburger Hill* finds myth, the *Myth of Sisyphus*, in its documentary style. Kael notes how *Hamburger Hill* is so different from all of the other Vietnam War films:

> What makes the film distinctive is that it doesn't provide the viewer with any shelter. You don't get melodrama to fall back on; you don't have the reassurance of plot. "Hamburger Hill" doesn't offer the jingo heroism of "Rambo," or the impassioned metaphorical good-and-evil of "Platoon," or the neat parcel of guilt supplied by "Full Metal Jacket."[30]

Kael is right that *Hamburger Hill* has no plot. Its characters are faceless and disposable as were the real soldiers in Vietnam. It is a slice-of-life movie with no story, no structure, no favorites (stars) played. In its conception it mirrors the anonymity and confusion of the grunts in the Vietnam War. Its greatest triumph is the way in which its factuality, its documentariness, ultimately takes on symbolic and mythic qualities, the way in which a realistic depiction of life elevates itself to the level of art, the way in which the holograph of history demands interpretation.

One other documentary quality of *Hamburger Hill* is the way in which its verbal interludes are comprised of set speeches of the sort that the interviewee talking heads in documentaries deliver. At intervals, charac-ters get to take over the screen in close-up and deliver a speech on some subject close to their hearts, such as racism, the loss of meaning, or the emptiness of going home. These speeches emphasize the loneliness and nihilism of these abandoned grunts in the Ashau Valley.

But the documentarylike quality of *Hamburger Hill* is not the only way that it differs from the other films of this year. Each of these films is different in setting, which affects their textuality. The grunts in *Platoon* are suffocating in the jungle, especially at night. *Full Metal Jacket* is street warfare in the city of Hue. But *Hamburger Hill* is set in the hill country, where the enemy controls the high ground and the American soldiers must fight not only themselves and the enemy, as in *Platoon* and *Full Metal Jacket*, but also the terrain and the elements, specifically the rain that makes their uphill assaults in sliding mud almost impossible. This context of the landscape of *Hamburger Hill* adds to the sense of nihilism by offering images of the very soil of Vietnam turning against the American soldiers. Like *Go Tell the Spartans* of the first phase, *Hamburger Hill* is in danger of becoming another "Forgotten Vietnam War Film."[31] It deserves better critical treatment. Especially in its combat scenes, *Hamburger Hill* is a horribly realistic film. But it is a fine film because its slow, relentless repetition of the events of life in the war, its emphasis upon the disposability of its characters, its verbal outbursts of bitterness and racial hurt, its final images of men constantly fighting an uphill battle, all expand into metaphors for the war itself, for the whole episode in American history. The Vietnam War as a meaningless uphill battle fought by disposable troops under the worst possible conditions is what *Hamburger Hill* in all of its symbolic nihilism represents.

Hamburger Hill is an utterly fragmented, slice-of-life film for its first forty minutes. As in *Platoon* and *Full Metal Jacket*, there is a "naming of parts" of the Vietnam War, but not until the platoon embarks by chopper into the Ashau in montage and the date "10 May 1969" comes up superimposed upon the screen does the film take on any structure. For these grunts, it really makes no difference what day it is, what date. They do not care. All the days are the same. The whole uphill battle of staying alive in Vietnam runs together. *Hamburger Hill* really has no structure, no story. Its nothingness builds from beginning to end.

Two scenes especially express this nihilism. In the first, the blacks of the platoon mourn the death of Mac (Don James) who had said only moments earlier that he was "too short for this shit." They form a circle and, knocking fists, chant the litany of nihilism in Vietnam:

> It don't mean nothin'.
> Come on man, you owe it to yourself.
> Don' mean nothin'. Not a thing.
> Don' mean nothin'.

This chant of nihilism is the only way they can cleanse their minds of the death that is all around them.

The second scene of utter nihilism involves a verbal exchange between the two white sergeants, Worchester (Steven Weber) and Frantz (Dylan McDermott), who are different from the two Manichean sergeants in *Platoon*. They echo the nihilistic sentiments of Animal Mother's speech rejecting the word "freedom" in *Full Metal Jacket*, but they also mourn the death of Mac:

> FRANTZ: All he wanted to do was go home in his jumpboots. You believe they called him a jerk. Or worse.
>
> WORCHESTER: Well, you know, people get hurt over here.
>
> FRANTZ: Oh, c'mon. Don't tell me he died for God, country and the 101st Airborne.
>
> WORCHESTER: Hey man, I'd never say that shit to anybody. Danny didn't die for anything. Didn't leave his guts on a goddam trail in the goddamn Ashau Valley for hometown, a medal, any of that bullshit. Planked his automatic weapon and took it out for you and third squad. And don't give him anything less.

Once again, two grunts acknowledge that what they are doing has no meaning outside of the acting itself within the context of life in the platoon, in the war.

Besides the relentless nihilism of *Hamburger Hill*, a second theme, that of race, of why so many blacks are in Vietnam, echoes through the speeches of the talking heads. One of the indefensible aspects of the history of the Vietnam War films from the mid-seventies to 1987–88 is their consistent ethnocentrism. In the films of the first phase, only *The Boys in Company C* and *Apocalypse Now* acknowledge that there even were blacks fighting in Vietnam. Except for *Some Kind of Hero*, which is about a returned black POW played by Richard Pryor, none of the films of the second (comic book) phase explore or even acknowledge the racial theme. Not only are these films of the first two phases ethnocentric, but they are also what William Duiker calls "Amerocentric";[32] that is, they focus solely upon the American side, the American emotions, the American deaths in the Vietnam War. In a sense, all of these Amerocentric films are themselves racist in failing to recognize the Vietnamese as human beings. By far the most overtly racist in this "Amerocentric" regard are *The Deer Hunter* and *Rambo II*. In *Platoon*, *Full Metal Jacket*, and *Hamburger Hill*, however, blacks are given full characterization and full thematic voices. J. Hoberman half agrees:

> *Hamburger Hill* allows a taste of black rage, albeit focusing on micro-incidents of racial tension rather than addressing the essentially racist underpinnings of the war. The black cop from *Off Limits* notwithstanding, as yet there has been no Vietnam film made from a black point of view, although overrepresented as they were in the worst assignments, black

grunts were far more politically radical and radically disaffected than were whites."[33]

Though Hoberman makes two assertions, one about "the essentially racist underpinnings" and the other about "black grunts" being "far more politically radical," which are so general that they are neither provable nor even arguable, he is right that *Hamburger Hill* and *Off Limits* come the closest to presenting a true black point of view on the Vietnam War.

When Doc (Courtney B. Vance), the most articulate spokesman for the black point of view in *Hamburger Hill*, who declares that they are all fighting for "the United States of White America," is wounded, he has the following exchange with Sergeant Frantz:

DOC: It's alright, blood. I don't feel a thing. I am *beaucoup* doped up.

FRANTZ: Doc. Now. C'mon now, Doc. You owe this to yourself. (Trying to persuade him to hang on until the chopper gets there to evac him.)

DOC: Won't be happy 'til he gets all my people killed.

FRANTZ: Hey, how you gonna act, Doc? How you gonna act when you get back to the real world.

DOC: I'm just what the world needs, another nigger.

FRANTZ: Now, c'mon, you stop that shit.

DOC: I'm not shitting you, blood. We're all no-good dumb niggers on this hill, blood and soul type.

For Doc, in this dying speech, the issue of race in Vietnam becomes a metaphor for the larger rejection of all the soldiers fighting the war. "We're all no-good dumb niggers," Doc says, and it makes no difference what color one's skin may be, rather it is a state of mind, a state of America's mind toward the soldiers in Vietnam. Like the blacks in American history, the soldiers of Vietnam have been rejected by the society they have pledged to defend. In one of the early assaults on the hill, helicopter gunships fly over to provide support, but they think the Americans are the enemy and they open up with what is absurdly called "friendly fire." Metaphorically, this absurd killing of Americans by other Americans represents the division of American society by the Vietnam War. The nihilism of that division is underlined even more powerfully when the American soldiers who are being fired on by their own gunships start firing back. As both *Platoon* and *Full Metal Jacket* earlier and *Off Limits* later stress, America from the beginning was its own worst enemy in Vietnam.

Another of the talking heads of *Hamburger Hill*'s documentary style, Sergeant Worchester, elaborates on this "niggerness" of the American soldiers in Vietnam:

You're right about how they love everybody back there. They tattoo it to their foreheads. They wear love buttons on their flowered shirts. Yeah, they love everybody back there. Cats, dogs, niggers, spics, kikes, wops, micks, grease-balls. Yeah, they're real fond of Luke the Gook back home. You believe that. They got buttons for him too. They love everybody but you! I was med-evaced after Dak To. There was a hill. And we were met in Oakland by pretty little things—you know what I mean—they had hair down to their asses, you know—and they had bags full of . . . dog shit. Well, don't mean nothin'. I'm back in the Nam now. Nothin' gonna ever bother me again.

For the dying soldiers in *Hamburger Hill*, the villains of the piece are not the enemy in their bunkers at the top of the hill raining down death, but the American society that has hung them out here by themselves to die.

What John Irvin's *Hamburger Hill* does in its chosen pace and style is mirror life in the Vietnam War. At times it is fragmented, repetitive, and meaningless because that is what the experience of Vietnam was like. At other times it is frantic, hopeless, and horrible because that is how Vietnam was. The movie is like a documentary that builds to one set of symbolic images: the relentless series of Sisyphean assaults on the hill. Like life and death in the Vietnam War, *Hamburger Hill* "don't mean nothin'," but of all these films of the 1987–88 phase it is the only one that does not try to mean anything. If "don't mean nothin'" is the nihilistic catch phrase of the war, then the documentaryness of *Hamburger Hill* captures it perfectly.

Gardens of Stone

Of all of the films in this 1987–88 third phase, Francis Coppola's *Gardens of Stone* is the most austere and symbolic in its representation of the nihilism of the Vietnam War. Since the weddings and baptisms and cocktail parties of *The Godfather I* and *II* in the early seventies, Coppola has always been the master of symbolic ritual in American motion pictures. Like the theme of ritualized language as presented by Kubrick in *Full Metal Jacket*, the theme of ritual as a means of distancing America from the terrible nihilistic reality of the war, protecting America's innocence, is the central symbolic theme of *Gardens of Stone*. The fake ritual in this film is the full-dress military funeral that symbolizes the death of America in Vietnam, the point in American history when the American dream died and "the green breast of the new world"[34] turned to gardens of stone.

The daily full-dress burials by the U.S. Army "Old Guard" take place in Arlington National Cemetery in 1968–69 at the height of the Vietnam War. They are intended to make up for the meaninglessness of the war, for the nothingness of the anonymous death that the plain military stone marker commemorates. "Where have all the flowers gone," Bob Dylan wrote while this war was going on, "where have all the young men gone?" The garden of stone that is the setting of Coppola's film answers Dylan's question.

The career soldiers who conduct these phony military rituals are acutely aware of the terrible contradiction between the order and beauty of the funeral ritual and the confusion and nihilism of the war. "Welcome to show business, soldier," Sergeant Clell Hazard (James Caan) sarcastically greets a new member of the funeral cortege. "Why madam, we are the Old Guard. We are the nation's toy soldiers. . . . We are the Kabuki Theater," Sergeant Major Goody Nelson (James Earl Jones) laughs. But even as these career soldiers mock the military ritual charade that they take part in every day, they realize that their job is a bizarre cover-up for a war that is in utter chaos.

When young Jackie Willow (D. B. Sweeney), a protégé of Sergeant Hazard, says he wants to command a line unit in Vietnam, the old sergeant barks back, "there is no front line in Vietnam. Not like the other wars. Hell, it's not even a war. Nothin' to win. No way to win it." Later in the film, Sergeant Major Nelson echoes Sergeant Hazard's nihilistic views: "There ain't no front in Vietnam. . . . It's a funny little war, kid. Things have changed." Both of those speeches are direct echoes of the central speech on the nature of the war delivered by Major Barker (Burt Lancaster) in *Go Tell The Spartans* ten years before. The Arlington National Cemetery, where these cynical soldiers work, is a symbol of America's attempt to ritualize the nihilism of death in Vietnam.

Near the end of *Gardens of Stone*, Sergeant Clell Hazard, as part of an elegy in a funeral ritual says, "there will be no tombs for the unknown soldiers of Vietnam. We have gotten better at identifying our soldiers, but do we really know them." That is what Coppola's *Gardens of Stone* is really about, getting to know the soldiers who fought and died in Vietnam. The stones in Arlington National Cemetery are spare and uniform and face-less, but the Vietnam War Memorial is like no other war memorial in the land. It is a brooding black V, like the wings of an ominous bird, set in a shallow valley on the Mall, transparent, reflecting those who stand before its black granite mirror, reflective of all those who served and died in the war. The more than fifty thousand names etched across its dark face make it a very personal war memorial. The reflection of the faces of those who look into it and see themselves overcomes the facelessness of the stones in Arlington. *Gardens of Stone* and the Vietnam War Memorial both focus upon an emotional need of everyone who is a member of the Vietnam generation, the need to know who the men who died in Vietnam were and to remember them as individuals, as real people, not as bodies in a count, stones lined up on a hill. What Coppola's film does is bring together a group of characters in the garden of America whose different identities and differing views on the war represent how that garden is being turned to stone by the Vietnam War.

Like both *Platoon* and *Full Metal Jacket* (as well as the documentary *Dear America: Letters Home from Vietnam*), *Gardens of Stone* employs a voice-over reading of letters home to project some of its thematic ideas. Late in the film, young Jackie Willow, who has gotten his wish to command a line unit in Vietnam, writes to Sergeant Hazard: "All anyone talks about in Vietnam, all we see and hear about are demonstrations. This war seems to be tearing us all apart, the whole country." What the film does is project upon a group of well-realized characters each of the emotional and political stances taken toward this Medusa war that is turning the garden of America to stone. Clell Hazard is a career Army man who doesn't like and doesn't believe in the Vietnam War. He hates the war because it is a military mistake that is damaging the credibility of his family, the U.S. Army. He falls in love with Samantha Davies (Anjelica Huston), a *Washington Post* reporter who protests the war in the streets. In the Army he is referred to as "the peacenik Sergeant." In the streets she is referred to as a radical. In truth, they are both simply people trying to express their feelings about a very complex problem. "Clell sees this war as bad judgment," Sam tells Jackie. "I see it as genocide." Jackie Willow is like a son to Clell Hazard and yet they totally disagree on the war. *Gardens of Stone* is a real "generation gap" film, to resurrect a true sixties term. The generation gap in this film, however, is within the military. Jackie is young, an Army brat, gung-ho to get into the action. He believes in the myth that "a soldier in the right place at the right time can change the world." Clell Hazard only believes in his family, the Army, and he sees it taking a real beating in Vietnam. He buries twenty family members a day in the garden of stone and he does not know what to do about it. He decides that the only way he can help is to try to teach the Vietnam War better, to give the young men he teaches more of a chance to survive. Unlike the grunt veterans in all of the previous films of this year of Vietnam, Hazard wants to teach the "FNGs," but he too learns that the war is unteachable. He sets out, through teaching, to save just one young man, Jackie Willow, and he fails. As Clell and Goody have argued throughout the film, the Vietnam War *is* different. It is a Medusa war that is turning the whole nation to stone.

Each of the characters in Coppola's film argue their differing views of the war, but nothing is ever resolved. The film ends the only way that a Vietnam War film of the late eighties can end, in nihilism. Rachel (Mary Stuart Masterson), Jackie Willow's young wife and eventual widow, best expresses how the Medusa war turns America's men to stone. "Bonnie Fowler's man came home different," Rachel tells Sam. "Men come home crazy and broken and cold, but that's not my Jackie." Jackie himself expresses the loss of his idealism, his belief in the war, in a letter to Sergeant Hazard: "It's hard to believe that I'll be back so soon. It's hard to believe anything. . . . It's so hard to believe that she still loves me. That there is any love anywhere. . . . I've learned so much, Sarge. I've learned that I can't protect the kids. It's my sworn duty to protect them and I can't. . . . But after this, I don't know anything anymore." Ultimately,

Gardens of Stone is about this naïveté, the warrior's grand illusion that "a soldier in the right place at the right time can change the world." What *Gardens of Stone* subtly, almost philosophically, points out, and what the career soldiers, Hazard and Nelson, know full well, is that Vietnam is neither the right place nor the right time. It is exactly the point that Major Barker made in *Go Tell the Spartans* (1978) a decade earlier.

In the eighties, the Vietnam War is still a social issue, but it is a dead, cold issue, something not to be lived but to be reflected upon. Whereas *Platoon* and *Full Metal Jacket* and *Hamburger Hill* are films for the young that concentrate upon telling them what it was like and how not to be deceived by tunes of glory, *Gardens of Stone* is a film for middle-aged people who want to remember and analyze how they feel now about a war that tore our society apart. *Platoon* is a film about the body with all its action and confusion on the brutal surface. *Gardens of Stone* is about the mind of the career soldier and the mind of the nation in the time of Vietnam.

Good Morning, Vietnam

In contrast to *Gardens of Stone*, *Good Morning, Vietnam*, is the only one of the six Vietnam War films released in 1987–88 that trivializes the war and the issues of the war. *Good Morning, Vietnam* does not even qualify as a movie. Its characters do not have as much substance as the comic book characters of the second phase of the Vietnam War film history. It is a shallow, plotless combination of a Robin Williams comedy concert and an extended music video masquerading as a biopic. The movie purports to be the story of off-the-wall Armed Forces Radio disc jockey Adrian Cronauer's (Robin Williams) year of spinning records "from the Delta to the DMZ." Cronauer was a talented, inventive, and irreverent DJ who surfaced in Saigon in 1965 and changed the makeup of Armed Forces Radio, what it said and the music it played to the grunts in-country listening on their portables, their helicopter radios, over their patrol boat loudspeakers, in their trucks and Jeeps. Cronauer has a rapid-fire satiric delivery, the ability to create outrageous characters and do brilliant impressions, and an utter disdain for the music of Ray Conniff, Lawrence Welk, Montovani, Perry Como, and Frank Sinatra, with which Armed Forces Radio was anesthetizing the airwaves before Cronauer's arrival. Michael Herr in *Dispatches* says that Vietnam was the first rock-'n'-roll war. *Good Morning, Vietnam* purports to be the story of the man who made it so.

Really, *Good Morning, Vietnam* is simply the first extended rock video to use Vietnam as a backdrop. Like the comic book adventures of *Rambo*, *Good Morning, Vietnam* does not dramatize or explore the Vietnam War but rather only uses that war. It is one long montage sequence, a fusillade of images to the accompaniment of either sixties rock-'n'-roll (the Stones, the

Supremes, the Beach Boys, the Doors, Jimi Hendrix) or Robin Williams "autogetum" comedy monologue.

Good Morning, Vietnam fails as a Vietnam War film because it depends completely on monologue rather than the kind of dialogue that can explore such a complex issue as the Vietnam War. In this sense, it is directly the opposite of *Gardens of Stone*. In Coppola's film, characters representing differing points of view are consistently paired off so that they can carry on dialogue that reveals the themes of the film. *Good Morning, Vietnam* is dominated by Cronauer's semipolitical schtick that never makes more than a superficial pass at exploring the basic issues of the War. All remains zanily monologic.

But *Good Morning, Vietnam* also makes no attempt to set up any metaphoric representation of theme, such as that of the firefight representing confusion and chaos in *Platoon* or that of the failure of words in *Full Metal Jacket* or the metaphor of race as expanded to define the rejection of all the soldiers in Vietnam by their own country in *Hamburger Hill* or the imagery of the garden of America being turned to stone by that Medusa war in *Gardens of Stone*. *Good Morning, Vietnam* simply is not aware of the nihilism that every other Vietnam War film of this 1987–88 period stresses.

In *Good Morning, Vietnam*, the war is a doo-woppin' good time, a lot of laughs and rock-'n'-roll. There is only one genuine scene in the whole film. It occurs during a traffic jam in downtown Saigon where Cronauer, who by this time has become a warwide celebrity, finds himself in the middle of truckloads of American grunts on their way into battle. He does his DJ rap and kids with individual soldiers. As the scene unfolds, he begins to realize that the only real importance of his life in the war lies in the smiles he brings to the faces and the emotion his music brings to the fragile lives of these young men who are going out to die. As the traffic jam breaks up and the trucks loaded with doomed men pull away, the camera stays on Cronauer's face as it subsides from the exhilaration of performance to the perception of grim reality. It is the only truly emotional scene in the film, and it reminds of a similar scene in Peter Bogdanovich's *Saint Jack* (1981) as a line of young American soldiers board the bus in front of Jack's whorehouse as their R-and-R comes to an end and they have to return to Vietnam.

Many critics compared *Good Morning, Vietnam* to Robert Altman's *M*A*S*H* (1970), but that comparison does a great disservice to Altman's Vietnam black comedy. *M*A*S*H*, even though set during the Korean War, was really about Vietnam. It was the only major American film besides John Wayne's right-wing propagandist *Green Berets* (1966) to confront the issues of the war while that war was in session. *Good Morning, Vietnam* is a distinctively eighties aberration that takes the Vietnam War and turns it into a music video.

Off Limits

The final Vietnam War film to be released in that sixteen-month period of 1987–88 goes to extremes of obscenity and violence to portray the nihilistic power of the Vietnam War. *Off Limits* is obscene in its images of dehumanization and sexual psychopathy. It gives a strong sense of real, not imagined, evil. Its nihilism overcomes any attempts its characters make to sentimentalize the obscenity of the Vietnam War. *Off Limits* is a descent into hell that assaults the senses and sensibilities of the audience. As a buddy-cop film, it could have been set in San Francisco or L.A. or in Miami as on TV, but it is set in Saigon in 1968 and that completely changes the context of violence. Big city violence is one thing, but big city violence in the midst of the Vietnam War is something altogether different.

The world of Joseph Conrad's *Heart of Darkness* is the world of *Off Limits*, a world of "no restraint." Every sin against humanity is committed in this cess pool of Saigon. No prisoners are taken. Men, women, children—everyone is fair game in the perverse line of fire of the war. There are no real heroes, just madmen of all sorts off limits morally in every possible way. The film presents a vision of Vietnam as America's *Inferno*. It pursues evil to the seventh circle of a ten-year hell and confronts the devil himself, who turns out to be an American. The plot of *Off Limits* reads as a political critique of American involvement in Vietnam. The film's nihilistic theme is similar to the theme of *Platoon*: In Vietnam Americans are their own worst enemies.

McGriff (Willem Dafoe) and Perkins (Gregory Hines) are two street cops, members of the CID (Criminal Investigations Division) of the U.S. Army in Saigon. Their boss, Staff Sergeant Dix (Fred Ward), assigns them to the case of a murdered prostitute found with the uniform insignia of an American officer clutched in her hand. As in the novels of Dashiell Hammett, Raymond Chandler, and Ross MacDonald, the two detectives have no idea what they are doing; they are just doing it. Their investigation first uncovers an American cover-up of the murders of five other prostitutes and they realize they've got a case of Colonel Jack D. Ripper on their hands.

As they descend into the ugly pit of these sex murders, they meet Sister Nicole (Amanda Pays) who takes care of the children of the dead prostitutes at an orphanage. Next, they fly to Khe Sanh to interview the last investigator who was taken off the case when he got too close. Then they meet Colonel Armstrong who is their prime suspect. Their investigation gets more labyrinthine.

Because *Off Limits* is a hard-boiled detective mystery, it is in the detecting that the central Vietnam War metaphor unfolds. All the time it has been a smiling American who was committing the despicable crimes. *Off Limits* is not just another action movie like *Lethal Weapon* (1987) or the Dirty Harry movies. It is a tortuous metaphoric examination of America gone psycho in Vietnam.

The opening scene in *Off Limits* is of a faceless American officer committing an obscene war crime. After sex, he blows a Vietnamese hooker's head off with a .45 at point-blank range as her baby sleeps next to the bed. "Saigon, sheeit," Captain Willard (Martin Sheen) says at the beginning of *Apocalypse Now.* "I'm a cop in the cess pool of the world," Sergeant Perkins says early in *Off Limits.* Later, Perkins and McGriff's boss, Staff Sergeant Dix, describes Saigon in the same utterly nihilistic terms: "Gook whores. I mean, you really give that big a shit? . . . You're floatin' in a big sea o' shit and instead of stayin' in the boat you reach over and pick up this one little turd." There are no limits in Saigon in 1968. It is hard to pick out the bad guys because everyone is a bad guy. As they begin their investigation, McGriff asks, "you know who our suspects are?" and Perkins answers, "Everybody in Saigon" as if it were a foregone conclusion. In a tone of utter cynicism, McGriff expands upon Perkins's nihilism: "Civilians, troops, gangsters, cowboys, deserters, refugees, dopers, black marketeers. God I love this town. I really do."

As Perkins and McGriff interview witnesses and confront suspects, they find that everyone is sinking in this cess pool of nihilism. The Marine (Keith David) who saw the killer says, "I don't trust no motherfuckers at this point." He refuses to talk to anyone but a general and is killed by sappers before he can identify the killer. The last CID man to investigate the case of the murdered hookers would rather be in Khe Sanh under fire during the TET offensive than return to Saigon where his own people could kill him. When McGriff and Perkins approach this zombie in Khe Sanh, they identify themselves as CID-Saigon and he screams, "are you here to waste me?" Perhaps the most symbolic scene of this plague of nihilism that has infected everyone in the world of this film involves the prime suspect in the murders, Colonel Dexter Armstrong (Scott Glenn), a brilliant young West Pointer on track to become a joint chief. Armstrong is a sadistic sexual pervert who reminds of Colonel Kurtz in *Apocalypse Now.* He is one of the "best and the brightest" from Kennedy's Camelot, who has descended all the way into the heart of darkness. He has his "children," U.S. Army soldiers, kidnap McGriff and Perkins to Can Tho, where he takes them up in one of his helicopters. Armstrong shows himself a true Conradian "lusty devil" and his chopper is the Sixth Circle of Hell. After he throws three Viet Cong out of the chopper, in an act of lunatic nihilism he throws himself out. This scene proves that in Vietnam Americans truly are their own worst enemies. But the Seventh Circle of Hell still awaits Perkins and McGriff.

Back in Saigon, the clearest insight into the self-defeating dilemma of America in Vietnam is offered by the ARVN Colonel Lime. It is one of the rare instances in the Vietnam War film history when a Vietnamese is allowed to speak out about of the war. In fact, three Vietnamese characters—Colonel Lime, Lan a prostitute, and a female Viet Cong—are given voices in this film, thus making it one of the few holes in the wall of Amerocentrism that has hitherto enclosed the Vietnam War film history. Early in *Off Limits*, Colonel Lime warns McGriff: "Your passion is misdirected, Sergeant. The men who killed your friend work for the same people you do." Later, Lime once again tries to warn the detectives that Americans are their own worst enemies in Vietnam: "You despise me because you think I am corrupt when in reality you are too innocent to see corruption which is right before your eyes. You're only in danger for your life from those above you."

Just moments before making this prophetic statement, Lime had confronted Staff Sergeant Dix in the middle of an angry mob with all of his squad's guns leveled at the Americans. "You are outgunned today, Sergeant," Lime gloats. "Goddam, when will you people ever learn," Dix laughs in Lime's face. "We are never outgunned," Dix arrogantly asserts as a helicopter gunship levels off over the Saigon street with Colonel Lime in its gunsights. Perhaps Americans "are never outgunned" in Vietnam, but they still cannot win because they are their own worst enemies. The constant reiteration of this theme becomes a metaphor larger than this dangerous Saigon mystery. *Off Limits* is really about why America failed in Vietnam, about how America defeated herself, about the landscape of America's deepest descent into her own heart of darkness.

Sooner or later, even these two detectives who think they can keep order in 1968 Saigon, must succumb to the utter nihilism of the war. On the way to the airport, being run out of town so that their American comrades can cover up the murders, they acknowledge the nothingness of their lives in the war:

PERKINS: Well then fuck their insect hookers. I refuse to give a shit.

MCGRIFF: We weren't doin' it for them. We were doin' it for us. To give it all some kind of fuckin' meaning.

PERKINS: Leavin' this place outside a plastic bag is all the meaning I need.

The problem with trying to give the Vietnam War meaning is that there is no meaning to America's presence in Vietnam. Some can find meaning in staying alive, but others like Armstrong realize that there is no possibility of meaning, and they throw themselves out of helicopters. Immediately upon acknowledging their inability to find meaning in the war other than being alive, sappers sent by their own commanding officer try to kill Perkins and McGriff. After escaping this attempt to annihilate even their meager sense of meaning, the two decide to fight back motivated by an almost Sisyphean despair.

At the end of *Off Limits*, the two detectives, as Odysseus did, descend into the underworld of a Viet Cong tunnel complex in search of truth. There, Nguyen the Viet Cong identifies Staff Sergeant Dix as the murderer. The film ends as *Platoon* did, with the two Americans killing one of their own who has succumbed to the heart of darkness. As a murder mystery set on top of a large political powderkeg, *Off Limits* is brutally realistic and deeply nihilistic. It belongs with *Platoon*, *Full Metal Jacket*, and *Hamburger Hill* as a text of the symbolic nihilism of the Vietnam War.

In *Going After Cacciato*, Paul Berlin's naïve father as he sends his naïve son off to Vietnam suggests "You'll see some terrible stuff, I guess. That's how it goes. But try to look for the good things, too." But in *Platoon*, *Full Metal Jacket*, *Hamburger Hill*, and *Off Limits* the characters can find no good things to balance off the nihilism and death. The only possible positive event in a soldier's day is waking up, realizing that he has survived yet another day in the meaningless void. It was only a matter of time until the films depicting the Vietnam War got around to facing up to the nihilism of the experience that the books about the war have been confronting all along. The Vietnam War films of 1987–88 thus form a coherent text for reading the war.

3

The "Coming Home" Films

I N T H E T H R E E - P H A S E history of the Vietnam War films, the theme of "coming home" has been, from the beginning with *Taxi Driver* in 1976, the most scrutinized aspect of the war. In the first, epic, phase, every film, with the exception of *Go Tell the Spartans* (1978) and *Apocalypse Now* (1979), was more interested in bringing the war and its casualties/survivors back to American soil than with exploring the nature of the war as it was fought in-country Vietnam. In *Taxi Driver* (1976), *Rolling Thunder* (1977), *Who'll Stop the Rain* (1978), and *Heroes* (1977), Vietnam veterans actually relive the firefights of their in-country experience on the Main Streets of America itself. In *Coming Home* (1978) and *The Deer Hunter* (1978),[1] Vietnam veterans searched for ways to heal the unhealable wounds of the war and struggled for visibility and reassimilation into an American society that had turned them into a whole generation of invisible men. What the "coming home" movies of that first phase did was identify the problems of the Vietnam veteran in postwar American society. They defined his sense of rejection, his invisibility, his physical and psychological wounds.

Conversely, in the third, symbolic nihilist, phase of the Vietnam War film history, the theme of "coming home," with the single exception of *Gardens of Stone*, is ignored. All of these films are set in-country Vietnam. Thus the major veterans' issue of the eighties was not even examined in the retrospective deconstruction of these 1987–88 third phase films.

The second, comic book, phase of the years 1980–86, however, is almost universally concerned with the "coming home" theme (as in *First Blood*, *The Stunt Man*, *Some Kind of Hero*, *Birdy* and *Cease Fire*) or ironically, with the "coming home" followed by the "going back" (as in *Uncommon Valor*, the *Missing in Action* series, *Rambo II* and *The Killing Fields*). However, as their comic book designation implies, the majority of these films approach the complex problem of "coming home" from an exploitative and simplistic fantasy perspective. The complexity of the "coming home" issue involved the physical, psychological, racial, and social problems of Vietnam veterans trying to cope with life in a society that for a decade had denied their existence.

First, the "coming home" issue involved dealing with the physical problems of an overburdened, nonresponsive Veterans' Administration medical establishment's poor handling of wound treatment and utter denial of Agent Orange contamination. Second, the "coming home" issue involved the psychological problems of Post Traumatic Stress Disorder (PTSD) and the often attendant "survivor guilt syndrome." Third, the racial issues of the acceptance of Vietnamese refugees and Amerasian children in American society, as well as the realization of the class prejudice that had obtained in the induction procedures during the war, a prejudice that had placed an inordinate burden of the actual combat upon black, Hispanic, and poor white soldiers, further complicated the issue. Finally, the social problem, heavily exploited by the American media, of the time-bomb potential for street and domestic violence by Vietnam veterans turned those veterans into social pariahs in a burgeoning yuppie society. All of these aspects of the "coming home" issue were alive in American society in the early eighties. Most of them were crudely exploited in the films of this comic book phase. These films sold themselves on the premise that they were analyzing the wounds that first phase films like *Coming Home* or *The Deer Hunter* had identified. Unfortunately the tools that these films used involved the most rudimentary pop psychology, or worse, a Reagan-era propagandist revisionary chauvinism that turned these serious issues into either comic book fantasies or political allegories. All of this movie exploitation of the stereotypes of the Vietnam veteran culminated in the Rambomania of 1985–86.

Charles Haid, a Vietnam veteran who played Officer Andy "Cowboy" Renko on the TV show "Hill Street Blues," in a newspaper interview, said that *"Rambo* is an irresponsible fantasy and the shame of our industry" (*USA Today*, 27 June 1985). David Halberstam, another Vietnam vet and author of the Pulitzer Prize-winning *Best and the Brightest* (about the Vietnam era generation), used much stronger words: "It's a disgrace. It dishonors every veteran of that war, dead or alive. It is everything bad about us and says nothing of the good about us." (*New York Times*, 12 July 1985). Finally, one other Vietnam veteran, Robert K. Brown, the publisher of *Soldier of Fortune* and *Combat Weapons* magazines, when asked why *Rambo* was so popular, answered: "The whole premise of the movie reflects the attitude of the American public now about the Vietnam War." When asked "Doesn't a movie like that fuel the myth of the mercenary rather than show what the actual war was like?" Brown answered: "That one does. I would call it a fantasy movie but . . . One of the big things about *Rambo* was when you stepped back and looked at it after it was all over, you said, 'Aha, the guys in the white hats won one for once'" (*USA Today*, 5 September 1985).

A large percentage of the Americans who paid more than $200 million to see *Rambo II* probably agree with Mr. Brown's chauvinistic sentiments. The reason they agree is that *Rambo II* (and others like it) and magazines and newspapers and the electronic news media and even the great communicator in the White House conditioned them to agree by exploiting popular stereotypes to elicit that chauvinistic response. As Haid and Halberstam intimate, perhaps the only ones who did not succumb to this inflated stereotype were the Vietnam veterans themselves.

For six months in 1985, Rambo was everywhere. In a wonderful exercise in pop psychology, Steve Randall, the executive vice-president of Tri-Star Pictures tried to convince that *Rambo* was just what the psychiatrist ordered for America: "It's a healthy response because they're able to vent their frustration in the movie theater and not out in the streets" (*USA Today*, 25 June 1985). Randall is declaring that Hollywood has openly entered the field of psychotherapy on a national scale. With an actor in the White House it is only a brief extension of a possible logic to posit Hollywood as the psychiatrist to the inferiority complex of the country.

In the throes of Rambomania, the American movie industry and the American media reached the apex of their deployment of a distorted set of stereotypes of the Vietnam veteran. The most positive thing to be said about the film representations of the Vietnam veteran since *Taxi Driver* in 1976 is that the movies helped strip off the cloak of invisibility that America had draped over the Vietnam vet. But in stripping off that cloak, the movies distorted rather than clarified the identity of the more than four million Vietnam veterans.

Travis Bickle (Robert De Niro), the original urban cowboy, a little big man survivor of the mid-twentieth-century Little Big Horn, shows up in Martin Scorsese's *Taxi Driver*. Travis's swaggering pride in his arsenal of handguns, his cathartic search-and-destroy mission into the brothels of New York, set the tone for the image of the Vietnam veteran. In *Rolling Thunder*, former POW Colonel Charles Rane (William Devane) and Johnny Vohden (Tommy Lee Jones), his pal from Vietnam, are violently disturbed and sexually impotent. All that can make them feel better is a good dose of search and destroy in a Mexican brothel. Jack Dunne (Henry Winkler) in *Heroes* escapes from a mental hospital and crosses the country to experience his nervous breakdown in the war-torn streets of Eureka, California. Nick Nolte plays Ray Hicks in *Who'll Stop the Rain* (adapted from Robert Stone's *Dog Soldiers*), an American Samurai who lights up the New Mexico desert the way he had lit up Vietnam earlier. In 1978 and 1979 Bruce Dern made a career out of playing psychotic and confused Vietnam veterans in movies like *Black Sunday* and *Coming Home*. Finally, in one of the best and most controversial Vietnam War films, *The Deer Hunter*, Nick (Christopher Walken) cannot escape the obsession with his Vietnam experience and becomes a man doomed to repeat his own death until he finally receives it. In all of these movies, ultraviolent catharsis and suicide are offered as *the* common options for the sufferer from Post Traumatic Stress Disorder (PTSD). All of the protagonists are doomed victims of their own past experience.

Coming Home, perhaps, presents the most confusing compendium of the Vietnam veteran experience. One of the many vets in the film, the wheelchair-bound Luke (Jon Voight), is presented realistically and sympathetically, but two others commit suicide, thus making Luke's progress toward health and stability seem the exception to the Vietnam veteran rule. The last third of *The Deer Hunter* also grapples with the problems of returned veterans, but it suffers from the same dispersed confusion that plagues *Coming Home*. This segment is irreparably marred by the fantastical playing out of the survivor guilt syndrome when Michael (Robert De Niro) returns to 1975 Saigon to find Nick. Strangely enough, this last fantastical section of *The Deer Hunter* prefigures the new direction that the stereotyping of the Vietnam vet takes in the movies of the eighties leading up to *Rambo II*.

The portrayal of the Vietnam War veteran in the movies evolved into something completely different in the early eighties. The phase of the Vietnam vets' vulnerability, confusion, and psychological imbalance partially ended and the age of the "supervet" began. In 1981 American film stopped lamenting the plight of the Vietnam vet and began mythically heroizing both the war and the men who fought it in a series of rightist fantasies of revenge, triumph, and expiation. The films were *Uncommon Valor*, the *Missing in Action* series, and *Rambo II*, the sequel to the earlier "violent vet" film *First Blood*. These films have the same plot, play out the same survivor guilt fantasy, exploit the same new image of the Vietnam vet as an undervalued superhero who jumps at the chance to rehistoricize himself and his country.

It was also in the early eighties that television discovered the Vietnam vet. Thomas Magnum and his sidekick T. C. were the first real Vietnam vets on TV. For the first two years, their flashbacks to Vietnam punctuated almost every show and then real remnants of Vietnam out of Magnum's past started washing up on the beaches of Hawaii until finally he had to go back. Matt Houston also had to go back to rescue some of his war buddies from a POW camp. Raynor Sarnac on 1984's short-lived "Call to Glory" also had to go back. Lieutenant Hunter and Joe Coffey of "Hill Street Blues," Rick Simon of "Simon and Simon," Gonzo Gates of "Trapper John, M.D.," Stringfellow Hawke of "Airhawk," and Sonny Crockett of "Miami Vice" are other TV supervets, all subject to different degrees of violence, portrayed with different degrees of malaise. One thing, however, can be said for TV as opposed to the movies. TV gave some Vietnam vets a sense of humor; partially softened the violent vet stereotype. In the movies, only Richard Pryor's *Some Kind of Hero* comes close to showing the black humorist's approach to life of so many Vietnam vets. Late in the decade, following the phenomenal success of *Platoon* and the other films of the 1987–88 year of Vietnam at the movies, two TV series set in-country Vietnam—"Tour of Duty" and "China Beach"—found success.

But the movies and television were not the only villains in the exploitation of the "coming home" issue and the reentry problems of Vietnam veterans. The most consistent, everyday villain was the print medium. Newspapers and magazines continue to note when a criminal act has been committed by a Vietnam veteran. Somehow the Vietnam vet burglar or rapist or mass murderer is much bigger news than the garden variety burglar, rapist, or mass murderer.

In *Taxi Driver* the Vietnam vet surfaced as a deranged psychotic, and across the eighties decade that "violent vet" image has changed little in substance yet a great deal in social perception. Whereas in the seventies the "violent Vietnam vet" was perceived as a threat to society, in the eighties the "violent Vietnam vet" has become a "heroic" and "mythic" figure, but not in the classical literary terms of Greek and Roman myth. Rather, the Vietnam vet stereotype has undergone a pop-culture mythicization, has been turned into a comic book hero right up there with G.I. Joe and Sergeant Rock. Perhaps motion pictures, as one social commentator put it, "dewimped the American hero," but in the process they once again denied the humanity of the Vietnam vet. The heroizing of the Vietnam vet is not a compliment, rather it is the same denial of his basic humanity and intelligence that the obsession with the "violent vet" stereotype of the late seventies was.

American culture has always been attracted to the simplicity of the labels of *polarization*: right/left; hawk/dove. We invented the Western movie with its white hat/black hat characters to satisfy this polarization urge and we sustained the black/white opposition of slavery for three hundred years and segregation, the American version of apartheid, for another one hundred years. In the late seventies and early eighties, the Vietnam vet has become one of the central objects of this American fondness for polarized stereotyping. As a result, he has been held in bondage to the media. H. L. Mencken once wrote: "No one ever went broke underestimating the taste of the American people." *Rambo II* has proved Mencken's axiom better than any carnival freak show or national pornographic industry ever could. In the stereotyping of Vietnam vets, the American public has exercised a range of bad taste that stems directly from changes in the political motives of America's tastemakers, the media. Since 1976, the Vietnam vet has evolved from an invisible man to either a walking time bomb or a suicidal depressant to an ultraviolent comic book superhero working out the ultimate in survivor guilt fantasies. Each of these images is but a political caricature that uses veterans as pawns for the therapy of national psychoses.

On Veterans Day, 1984, John Wheeler, the author of *Touched with Fire: The Future of the Vietnam Generation* wrote in *USA Today*: "We can each take specific steps to speed the national assimilation of the Vietnam War. One step is to lay aside the battle fatigues. . . . the overwhelming majority of

Vietnam veterans are not found in fatigues, even on patriotic holidays. They can be identified by their growing leadership in the nation's public and private life."

Vietnam vets in the eighties have gone well beyond the fantasy of sending Bo Gritz to try to find, Rambo-style, surviving POWs in Vietnam. Rather, they are lobbying hard for the resolution of three major partisan issues:

1. Diplomatic resolution of the MIA/POW issue
2. The Agent Orange issue
3. The issue of the plight of Amerasian children

They are pursuing their goals as intelligent people with a cause have always pursued their goals, through education and action within the channels of the American political system.

But thanks in part to the simplistic stereotyping and the right-wing propagandizing of the movies of the comic book phase of the Vietnam War film history, Vietnam veterans, in the words of psychologist Charles Figley, find themselves still "strangers at home."[2] Don Bellisario, a former Marine and executive producer of television's "Magnum, P.I." and "Airhawk," argues that the "Vietnam vet is probably the most complex we've had in this century" and "he has gone through such a tormented and pendulum existence. . . . that makes for a far more interesting character" (*USA Today*, 27 June 1985), but that knowledge does not seem to have influenced the fantasy revisionism of the "let's go back and do it right this time" propaganda of TV's Rambomania spinoffs. The comic book phase of the Vietnam War film history began with a single polemic speech in the initial Rambo movie, *First Blood* (1982), then seemed to take on political life of its own. Throughout the early eighties, the image of the Vietnam vet evolved out of rejection and invisibility into patronizing political heroization. The Vietnam vet went from being an invisible man to a walking time bomb to a sympathetic victim to a cartoon character.

Simplistic as this comic book phase designation may sound, the "coming home" movies that appeared between 1980 and 1986 examined the issue of the Vietnam veteran in American society from four different perspectives. First, the most positive, least cartoonish group of movies explored with varying degrees of resistance to exploitation the psychological inability of the Vietnam vet to leave the war behind and regain unencumbered normality in American society. Films like *The Stunt Man* (1980), *Cutter's Way* (1981), *Some Kind of Hero* (1981), *Birdy* (1985), *Cease Fire* (1986), and even to some extent *First Blood* examined this imprisonment by the past. The second set of "coming home" films, however, the survivor guilt fantasies, took directly the opposite view. Films like *Rambo II*, *Uncommon Valor* (1983), the *Missing in Action* series (1984, 1985, 1987), all harking back to the final Saigon section of *The Deer Hunter* (1978), opted for a comic book heroization of the Vietnam supervet motivated by Reagan administration historical revisionism. A third group of films, including the *Lethal Weapon* series (1987, 1989), *The Presidio* (1988), and *Shakedown* (1988), explored the anomaly of the violent vet finding a legal outlet for his violence behind a badge. An irony of these films is that in most cases both the cop heroes and the villains turn out to be Vietnam vets. Finally, the fourth set of films which view the Vietnam vet "coming home" focuses upon differing forms of Vietnam War racism within American society. While films like *Alamo Bay* (1985) and *The Year of the Dragon* (1985) examine American racism toward the oriental villains of the Southeast Asia melodrama, others look at the racism toward black Vietnam veterans both within the military and the society at large. Thus there is a diversity of thematic perspective within these "coming home" films of the comic book phase, but with a few exceptions (*The Stunt Man*, *Birdy*, *The Killing Fields*), these films stereotype and exploit the image of the Vietnam veteran.

The "Strangers at Home" Films

First Blood, the movie that introduced the character John Rambo, crosscuts consistently between two textual intentions. On one hand, it is a comic book action fantasy that exploits the Hollywood stereotype of the supervet for the purpose of motorcycle and car chases, automatic weapons gun-fights, Southern sheriff cliché violence (though set in the Oregon north woods rather than the Kentucky hills of the book from which it is adapted), and fiery explosions. On the other hand, for long stretches, *First Blood* is a talky movie, a debate that focuses upon revisionist historical analysis of what happened in Vietnam, why America lost, and the postwar situation of the Vietnam vet who has been made into a "stranger at home" by American society. In these analytic dialogue exchanges and extended polemic speeches, the comic book exploitation of the action scenes gives way to a rather serious and thoughtful social text. Because *First Blood* does this precarious balancing act, it cannot immediately be written off as a comic book (as can its two sequels).

There are two reasons why *First Blood* carries more textual intentionality than its sequels. First, it is adapted from a thoughtful text, David Morrell's novel of the same name. There is an evident and conscious attempt on the part of the *First Blood* screenwriters to capture the historical, social, and psychological complexity of the book's text and central character. But, second, unlike the John Rambo of 1985 and 1988, this first John Rambo has not yet been exploited into a greased-up comic book hero. *First Blood* does not end in violent comic book action but rather in one long, human speech in which John Rambo verbalizes, first, his historical vision of what happened in Vietnam, then, his sense of himself, and all the other Vietnam veterans as a "lost generation" within American society.

After the holocaust on the Main Street of small-town America and the final violent confrontation with bullheaded Sheriff Teasle (Brian Dennehy), Colonel Trautman (Richard Crenna), Rambo's commanding officer in Vietnam, tries to talk his "boy" out of this firefight. In response to Trautman, Rambo, after spending the whole film in silence, finally gets to tell his side of the story. It is a speech in which Rambo's humanity attempts to override the film's other, competing text of violent comic book action:

TRAUTMAN: It's over, Johnny. It's over.

RAMBO: Nothing is over! Nothing! You just don't turn it off. It wasn't my war. You asked me, I didn't ask you. And I did what I had to do to win. But somebody wouldn't let us win. Then I come back to the world and I see all those maggots at the airport, protestin' me, spittin', callin' me babykiller and all kinds of vile crap. Who are they to protest me, huh? Who are they? Unless they been me and been there and know what the hell they're yellin' about.

TRAUTMAN: It was a bad time for everyone, Rambo. It's all in the past, now.

RAMBO: For you! For me civilian life is nothin'. In the field we had a code of honor. You watch my back, I'll watch yours. Back here there's nothin'.

TRAUTMAN: You were a member of an elite group. Don't end it like this.

RAMBO: Back there I could fly a gunship. I could drive a tank. I was in charge of million-dollar equipment. Back here I can't even hold a job parkin' cars. (Rambo breaks down and begins to weep.) I can't get it outa my head. I seen it for seven years. Every day's like that. Sometimes I don't even know where I am. I don't talk to anybody. Sometimes a day, a week. I can't put it outa my mind.

Trautman repeatedly argues that the Vietnam War is over, but for Rambo and his fellow veterans it is not. Rambo's argument begins historically— "Somebody wouldn't let us win" followed by his description of his reentry into the "world"—but ends psychologically with his graphic description of the rejection, alienation, nothingness of life for the veteran in postwar America. Only at the very beginning, and here at the end, of this exploitation film is character allowed to emerge. All of the "coming home" veterans' issues erupt in Rambo's climactic speech, and ironically, their final liberation justifies all of the comic book action and supervet stereotyping that the film has had to slog through to reach them. Though the contest is close, character ultimately holds exploitation at bay.

First Blood, then, is a bitextual film in which the metaphoric and psychological verbal offsets the exploitative visual. John Rambo's alienated silence heightens the power of his final verbal outpouring. For seven years he has been a voiceless invisible man. Now he finally has a chance to speak out. But the dialogue of the other characters in the film also weaves a web of metaphor around the historical revisionism of the Vietnam War and the situation of the Vietnam veteran in eighties society. *First Blood's* opening image is of a man walking down a lonely country road with a knapsack on his back. His hair is long. He is unshaven. He wears a U.S. Army fatigue jacket and blue jeans. The image aligns Rambo with a whole history of American outcasts, from the hobos of the Great Depression to the beats of Jack Kerouac's *On the Road* to the wandering youth of the sixties. "Who is he?" the image asks. It turns out he is a Vietnam vet trying to visit an old Army friend. But his friend has not survived. He has died of "cancer. Brought it back from Nam. All that Orange stuff they spread around." Later, when Colonel Trautman asks about this other survivor, Rambo answers, "Got himself killed in Nam, didn't even know it. Cancer ate him down to the bone." This opening scene is but the first indication that Vietnam is still going on.

Walking into a small Oregon town, the film's ironies begin to build around Rambo. The town is named "Hope." The town's Sheriff Teasle (Brian Dennehy), wearing the American flag on the shoulder of his uniform jacket, confronts Rambo at the city limits. "You know, wearin' that flag on that jacket, lookin' the way you do, you're askin' for trouble around here, friend," the Sheriff grins at Rambo. When Rambo refuses to be run out of town, the Sheriff arrests him. In the jail, both Rambo's mythic iconography (his huge hunting knife reminiscent of the American frontier) and his psychological burden (flashbacks to a prison camp in Vietnam) begin to surface. Rambo's scars signal his prison camp past even as the brutal cop's nightstick and firehose link that past to the present. Like so many Vietnam veterans, John Rambo consistently exists in two time zones, the historical past in Vietnam and the alienated present in American society where all the realities of Vietnam seem to be coming back, except that now America is the enemy and vets have become a new species of Viet Cong. In the film's final exchange when Colonel Trautman says, "It's over, Johnny," he means the private war of the present, but when Rambo answers, "Nothing is over," he in turn is not talking about the present at all but rather the war of seven years before.

When Rambo explodes under the sadistic treatment of the cops and escapes to the mountains, the comic book mythicism of the film takes over. Rambo becomes a stone age man aligned against the technology and firepower of the late twentieth century. The metaphor is unmistakable. In one scene he even throws a rock at a helicopter. Yet the metaphor is askew. Yes, Rambo has returned to Vietnam, or more to the point, has reconstituted Vietnam in American society, but that return/reconstitution has reversed his role. Whereas in Vietnam with all the backing of million-dollar American technology, he was hunting and killing the Viet Cong, in this metaphorical Vietnam, he has become the primitive Viet Cong that American technology is attempting to "bomb into the Stone Age." America has become the enemy, and the Vietnam veteran the primitive outgunned guerrilla. This cliff scene that ends with Rambo throwing a rock at a helicopter links with Rambo's earlier exchange with Sheriff Teasle about the proprieties of wearing the American flag on one's jacket. Both scenes define the theme of the betrayal of the American soldier during the war and of the veteran after the war by his own country. Once again, as in both *Platoon* and *Hamburger Hill*, America is portrayed as being its own worst enemy.

Colonel Trautman's first speech in *First Blood* confirms the ironic Viet Congness of John Rambo. This speech metaphorically alludes to, first, America's historical need for and refusal to accept help in extricating itself from the Vietnam War and, second, Rambo's social situation as a primitive guerrilla fighter within American society.

TRAUTMAN: The Army thought I might be able to help.

SHERIFF: Well, I don't know in what way. Rambo's a civilian now. He's my problem.

TRAUTMAN: I don't think you understand. I didn't come here to rescue Rambo from you. I came here to rescue you from him. . . . That boy's a heart attack. He may be the best that Special Forces ever produced. Whatever you're planning to throw at him here, he's been through a whole lot worse in worse places than this. . . .

SHERIFF: Colonel, you came out here because one of your machines blew a gasket.

TRAUTMAN: You don't seem to want to accept the fact that you're dealing with an expert in guerilla warfare. With a man who's the best, with guns, with knives, with his bare hands. A man who's been trained to ignore pain, to ignore weather, to live off the land, to eat things that would make a Billy Goat puke. In Vietnam his job was to dispose of enemy personnel, to kill, period. War of attrition. Well, Rambo was the best.

Trautman clear-sightedly predicts the victory of the primitive guerrilla fighter over all of the massed technology of American society. He is a perceptive student of history. Sheriff Teasle, stereotypically, yet also true to historical accuracy, dehumanizes Rambo as a "machine" that "blew a gasket," as a "civilian . . . problem now." Trautman, conversely, characterizes Rambo in human terms: "a heart attack," "an expert," "a man who's the best . . . with his bare hands." Both the past historical confrontation in Vietnam and the present social confrontation on the streets of America are between men and machines, between primitive individualism and dehumanizing repression. Later when Trautman raises Rambo on the radio, he says, "Well, look John, we can't have you runnin' around out there wasting friendly civilians." Rambo does not hesitate in his reply: "There are no friendly civilians, sir." His answer sums up the overwhelming sense of alienation within American society of the Vietnam veteran.

On different levels of meaning, *First Blood* metaphorically represents themes of historical revisionism toward the Vietnam War and of America's technological ineffectuality in that war against a primitive enemy, but the most important theme of the film is neither historical nor political; it is social. The ultimate ludicrousness of American society's rejection of its Vietnam veterans is spelled out by Colonel Trautman: "Vagrancy, wasn't it? That's gonna look real good on his gravestone. Here lies John Rambo. Winner of the Congressional Medal of Honor, Survivor of countless missions behind enemy lines, killed for vagrancy in Jerkwater, U.S.A." Perhaps *First Blood* is really a black comedy like *M*A*S*H* (1970) or *Catch-22* (1970), laughing through the blood at America's confusion.

But John Rambo is by no means the only Hollywood-generated Vietnam veteran to articulate his sense of being a "stranger at home." Three other films, *Birdy* (1985), *Some Kind of Hero* (1981), and *Cease Fire* (1986), are psychological case studies of Vietnam veterans' problems of reassimilation into American society. Each is different in its approach to the trauma of the "coming home" situation. As Pauline Kael writes, *Birdy* is "all metaphor" (*New Yorker*, 11 February 1985). If *Birdy* is the most visually and verbally representative, then *Some Kind of Hero* is the most ironic and cynical. Its black comedy slashes mercilessly (and hilariously) at the utter insensitivity of American society (the military, the media, the financial sector, the family) toward the reentry problems of Vietnam veterans. Of the three, *Cease Fire* is the most clinical and the least imaginative in its case study of PTSD.

As in *First Blood*, Vietnam itself and the rejection of the Vietnam veteran when he came home are the motive for all of the turmoil in *Birdy*. Also, as in *First Blood*, that motive is finally explained in a climactic speech late in the film when Al Colombato (Nicholas Cage) spills out all the frustration of his rejection by the society he went to war to protect. Kael, who reads *Birdy* as a film about a boy who wants to fly ala Robert Altman's *Brewster McCloud* (1970) rather than as a film about the aftermath of Vietnam, sees this climactic theme statement as a major flaw: "Talking to the unresponsive Birdy, Al suddenly delivers an impassioned antiwar statement. It's totally out of character, and you're groaning at the moviemaker's intruding in this way" (*New Yorker*, 11 February 1985). However, if the film is accepted as a "coming home" film, that climactic speech becomes almost mandatory. What these "strangers at home" films are all directed toward is the movement of the Vietnam veteran out of silence; in psychological terms, into the articulation of his traumatic frustration and the reassertion of his identity as a human being.

The final speeches of John Rambo and Al Columbato are a necessary therapeutic hurdle that the Vietnam veterans must jump in the process of humanizing their lost selves and reentering the society that has dropped that cloak of invisibility over them. Early in *Birdy*, Al, who has just had reconstructive surgery after having half of his face blown off in Vietnam, looks at his bandaged countenance in a mirror and, when his doctor asks him how he feels, answers, "like the invisible man." He reiterates this loss of identity because of Vietnam in that final speech when he decides that he wants to stay in the military asylum with his catatonic friend Birdy (Matthew Modine):

> AL: I can't go out there. I couldn't make it. They got the best of us, Birdy. We're both totally screwed up. I mean, we haven't had anything to do with running our lives. Fuck! I was always so damn sure about being myself and how nobody was gonna make me do anything I didn't want. And now here we are. They finish you off with a discharge or put you on a casualty list. It doesn't matter how special you are or were. I feel like one of those dogs that nobody wanted, remember? . . . And then I realized that it was my own skin that was burning and I couldn't even touch the pain. I don't even know what I look like anymore, Birdy. I don't know if it's me under these bandages or if some Army meatcutter thinks this is me. . . . I just want it to be Al under here. Not some sewn-together freak. Shit, what's so great about their fuckin' world anyway. We'll just stay here and keep the hell out of it.
>
> BIRDY: (who has not spoken at all in the whole present time of the film) Al, sometimes you're so full of shit.

The film both accepts the plight of the alienated Vietnam veteran and rejects it. This issue of alienation is a reality in American society, but all these films can do is state it. They cannot really deal with it. They opt either for Rambo's violent action or for Birdy's psychic withdrawal into a possibly better, freer world. Vietnam has grounded a whole new "lost generation" of young Americans, and the title character of Birdy represents their desire to once again soar above their lostness and invisibility at home.

All through *Birdy*, carrier pigeons, whose existence is based upon the premise of "coming home," serve as symbols of what Al and Birdy post-Vietnam are trying to do. When Birdy first shows Al his pigeons, Al asks, "What are you trainin' 'em for, to carry messages, like in a war?" Al and Birdy are both pigeons forced to take flight to Vietnam who are now struggling to return home with the message of that war. Repeatedly symbolic scenes of birds not being allowed to return home represent the barriers that the society has thrown up for Vietnam veterans. Early in the film, Birdy's malevolent mother will not allow his pigeons to return home. First she tries to poison them and then she has the butcher kill them. Later as Al is going off to Vietnam, Birdy watches from his bedroom window. When his pet canary, Perta, the love of his life, escapes through a crack at the bottom of the window, Birdy, knowing that she will try to come home immediately, tries frantically to raise the window but cannot. Perta flies full force into the glass pane and is killed trying to come home. This motif is but one example of the successful metaphoricality of *Birdy*.

Both of the central characters, though their views of the world (Al always looks down on the city, while Birdy always looks up at the stars) are totally different, have found via Vietnam that they no longer fit into what seemed the simple world of their childhood in Philly. Both realize, as they think back on those years, that those years were not simple at all. And then came Vietnam and growing up before their time and coming home and being different. In the gym at the VA hospital, Al first watches a paraplegic shoot baskets from a wheelchair, then a legless man climb a rope, and he thinks: *Funny. In any other war we woulda been heroes. We really didn't know what we were getting into with this John Wayne shit.*

Al, with his bandaged face, is supposed to be a therapist for the catatonic Birdy, but he begins to realize that he is every bit as much a patient as his silent friend. He realizes that all Vietnam vets are patients. "You gotta come back, Birdy," Al pleads with his friend to reject his silent catatonia. "I'm scared, Birdy," Al says. "I'm more scared now than I ever was in the war and I was more scared there than anybody I knew." As did Tim O'Brien's novel *Going After Cacciato*, *Birdy* explores the possibility of escaping the psychological wounds of Vietnam via a flight of imagination and, in the end, rejects that possibility. As was the case in *First Blood*, the whole film leads up to Al's climactic speech about Vietnam, which Birdy rejects. But Alan Parker does not end *Birdy* on this speech and a slow fade as *First Blood* ended. The climactic speech is followed by a silly, comic book chase culminating in a ridiculous sight gag that undercuts whatever power the film had previously generated. As Jack Matthews (*USA Today*, 13 December 1984) put it: "I felt as if I had just poured my heart out to my psychiatrist and he mooned me."

At least in *Some Kind of Hero*, one is prepared for the mooning of the "coming home" issue. If *First Blood* was the coming home of Sergeant Rock, then *Some Kind of Hero* is the comic book coming home of a black Bugs Bunny. If *First Blood* portrays the "coming home" theme as action-adventure, and *Birdy* portrays it as psychological case study, then *Some Kind of Hero* is screwball comedy's contribution to that theme. Remember Cary Grant donning those feathery ladies' nightclothes in Howard Hawk's *Bringing up Baby* (1938) and *Monkey Business* (1952)? In *Some Kind of Hero*, Corporal Eddie Keller (Richard Pryor) reprises that exact scene and follows to the letter the McGuffin pursuit scenario of the screwball genre.

In fact, *Some Kind of Hero* reprises a number of scenes from earlier films. When he decides that he is sick of being rejected by American society, Eddie Keller buys a toy squirt gun and, like Travis Bickle in *Taxi Driver*, rehearses a bank robbery in front of the mirror. Unfortunately when he actually does try to rob a bank, he wets his own pants with the squirt gun and everybody laughs. Despite the screwball situations, *Some Kind of Hero* still makes telling points about the difficulty of a Vietnam veteran's "coming home."

Some Kind of Hero is structured in three parts. Part one takes place in-country Vietnam, where on his first day in combat, Eddie Keller is caught with his pants down (literally) and marched off to an NVA prison camp. He spends two years as a POW. Part two is the "coming home" section of the film, and part three is the screwball chase after a briefcase full of negotiable bonds. By far the most interesting in its cynical black humor is the second section in which Eddie returns home and experiences a succession of disappointments, rejections, betrayals, and social hostility.

As the plane bringing Eddie Keller home from Vietnam touches down, Colonel Powers (Ronny Cox), the Army psychiatrist, says "OK, Eddie, we're home." But everything is not "OK." First, the media descend upon Eddie and start putting words into his mouth, cajole him into kissing the ground and feeling like a fool. Later the media will again interview Eddie after he has witnessed a bank robbery by another 1st Air Cav vet. When Eddie starts talking about how the bank would not give him a loan and how the bank was robbed by other veterans like himself, the media does not want to hear it. Second, Eddie is rejected by his own family. His wife has found another man and with the help of her new lover has lost Eddie's business and all of his money. "We'll pay you back, I swear to God. We'll pay you back," she promises emptily as Eddie laughs and cries at the same time. Third, when he goes into a bank to get a loan to pay his mother's nursing home bills, the sign says "We Never Say No." Unfortunately they have no trouble saying "No" to Eddie. Fourth, as Eddie sits in a bar, two guys start mocking his uniform and hassling him about losing the war. On his first day in Vietnam, Eddie was captured by the enemy, and on his first day back home he is rejected by the media, his family, an American financial institution, and the general public. *Some Kind of Hero* is a checklist of all the kinds of rejections a Vietnam veteran experiences when he comes home. What is most puzzling about *Some Kind of Hero* is the fact that race is never, in any way, allowed to become an issue.

What all three of these "strangers at home" films—*First Blood*, *Birdy*, *Some Kind of Hero*—have in common is their thematic stress that the only way Vietnam vets can survive the psychological horrors of PTSD and the social horrors of "coming home" is through solidarity with other psychological and social outcasts. John Rambo must be med-evaced out of his private postwar war by his Vietnam comrade in arms, Colonel Trautman. Birdy's childhood friend Al, externally scarred by Vietnam as seriously as Birdy is internally scarred, becomes the vehicle of Birdy's liberation from the VA psycho ward. Eddie Keller's only friend in the American society to which he returns turns out to be a hooker whose profession, ironically, Eddie criticizes in the same manner that those men in the bar mocked his uniform and service in Vietnam. Each of these films reaches for but never grasps a solution to the "coming home" problem. At the end of each, the troubled veteran is left suspended in the vacuum of a vague unresolved issue. This vagueness is best exemplified in one brief exchange in *Some Kind of Hero* between Eddie Keller and Colonel Powers, his Army psychiatrist:

COL. POWERS: What do you expect me to do?

EDDIE: The right thing.

Eddie's plea for some vague moral resolution is emotional but ineffectual. A society needs much more specific direction for dealing with the problems of its rejected minority groups.

One other film, *Cease Fire* (1986), is much more psychologically melodramatic in its attempt to portray the torments of Vietnam veteran PTSD. It is a comic book movie in the hand-wringing soap opera style of Brenda Starr or Mary Worth. Lacking the war comic exaggeration of *First Blood*, the metaphoricality of *Birdy*, and the cynical frenetic Bugs Bunnyness of *Some Kind of Hero*, *Cease Fire* also fails in its realism. Like a bad "disease of the week" made-for-TV movie, *Cease Fire* collects all the symptoms of a Vietnam veteran's PTSD situation and melodramatizes them. *Cease Fire* is pure social exploitation, a chance to show bombs going off in a character's mind and then show that character becoming a bomb timed to go off in society.

Tim (Don Johnson) is an unemployed Vietnam vet, who is flashbacking to the point that he turns his own living room into a war zone complete with live ammunition and sharpened bayonets. This is a whole new twist to the concept of Vietnam as a "living room war." Tim cannot hold a job, is drinking too much and has started to beat up his wife, Paula (Lisa Blount). He looks for friendship from another Vietnam vet, Luke (Robert F. Lyons), but unlike the positive relationship between vets in *First Blood* and *Birdy*, this one is destructive. Luke's own PTSD problems are as bad as Tim's. In the best TV-melodrama fashion, Tim is rescued by the understanding and love of a good woman, but his rehabilitation skirts the real issue, that PTSD's stubborn resistance to treatment lies not within the individual mind but within the collective mind of the rejecting society as well.

Of all the "strangers at home" films, two stand out as the most stylish and intelligent, though also possessed of their comic book aspects. Those two are the cockeyed film noir *Cutter's Way* (1981) and the antiwar metamovie *The Stunt Man* (1980). The central character in each is a Vietnam veteran unable to find an identity in postwar society, subject to outbursts of senseless violence, armed with a cynical sense of humor, and caught in a social situation that in highly metaphorical ways parallels his former situation as a soldier in Vietnam. Alex Cutter (John Heard) in *Cutter's Way* chooses to become an unmanned postmodernist caricature of the forties' hard-boiled detective in a metaphoric Vietnam War revenge scenario. Cameron (Steve Railsback) in *The Stunt Man* mixes up his real past life in Vietnam with his present metalife as a multiple identity stunt man making a war movie. Neither film has any scenes set in Vietnam, no flashbacks.

Neither protagonist talks in any detail about his experiences in Vietnam. Yet in both films, the wounds of Vietnam are still open, the arrogance of American society toward veterans still evident, and a clear political statement of how Vietnam veterans feel about the society that sent them to Vietnam and subsequently rejected them when they came home still needed. Of all the "strangers at home" films, these two are the most consciously metaphorical, mythical.

Cutter's Way is an elaborate metaphor that works out a single thematic truth: that American society has refused to take responsibility for the Vietnam War by placing all the blame for its conduct, results, and aftermath upon the soldiers who fought it. Motive gives motion to this metaphor and that motive is revenge, Alex Cutter's mad, Ahab-like obsession for making those two factions of American society who made the Vietnam soldier's life miserable—the fat-cat military-industrial establishment and the antiwar movement—pay. *Cutter's Way* expresses the need of Vietnam veterans to force America, both the political right as represented by J. J. Cord (Stephen Elliott) and the political left as represented by Richard Bone (Jeff Bridges) to take responsibility for what it did to them.

As political allegory, the characterization of *Cutter's Way* is unmistakable. The plot is a conventional comic book murder scenario. On a dark and stormy night, Richard Bone catches a glimpse of a large man stuffing something into a trash can. The next morning the body of a sexually assaulted, brutally murdered, teenage girl is found. Bone is suspected, tells his vague witness story, is released, but the next day in the company of his Vietnam veteran friend Alex Cutter, he spots a large shape that he thinks might be the murderer. That familiar bulk belongs to one of the city's richest and most prominent citizens, who is riding his white horse down Main Street in the Santa Barbara Fiesta Parade. The complexity of *Cutter's Way* does not lie in its mystery plot but in the subtext that the characterization of these three central figures embodies. On the surface, *Cutter's Way* is a movie about a murder, but in reality it is an extended metaphor about both the placing and the accepting of responsibility for the Vietnam War.

Richard Bone is a latter-day hippie, aimless, uninvolved, interested in making love, certainly not war on J. J. Cord. Early in the film, Alex Cutter unequivocally characterizes Bone: "You're watchin' Richard Bone doin' what he does best, walkin' away." Bone represents that segment of the Vietnam generation that avoided the draft, then vilified the soldiers when they returned from the war. Later Mo (Lisa Eichorn), Alex Cutter's wife, just before she is firebombed in her home, another innocent victim of the war, asks Bone:

MO: Where's Alex?

RICHARD: He's fightin' the good fight.

MO: What about you?

RICHARD: I chickened out.

Richard Bone is that segment of American society that needs to be educated in the history of their generation. When Alex Cutter's brother Georgie asks Richard the same question that Mo asked—"Where's Alex?"—Bone replies in the same detached way: "Alex? He feels the world is short of heroes and he's tryin' to fill the gap." For Richard Bone, irresponsibility, disengagement, is his way of life. Unfortunately what Georgie tells him—"Sooner or later you gotta make a decision"—is ultimately true. Both circumstances (his being at the wrong place at the wrong time to witness the disposal of the body) and the moral force of Alex draft Richard Bone into the war. Eventually there is no way he can dodge that draft.

One small scene defines the difference between playing at war and actually fighting a war. As Cutter and Bone are waiting to put pressure on J. J. Cord, Bone stalls by aimlessly firing a BB gun at an ace of spades in a pier shooting gallery. Cutter, impatient with Bone's stalling and never hitting the target, pulls a .45 out of his belt and blows the card away. Aimlessness is not Cutter's way and this small scene of nonavoidance makes that unmistakably clear. If you are going to fight a war, you cannot do it by avoiding the issues, stalling for time in the hope that the enemy will go away. But if Bone represents the uninvolved left, then Cord represents the overinvolved right of the Vietnam era.

From his first appearance on-screen, Cord is iconographically represented as a fascist. Riding on a white horse as the honorary Presidente of the Fiesta Parade, Cord, head shaved like Il Duce and wearing black, opaque SS sunglasses, is shot from a severely low angle that emphasizes his power. The visual iconography of Cord's ironic white horse and menacing sunglasses is repeated throughout the film. The opening image of the film is a young girl in a white dress in the parade dancing in slow motion down the center of the street. The white innocence and freedom of the dancer's dress transfer to the subdued whiteness of the horse beneath Cord. Early in the film, Richard Bone must stop his car to allow a riderless white horse to pass in the street, and then, mere moments later, he witnesses the disposal of the body of the mutilated young girl. In the last scene of the film, Cord, confident that Richard Bone does not have the nerve to pull the trigger of Alex's .45, arrogantly puts on his opaque sunglasses as a way of closing out the real, moral world. Both Richard Bone and J. J. Cord are type characters, comic book caricatures of the aimless hippie and the arrogant fascist politician, but Alex Cutter is much more complex.

Most of the Vietnam veterans of these "strangers at home" movies bear distinctive war wounds. John Rambo's back is scarred. Al Columbato's face is half blown off and Birdy's body is contorted into the posture of a caged canary. Luke, Tim Murphy's vet friend in *Cease Fire*, is hallucinatory and suicidal. But none is as visibly wounded as Alex Cutter. He is a one-eyed, one-legged, drunken, wife-beating, suicidal Vietnam vet hungry for revenge upon a society that refused to take any responsibility for putting him in Vietnam and turning him into a cripple.

"It must be tough playin' second fiddle to a one-eyed cripple," Mo taunts Richard Bone early in the film. "He's not your ordinary one-eyed cripple," Bone answers, and indeed, Cutter certainly is not. Alex Cutter's first words in the film are drunken but set yet another subtextual context for interpreting the film. When Bone enters the bar, Alex greets him with, "Ahoy maties, Ishmael returneth." He then launches into a tirade of literary gibberish that quotes *Moby Dick*, *Hamlet*, Karl Marx and ends with a "Rastus" joke. With his piratic eye patch and his wooden leg (cane), Alex Cutter is a cross between the mythic Captain Ahab and the comical Long John Silver. This association of Cutter and Bone to the contexts of American myth is supported when moments later Cutter's wife, Mo, greets Richard Bone with the words, "Poor Richard." The mythic associa-tion comes clear later in the film when Cutter obsessively closes in pursuit of Cord who is repeatedly associated with whiteness and whose powerful bald forehead looms over them like the brow of Moby Dick.

Next to Joseph Conrad's *Heart of Darkness*, the one literary allusion that most often surfaces in the Vietnam War literature and film is to *Moby Dick*. Both Thomas Myers and John Hellmann have noted how the mythic quest for the white whale is emplotted in the best Vietnam War fiction, partic-ularly John Del Vecchio's *13th Valley*.[3] In Francis Coppola's *Apocalypse Now*, the camera's shadowy stalking of Colonel Kurtz (Marlon Brando), his rising out of depths of darkness to fascinate Captain Willard (Martin Sheen), also conjures the *Moby Dick* allusion.[4] In Oliver Stone's *Platoon*, the voice-over narrative explicitly compares Sergeant Barnes (Tom Berenger) to Captain Ahab. In *Cutter's Way*, however, the Ahab association is handled in such a broadly comic and obvious manner that it escapes all the pretention that Stone's later allusion to the myth in *Platoon* suffers under.

Alex Cutter is a comic book Captain Ahab obsessed with his revenge quest to place the responsibility for his mutilation in the Vietnam War and, by implication, America's mutilation in the Vietnam War upon someone. Richard Bone is, indeed, his innocent Ishmael whom he convinces to sign on for his fanatical quest for justice. Once Alex Cutter sets his sights on the whiteness of his whale, J. J. Cord, there can be no turning back and all Bone can do is ride the crest of Cutter's violent wave until it spits him out.

The title was originally *Cutter and Bone* with a wordplay on the idea of cutting right to the bone of life, meaning reality, a wordplay upon the imagery of amputation in which Alex Cutter, the Vietnam amputee, cuts away all of Richard Bone's supercilious avoidance of the moral issues of life. But the final title, *Cutter's Way*, changed for the film's re-release, is less obscure and more appropriate. Doing things Alex Cutter's way is doing things right, pursuing a moral conviction all the way (as America did not do in Vietnam). For Alex Cutter, there is only one way to explain America's failure in Vietnam and America's rejection of the men, crippled like himself, who fought there. In Cutter's way of looking at it, those things happened because no one wanted to take on any responsibility:

ALEX: Don't give me any lectures on morality. In fact, in fact Rich, let me give you one. . . . I watched the War on TV just like everybody else, OK. Thought the same damn things. You know what you thought when you saw a picture of a young woman with a baby lying face down in a ditch, two gooks? You had three reactions, Rich. Same as anybody else. First one is easy. I hate the United States of America. Yea, you see the same damn thing the next day and you move up a notch. There is no God. But you know what everybody finally says? What you finally say? No matter what? I'm hungry. I'm hungry, Rich.

RICHARD: So you pick out somebody and you blackmail him.

ALEX: I didn't pick him out. You did. And he isn't somebody. He's responsible.

RICHARD: For the girl?

ALEX: For everything. They're all the same.

RICHARD: So let's blow up AT&T, eh?

ALEX: You know why they're all the same, Rich? Because it's never their ass that's on the line. Never. It's always somebody else's. Always yours, mine, ours. So leave off the morality, OK. And don't write me off as a money-grubbin' bastard altogether.

As in the culminating speeches in *First Blood* and *Birdy*, Cutter's movement through the philosophical vortex of existential man in a Marxist world to an island of lucidity in a politics of responsibility defines the mindset of yet another Vietnam veteran trying to find a clean, well-lighted place in postwar American society. Cutter's way is to force someone else to take on the responsibility for Vietnam that was forced upon him and his fellow veterans when they were drafted. Cutter enlists Bone, Ahab signs his Ishmael on, to force America to take responsibility for its actions instead of hiding behind its power and respectability, sloughing all its guilt off on its scapegoat, the veterans who fought honorably for its empty ideals.

Of all the "coming home" films of the 1980–86 period, *Cutter's Way* offers the most radical political message couched in genre metaphor. It is a virulent indictment of American society's attitude toward the soldiers who fought in Vietnam. Its brutal murder mystery text is of little consequence, but its two subtexts—one political, one mythic—define the hostility that exists between Vietnam veterans and an American society that refuses to accept its responsibility.

The primary text of *The Stunt Man* is also about a failure to accept responsibility, in this case responsibility for the death of a stunt man during the making of a movie. Like Graham Greene's novel *The Quiet American*, which in 1954 caricatured the first American CIA excursions into Vietnam, Richard Rush's *Stunt Man* will always be bathed in a weird prophetic light. Two years after *The Stunt Man*, on the set of *Twilight Zone: The Movie*, while filming a sequence about the Vietnam War, actor Vic Morrow and two Vietnamese children were killed when a stunt scene went bad and a helicopter crashed on top of them. In its portrayal of a similar stunt accident, in its egomaniacal director character, in its helicopter antics, and in its whole cover-up scenario, *The Stunt Man* bears an eerie prophetic similarity to the John Landis-directed *Twilight Zone* tragedy of 1982. But the real voodoo of linking *The Stunt Man* to the *Twilight Zone* tragedy is thematic. *The Stunt Man* is a film about life and art getting all confused to the point that illusion becomes reality, reality is nothing but an illusion, and nothing is ever what it seems to be. In the *Twilight Zone* tragedy, that is exactly what happened. The illusion of Vietnam turned into reality. Death intruded upon art. A mere movie got too real.

But *The Stunt Man* is not the most important of the "strangers at home" films simply because it is blessed with the gift of prophecy. Many films — from *Casablanca* (1942) to *The China Syndrome* (1979) — have verged upon prophecy. *The Stunt Man* is important because it is the only one of these "coming home" films that deals with the most elemental disorientation that Vietnam worked upon the men who fought there; that is, the inability of the Vietnam veteran to distinguish between reality and illusion, the paranoid conviction of the spooked Vietnam veteran that nothing is ever what it seems to be. In the mid-seventies, another metaphoric Vietnam War film, *Chinatown*, explored this same theme of historical paranoia.[5]

Pauline Kael seems to think that *The Stunt Man* is merely about "paranoia and moviemaking" (*New Yorker*, 29 September 1980), when in fact, it has a much wider theme. *The Stunt Man* is about the paranoia with which Vietnam infected American society, the insecurity that reality is but an illusion, that nothing is ever what it seems. *The Stunt Man* has been interpreted as metamovie (a self-reflexive movie about moviemaking)[6] and as psychoanalytic romp through the mazes of paranoia,[7] but it has yet to be read as the intricate metaphoric "coming home" from Vietnam film that it is. *Vietnam: The Movie* as immortalized in both Michael Herr's *Dispatches*[8] and in Stanley Kubrick's *Full Metal Jacket*,[9] here gets its fullest rendering, previewed only by that wisp of a scene in *Apocalypse Now* in which Coppola himself, posing as a TV cameraman, walks Fellini-like into one of the battle scenes of his movie chanting the goofy mantra, "don't look at the camera, don't look at the camera, keep fighting." In a world of "Is it real? Or is it Memorex?" how does a Vietnam veteran learn to grasp the reality of postwar life? Or, better, is it possible for postwar life ever to be real? These are the unique questions that *The Stunt Man* explores.

Two snatches of music dominate the sound track of *The Stunt Man*. One, a jangly circus anthem, governs the pace of the film, ushers the film out of the symbolic, metaphysical mode of the dialogue passages into the zany, out-of-control, illusion game of the action passages. This circus music functions in much the same way as the *Jaws* theme that signals the impending presence of the murderous shark. The second musical reprise, however, is a haunting ballad that at crucial moments asserts that reality can never be anything more than an illusion because all of life is but an illusory game, like a movie. The song contemplates how reality and dreams are of little use in a world in which nothing is what it seems to be. This song links *The Stunt Man* to the major films of the previous decades, *Blow-Up* for the sixties and *Chinatown* for the seventies, which deny the concept of reality, which see the world as an ongoing game played by illusionists for no purpose but to keep the game going.

Three major thematic points are made in this haunting theme song. It points to those "pieces of your past" from the Vietnam veteran Cameron's (Steve Railsback) time in the war that he repeatedly uses as similes for what is happening on the film set. It defines the world as "out of reason, out of rhyme" where "nothing is what it seems," echoing the crucial thematic line of dialogue of *Chinatown*. And finally, it poses the question—"what good are your dreams?"—which aligns it with a body of literature that, as in *The Great Gatsby*, examines the ephemeral qualities of the American dream.

Of all the works in the Vietnam literature canon, the one to which *The Stunt Man* has the closest ties is Tim O'Brien's *Going After Cacciato*. In that novel and in *The Stunt Man*, a young man finds that the only avenue of escape is through his imagination, through creating a grand illusion that can replace the brutal reality of the war.

Cameron (the pun is on "camera on"), the fugitive Vietnam vet who stumbles onto an elaborate war movie set while fleeing the police, has only one point of reference, the Vietnam War, for characterizing his actions in a supposedly real world. As he views the bloody carnage of a movie set battle, Cameron for a moment thinks that he is back in Vietnam and screams "Medics!" When a young tourist says, "Why do they always use so much blood? Ruins the realism, don't you think?" all Cameron can reply is "Asshole!" To Cameron, the tourists' cavalier, cynical reactions to the seeming gore and death of war is indicative of that American sense that Vietnam was just an illusion, a poorly made movie that flopped at the box office. In this American social metamorphosis of the reality of Vietnam into the illusion of *Vietnam: The Movie*, the soldiers, the Vietnam veterans, become the stunt men who doubled for the more valuable "stars" of the society. These stunt men took all the risks, while the others stood back and watched until it was time to step in for the love scenes. The film extends this metaphor of the Vietnam vet as stunt man for America. In the metaphor, the vet did the dirty work that others did not want to do. The risks involved in their stunts constantly escalated. The stunt man grunts were deceived during the war, and then when it was all over, those stunt grunts were not paid off for their work. It is a meticulously constructed metaphor for the American soldier in Vietnam.

"Ever done any stunt work?" the head stunt gaffer (Chuck Bail) asks his pupil, Cameron. "Got outa Nam in one piece. That's a hell of a stunt," Cameron the wiseguy answers. "Ancient history," the gaffer scoffs. "Seems like yesterday to me," Cameron corrects him. Cameron then goes on to address him as "Sergeant" as the stunt man boot camp begins. This "Sergeant" of illusion gets mad at Cameron for not taking this training seriously: "It's a little different when you're runnin' over those roofs and they're pumpin' tracer bullets over your head." But Cameron laughs: "I was runnin' for twenty-six months with guys shootin' at my head, not over my head. I'm here. I'm alive. I knew daredevils and I got nothin' against 'em except they're all dead." As metaphorical text, *The Stunt Man* is about the manner in which American society not only conducted the Vietnam War like a movie but actually turned social history into an illusion, scripted and acted out social history for the cameras of the media. Thus *The Stunt Man* is eerily prophetic in yet another way. Released in 1980, it predicts the Reagan administration, with all of its movielike qualities, fueled by photo opportunity scheduling and the orchestration of "sound bites" by "spin doctors" in which a real actor is actually playing the lead role in social history.

At the center of *The Stunt Man*'s metaphor hangs the dangling man, the Vietnam veteran who is expected to step off the set of the war and resume his old invisible identity. The dilemma of this expectation, however, lies in the fact that for the Vietnam vet and the stunt man this easy withdrawal and forgetting often does not work. "I knew a guy once, stepped on a bouncing betty booby trap," Cameron generates another metaphor. "Stepping on it wasn't the problem 'cause it's when you step off it that it explodes. So, all he could do was just stand there." That is precisely the situation of the Vietnam vet in postwar American society. He is immobilized because, first, he cannot get away from the war, cannot escape the booby traps always on the verge of detonating inside his mind; and second, American society has walked away from him, left him standing there alone waiting for his memories and his postwar sense of rejection to blow him away. When, in *The Stunt Man*, the movie's site producer asks the director, "What have you been feeding that soldier boy, brave pills?" the answer is, "It's not what he eats, but what's eating him that makes it so interesting." And later, "you read in some paper about some land mine that was left over from some war. He's one of them."

As the movie within this movie *The Stunt Man* relentlessly offers metaphor after metaphor characterizing the postwar situation, both social and psychological, of the Vietnam veteran, and (by metaphoric extrapolation) the war goes on, the stunt man/soldier begins to see the light, begins to realize how the director/the society is exploiting him. The Vietnam War subtext is clear in Cameron's perception of his stunt man situation: "It doesn't change the fact that the man is crazy. If he had his way, there wouldn't be a soldier left by morning. But I'm the only soldier he's got on hand. I don't even know if he knows why he's doin' it, but it's a great idea. A genuine dumb grunt cashing in before your very eyes, the real McCoy. Kill two birds with one stone. It's got nice logic to it. Trouble is, both birds are me." In this speech, Cameron has the movie and the war all mixmastered together into a frantic metaphor that finally arrives at the one overpowering truth: No matter what, whether in the real war or in the illusory war back in society, the one left standing on the mine is the veteran. In the seventies, American society truly tried to kill two birds with one stone in its dealings with Vietnam veterans. First, it tried to kill them off in the real war; then, it tried to make them disappear when they got home.

Cameron's comment, "Trouble is, both birds are me," is especially ironic when considered in context with the very first words of the film. When a bird flies into the windshield of a helicopter in that marvelously kinetic opening sequence, the chopper pilot yells, "That goddam bird just tried to kill us!" At that moment, a disembodied hand raises an apple for a bite and the disembodied voice of the film director says: "That's your point of view. Did you stop and ask the bird what his was?" That is what *The Stunt Man* is all about, looking at the world from the point of view of the bird, the Vietnam veteran, whom everyone seems to be trying to kill off.

As in the other "strangers at home" films, the point of view of the bird (the Vietnam vet) finally gets expression in a final explanatory speech. Cameron's speech near the end of *The Stunt Man* is strikingly similar to those of John Rambo in *First Blood*, of Al Columbato in *Birdy*, of Eddie Keller in *Some Kind of Hero*, and of Alex Cutter in *Cutter's Way*. All of these speeches touch upon the same four points, form an identifiable Vietnam vet rhetoric: (1) what it was like in Vietnam; (2) what the veteran expected when he got home from Vietnam; (3) how America reneged on its payment to the Vietnam veteran; (4) how that Vietnam veteran as a result feels identityless in American society. Cameron's version of this set speech is different only in that it is delivered with more wry humor than were the desperate speeches of the other "strangers at home."

When Nina (Barbara Hershey), his actress-lover, asks him "Who the hell are you?" Cameron answers:

> Somebody trying to stay alive. . . . I did the same as everybody else. Just one of the boys. I shot my M-16 at every sound. Course, I didn't know if I was killin' gooks or cherries. New boys from the states. We called 'em cherries.

'Cause they were for about fifteen minutes. So after the war I went home and I guess I expected somethin'. Free car wash. Double blue chip stamps. Instead, they looked at me as if I was gonna start killin' babies or somethin'. I was supposed to be gettin' married. Run an ice-cream parlor. . . . I'm beginning to feel like something Sam wrote. I'm not real. I'm some goddam flyer from World War I that has to go off some bridge and die because some script says so. If they just tore out that page. Just ripped it out, you know. I'd be fine. If they just crossed it out and wrote something else.

This obligatory culminating speech is the clear measure of the intertextuality of all of these "strangers at home" films. Each returned veteran has been brutalized by the war, rejected by society, and left to wander identitiless in the postwar wasteland. Unlike in *First Blood*, however, which abruptly ends with Rambo's speech, or *Birdy*, which rejects Al Columbato's speech as self-pity, or *Some Kind of Hero*, where the speech is subsumed in the madcap comic book antics, or *Cutter's Way*, where Alex's speech becomes just another aspect of noir-ish despair, *The Stunt Man*, through Cameron's speech, actually searches for a solution. That solution, ultimately, is unsatisfactory because it lies in the same realm that the only solution to the problems of Paul Berlin in *Going After Cacciato* did, the realm of imagination. The only way that Cameron can find a new identity is to become one with the illusion, reject the historical reality of Vietnam for the new imaginative reality that he has learned to live with on the movie set, a reality in which "nothing is ever what it seems." In other words, Cameron, in the words of Stein in Joseph Conrad's *Lord Jim*, must "in the destructive element immerse."[10] He must allow himself to become like God and create a world in which he can exist.

Like *Cutter's Way*, *The Stunt Man* parallels its social subtext with a strong mythic subtext anchored in the characterization of Eli Cross (Peter O'Toole), the director of the movie within the movie. Cross becomes Cameron's mentor, who will teach him how to become like God through the power of imagination. For Cameron, postwar America is paradise definitely lost and Eli Cross is both God and Satan in this postlapsarian world. The Edenic myth is present from the opening sequence. When Cross in his helicopter takes the single bite out of his apple, then throws it out the window, he triggers the chain reaction of events that will cast Cameron, the film's Adamic figure, out into the fallen world of the movie within the movie, "where nothing is what it seems." Later, this opening Edenic allusion is repeated. Nina offers Cameron an apple. He takes one bite and throws it away. Immediately upon completing this symbolic gesture, Cameron accuses his Eve of her original sin. "Aren't you going to congratulate me?" Nina innocently asks. But Cameron has eaten from the tree of knowledge and answers: "What should I congratulate you for? The fuckin' scene or fuckin' the director?" After Nina runs out in tears, Sam (Alan Goorwitz) the screenwriter asks in disbelief: "Was she supposed to be a virgin?" In the shock of recognition, Cameron softly answers, "Yeah."

This Edenic myth metaphorically complements the social subtext. Cameron as betrayed Adam and Nina as fallen Eve are allegories for the veteran's realization of America's loss of virginity and original sin in Vietnam. After Vietnam, America can no longer claim to be the new Eden, and no one is more aware of their expulsion from the garden than the veterans. Vietnam was America's apple out of which she could not resist taking a bite. Ultimately, however, Vietnam had to be discarded when the mistake became painfully evident.

In this Edenic myth, Eli Cross plays a dual role. He is both tempter and savior, both good and evil, God and Satan. As Satan, he leads his protégé, Cameron, to realize the fallen state of a paranoid postwar American society. "Maybe that's what this movie is really about," Cross argues. "Guys like him. Scared shitless. Whistling in the dark. Thinking everybody's your enemy." Whether he is referring to his own movie within the movie or the metamovie he is within, in either case he is also referring to America after Vietnam, the social movie in which everyone's "whistling in the dark" and looking over his shoulder because "everybody's your enemy." This Satan realizes that his movie must play to an utterly corrupt audience. "I know a man who made an anti-war movie, a good one," Cross continues his pillorying of fallen America. "When it was shown in his home town, Army enlistments went up 100 percent." As Satan, Eli Cross is like an earlier namesake, Noah Cross (John Huston) in *Chinatown*, who shared that cynicism about American society and its fallen dream. As Satan, Eli Cross pulls no punches about the fallen state of post-Vietnam America.

As God the Father, however, in this Edenic myth, Cross offers Cameron instruction in man's only godlike power, imagination, as the means of rising above the fallen world. In *The Stunt Man*, as in *Going After Cacciato*, the power of imagination can liberate fallen man from the horrors of war and allow him, as it did Gatsby, to create a new identity "out of a platonic conception of himself."[11]

Eli Cross as the God figure of this myth is both visually and verbally identified. He is repeatedly shot from a severe low angle so that he looms over the camera and the characters. He is the only character who is liberated in space, who can fly. When not cruising around in his chopper (which constantly causes Cameron to flinch because it reminds him of Vietnam), Cross is swooping and gliding, rising up into, and dropping down out of, the sky on what he calls "the ride of the century on Eli's killer crane." He also controls time; when told by Cross to "wait a minute," an assistant director asks, "is that an Eli minute or a real minute?" Near the end of the film, when the crucial scene is about to be shot, Cross gives his Sermon on the Mount: "We must have this shot. I therefore order that no camera will jam or no cloud will pass before the sun." As God, he rules the very elements. In fact, as a twentieth-century God with all the illusionary magic of the movies at his disposal, Cross has become what Adam hoped eating from the tree of knowledge would allow him to be. "If God could do the tricks that we can do, he'd be a happy man," Eli declares.

Despite all the mechanical magic and the force by which his illusions subdue reality, Eli's most godlike power is the power to bestow identity upon men. "You shall be a stunt man who is an actor who is an enemy soldier who is a character in a movie," Eli assures Cameron. "Who'll look for you among all those?" When Cameron stumbles on to this magical holograph of a movie set, he is an aimless, wandering, anonymous Vietnam vet like John Rambo in *First Blood*, but Eli Cross gives him a whole new existence.

Eli's mythic powers, however, are not limited to an Edenic allegory. He invites Cameron into his magical world of imagination allusively: "That door is the looking glass and inside it is Wonderland. Have faith, Alice. Close your eyes and enjoy." If anything, Eli Cross is the Mad Hatter and the postlapsarian world that he cajoles Cameron into believing can be subdued by imagination is a world of divine madness, a quixotic world where men are "so mad we'll do anything. Fight wars. Fight windmills. Go off bridges."

This fighting of imaginary windmills, Vietnam veterans trying to reenter a society of which they are purportedly a part, is the theme both of *The Stunt Man* and of Eli Cross's movie within the movie. When Sam the screenwriter tries to define what Eli's movie is about, Eli is compelled to correct him by means of mythic allusion:

> SAM: Way back then when you were so charged up about making a big anti-war statement, they wouldn't let you. Now they'll let you, but Vietnam is long since gone and it's too late.

> ELI: This movie isn't about fighting wars. It's about fighting windmills.

As a "coming home" from Vietnam movie, *The Stunt Man* portrays the Vietnam veteran as an innocent in a mad, magical Wonderland learning the powers of imagination from an unpredictable god in order to qualify to joust with the windmills of his social rejection. As mythic figure, Cameron is Adam, who is Alice in Wonderland, who is Don Quixote. Like each of his mythic alter egos, he enters a new, magical, yet illusory and fallen world to which he must learn to adapt by applying the only godlike power he has, his imagination.

But, on another plane of this holograph of a film, Cameron is not Adam eating his apple, is not Alice passing through the looking glass, is not Don Quixote; he is, rather, a veteran of the original sin of Vietnam (which destroyed forever the American dream), who has been forced to find some accommodation in a hostile postwar world.

Of all of these "strangers at home" films, *The Stunt Man* is the most stylish and sophisticated because its message does not stridently overwhelm its medium. The culminating soliloquies of *First Blood* and *Birdy* are last-ditch attempts to placard meaning across the face of conventional cartoons. *The Stunt Man*, however, meticulously builds an elaborate literary metaphor out of similar "coming home" material. It eschews the physical realism of *First Blood* and the psychological realism of *Birdy* for an unpretentious (and postmodernist) admission that realism is a dead end and the illusion of imagination offers greater possibility in the post-Vietnam world. As Eli puts it: "We need something crazy. We're shaking a finger at them, and we shouldn't. If we've got anything to say, we should slide it in when they're laughing and crying and getting off from all the sex and violence. We should do something outrageous, like catching the authentic stench of madness behind all that good clean fun."

What *The Stunt Man* does that the other "strangers at home" films of this "coming home" comic book phase of the Vietnam War film history do not do is construct a multilayered, holographic metaphor that moves kinetically (never stopping to pretentiously preach) both to represent the crisis of identity of the Vietnam veterans, America's stunt men, and to offer a solution to that crisis. All of the other "strangers at home" films avoid solutions, except for *Cutter's Way*, which posits revenge-motivated violence as its comic book solution. Of all the "strangers at home" films, *The Stunt Man* is the only one that moves beyond conventional realism and creates a viable metatext for the existential dilemma of the Vietnam veteran.

The Survivor Guilt Fantasies

"Sometimes, in odd places, it all comes back," Pete Hamill writes:

> You are strolling the sidewalks of a northern city . . . eyes glazed by the anonymous motion of the street. A door opens, an odor drifts from a restaurant; it's *ngoc nam* sauce, surely, and yes, the sign tells you this is a Vietnamese restaurant, and you hurry on, pursued by a ghost. Don't come back, the ghost whispers. I'll be crouched against the wall, grinning, my teeth stained black from betel root. Vietnam.[12]

That ghostly VC's warning, "Don't come back," is one more echo of the good advice that America has ignored since Graham Greene's *Quiet American* in 1954 when her Vietnam tragedy was but beginning.

In the eighties, American movies have continued to ignore that advice as the American political and military policymakers from 1960 to 1973 did. So many films of that second phase of the Vietnam War film history rush in where Hamill and other veterans fear to tread. These films ignore the ghostly warnings of the past and create fantasies about returning and this time winning that first war that America ever lost.

Psychologists have confirmed that many Vietnam veterans entertain this fantasy of returning to Vietnam, but the fantasy is motivated not by embarrassment over the loss or by chauvinism but rather by guilt for having survived the war, while so many of their buddies, whose ghosts speak to them in their dreams, are dead. This "survivor guilt syndrome" is a major burden amidst the baggage that veterans brought home from that war. Frank Friedel writes: "one finds all of the varied responses to combat service that earlier soldiers have experienced, from becoming 'war lovers' to suffering shocked revulsion against killing, and especially feeling guilt over not somehow preventing the death or wounding of a buddy."[13] Clark Smith seconds Friedel's emphasis upon guilt: "Underlying post-Vietnam syndrome is a nagging *aggravation* complicated by contemporary anxieties, frustrations and persuasions. The aggravation is compounded by the manifold aspects of guilt: survivor guilt, war guilt, criminal guilt, complicity guilt."[14] After coming home from Vietnam, "usually within the first year and a half . . . the individual veteran began questioning himself and his role in the war. . . . The questions most often asked were: What's the war really about? For what did my buddies die? . . . Why do I feel depressed even though I've survived? Why must I feel so much guilt and pain for an unjust war?"[15]

Those questions pertain directly to "survivor guilt," a widely shared characteristic of the "coming home" experience of the Vietnam War veteran. Thus Hollywood's eighties fascination with the problems of those veterans made "survivor guilt" fair game for filmic exploitation. The only problem was how to make internalized feelings of guilt available and entertaining to a mass audience. Those internalized guilts had to somehow be externalized, objectified, in some sort of action that could be filmed. The inevitable result was Hollywood doing what it does best, elevating fantasy to the level of reality. If Vietnam veterans felt guilty about surviving and leaving their buddies behind, why not let them go back, rescue their buddies, and thus assuage that guilt?

Simultaneous with this early eighties discovery of the possibilities of the "survivor guilt" theme was the popularity of Reagan administration-orchestrated chauvinism. This political scenario preached the necessity of America returning to its pre-Vietnam prominence as a military power. Both Hollywood's comic book objectification of Vietnam veteran psychology and Reaganism's revisionist view of history were variations on an absurd fantasy. Neither Hollywood nor Reagan acknowledged the fact that you can't go home again, and the result was Hollywood movies and Washington press conferences full of comic book characters fighting comic book miniwars. One critic described eighties politics thusly:

> Ten years later, the anti-Communist sermon is again the dominant factor in our foreign policy. Those little men with the quartz eyes and pink hands who sit in safe Washington buildings are again signing papers that allow young men to go off and kill and die, in Beirut or Grenada or the hills of

Nicaragua. The conquest of Grenada, which proved definitively that a nation of 235 million could overwhelm a country of 110,000, was greeted as a famous victory. The president was hailed as a firm leader, and medals dropped from the Pentagon like snow.[16]

Everyone, including Hollywood and Ronald Reagan, knew that going back to Vietnam and changing what happened was a guilt-fueled pipedream, but in the early eighties, American society still was not ready to accept the loss or live with the guilt. The Hollywood comic book exploitations of the survivor guilt fantasy — *Uncommon Valor*, the *Missing in Action* films, *Rambo II* — were among the most successful box office hits of that 1980–86 period. The American people also fully funded the Reagan movies that refought Vietnam with varying levels of success in Grenada, Central America, and Beirut.

These "survivor guilt" fantasies contributed to the supervet stereotype. Reinserted into Vietnam, this American soldier was not handicapped by any of the illusions or inexperience of that previous inept war. This American soldier had in that ten-year interim become a guerrilla fighter par excellence, even better than the Viet Cong themselves. But, as had been the case in his first tour of duty in Vietnam, this latter-day grunt's greatest enemy was on the home front, the CIA and the politicians who would not let him fight and win.

What Hollywood did was take the guilt feelings of Vietnam veteran psychology and exploit them into a propagandist, militarist fantasy that an insecure American society, at the urging of a popular movie star president, blindly accepted. Pete Hamill best characterizes the reality of the veterans' feelings: "I'm never surprised when I meet once-young men who want to go back. For a day, a month, an hour. They want to see Vietnam when its beauty does not hold the potential of death." In fact, on 14 January 1989 six former combat Marines got their wish to return to Vietnam in peace. The Associated Press characterized their sight-seeing visit as a "patrol into the past, a journey to heal their own pain."[17] Most Vietnam combat veterans have suffered from "survivor guilt" problems, but few have ever expressed any interest in going back to Vietnam to fight in the way that those happy warriors in *Uncommon Valor* go or John Rambo goes.

All of the "survivor guilt" films of this "coming home" comic book phase of the Vietnam War film history have plot and character specifications that they share. All focus upon troubled veterans still plagued by the past, still flashbacking to their in-country experiences. All focus on the idea of reluctant warriors drawn into action by "survivor guilt." All portray the American government, specifically the CIA, as the Judas in the Resurrection scenario, the betrayer who wants the MIAs to stay dead rather than be brought back to life. In each, the Americans become like the Viet Cong, yet all resemble Western genre films in their Amerocentrism and racism toward the Indian (in this case Oriental) hordes who bite the dust. Ultimately though these films laboriously wrestle political and psychological themes and motives around, they are no more than the most conventional vehicles for presenting commando comic book action. They exist only for the fighting and the fireworks. All of them follow the same plot and polemic structure. Each is divided into three dramatic acts. Act 1 involves recruitment to the cause, rededication to the past. Act 2 involves training for the mission, the return to Vietnam. These first two acts bear the brunt of the polemic definitions of "survivor guilt." America's national guilt has occasioned this fantasy attempt to refight and rewin the war. These preliminary acts define who the heroes (those left behind), the antiheroes (those going back to assuage this guilt), and the villains (representatives of the federal government) are. These preliminary acts define the motives and responsibilities of "survivor guilt." The final acts of each of these films in which the commando missions are carried out are the more predictable and least interesting parts. Each film ends with an apocalyptic battle that pits the guilty veteran commando(s) against the Oriental hordes much as *Fort Apache* (1948) or *They Died with Their Boots On* (1941) ended.

The newspaper advertisements for *Uncommon Valor* (1983) screamed, "C'MON . . . WE'RE GOING HOME," followed in smaller print by "in the most important mission of their lives, they're going back to get their buddies who were left behind." Pauline Kael in her strangely divided review (*New Yorker*, 23 January 1984) at one point calls it "cheap jingoism" and at another point calls it "a middle-of-the-road right-wing fantasy." That last phrase embodies her indecision. How can a film be both "middle-of-the-road" and "right-wing" as well as a "fantasy"? Kael reveals in the uncertainty of her prose either her own inability to grasp the film or the film's own inability to place itself. The latter is the guilty party. Kael's prose is contradictory, but so is *Uncommon Valor*. It does not know what it wants to be, a social statement or a commando shoot-em-up. In trying to be both, it ends up being just another *Men at War* comic book.

Kael's waffling review captures well the mixed motives of *Uncommon Valor*. The film is caught between an honest attempt to portray the psychological ravages of the "survivor guilt syndrome" and the political temper of Reagan revisionism that tried to convince the American people that the Vietnam War could be refought in places like Grenada, Beirut and Central America. Psychology and politics clash in *Uncommon Valor*, but what makes this film so different from *Rambo II* (to follow) is that Psychology actually puts up a fight against Reaganism's "cheap jingoism." *Rambo II* sells out to political propaganda from frame one.

The first hour of *Uncommon Valor* is exclusively devoted to dispensing issue information on the POW-MIA question and on the "survivor guilt syndrome." Colonel Rhodes (Gene Hackman) is known as "that ol' Colonel

MIA" by congressmen and military bureaucrats in Washington. To one of these bureaucrats Rhodes says over images of him wandering through Bangkok trying to get information about his MIA son:

RHODES: Look, there are 2500 men still unaccounted for and more than 400 live sightings.

VO: Look, Colonel Rhodes, I told you there was nothing I could do.

RHODES: Aw dammit, that's all I ever heard in Washington. Nobody can do anything.

This exchange makes it clear that the villains of this piece are going to be a governmental bureaucracy that does not care representing a nation that wants to avoid memories of its failures in Vietnam.

Early in the film, the federal government takes a passive role in trying to block Colonel Rhodes's mission into America's past, but later, after the proposed rescue mission has gotten financial support from rich private business interests (which echo both H. Ross Perot's private international adventuring and the financing of Ronald Reagan's political career), the government resistance becomes more active. The CIA places Rhodes under surveillance, bugs the sponsoring businessman's offices, and ultimately intervenes to stop the mission.

If the government is the villain in these "survivor guilt" films, then how can those films also be an endorsement of Reagan administration chauvinism? The answer lies in Reagan's departures from the liberalism that got America into Vietnam (read Democrat administration) plus Reagan administration support for "cowboying" in international affairs as best represented by Oliver North. There is, of course, contradiction in all of this. The Reagan administration is the government. The government is the villain in these films. All through the eighties, especially when the country was in the throes of Rambomania, the great communicator in the White House repeatedly aligned himself with Vietnam veterans. He did this by expanding the need of the individual Vietnam veteran to overcome his guilt into therapy for a national psychosis over Vietnam.

In a long speech, unendingly preachy if not delivered by a brilliant actor like Gene Hackman, Colonel Rhodes characterizes the American government as corporate villain:[18]

> There is a bond between you men. As strong as the bond between my son and me. Course, there's no bond as strong as that shared by men who have faced death in battle. You men seem to have a strong sense of loyalty because you're thought of as criminals because of Vietnam. You know why? Because you lost. In this country that's like going bankrupt. . . . You cost too much and you didn't turn a profit. That's why they won't go over there and pick up our buddies and bring them back home. Because there's no gain in it. You and I know that the books are still in the red. And the politicians know too. The same politicians that never lost a single son in Vietnam, not one. Now

they say they've been negotiating for ten years. Well, the other side's not buying. Gentlemen, we're the only hope those POWs have. So we're going back there. And this time, this time, nobody can dispute the rightness of what we're doing.

This speech's rhetorical strategies present two themes central to the film's complex definition of the relationship of the Vietnam veteran to his government.

First, Rhodes characterizes Vietnam veterans as a family of outcasts in American society and sets himself up as a father figure. He then defines that family relationship in terms of the bonding, first, of combat and, second, of the criminality that American society imposed upon Vietnam veterans when they came home. Psychological studies show that it is combat veterans as opposed to support personnel who experience "survivor guilt" problems. After establishing this family metaphor, Rhodes counters it with a corporate, economic metaphor to characterize the relationship of the society and especially the government to those veterans. The veterans are no more than numbers on a balance sheet, and the CEOs, the accountants, who run the corporation, have rejected them because they failed to turn a profit. Rhodes's speech ends with his third rhetorical strategy, that of the evangelist who rejects materialism for the religious virtues of "hope" and "rightness." What is most ironic and contradictory about this speech (and this film) is the manner in which it, first, establishes this "survivor guilt" as a "family" responsibility and then elevates that "survival guilt" to a metaphorical national guilt for having lost in Vietnam. Reagan exploited that national guilt complex into an aggressive strategy for international adventuring in the eighties. Whereas George McGovern characterized the Johnson administration's pride in ignoring the lessons of history, the Reagan administration proved its willingness to exploit history to justify its foreign policy.[19]

Colonel Rhodes is the vehicle for presenting both the POW-MIA issue and the political aspects of the "survivor guilt syndrome," including the idea of national guilt, but it is the members of his commando squad, the Vietnam veterans who in the harrowing opening scene witness their buddies getting left behind in a rice paddy saturated with VC, who articulate the psychological themes of the film. Each makes his private point about how "survivor guilt" works in the lexicon of the Vietnam veteran who ten years later is still trying to come home.

The wife of Wilkes (Fred Ward), the tunnel rat, speaks for her husband:

WIFE: Look, you've got no right to be here. It's taken me ten years to get that war out of his head.

RHODES: Looks to me like it's still in his head pretty strong.

WIFE: Oh, that's very deep. Gee, where were you all the days he sat for hours just staring at the walls.

The wife of Charts (Tim Thomerson), who has spent his ten years hiding behind his sunglasses, feels differently: "Ya know, maybe you should take him back to Vietnam. He sure as hell doesn't give a damn about anything around here." Johnson (Harold Sylvester), a decorated chopper pilot, tries to deny his guilt:

JOHNSON: Lost a lot of good friends.

RHODES: How many?

JOHNSON: Oh, I don't remember. It just seemed like everybody.

RHODES: You lost eleven men and nine aircraft. You were shot down on your first attempt. And you volunteered to go back and pick up that pilot. Why?

JOHNSON: Well, if you know all that, Colonel, why don't you tell me?

RHODES: I'm askin' you why?

JOHNSON: Because it was my job, that's why. We had to go back in there. We couldn't let good men die for nothing.

RHODES: That's exactly why we're gonna go back now, to get those good men you're talkin' about.

JOHNSON: Wait, back up, back up. You cannot lay that kind of guilt on me. No. I'm sorry but the answer is no. What do you want from me? I run half of this hospital. I lead a good life here. I'm off to Bermuda next week, and not off to some fantasy war. I cannot save the damn world, Colonel.

Despite his protestations, Johnson goes back. He knows it is a "fantasy war," but he chooses to fight it anyway. They all are compelled by their guilt. Only Blaster (Reb Brown) and Sailor (Randall "Tex" Cobb), an aimless beachboy and a crazed biker, show no hesitation. They go back for the fun of it as good war lovers should. Of all the vets, Wilkes has the most acute psychological problems. He and Rhodes find their common ground in nightmares:

RHODES: My nightmares all had to do with the Chosin Reservoir. The ground was so hard we couldn't bury the dead. . . . For years I'd wake up with those dead frozen faces staring at me.

WILKES: They ever go away?

RHODES: No. I finally made friends with 'em though.

In *Uncommon Valor*, the Vietnam veterans seem unable to make friends with their ghosts. All need to go back to the war and bring those ghosts back to life.

Perhaps what is most curious about *Uncommon Valor* (and *Rambo II* later) is the way these veterans go back not as an American army but as guerrilla fighters, as Viet Cong. In concert with the film's subtext—going back and doing it right this time—this fighting the Viet Cong with their own tactics is a clear indictment of the way the Vietnam War was originally fought. In training, Rhodes tells his squad: "We'll be eating nothing but Vietnamese food from now on. We don't wanna be tramping through the jungle smellin' like Americans."

Two recurring symbolic images capture visually the "survivor guilt syndrome" in *Uncommon Valor*. Those images are introduced in the opening scene before the credits. Set in a firefight in the past in Vietnam, the image of a soldier carrying his buddy to safety and the image of a hand outstretched to pull a buddy to safety are given symbolic significance by the camera lingering upon those gestures. The first image, also prominently featured in the print advertisements for the film, is a Vietnam era version of the logo for Father Flanagan's Boys' Town: remember "He's not heavy, fadder; he's my brudder"? That image is repeated three times in the film: in the opening scene, in the training sequence at the end of a brutal fight between Sailor and young Kevin Scott (Patrick Swayze) as a sign that the kid has won acceptance into the platoon, and in the final rescue where Sailor this time succeeds in carrying one of his buddies to safety. Almost exactly the same sequence of recurrence is used with the hand-out-stretched image. It is first encountered in the opening sequence as grunts try to pull their buddies into the helicopters. It appears again in Colonel Rhodes's flashback dream to when his own son was little, scared of a storm and wanting to be pulled into bed to sleep with his parents. It appears lastly in the final firefight as hands reach out to pull the squad and the rescued prisoners into the helicopters. In words and images, these two symbolic acts of bearing the burden and stretching out your hand capture the emotional ties at the heart of the "survivor guilt syndrome." These were the symbolic acts that those men were trained to carry out and their frustration in failing in them has occasioned the survivor guilt. If there is *any* doubt as to the political and psychological subtexts of *Uncommon Valor*, one small exahange in the midst of the final apocalyptic action should negate it. Colonel Rhodes orders Johnson, the chopper pilot, "you give me a count of sixty and then you go." Johnson finally refuses: "No, we can't leave anybody behind *this time* [my italics]."

Despite its doubleness, its informative handling of the "coming home" problems of veterans versus its fantasy revisionism in comic book action, *Uncommon Valor*, when compared to the three almost nonverbal *Missing in Action* films and *Rambo II*, is an eloquent statement of the issues and guilts of Vietnam combat veterans. The *Missing in Action* films betray no such eloquence and a mere whisper of political subtext. Their Colonel Braddock (Chuck Norris) is much more the comic book killing machine than Colonel Rhodes in *Uncommon Valor* would ever aspire to be. In fact, Braddock is, quite literally, based upon a comic book character. Spider-man is the metaphor that defines the enigmatic, almost totally silent character of Braddock.

Early in *Missing in Action* while watching a Spiderman cartoon on TV, Colonel Braddock dials up the state department and, after refusing their overtures for months, consents to go on a diplomatic mission to discuss the MIA issue with the Vietnamese. Once in Ho Chi Minh City, Braddock decides on some nighttime recon, but the only way to evade Vietnamese surveillance is by doing a Spiderman act down the face of his hotel. When the pretty young state department aide asks, "How are you going to get out of here anyway?" he answers with his typical conciseness, "Fly." That one-word answer belongs in a comic book bubble inflating out of Spiderman's mouth. Returning from his nighttime adventures possessed of the location of the MIAs and with the Vietnamese army on his heels, he gets back to the alibi of the young woman's arms by again Spiderman-ing it up the side of the building. If there were any doubts of the comic book nature of this phase of the Vietnam War film history, this direct choice of a hero's metaphorical role model puts those doubts to rest.

Missing in Action is more than a clone of *Uncommon Valor*. Its plot structure is so similar that it looks suspiciously like an unrepentant ripoff. In fact, *Missing in Action 2: The Beginning*, a prequel set in the Vietnamese prison camp from which Braddock escaped, was made at the same time as *Missing in Action* and was supposed to be released first. But with the success of *Uncommon Valor*, the producers changed the order of release of the two films in order to capitalize upon this interest in the "return to Vietnam" theme. The only major difference is that in *Uncommon Valor* a team goes back, whereas in *Missing in Action* Braddock goes back alone. Like *Uncommon Valor*, *Missing in Action* begins with a flashback to a firefight in which Braddock carries one of his men out just as Sailor did. The details of this scene, from the exploding chopper to the men left behind, mirror the same scene in *Uncommon Valor*. After this view of the past, the trail back to Vietnam and the rescue of the MIAs are exactly the same as they were in *Uncommon Valor*. Braddock finds out where the MIA prison camp is located, then goes to Bangkok where he gets help from an old Army buddy and bargains for guns just as Colonel Rhodes did. Whereas in *Uncommon Valor* the pyrotechnic rescue mission was a conventional, split-second commando raid, and later, in *Rambo II*, the rescue will be an almost medieval warrior quest, in *Missing in Action* the rescue is more James Bond-like with its fancy weaponry, its high-powered assault raft, its choreographed martial arts combat. *Missing in Action* is similar to *Uncommon Valor*, but it is still only a shadow of that film in substance and meaning. Except for a few silent grimaces and hand-wringings by Braddock early on in his motel room, where he has withdrawn to mope and watch Spiderman cartoons, *Missing in Action* gives no representation of the "survivor guilt" issue. No one really ever knows what motivates Braddock to return to Vietnam. In the third film of this series, *Braddock: Missing in Action III*, the motive is clear but utterly personal. He returns to rescue his

Vietnamese wife and their Amerasian son, who have conveniently resurfaced for this sequel.

If the three *Missing in Action* films do not really face up to the "survivor guilt" aspect of the "coming home" films, *Rambo II* takes that "survivor guilt" and handles it in such a way that it becomes easily exploitable by the Reagan jingoism of the eighties. *Rambo II* attempts no stronger assertion of the MIA issue or takes no more radical stance on the political handling of the Vietnam War itself than did either *Uncommon Valor* or *Missing in Action*, yet because of the visibility of its star and its incredible box-office popularity it became the catchword of eighties social history whenever any Vietnam War issue was raised. However, of all of these films, *Rambo II* is the one that has been most widely recognized as an intentional comic book characterization. Film critic Pauline Kael refers to *Rambo II*'s Sylvester Stallone as "our national palooka" and argues that *Rambo II*'s "comic strip patriotism exploits the pent-up rage of the Vietnam vets who feel that their country mistreated them after the war" (*New Yorker*, 17 June 1985). Richard Schickel (*Time*, 2 June 1986) seconds Kael: "All action movies may aspire to be judged not on the basis of how well they imitate life, but on how well they imitate the genre's ideal form—a Road Runner cartoon." Martha Bayles agrees:

> One of the tragic ironies of the Vietnam War was that our efforts to wage it "humanely" resulted in a series of half-measures that, it can be argued, only prolonged the agony. The brooding figure of Rambo is a walking embodiment of this irony—which is why, for all his cartoonishness, he is not smug. Stallone taps popular patriotism, but he also taps darker emotions, such as the resentment many veterans feel toward their government for not waging war against North Vietnam to the hilt, and toward their countrymen for ridiculing or ignoring their sacrifices.[20]

The audiences were just as aware of the comic book qualities of Rambo as were the national critics. Outside a theater in Vienna, Virginia, Lynne Chapman, aged seventeen, told a *USA Today* (15 June 1985) interviewer: "It was like a comic book. He's Superman and that made it fun." From the beginning everybody knew that it was a comic book and being accepted on those terms gave *Rambo II* an unpretentious credibility that helped deliver its right-wing political, "survivor guilt" psychological, revisionist historical, messages.

Early in *Rambo II*, Marshall Murdoch (Charles Napier) "in charge of Special Operations from Washington" delivers the mandatory issue information speech that is the "Gentlemen, start your engines" of all of these "survivor guilt" films:

> Rambo, you're probably aware that there are 2500 Americans still missing in action in Southeast Asia. Now most of those boys are presumed killed, but to the League of Families, Congress and lots of Americans it's still a very

emotional issue . . . Rambo, you certainly don't know as much about me as I do about you. I haunched with the 2nd Battalion, 3rd Marines at Kontum in 1966. I lost a lot of good men, so I know what you and every vet feels. Now maybe the government didn't care. Now maybe certain segments of the population didn't care. My committee cares.

Every word that Murdoch mutters, down to his own war record, is a lie. As in the other MIA rescue films, the villain of *Rambo II* is the American government bureaucracy that has lost those possibly existent MIAs in its fog of red tape.

Rambo characterizes this betrayal of Vietnam veterans by their country as another kind of war:

RAMBO: When I came back to the States I found another war goin' on.

GUIDE: What war?

RAMBO: Kind of like a quiet war, a war against all the soldiers returning, the kind of war you don't win.

Later, after Murdoch has betrayed Rambo, Colonel Trautman (Richard Crenna) reiterates Rambo's conviction that the government and American society have betrayed all Vietnam vets:

TRAUTMAN: It was a lie, wasn't it? Just like the whole damn war. It was a lie. . . .

MURDOCH: Who in the hell do you think you're talkin' to, Trautman?

TRAUTMAN: A stinkin' bureaucrat who's tryin' to cover his ass.

MURDOCH: No, not just mine, Trautman. We're talkin' about a nation's. . . . Do you think somebody's gonna get up on the floor of the United States Senate and ask for billions of dollars for a couple of forgotten ghosts?

TRAUTMAN: Men . . . who fought for their country!

But in *Rambo II*, the American government and society is the villain in more than one way. The criticism of the American government and society in *Rambo II* extends to commentary upon how the war itself was waged, not just its aftermath. The first question that Rambo asks when the proposal of his going back to Vietnam is made is "Sir, do we get to win this time?" Ironically that question proves prophetic as the government stacks the deck against Rambo the same way it did the first time around in the Vietnam War. Trautman tells Rambo, "John, I want you to forget the war, the old Vietnam's dead." But Rambo knows better: "Sir, if I'm alive, it's alive." All the things that went wrong during and after the war cannot be forgotten by the veterans. The lack of support and ultimate betrayal of the Vietnam veteran is symbolized in a Sisyphean scene at the center of *Rambo II*. Dragging a rescued MIA up a muddy hillside, Rambo reaches the top just as Murdoch aborts the chopper evacuation mission and leaves him standing there to be captured by the swarming Vietnamese army. Once again, America has betrayed the grunt who did the job.

Perhaps the most telling criticism in *Rambo II* of how the Vietnam War was conducted explores the American overconfidence in firepower and technology. Before the mission begins, Rambo is assured "besides the monitoring devices you see here, you'll be issued every ultramodern piece of equipment we have to ensure your safety. Rambo, you can feel totally safe because we have the most advanced weapons in the world at your service." Yet he is rightly skeptical. "I've always thought the mind's the best weapon," he tells Murdoch. "Times change," Murdoch smirks. "For some people," Rambo hisses back. In the Vietnam War, there was no question that America had a tremendous hardware advantage, but it did not do any good. That is John Rambo's point. Since the war, America has tried to dehumanize the whole lesson of Vietnam. Vets like Rambo went there and came home and America must acknowledge that fact. At the end of the film, in an eloquent gesture, Rambo shoots to pieces the sophisticated computer system that has run this whole operation, symbolically assaults the American war machine that mismanaged the Vietnam War and failed to support the soldiers who fought there.

As an ironic counterpoint to this critique of America's hardware war and consistent with all of the other MIA rescue films, Rambo chooses to become a guerrilla fighter, a Viet Cong, to refight the war. Rambo, in fact, goes even further back in history, becomes a primitive warrior fighting all that twentieth-century hardware with knives, stones, bows, and arrows. After his female Vietnamese guide is killed, the camera ritualizes Rambo as he girds himself for war. As one by one in the rain he kills the Russian troops who have come to help their Vietnamese allies, Rambo becomes one with the primeval sludge, lives within it, and emerges only to kill. The comic book image merges Sergeant Rock with Conan the Barbarian. Like Conan, when captured, Rambo is tortured in the archetypal style of crucifixion. In *First Blood*, Rambo assumed the Christian pose when hung on a rock cliff. In *Rambo II* he is literally tied to a cross to undergo tortures. This Christ imagery will resurface in the death of Sergeant Elias in *Platoon*. All of these attempts to mythicize grunts fail because Christ imagery just does not work in war movies. The violence delimits its impact and ironically undercuts its meaning. But the pattern of the American soldier defecting to the likeness and tactics of his Viet Cong counterpart is repeated in these MIA rescue films. Leo Cawley analyzes this pattern in sociohistorical terms: "Our mass culture presents Americans as underdogs or as the allies of underdogs. Rambo, although an American, becomes the guerrilla fighter, the Vietcong in the jungle armed with will and primitive weapons who successfully battles helicopters and superior firepower."[21]

While *Rambo II* simply repeats the themes and political speeches of the earlier MIA rescue films, what is more interesting is the use that *Rambo II* has been put to in American society. Besides the media and retail merchandising bonanza of Rambomania, *Rambo II* catalyzed a frenzy of political exploitation that stretched to historical revisionism and national psychotherapy. "The Vietnam War has had an odd history in American films," James Hoberman writes. "Almost from the beginning movies wished the war over. Vietnam films were far less obsessed with battlefield sacrifice than with the plight of the returning veteran—using him as either the scapegoat or the redeemer of a guilty society."[22] Whereas the "strangers at home" films treated the Vietnam veteran as scapegoat, these "survivor guilt" films all treat the veteran as redeemer. Across the media in 1985, Rambo was alternately commended and flogged for de-wimping the American hero, for revising history, for restoring positive values to a nation that since Vietnam, Watergate, and the Iranian Hostage Crisis had been depressed by a negative self-image. Mike Clark (*USA Today*, 22 May 1985) laughs at Hollywood's presumption: "Those who take a sociological approach to film history will find *Rambo* a Comstock Lode—and load. Hollywood is apparently trying to atone for losing the Vietnam War by having Stallone singlehandedly wipe out scores of Vietnamese and their Soviet advisors."

In almost twenty years of trying to capture the Vietnam War on film (1966–86), no progress was made. Fortunately the Vietnam War films of 1987–88 did progress to a much more realistic view of the nature and meaning of that war. One "survivor guilt" film of the 1980–86 period that did rise above exploitation of the anguish of Vietnam veterans and Reagan administration jingoism was the personal memoir *The Killing Fields* (1984). Not really about Vietnam (though the Vietnam War that contributed to the fall of Cambodia is always in the background), it is a film about "survivor guilt," which is the emotion most central to the characterization of Sidney Schanberg (Sam Waterston), the *New York Times* reporter who was forced to leave his Cambodian friend Dith Pran (Haing S. Ngor) behind when evacuated from Phnom Penh in 1975 as Cambodia was falling into the genocidal hands of the Khmer Rouge. Of all the "survival guilt" films, *The Killing Fields* is the most powerful in its scope and the least exploitative in its polemic. But perhaps more important, it is the only film of this whole period that is not totally Amerocentric or outright racist in its treatment of the peoples of Southeast Asia.[23]

"Survivor guilt" fuels the characterization of the otherwise arrogant and abrasive Sydney Schanberg. In a voice-over opening that echoes Captain Willard's (Martin Sheen) opening "Saigon, Sheeit" to *Apocalypse Now*, Schanberg clearly sets the blame for what is about to happen in Cambodia: "Cambodia. To many Westerners it seemed a paradise, another world, a secret world. But the war in Vietnam burst its borders and the fighting soon spread to neutral Cambodia. In 1973 I went to cover this sideshow struggle for the *New York Times*." What this opening speech does is set a wider context for the "survivor guilt" theme than has been attempted in the comic book films. Whereas *Uncommon Valor* and *Missing in Action* had shown the American government as guilty for abandoning its soldiers in Vietnam, *The Killing Fields* assigns guilt to America for entering Southeast Asian politics with a blithe imperialist arrogance and then, after setting the wheels of military conflict in motion, abandoning the people of Southeast Asia to the bloodbath. Thus *The Killing Fields*, on a textual level, is a factual representation of the "survivor guilt" of Sydney Schanberg for having left his friend Dith Pran behind but, on a subtextual level, is a metaphorical representation of a national "survival guilt" for what happened to the people of Cambodia because of the Vietnam War.

There are two villains in *The Killing Fields*. Schanberg is the villain of the film's personal text. Throughout he is accused and berated by other journalists for, first, not getting Dith Pran out of Cambodia early enough (or, in other words, underestimating the situation intentionally in order to keep getting news) and, second, for leaving him behind when the Americans were evacuated. At every point, however, Schanberg's nagging "survivor guilt" is paralleled metaphorically to the guilt that America should be feeling for the Kennedy and Johnson administrations' going into Southeast Asia without knowing what they were getting into and underestimating the consequences of their action, and for the Nixon administration's widening the Vietnam War to Cambodia and then abandoning Southeast Asia to a postwar bloodbath. It is these two levels of "survivor guilt" thematics that make *The Killing Fields* the most incisive and nonexploitative of this set of films.

While they are in Cambodia, Dith Pran is Sydney Schanberg's voice. Schanberg cannot speak the Cambodian language and Dith Pran speaks for him even to the point of saving Sydney's and three other journalists' lives when they are all arrested by the Khmer Rouge who are indiscriminately executing people in the streets. But when Sydney tries to become Dith Pran's voice, he fails. He cannot get Pran out of Cambodia; he cannot convince Pran's wife that Pran is still alive; he cannot find Pran from the distance of New York City. It is when Schanberg gets back to New York after his close call in Cambodia that the film's linking of his personal survival guilt to a national survival guilt for what is happening in Southeast Asia kicks in.

In his New York apartment with a Puccini aria playing on the stereo, Schanberg looks at a videotape of, first, Nixon lying about American intentions toward Cambodia and, then, the real news footage images of what is happening in Cambodia after Nixon's widening of the war.[24] On the tape, Nixon insists: "There are no American combat advisors in Cambodia. There will be no American combat troops or advisors in Cambodia. We will aid Cambodia. Cambodia is the Nixon Doctrine in its purest form." Upon making this announcement, Nixon began the Vietnam War sideshow by bombing Cambodia and invading Cambodia with American combat troops.

A later extended scene, structured in three sections, takes place at a banquet at which Schanberg receives the Pulitzer Prize for his (and Dith Pran's) coverage of the secret war in Cambodia. In each of the three sections of this eloquent scene, Schanberg either chooses or is forced to confront the film's two established levels of "survivor guilt"—his own and the American nation's.

In the first section of this unabashedly polemic scene, Schanberg delivers an eloquent and heartfelt speech of acceptance of the Pulitzer Prize. He first accepts the prize for both himself and Pran and then places the guilt for what is happening in Cambodia:

> As they pondered their options in the White House, the men who decided to bomb and then to invade Cambodia concerned themselves with many things: great power conflicts and collapsing dominos, looking tough and dangerous to the North Vietnamese, relieving pressure on the American troop withdrawal from the South. They had domestic concerns as well which helps to explain why they kept the bombing of Cambodia a secret for as long as they could. And, they may be assumed not to have ignored self-interest in their own careers. What they specifically were not concerned with were the Cambodians themselves. Not the people. Not the society. Not the country. Except in the abstract as instruments of policy. Dith Pran and I tried to record and bring home here the concrete consequences of these decisions to real people, to human beings, to people who were left out of the administration's plans, who took the beating for them.

If there is any doubt that *The Killing Fields* is a polemic film about a form of national "survivor guilt" or that its intention is to promulgate an interpretation of American history, this speech dispels that doubt. Perhaps this film can be accused of ascending a soap box, but a better read is that the film is reporting a real speech on a real historical event that happens to capture the essence of the film's multileveled theme.

The same thematic duality between Schanberg's personal guilt and America's political guilt is inferred in the second section of this scene when Al (John Malkovich), the photographer who was with them in Phnom Penh when it fell, confronts Schanberg in the men's room:

AL: You know what bothers me?

SYDNEY: What?

AL: It bothers me that you let Pran stay in Cambodia because you wanted to win that fuckin' award and you knew that you needed him to do it.

SYDNEY: I didn't have any idea what was gonna . . .

AL: The fuck you didn't. The fuck you didn't!

Al says aloud what Sydney has been wondering about himself, wondering how much everyone knew (individuals like himself and the government) and yet still decided to ignore.

In the third section, Schanberg emerges from his men's room confrontation with Al to confront the TV cameras. An interviewer asks from a national perspective the same question that Al was asking from a personal perspective. "How do you respond to the accusations that you and other journalists underestimated the brutality of the Khmer Rouge and so share the responsibility for what happened in Cambodia afterwards?" the newswoman asks. "We made a mistake," Schanberg answers. "Maybe what we underestimated was the kind of insanity that seven billion dollars worth of bombing could produce." Schanberg makes it clear that he is only responsible for half of the "survivor guilt," that the Nixon government that caused the widening of the war to Cambodia is also responsible.

The structure of the second half of *The Killing Fields* is a straightforward one. Scenes of Schanberg in New York coming to grips with his own guilt feelings while simultaneously defining the guilt of America for the horrors of Cambodia are alternated with Dith Pran's journey through those horrors. In Cambodia, Pran talks to Sydney in his mind; in New York Sydney struggles to assuage his "survivor guilt." In a confession to his sister, Sydney admits to his inability to communicate with his own voice, Dith Pran. "I never really gave him any choice," Sydney confesses. "I never really discussed it with him. He stayed because I wanted him to stay."

But *The Killing Fields* is an important film for another reason besides its dual perspective upon the "survivor guilt" theme. It is one of the few films of the eighties to break from the Amerocentric and ultimately racist view of history, literature, and the media toward the Vietnam War and its aftermath in Southeast Asia. Early in *The Killing Fields*, Schanberg and Dith Pran manage to make their way to a village that the Americans have bombed by mistake and are trying to cover up. The people lead the American journalist around to show him their wounds, their deaths, the rubble of their world. It is a rare instance in eighties American film when the other side is given the opportunity to speak for itself. The Vietnamese mowed down in *Uncommon Valor*, *Missing in Action*, and *Rambo II* are not given any lines, nor are the Vietnamese portrayed as brutal sadists in *The Deer Hunter*.[25]

At the end of *The Killing Fields* when Sydney Schanberg and Dith Pran meet in Thailand, Sydney asks, "Forgive me?" Smiling, deferential as always, Pran answers, "Nothing to forgive, Sydney, nothing." Is it true? *The Killing Fields* poses the question of "survivor guilt" that many of the other Vietnam War films of this 1980–86 period also posed and explores that question in depth as opposed to the superficial, comic book, propagandistic explorations of the other films; but one terrible irony remains. Though not the case for Sydney Schanberg, most of the time the person experiencing "survivor guilt" has no one whom he can ask for forgiveness.

The New Racism Post-Vietnam

In the late seventies and early eighties, a new strain of racism, its seeds planted in World War II and Korea and germinated in Vietnam, began to bloom in American society. The new racism chose as the target for its bigotry the growing Oriental population in eighties America. This Oriental minority consisted of both immigrants and visitors. The immigrants were principally Vietnamese and Cambodians who had fled Communism, political persecution, and genocide in their native countries and, as boat people, had faced great danger in their pursuit of the American dream. The visitors were Chinese, Korean, Phillipino, and Japanese students as well as Japanese businessmen and industrial managers in joint business ventures. The motives for this new racism grew out of two types of American insecurity: first, the insecurity occasioned by the loss of the Vietnam War to an outgunned guerrilla force and, second, the insecure perception that America was losing the economic, industrial, and trade war to the Japanese. This American inferiority complex triggered resentment of orientals in American society, who, both as evidenced in their war victory and their economic victory, had gained a reputation for being smarter, subtler, and more productive (i.e., harder-working) than Americans. While eighties films such as *Ragtime*, *A Soldier's Story*, *Betrayed*, and *Mississippi Burning* portray the old racism against blacks as a backlash against the economic and political power which blacks had attained, another group of films, linked to the Vietnam War, portrayed this new racism against Asian Americans.

The charge of racism in Vietnam War films takes two forms aligned directly to the old racism against blacks and the new Amerocentric racism against the Asian peoples. The old racism was evident in the first phase of the Vietnam War film history when less than token acknowledgement of black soldiers in Vietnam was made. The new racism targeting Orientals was more evident in the first and second phases of the Vietnam War film history. Only in the third phase of 1987–88 did Hollywood begin to confront these two forms of Vietnam War racism.

Francis Coppola's *Apocalypse Now* in 1978 was the first American film to demonstrate any consciousness that blacks fought in Vietnam. Vietnam War films, including *Coming Home* and *The Deer Hunter*, had preceded *Apocalypse Now*, but with the exception of a single character in *The Boys in Company C* had all been lily white. Blacks are everywhere in *Apocalypse Now*, represented by major characters, Clean (Larry Fishburne) and Chief (Albert Hall), who are the first to die, and by numbers, all those burned-out black grunts pinned down at the Do Long Bridge. But in *Apocalypse Now*, if there is a consciousness of blacks, there is certainly no black consciousness, no strong voices declaring black perspectives on the war. In the Vietnam War film history, the consciousness of blacks is short-lived. *Some Kind of Hero* has a black central character but espouses no racial theme. In other "coming home" films of that second phase, there is little evidence of blacks, not in *Cutter's Way* or *Birdy* or *The Stunt Man* or *Cease Fire*. At the beginning of *First Blood*, reference is made to a black man who died of cancer owing to Agent Orange. *Uncommon Valor* has one black character, but the *Missing in Action* films and *Rambo II* return to the unbroken whiteness of the first phase.

The charges of Amerocentric racism in Vietnam War films were first raised against *The Deer Hunter*. Those charges were motivated by that film's one-dimensional characterization of the Vietnamese as sadistic degenerates, avid gamblers on life and death in the game of Russian roulette. Contrary to the metaphoric excursion into fantasy of *The Deer Hunter*, no evidence exists that Russian roulette was a Vietnamese pastime or betting sport. Briefly, *Apocalypse Now* presents a glimpse of life in a Viet Cong village, but that village is soon devastated by Colonel Kilgore's (Robert Duvall) Air Cav assault.

In the second-phase films of the early eighties, the Vietnamese, like the Indians in all those John Ford Westerns, once again became the cannon fodder of the American military. Pauline Kael, reviewing *Uncommon Valor* (*New Yorker*, 23 January 1984), writes:

> A reasonably accurate test of whether an action movie is racist: Do the white heroes slaughter people of color in quantity, either effortlessly or triumphantly? . . . *Uncommon Valor* . . . *is* racist. The Communist soldiers are depersonalized; they're presented in much the same terms as the Japanese in Second World War films such as *Bataan* (1943). They're little yellow-peril targets.

Andrew Sarris agrees with Kael. Comparing the Vietnam War films with World War II films (*Village Voice*, 8 September 1987) he argues:

> The Vietnamese, both ours and theirs, thus oozed out on the screen from a long line of Fu-Manchu Yellow Peril prejudices. They were the Other, like all the indigenous Indian tribes who stubbornly resisted our Manifest Destiny. When John Wayne traded in his cowboy hat for a green beret in his much-despised *The Green Berets* in 1968, he was merely applying the Tonto Principle to our foreign policy in Southeast Asia.

Leo Cawley (*Village Voice*, 8 September 1987) takes a stronger stance against this Amerocentrism. Whereas Kael defined it and Sarris cynically pinned down its ancestors, Cawley points toward ways of solving it:

> And, of course, there are the Vietnamese. It would seem lopsided if the films kept focusing exclusively on our story. Will we keep thinking the tragedy is that of the invader, of his painful self-knowledge, his loss of innocence, his recognition of limits? This suits the national character so depressingly well. It would be interesting to take other lives into account.

There should be scenes about the legions of whores and barbers and laundresses and spies who were all the Vietnam American troops ever knew. . . . And what about our "allies," the ones we went there to defend? Who were those people whose daughters wore white *ao dais* and rode bicycles? . . . There could be a film about their experience. Our memorial wall in Washington has 58,000 or so dead on it. The Vietnamese suffered more than two million dead. Allowing for the greater number of dead and the fact that there are fewer—one fifth as many—Vietnamese than Americans, their memorial wall of names, if they had one, would be 200 times larger than ours.

Thus this new American racism is present both in the society and in the films of the eighties. Southeast Asian hordes have replaced the rampaging Negroes of D. W. Griffith's *Birth of a Nation* (1915) and the waves of faceless Indians of John Ford's thirties and forties Westerns as the racial other. Many movies of the early eighties mindlessly promulgate the new racism, but few challenge it. One that does is Louis Malle's *Alamo Bay* (1985).

Racism against Vietnamese immigrants to America is the primary text of *Alamo Bay*. The redneck fishermen on the Gulf Coast of Texas hate the Vietnamese because of, first, veteran frustration and hatred occasioned by the loss of the Vietnam War and, second, insecurity in the face of the hard work ethic and economic success of the Vietnamese immigrants (which metaphorically parallels the industrial and trade dominance of Japan over the United States in the eighties).

Louis Malle, like his countryman Alexis de Tocqueville in the nineteenth century, presents *Alamo Bay* as an observation and commentary on the state of American society. The setting is the supposedly "New" South, but little is "new" except that the Ku Klux Klan has a new target for its racism, the Vietnamese. Early in *Alamo Bay*, Shane Crenshaw (Ed Harris), the bigoted redneck antagonist of the Vietnamese immigrants in this small fishing town, complains:

SHANE: Hey Luis, that's not much shrimp for ten hours' work. These gooks been rapin' the bay.

LUIS: It's a fact. It's like the range. There's only so many fish. You overgraze it and everybody goes belly up.

It is no coincidence that Malle has chosen modern-day Texas as the setting for making his statement about the new racism. His intentional drawing of a parallel to the open range wars of the nineteenth century places his social commentary directly within the context of American myth, the context so familiar to audiences of western movies of the thirties and forties. There is, in fact, a comic subtext all through *Alamo Bay* that culminates with the heroine Glory (Amy Madigan) declaring with a grin that her Vietnamese friend Dinh (Ho Nguyen) is "the last real cowboy in Texas."

Alamo Bay examines the aging of the American dream. At one point,

Dinh teaches the Vietnamese children to play baseball, a hopeful sign of their assimilation, but the overall tone of the film suggests that the American dream is no longer open to immigrants. Like Costa-Gavras's *Betrayed* (1988) and Alan Parker's *Mississippi Burning* (1989), films by foreign directors exploring American racism, *Alamo Bay* chronicles the attempts of white supremacist groups to close off the American dream to minority members of the American community. American racism in the eighties seems a subject to which foreign directors are attracted. Perhaps the reason is the inability of Americans to face one of the nation's ugliest social realities.

The opening image of *Alamo Bay* is much like the opening image of *First Blood*—a Vietnam veteran walking a road alone, looking for a place. The major difference is that in *Alamo Bay* the fugitive from the Vietnam War is Vietnamese and is smiling, hopeful. Printed across this opening image are the words: "In the years following the fall of Saigon, a million Vietnamese fled their country, many of them hoping to find a new life in the USA. This story is inspired by a series of incidents which took place on the Gulf Coast of Texas in 1978 and 1981." The image and the words point to the two motivating factors in the new racism frustration over the loss of the Vietnam War and frustration over the loss of American economic superiority to Japan. Shane Crenshaw embodies both motives. He is a Vietnam veteran who hates the "gooks" he fought and the government who would not help him when he got home from fighting its war. He is also a self-employed shrimper who is in danger of losing his boat, his wife, and his run-down little piece of the American dream. Both motives feed his racism toward the Vietnamese immigrants who have settled in Port Alamo. Naturally the Ku Klux Klan is more than willing to send in organizers to exploit that racism complete with white sheets and hoods, burning crosses, and the forcing of the whole refugee village out of town.

That the Vietnam War is still a sensitive issue in East Texas is the first subject broached by the truckdriver who picks up Dinh, the Vietnamese hitchhiker: "Yo're luckier'n a pig ah picked you up," the truckdriver grins stupidly. "Some o' these ol' boys round here drive right over the top o' you, son. Vietnamese, ain't ya? Alright. Had a good time over there myself. Good lookin' women. Dynamite drugs." Shane Crenshaw, however, is not nearly so sanguine about the war and these new immigrants. After being turned down for a bank loan, he screams out his frustration: "You know what's the trouble with the fishin' industry here in this town is the trouble with the goddam government. We defend everybody all over the world, but there's no protection for any Americans, and that ain't right." Most of the townspeople of Port Alamo agree with Shane's angry assessment. At a town meeting, a woman states succinctly the two reasons for this outbreak of racial hatred: "My boy fought the VC over there and now they're right here in Texas takin' the bread outta our mouths."

It does not take long for the racism to escalate out of the town council into the violence of the streets, and *Alamo Bay* becomes a film in which the ugly American is at his ugliest. Shane confronts his girl friend, Glory, over her friendship with Dinh:

SHANE: You gonna ride down Main Street with that gook?

GLORY: He's not a gook. Yes, I am gonna ride with him.

SHANE: (screaming) Communist cunt!

Shane sees the Vietnamese as responsible for every failure of his life: in war, in business, in love. He reacts with blind racial violence. On his boat he flies the American flag upside down above the upright flag of the Confederacy. He puts the Ku Klux Klan, armed and in full regalia, on boats. He starts shooting at the Vietnamese and makes mad assertions of his own Manifest Destiny. He screams at Glory, "Why don't you go back to your gooks and your gook business." He screams at the Vietnamese Catholic priest: "Keep your goddam gooks outta my family's fishin' grounds." He screams his frustration and then brings the Vietnam War back to Main Street America.

Most of the early part of *Alamo Bay* is an alternation of scenes of life in an American redneck's family with scenes of life in a Vietnamese immigrant's family alternated with crosscuts between the Vietnamese boat and the American boat fishing for shrimp. The result of this paralleling of images is a positive realization (that the two cultures are not really that different) and a negative realization (that the two cultures are living side by side but are certainly not living together). The Ku Klux Klan burns a cross outside the Vietnamese enclave and chants "Death to the gooks. Death to the Cong." Blind racism transforms these Vietnamese refugees from Communism into Communists. Blind racism turns our allies into our enemy.

The Klan-organized racism that drives the Vietnamese out of Port Alamo is based upon the misperception and distortion of history. As the Vietnamese community is bused out of town, the Klan organizer shakes hands all around and brags: "Y'all remember now, nobody from the Third World can hold a candle to us unless we tie our hands behind our backs. History is with us." His Amerocentric expropriation of history defines international relations as a game in which America has, in situations like the Vietnam War, handicapped itself. His expropriation of history mirrors the Amerocentrism and ethnocentrism of the vast majority of the films in the Vietnam War film history.

Alamo Bay examines the tremendous resentment of the Vietnam veteran toward a war he was not allowed to win, toward a government and a society that refused to reward him for risking his life to protect it, toward those Asian races, both Vietnamese and Japanese, that he sees as a threat to America's economic superiority. The Texas Gulf Coast rednecks find an outlet for all of these Vietnam War and society-engendered resentments in the old forms of racial violence aimed at new targets. *Alamo Bay*, in its analysis and *E.T.*-like (Dinh is a cheerful, saintly, wide-eyed alien) condemnation of America's new racism, is the exception rather than the rule of eighties film representations of the racial hatred that grew out of the Vietnam War. Throughout the eighties, the new racism toward Orientals in American society did not abate. In 1985 Michael Cimino's *Year of the Dragon*, whose central character is a Vietnam vet, raised a media outcry against its portrayal of the Chinese gangster community in New York. A similar outcry had been raised in 1978 about Cimino's brutally negative portrayal of the Vietnamese in *The Deer Hunter*.

Year of the Dragon followed in the footsteps of *Rambo II* as a "comic book" one-man war against the evil Asian hordes. The only difference was that the war was not being fought in Southeast Asia but rather on the streets of New York's Chinatown. Rambo as Sergeant Rock is transformed into the ironically named Stanley White (Mickey Rourke) playing Dick Tracy shooting evil Oriental gang members and drug dealers into Swiss cheese. White is a Vietnam vet who accuses his Chinese American girlfriend's race of helping the North Vietnamese in the long-gone war. The film's allusions to the Vietnam War as motivation for White's violence and racial hatred are tenuous at best, and Cimino's need to again connect the Vietnam War to an anti-Asian statement is suspicious at least. From the day of *Year of the Dragon*'s release, Chinese Americans picketed theaters across America. This stimulated a media focus that pushed the distributors to attach a disclaimer to the film: "This film does not intend to demean or ignore the many positive features of Asian-Americans [*sic*]." That disclaimer was not enough, however, to offset the negative portrayal not only of the Asian American gangsters, but of the whole Asian American community that is the backdrop for Stanley White's one-man war. In the wake of these charges leveled at Cimino, Hollywood counterattacked by stressing the highly positive images of Asian Americans in films either already in release or in production when *Year of the Dragon* was released in 1985. The films mentioned were the *Karate Kid* films (1984, 1986), *Remo Williams: The Adventure Begins* (1985) in which Joel Grey plays a Korean mystic, and *Gung Ho* (1986), a comedy in which the Japanese take over an American automobile factory. The fact remains, however, that *Rambo II* and *Year of the Dragon* are embarrassing examples of this new racism that *Alamo Bay* defines and all the *Gung Ho*'s in production cannot laugh off.

The new racism against Asian Americans stemming from the dual motives of Vietnam War frustration and economic frustration is the most complex form of racism in American films in the eighties, but other forms—the old racism against blacks and new economic racism mainly against Hispanics—are also represented. Charges of the Reagan administration's return to pre-1964 attitudes toward black Americans plus the international political interest in South African apartheid occasioned a number of film treatments from both a historical and a contemporary perspective of eighties racism. Another group of films focused on the illegal immigration and racial exploitation of Hispanics along the Mexican border.[26] After the breakthrough successes of the civil rights movements of the sixties, and the steady advances in opportunity for all races in the seventies, the eighties under Reagan more and more was perceived as a withdrawal from the previous two decades support of racial equality and equal opportunity in American society. American film both fed this new racism (as in *Rambo II* and *Year of the Dragon*) and attempted to raise the consciousness of American society (as in the border movies and films like *Betrayed* and *Mississippi Burning*) against both the reemergence of the old racism against blacks and the emergence of this new racism against Asian Americans and Hispanic Americans.

The Violent Vet

Though the controversy that surrounded *Year of the Dragon* focused upon its racist portrayal of Asian Americans, that film also presented a negative stereotype of the Vietnam veteran. Tim O'Brien, author of *Going After Cacciato*, writes, in an essay titled "The Violent Vet," about this stereotype:

> The typical Vietnam veteran is bonkers. Outright dangerous: a shell-shocked, frazzle-brained, doped-out psycho. In late-night reruns of *Barretta* or *Kojak*, you'll recognize the Vietnam vet by his demented eyes and twitching trigger finger, the robber in a whole decade of cops and robbers shows, the kidnapper and hijacker and rapist. . . . Haunted by his complicity in an evil war, the combat veteran is given to fits of violence, succeeded by periods of almost catatonic depression, succeeded by more violence. . . . The typical Vietnam vet turns cynical, bitter and angry; he is surely suicidal, probably murderous. . . . Anyhow, that's the TV version. More recently, this sorry stereotype has been updated, though hardly sanitized, in such major films as *Apocalypse Now*, *The Deer Hunter*, *Coming Home*, *Who'll Stop the Rain*, and *Heroes*.[27]

O'Brien is writing in late 1979, but by the late eighties that stereotype of the Vietnam vet as violent, unstable, suicidal, and criminal had changed in one significant perception. By the late eighties in films the violent vet, still a walking time bomb, is likely to be on the right side of the law. He is still violent and unstable, but American society has given him a license to direct that Vietnam-generated violence toward the criminal element of society.

Stanley White, the cop in *Year of the Dragon*, is a prime example of the movie stereotype of the violent vet. His hair is prematurely gray due to the horrors of combat in Vietnam. He is also the most decorated police officer in New York City. But he cannot deal with authority, and the violence of being the crimebuster of Chinatown exhilarates him. He is a war lover who now that he has come home is unable to come down off that violence high. Most of the violent vets in eighties films are cops who replace their violent lives in the war with violence in peacetime. The police force is where that war violence can be legally duplicated. Stanley White is the archetypal "violent vet." He is most at ease, most alive, in the midst of a firefight in a hostile Asian neighborhood. He is out there alone, abandoned by the government that has asked him to fight their dirty little war. He decides, as Colonel Kurtz did in *Apocalypse Now*, to operate without restraint. He has found a way to metaphorically reduplicate the Vietnam War acceptably in American society.

Unlike Stanley White, many of the soldiers who came home from Vietnam missing the violence did not end up on the right side of the law. The "violent vet" films of the eighties fit the comic book profile of the second phase of the Vietnam War film history. These eighties vets are more one-dimensional than the ambivalent "violent vets" of the films of the late seventies. They are either violent good guys or violent bad guys. There is no middle ground. Whereas Travis Bickle (Robert DeNiro) in *Taxi Driver*, Colonel Rane (William Devane) and Johnny Vohden (Tommy Lee Jones) in *Rolling Thunder*, and Ray Hicks (Nick Nolte) in *Who'll Stop the Rain* are all caught between a society that does not care about them and criminals who want to kill them, the violent vets of the eighties are inclined to take sides. They choose to be either cops or robbers, but the one thing that does not change is the supposed motive for their choice, their love for violence.

With so many films like *Lethal Weapon* (1987) and *The Presidio* (1988) taking their cue from television's "Miami Vice" and lining up Vietnam vet cops against Vietnam vet criminals, there is a real ambivalence toward the propensity for violence that those vets brought home from Vietnam. Is that violence OK if it is channeled into law enforcement? Are these violent vets sane? Disturbed? Valuable to society? Are they booby traps wired by the war to go off when they get back into society?

Lethal Weapon (1987) is loaded with violent Vietnam vets and is one of the best examples of this particular comic book stereotype. The film is all buddies and bodies. The buddies are two L.A. cops. Roger Murtaugh (Danny Glover) is a Vietnam vet and a family man who keeps sighing, "I'm too old for this shit." He is stable, not exceptionally violent, though an excellent cop who does not hesitate to fire his gun. Murtaugh's new partner, Martin Riggs (Mel Gibson), also a Vietnam vet, is a suicidal murder machine. Soon, there are so many corpses strewn across the L.A. landscape that it resembles Hue during TET in 1968.

If Moe Howard of the Three Stooges was a psychopath with a Magnum and a machine gun, he would be Martin Riggs. Riggs is utterly certifiable. In addition to carrying around the weight of Vietnam, Riggs's wife has died the year before. It is Christmastime and he sorely misses her. Murtaugh is not nearly as disturbed. In fact, he wants to dissociate himself from Riggs's unstable violence. He tries to get a new partner; he begs Riggs to calm down; he tries to talk to him about Vietnam. Nothing works and the war keeps breaking out in downtown L.A. But Murtaugh also has Vietnam coming back into his life. The daughter of one of his Vietnam buddies, a high-class hooker, has supposedly jumped to her death from a high-rise apartment. Murtaugh is driven to find out what really happened.

To add to the "violent vet" symmetry of *Lethal Weapon*, the antagonists of Murtaugh and Riggs are also Vietnam vets, two former CIA spooks. They are cold, emotionless killers who fit well a pattern of eighties villainy defined by Dennis Hopper in *Blue Velvet* (1986), John Glover in *52 Pick-Up* (1987) and Willem Dafoe in *To Live and Die in L.A.* (1986). Mr. Joshua (Gary Busey) and Captain McCallister (Mitchell Ryan) are involved in the L.A. porno industry. *Lethal Weapon*'s greatest irony is that the Vietnam vets that overpopulate the film, whether good guys or bad guys, are all really not that different. There is a symmetry to the film's violence. Riggs and Mr. Joshua are psychos. Murtaugh and Captain McCallister are more controlled and rational but still have no trouble participating in the violence. *Lethal Weapon* is the extreme case of the persistence of the "violent vet" stereotype in American film.

The Presidio is another film almost exclusively populated with Vietnam vets, but it is not as extreme in its exploitation. The "violent vets" of *The Presidio* also are lined up on both sides of the law, and as in *Lethal Weapon*, the war is coming back to haunt them. As in Coppola's *Gardens of Stone*, the bad taste of Vietnam is still in the mouths of the central characters in *The Presidio*. An old lifer sergeant, McClure (Jack Warden), who won the Congressional Medal of Honor in Vietnam, sums up his difficulty in reentering American society: "I had an easier time winning that medal than I've ever had wearing it." His commanding officer, an irascible Scots American, Major Chandler (Sean Connery), is more sociologically perceptive than McClure as he defines the role of the military in an American society that neither respects them nor acknowledges the value of their contribution. One night, both drunk, Chandler tells the truth to McClure: "You see, America is this big fancy house and we're the Doberman Pinschers." But despite these attempts to analyze the problems of reassimilation into society of Vietnam veterans, *The Presidio* ultimately falls back on the old stereotype. When baited in a bar by a big, boorish biker for his uniform and for losing the war, Chandler takes the unsuspecting thug apart using only one thumb.

As in *Lethal Weapon*, in *The Presidio* the violent vets are criminals as well. The plot turns on a syndicate of former Vietnam vet black marketeers smuggling diamonds into America in the distilled water bottles of American military bases. These Vietnam vets are not nearly the psychopaths of

Lethal Weapon, however. In comparison, they are almost fatherly, perhaps simply despaired.

Back in 1979, Tim O'Brien wrote:

> The nation seems too comfortable—even dependent upon—the image of a suffering and deeply troubled veteran. Rather than face our own culpabilities, we shove them off onto ex-GIs and let them suffer for us. . . . The vet is a stand-in for the collective conscience. Moreover, by focusing sympathy and attention on the men who fought the war, we avoid many of the more difficult issues about the war itself. . . .
>
> The cinematic stereotypes of the Vietnam veteran—and the nation's willingness to accept it—seems tied to this same process. A way of atoning. A way of coping.[28]

Though attitudes toward Vietnam vets have changed since 1979, and though the media has toned down its stereotyping of the "violent vet," not much has changed in the films of the eighties except that the "violent vet" is now as likely to be good guy as he was bad guy ten years ago. The suspense thriller and the buddy-cop action genres love their violent Vietnam vets in the roles of both hero and villain.

The film *Mask* (1985) is the true story of Rocky Dennis, a young man with a deforming nerve disease who triumphs over all the problems that other people impose upon him. Rocky (Eric Stoltz) triumphs by simply being himself. Peter Bogdanovich made the film in a socially sensitive way. Unlike an earlier film about the same disease, *The Elephant Man* (1980), the camera never avoids Rocky's deformity, neither exploits it nor romanticizes it. After ten minutes of *Mask*, Rocky has become just Rocky. The film audience has seen through the "mask" of his deformity and has accepted him as a person. That is the kind of film that needs to be made about Vietnam vets. The American media have stigmatized the image of the Vietnam vet with all different sorts of distortion. Vietnam vets are not utterly lost or totally guilt ridden; they are neither Travis Bickle nor Rambo; they are neither comic book revenge masters nor suicidal depressants. Vietnam vets are simply people, people who survived and who are, in most cases, moving forward, not living in either a media-stereotyped past or a comic book fantasy.

Thus the films of the eighties, though almost a decade removed from the Vietnam War, continued to be obsessed with it. The different phases of their contemplation of that "dirty little war" came to dominate the film consciousness of both the late seventies and the whole decade of the eighties. The Vietnam War film history is but one indicator that qualifies that war as the most important event in the social history of America in the last three decades. But why in the eighties is the "re-presenting" of the Vietnam War as an issue of social history still necessary? Why in 1987–88 is Vietnam the central focus of sixteen months of films? The answer lies in what John Fowles in his novel *The Magus* calls the need for "disintoxication." The botched Vietnam exorcisms of both the films of the early eighties with their comic book heroes and the Reagan administration jingoism forced a continuing and more thoughtful "disintoxication." The "coming home" of Vietnam veterans was the most prominent problem. Real events, such as the power of the Vietnam War Memorial being built in Washington and similar "dirty little wars" being fought in Central America and the Middle East, kept the Vietnam War alive as a social issue. But perhaps more powerful than any other motive in explaining the continuing interest in the Vietnam War in American society is simply unsatisfied curiousity. Going on twenty years after America's involvement in Vietnam ended, that war is still a text that Americans are having a great deal of trouble reading and understanding, a text that demands more and fuller and more honest interpretations.

4

The Terrorism Film Texts

I N THE SEVENTIES, the villains, both in society and in films, were the corporations. Their profit- and power-obsessed corporate mindset instituted open hostilities against the individualism of the Sixties.[1] In the eighties, corporate villainy still flourishes both in society and in films like *Wall Street* (1987) in which a ruthless stock speculator manipulates companies and individuals in imitation of the Ivan Boesky insider trading scandal, or like *Silkwood* (1983) in which a faceless corporation murders by exposing its workers to radiation and by running them off the road at night. But though corporate villainy still exists in the eighties, a new species of villain—less profit-possessed, more politically motivated—has emerged.

In the seventies, the most popular film genre was the disaster movie that used natural disasters—fires, floods, earthquakes, tidal waves, meteors, volcano eruptions, shark attacks, airplane crashes—for its dramatic catalysts. These film disasters symbolically mirrored the social paranoia of the decade itself, which had to somehow deal with the disasters of Vietnam, Watergate, the corporate-induced oil shortage and Three Mile Island. In the eighties on film, disasters still occur, but they are no longer natural disasters that symbolize social disorder. Rather, they are man-made and politically motivated disasters. The new villain of the eighties and the focus of the new species of disaster film is the terrorist.[2]

While the Vietnam War was still a powerful social issue in the eighties, it was not still being fought. Similarly, there were no major governmental scandals like Watergate until late in the decade. Yet two events, one at the beginning of the decade, the other near the end, became the eighties equivalents of Vietnam and Watergate. The first, the Iran Hostage Crisis of 1979–80 and the second, the Iran-*contra* scandal of 1987–88, dubbed by the press "Iran-gate," were two sociohistorical events that were the result of a clandestine terrorist war that had begun with the Baader-Meinhof Gang in Germany, the Red Brigades in Italy, the IRA in the Anglo-Irish world, and the PLO in the Middle East in the sixties and had made scattered headlines, such as at the Summer Olympics at Munich in 1972, throughout the seventies. In the eighties, this terrorist war escalated, became nationalized and politically legitimized. Terrorism became "government terrorism," violent acts against the innocent populace of a country or the world sponsored by governments such as Iran, Libya, or a number of South and Central American "death squad" governments. In fact, the history of America's foreign policy in the eighties is more often than not a history of reactions to international terrorism.

The eighties decade was ushered in by the Iran Hostage Crisis. The most elaborate act of world terrorism yet conceived, it brought down the Carter administration as Watergate had brought down Nixon. Not simply the holding hostage of individual Americans, it was the holding hostage of the American nation by Iran. It signaled the beginning of the age of international governmental terrorism.

A *New York Times* analysis in late 1983 declares that year's escalation of Middle East terrorism "to be part of a regional campaign by Iranian-sponsored groups to strike at American interests, disrupt moderate Arab regimes and create fertile ground for the spread of the Islamic revolution that began in Iran." This revolutionary plot signaled "that a whole new form of terrorism seems to be brewing in the Middle East, with the U.S. and its allies the main targets."[3] Nineteen eighty-three was a year of continuous bombings all over the Middle East, culminating in the suicide attack in a truck loaded with six tons of explosives upon the Marine barracks in Beirut that killed 240 American soldiers. The frequency of these attacks was a clear signal that they were not isolated incidents but part of a coordinated effort directed from Tehran. Only two days after the attack on the Marine barracks in Beirut, President Reagan ordered the invasion of Grenada.

Without the Iranian Hostage Crisis and the terrorist attacks against American interests worldwide in the years 1979–83, there would have been no Grenada. Like every terrorist attack, Grenada was nothing more than a symbol, pure public relations, a controlled demonstration of the United States' striking capability against government terrorism. Through-out the rest of the eighties decade, similar counterterrorist deployment exercises would be offered in the form of attacks upon Iranian oil rigs in the Persian Gulf, of land and sea maneuvers based in Honduras, of rapid deployments of American troops to Panama to oppose General Noriega. These military maneuvers were, however, mere show because throughout the decade the United States never really developed any sort of foreign policy toward terrorism.

Terrorist action in the eighties was not, however, limited to the Middle East. In 1984, an American journalist was killed with four others by a bomb intended for the assassination of Nicaraguan rebel commander Eden Pastora, "Commander Zero." Though it was never determined who planted the bomb, the major suspects were either Sandinistan infiltrators of Zero's *contra* army or the American CIA.[4] Again a terrorist act was linked to government sponsorship.

But terrorist attacks were never limited to defined theaters of conflict like Beirut or Nicaragua. The terrorist war has always flourished most strongly when able to straddle international boundaries, when able to gain an international mobility that extends its symbolic power. Terrorism has always focused on the airways (or, as in the *Achille Lauro* hijacking, the seaways), where its message of violence can be directed against the whole world. The machine-gun and suitcase bomb attacks of the seventies against international airports were, in the eighties, superseded by airliner hijackings. In June 1985, TWA Flight 847 from Athens to Rome was hijacked. The terrorists took 39 hostages and killed 1, U.S. Navy diver Robert Stethem.[5] This hijacking was attributed to the same group that carried out the Beirut Marine barracks bombing in 1983 and, only four months later, would hijack the Italian cruise ship *Achille Lauro* in the Mediterranean Sea.[6] Then, in December 1988, all 259 people aboard Pan Am Flight 103 and 11 more on the ground were killed when a terrorist bomb exploded in mid-air over Lockerbie, Scotland. This most severe of all the airplane attacks was attributed to a Palestinian group hired by Iran to carry out terrorist attacks upon Americans.[7] What the success of these attacks upon airplanes proved was the unity of terrorist groups (especially in the Middle East) and the government sponsorship (by Iran, Syria, and Libya) of these loosely connected groups.

By the end of the eighties, Iran openly declared its sponsorship of terrorists acts worldwide. In early 1989 in San Diego, California, a pipe bomb blew up the car of Sharon Rogers, wife of the commanding officer of the *USS Vincennes* that had shot down an Iranian airliner a year earlier. Also in early 1989 proof was presented that Iran contracted the terrorist bombing of Pan Am Flight 103 that exploded over Lockerbie, Scotland. In February of 1989, Iran's Ayatollah Khomeini demanded the death of Salman Rushdie, author of the novel *The Satanic Verses*. In April 1989 Iranian Parliament Speaker Hashemi Rafsanjani, shown on Tehran TV leaning on an AK-47 assault rifle, urged Palestinians to "declare open war on American interests throughout the world." He went on to suggest, "Why don't you hijack planes in order to swap prisoners in Israeli hands, or blow up factories in Western countries."[8]

What the eighties saw on the evening news was not only an escalation of terrorist attacks but an increased openness of state terrorism. Iran, Syria, and Libya seemed to want the world to know they were responsible for sponsoring terrorist acts against the West. Late in the decade, a zany comedy film, *The Naked Gun* (1988), opened with a Summit meeting of all the world terrorist leaders. Arafat of the PLO wears a "Yasser is a gasser" pin. Gorbachev has a washable birthmark on his forehead. The Ayatollah Khomeini gets the Three Stooges treatment from Lieutenant Frank Drebin (Leslie Nielsen), the moronic defender of Western values who later must protect Queen Elizabeth from terrorist attacks during her visit to Los Angeles. *The Naked Gun* may be wacky, but it signals how common was the late eighties perception of terrorism as a highly organized international state conspiracy.

The Illusion of Safety

What the idea of a regional terrorist conspiracy places into perspective is the reality that terrorist acts, even "spectaculars" like the Beirut Marine barracks suicide bombing or the mid-air explosion of Pan Am Flight 103 over Scotland, are never an end in themselves. They are, rather, an ongoing tactic in a larger war of public opinion. This tactical function of terrorism in a larger war of words and postures explains why terrorist acts are rarely committed within the boundaries or in the skies above the continental United States. Paul Joyal, a U.S. government terrorism expert, asserts "that terrorists have made a tactical decision that such actions would be counter-productive." Rand Corporation theoretician Brian Jenkins argues that "many terrorist groups would consider attacking targets within the United States a major escalation that would provoke the wrath of the United States and prompt strong military retaliation." Joyal supports that view by noting "that small, determined groups through terrorist acts can achieve disproportionate effects."[9] What terrorism seeks to accomplish is not destruction of life and property but the intimidation of a national mind, the paranoid imprisonment of a nation within its own borders (where it considers itself safe).

Alan J. Pakula's film, *Rollover* (1981), dramatizes how three paranoiac aspects of late-twentieth-century life—universal anxiety, the illusion of safety, the fear of destabilization—have made the eighties especially vulnerable to terrorist tactics. On a TV interview program, Maxwell Emery (Hume Cronyn), America's most influential international banker, declares that the world goes "through regular cycles of anxiety." That predisposition to anxiety makes the eighties world vulnerable to terrorist tactics. Immediately following this "anxiety" speech, at a fancy New York cocktail dance, Emery and fellow banker Hubell Smith (Kris Kristofferson) watch as Lee Winters (Jane Fonda) is told that her husband has been murdered:

MAXWELL: What is it Hub?

HUBELL: Nothin'. I was just thinkin' about the illusion of safety.

The last shot of this scene pans away from the woman breaking down in tears to the ballroom below filled with elegant couples gliding unaware, secure. This ironic lingering pan shot reminds of the parties in *The Great Gatsby* (1974) or the Light Horse dancing the night before their departure for *Gallipoli* (1981). In all three contexts, the camera laughs cruelly at the dancers so unaware of the fragility of their existence.

Hub Smith's recognition of "the illusion of safety" in *Rollover* is exactly the fragile existence that terrorism exploits. Terrorist acts generate a paranoia that isolates and imprisons the targets of terrorist intimidation. *Rollover* does not deal with terrorism in the graphic way that films like *Nighthawks* (1981) or *Die Hard* (1988) do, but it does deal with the basic elements of terrorist theory.

Though *Rollover* is a film about international banking, its central theme of worldwide destabilization embodies the basic philosophical principles of terrorism. Terrorism is the tool of destabilization. It attacks on a physical level that "illusion of safety" in order to destabilize its target audience to the point where they are willing to listen to the rhetoric of terrorism. As Maxwell Emery, lecturing to a graduate class in international banking, notes: "The international character of banking today makes everyone vulnerable to everything. When someone sneezes in Zurich, we say 'gesundheit' in New York. The important thing to realize is that everything is interconnected." His New Historicist characterization of the reality of international banking parallels the reality of international terrorism. Terrorism is never anything more than a tool in the service of larger political or commercial scenarios. Terrorism is but one layer in the holograph of international power struggle.

Other films, notably *The Formula* (1980) and *Half Moon Street* (1987), offer a similar global political vision to that of *Rollover*. In all three films, terrorism is a useful tool of the international petrochemical industry, but the austere theoretical tone of *Rollover* examines the complexity of international conspiracy in the New Historicist manner that it deserves. *Rollover*'s high finance examination of "the illusion of safety" is a metaphor for the terrorist destabilization of the eighties world and offers a *point de départ* for a definition of the rhetoric of terrorism which it serves.

The Rhetoric of Terrorism

Terrorism is the dramatization of violent events directed toward innocent people in order to generate *words*. Terrorism is always a tool of public relations, an attention-getter that forces a specifically targeted audience to listen and react. Terrorism provides the platform for the delivery of speeches in support of a cause, a government, or a minority special-interest group. Thus terrorism is a rhetorical tool, a word tactic, that serves political ends by means of threat and blackmail. But terrorism is not just a political tool. It has also become part of the persuasive rhetoric of domestic profit industries, specifically the drug trade as plied by organizations modeled upon political groups: the drug smuggling cartel and the urban street gang.

Whether terrorism serves political causes or domestic profit groups, it catalyzes words that take three purposeful forms. In the wake of a terrorist act, the first rhetorical position taken is the claiming of responsibility. The terrorist act, at this stage, has been a tool for bestowing identity, for naming the group that claims responsibility. The second rhetorical position made possible by the terrorist act is the making of demands upon the target audience. The terrorist act, at this stage, has become a potentially recurring threat upon which blackmail is based. The third rhetorical position made possible by the terrorist act is that of negotiation. The terrorist act, at this point, has bestowed instant credibility upon a group that had previously had no negotiating position.

With these rhetorical motives in mind, terrorism serves three basic tropes effectively designed to capture the attention of three target audiences:

1. The world to publicize a political cause
2. An oppressed and potentially revolutionary proletariat under a totalitalitarian government (i.e., "death squad" terrorism) to maintain control
3. Rival business factions capable of invading a business territory (i.e., drug cartels and street gangs) to discourage competition

The three basic rhetorical motives of terrorism are predictably geographically distinctive. Political terrorism is very much a Western European-Middle Eastern phenomenon. Death squad government terrorism has been identified with South and Central American dictatorships, but more recently has been finding counterparts in other Third World areas, especially in emerging Africa. Finally, domestic commercial terrorism in defense of drug markets and territorial imperatives is an American urban phenomenon.

The Texts of Terrorism

Thus, as was the case with both the Vietnam War as a New Historicist holograph and the Vietnam War films, terrorism takes form in a number of different texts. The multitextuality of terrorism is a tool of a rather consistent rhetoric of terrorism that follows upon the impact of every terrorist act. The three most common terrorist texts are aligned to the rhetorical motives and geographical origins of terrorism. The *political* terrorist text is the classical terrorist scenario originating in Western Europe and the Middle East. Designed to draw attention to, and initiate debate upon, clearly defined political issues, it is the purest form of terrorism in which the act functions wholly as symbol. The *control* terrorist text is also political. This text employs death squad terrorism as a covert tool of fascistic government to intimidate potentially revolutionary masses. This is a populist terrorist text devolved out of necessity mainly in Central and South American dictatorships. Its function is in no way symbolic but purely intimidative. Its purpose is limited to maintaining the status quo. The third major terrorist text is the *commercial* text in which terrorism is used as a tool of one of the eighties' most profitable industries, the drug trade. This is an old-fashioned text imported in the nineteenth century to America with the deluge of immigrants from Western Europe. Throughout the twentieth century, this terrorist text has been the essence of American gangsterism from the bootleggers of the twenties to the organized syndicates of Capone and Luciano to Murder Incorporated to the corporate terrorism of the fifties as portrayed in Coppola's *The God-father, Part II* (1974) to the drug wars and gang wars of the eighties. It is a commercial text that, like the control text of death squad governments, is intimidative rather than symbolic. What all three terrorist texts share is their participation in a larger rhetoric of terrorism.

There were some terrorist films in the seventies, such as *Black Sunday* (1977), *Twilight's Last Gleaming* (1977), and *Two-Minute Warning* (1976), but their characterizations were generally psychotic and either apolitical or politically muddled. In these films, the terrorist was portrayed as a wronged individual pursuing a revenge scenario who has allowed himself to become the tool of some deeply backgrounded, unnamed political cause. This revenge-obsessed seventies terrorist was little more than a hitchhiker upon the vehicle of backgrounded political scenarios. In the eighties, the ideological texts of terrorism itself and a much more complex psychological profile of the terrorist than that of a one-dimensional psychotic are foregrounded in films.

An "innocents abroad" theme also took form in a number of eighties films in which terrorist acts are directed against individuals traveling in foreign lands. *The Amateur* (1982) is just such a movie. When his fiancée is executed by a terrorist before his eyes, on TV, a mild-mannered CIA computer whiz decides to take covert agent training in order to get revenge. Needless to say, when he finally goes on his mission into Eastern Europe the CIA is only using him as bait. In *Frantic* (1988), when the wife of an American medical doctor is kidnapped by terrorists at a convention in Paris, the American embassy refuses to even acknowledge her disappearance and the doctor must brave the Paris underworld on his own. Perhaps the most transparent of these "innocents abroad" movies is *Target* (1985). Walter Lloyd (Gene Hackman) is a quiet, taciturn man who runs a nice business in Dallas. His son, Chris (Matt Dillon), thinks that his father is old and boring. But when Walter's wife, Donna (Gayle Hunnicut), is kidnapped from her tour group in Paris, father and son must get together to rescue her. Luckily Walter is a tough former CIA agent and Chris is a hotshot motorcycle jockey, and they form a pretty good team even though their government will not even acknowledge their wife and mother's disappearance. Though these "innocents abroad" films deal with terrorism in an oblique way, they do not really confront the major sociohistorical issues of terrorism.

The films of the eighties have consistently focused on this new villain, the terrorist. While the terrorist film history is by no means as chronologically organized in its evolution as is the Vietnam War film history, yet it is clearly organized in terms of its three major texts and a number of recurring subtextual themes or tropes: the analysis of terrorist psychology, existential terrorism in which individuals are marked for violence, and governmental inadequency against terrorism. What too few of these films acknowledge, however, is the success that terrorism as a rhetorical tactic has had in the holograph of eighties history.

The Political Text Classical international political terrorism in the eighties (the Iran hostages, the U.S. servicemen's club bombings in Germany, the Marine barracks in Beirut, the TWA hijacking from Athens, the *Achille Lauro*, the Pan Am bombing over Scotland) was orchestrated from, and designed to cast focus upon, the Middle East, the most prominent theater of terrorism, where the terrorist superstars played out their dramas of word generation, asserted the rhetoric of terrorism. Responsibility was claimed, outrageous demands were made, and in most cases (excepting the servicemen's clubs bombings and the Lockerbie disaster), extended negotiations leading to policy changes occurred. What is, perhaps, most eighties distinctive about this particular set of terrorist spectaculars is that American intelligence was able to link each act to some Middle East-based terrorist superstar and was able to confirm that each act involved the loose cooperation of ideologically disparate terrorist groups. Since superstars are the bread and butter of the Hollywood film industry, the establishment of a new species of historical superstar was bound to catch the attention of moviemakers.

Also, the concept of wide-ranging international conspiracies involving terrorists of many different nationalities also caught Hollywood's attention. International terrorism was the flip side of the *Star Trek* coin. Whereas the *Star Trek* crew, composed of different Earth and galaxy nationalities, set out to restore order to a disordered universe, international terrorist consortia go where no man has gone before in the spreading of chaos for the purposes of political rhetoric. A series of films based upon these concepts of the superstar terrorist and the anti-*Star Trek* terrorist team examined the rhetorical intentions of eighties terrorism.

Nighthawks (1981) is one of the first films to flesh out this international terrorist superstar scenario. Wulfgar (Rutger Hauer), head of the Wulfgar Command, is an Ur-terrorist reminiscent of the Jackel in Frederick Forsythe's novel and Fred Zinneman's film *The Day of the Jackel* (1973). "International terrorism, gentlemen," Inspector Harp (Nigel Davenport) of Interpol lectures a special counterterrorist team, "is a worldwide organization and the man who runs like a thread through the majority of it all is one, Wulfgar." In the course of this meeting, Deke DeSilva

(Sylvester Stallone) asks "are you sure that this guy is even in the city?" Harp's answer confirms the rhetorical intention of terrorism: "He isn't comfortable in Europe. Where would he hide? Africa, Asia, the Middle East, South America? They've got enough revolutionaries. But if he wanted worldwide press coverage, New York, where else?"

In his first scene in *Nighthawks*, after successfully detonating a bomb in a crowded London department store, Wulfgar steps into a phone booth and launches into the rhetoric of terrorism: "United Press. I have an announcement to make for our international wire. The Wulfgar Command has just struck a blow against British Colonialism. Be warned that I have a long arm and I'm prepared to fight my enemies wherever they may be. Don't forget. There's no security." Wulfgar's tag line, "there's no security," echoes Hub Smith's thematic line about the "illusion of safety" in *Rollover*. Wulfgar's speech claims responsibility, asserts identity and is directed to the international press. As Harp later stresses: "What he wants most is press coverage. The media is their voice."

The rhetoric of terrorism in *Nighthawks* reaches its most persuasive point when it enters the negotiation stage. Wulfgar, who has hijacked the United Nations tramcar, confronts DeSilva, in a police helicopter, and Sergeant Fox (Billy Dee Williams), on the telephone, over the East River. The power of the rhetoric of terrorism to bring life to a halt is symbolically represented in the stalled tramcar hanging over the river and the helicopter hovering helplessly before it.

The *Star Trek* concept of international terrorist conspiracy is also evident in *Nighthawks*. One of Wulfgar's demands from the tramcar is that four imprisoned terrorists—a Palestinian, a German, a Japanese and an Irishman—be released. His support system of the Wulfgar Command is made up of IRA agents under the command of one Mercer in London, of a German-speaking woman whom he meets in a confessional in Madrid, and of the proprietors of a Palestinian grocery store in New York. All of the terrorist nationalities are represented.

But the concept of international terrorist image consciousness is also represented. After the London bombing, Wulfgar is censured by his IRA contact: "They want to talk to you about that bomb. Mercer says it was overdone. Several children were killed. It hurt the movement." The rhetoric of terrorism walks a thin line between capturing the attention of the world community and alienating that community by its barbarism. Unfortunately children always seem to be caught in the crossfire of terrorism, thus posing one of the rhetoric of terrorism's greatest argumentative problems.

The Little Drummer Girl (1984) begins with a suitcase bombing of an Israeli ambassador's home in Bad Godesberg, West Germany, in which small children are again caught in the political crossfire. Like *Nighthawks*, *The Little Drummer Girl* focuses upon the concept of a terrorist superstar and analyzes terrorism as a carefully staged drama of political public relations directed by the shadowy Palestinian superterrorist Kahlil. Adapted from John Le Carre's novel of the same name, *The Little Drummer Girl* is the first film taken from "contemporary fiction by a major writer depicting the Palestinians as a people with legitimate and deeply felt grievances."[10] In Le Carre's book, the "Palestinians cease to be merely stereotypical terrorists."[11] In fact, the superterrorist Kahlil has been identified in interviews by Le Carre as based upon Saleh Ta'amri. Ta'amri was Le Carre's escort while researching the novel through the southern Lebanese camps and was also the head of the Fatah's youth wing. Ta'amri was subsequently interred in an Israeli prison camp after the 1982 Israeli invasion.

While being evenhanded toward both sides in the Middle East terrorist tragedy, both book and film are also highly symbolic in their representation of terrorism as political theater. Perhaps, besides his factual researches, Le Carre, in the plot structuring and metaphorical conception of his novel, was most heavily influenced by John Fowles's novel *The Magus* (1965). The similarities in character, plot structure, and the concept of metatheater between the two books is striking. In Fowles's novel an eccentric millionaire stages an elaborate metatheater, a play within the play (or, in this case, novel), on an isolated Greek isle for the sole purpose of leading a young man to existential consciousness. *The Little Drummer Girl*, an eighties version of *The Magus*, has much bigger game to stalk. Its elaborate metatheater is created by Israeli intelligence for the purpose of reaching the superterrorist Kahlil and assassinating him. In fact, what the film is saying is that all organized terrorist and counterterrorist action is metatheater, a drama contrived to catch the conscience of the kings.

The kinship of Fowles's sixties novel and Le Carre's eighties version is signaled when early in the film the central character, an American actress named Charlie (Diane Keaton) working in England, is hired by a rich movie director to make a wine commercial on the Greek isle of Mykonos. Later, this mysterious film director turns out to be Marty (Klaus Kinski), the head of Israeli intelligence. After kidnapping Charlie, Marty explains:

MARTY: We want to offer you a job, an acting job.

CHARLIE: In what?

MARTY: Its a play. In a different kind of theater. The theater of the real. Its the biggest part you've ever had. The most demanding. And surely the most important.

Terrorism and counterterrorism are the "theater of the real" with a vengeance. The metaphor of raising plays within the real world to solve real problems, works especially well to embody the shadow world of both terrorist and counterterrorist. Ultimately both sides are only actors in a much larger international political theater, characters in search of authors who can release them from their revenge tragedy in the "theater of the real," who can write them out of the ongoing terrorist script of the eighties.

In *The Little Drummer Girl*, the rhetoric of terrorism eloquently backgrounds the characters playing their parts in the "theater of the real." The Israeli agent Gadi Becker (Yorgo Voyagis), who plays the role of Kahlil's brother Michel in the metaplay, delivers two speeches that define terrorism as political theater and justify its rhetorical existence. Giving a lecture in England, the character Michel, who will later be played by the actor Gadi, harangues his audiences:

> They call us terrorists! Why? Because we must deliver our bombs with our hands. We have no American planes to drop them from. No tanks to shell their towns. This Israeli tank commander who fires his cannon into our camps so that our women and children have their flesh burnt from their bones, this Israeli is called a hero. But when we strike back, the only way we can, with our hands, we are called terrorists. If these Israeli's will give us their planes, we will give them our suitcases.

This apologia adheres strictly to the formulaic rhetoric of terrorism. It first claims responsibility for terrorism, admits its identity, and then, by means of direct comparison to conventional warfare seeks to legitimize itself, even claim "heroism" as a motive for its action.

In fact, *The Little Drummer Girl* is filled with speeches of legitimization. The terrorists seek to legitimize their position with words. The Israeli counterterrorist metafictionists seek to legitimize their scenario of deceit and assassination with words. The individual characters, Charlie and Gadi, seek to legitimize the characters they assume in the metatheater of the real. The irony of this metatheatrical acting subtext in *The Little Drummer Girl* lies in the fact that the characters that Charlie and Gadi assume become much more real to them than their real (and confused) selves.

Gadi Becker playing the role of Michel tells Charlie about his past life:

> My father was the Mokhtar, the chief of the village where our family had lived for centuries. My father admired the Jews. My brother Achmed remembered bringing my grandfather's horse to the water and hearing wonderful stories from Jewish traders and peddlers. In 1948 do you know what happened to my grandfather's horse? He sold it to buy a gun to shoot the Zionists when they attacked our villages. The Zionists shot my grandfather instead. They made my father stand beside them when they did it, my father who believed in them.

"Is that true?" Charlie interrupts this Method actor's backgrounding of his character. "Do you know the word 'Day-el-Aran'?" Gadi answers.

In the village of Day-el-Aran on April 9, 1948, 254 women, old men and children were butchered by Zionist terror squads while the young men were working in the fields. In a few days nearly a half a million Palestinians fled the country. But my village stayed at my father's command and in 1967, that's when the Israeli tanks came to flatten our houses to make room for their own settlements. So we learn to fight the Zionists. Do you know the man who said the words "I fight therefore I exist." This Polish terrorist killed many British and many Palestinians. This proud winner of the Nobel Prize for Peace. He is the Prime Minister of my country Palestine which they stole and now call Israel. I love you. Share my cause.

When Charlie, who still cannot figure out this *Six Characters in Search of an Author* metatheater, asks "Who are you?" Gadi the actor replies with a question about Michel his character: "Does it play?"

This long speech makes *The Little Drummer Girl* the most polemic and historically didactic of the eighties terrorist film texts. This speech is a striking example of the historical voice finding dramatic form in a film text. Within the film's complex metatheatrical context, a focused history encompassing all three generations of the Palestinian problem is presented. This film makes a valiant attempt to offer a balanced view of the Israeli-Palestinian conflict and the manner in which terrorism, its tactics and rhetoric, lies at the heart of the history of the Middle Eastern question. When Gadi the actor finally steps out of Michel the character and answers Charlie the person's question, he admits that he is the tank commander who leveled that Palestinian village. In the world of *The Little Drummer Girl*, everyone is always on both sides of the Middle East terrorist question.

The Little Drummer Girl, both novel and film, is a complex blending of history and art. The premise of a theater of the real couples the artifice of acting with the realism of history and stresses the manner in which the imagination functions creatively in both realms. History becomes a stage upon which elaborate plays are acted out for the purpose of changing the history which has provided the original context for the play. Thus past history stimulates present art which influences future history.

The Little Drummer Girl's subtext of acting and the metatheatrical relationship between life and art supports its primary text of the complexities of the terrorist war being waged in the Middle East. All the terrorists in this film, all of the real terrorists in the Middle East, are actors in an ongoing political theater constantly making videos for the national network news.

But the film does not shrink from the dualities of the terrorist scenario in the Middle East. At one point Gadi admits: "Both sides have their madmen, their extremists. They have some that want to drive us into the sea. We have some that would wipe them out and have the weapons to do it." At another point Charlie screams: "Why don't you leave the poor fucking arabs alone? Give them back the land you stole from them?" Marty answers: "Where would you have us go? . . . back to the ghettos?"

The film recognizes that terrorism is more complicated than the duality of the Middle East question suggests. Kahlil and Michel, the terrorist superstars, are supported (as was the case in *Nighthawks*) by a multiethnic international terrorist network. A German courier delivers the suitcase bomb in the opening scene of the film. A Red Brigades motorcyclist picks up the car that Charlie delivers. Charlie gets her terrorist training in a Palestinian refugee camp.

It also recognizes the manner in which terrorism exploits the innocent. Marty tells Charlie how Michel uses women like herself: "One girl he actually used as a bomb. Put her on a plane with some nice looking luggage. The plane blew up. I guess she never even knew she had done it." That scenario rather eerily foreshadows the Lockerbie, Scotland, plane explosion some four years later. At another point, Marty characterizes one of Michel's terrorist recruits as "a Swedish halfwit who loves fucking and blowing people up." In human as well as pubic relations terms, terrorism is always an ultimately exploitative and false-acting scenario.

What is hardest for *The Little Drummer Girl* to recognize is the moral question involved in this Middle East war. "The question is" Charlie spits at her Israeli interrogators, "who's right and who's wrong. The Palestinians have been wronged. They've been driven off of land that has been their's for centuries and now they're herded into camps all over." What this film cannot ultimately decide, because no one—not John Le Carre nor the filmmakers nor the Israelis and Palestinians—can anymore, is who is right and who wrong. History has buried morality in the Middle East and terrorism with its amoral violence is the inevitable result.

But as *The Little Drummer Girl* moves toward its final bloody resolution, the one overpowering fact of this terrorist text becomes evident. When Charlie returns after supposedly delivering a bomb to a university auditorium in Friebourg, Kahlil exults: "A great victory. Michel died opening the case. Many Zionist supporters were wounded. Tomorrow the world will read that Palestinians will not wait to tell the news like the Jews." For Kahlil, the victory lies not in the destruction and death but in the verbal fallout from the bomb, the dispersal of words worldwide as recognition of terrorist power. *The Little Drummer Girl* in its complex examination defines terrorism as an international exercise in metatheater, a theater of the real choreographed for the purpose of generating international critical commentary by the news media. Life uses art to generate words, the theater of the real with a vengeance.

Deadline (1987), as does *The Little Drummer Girl*, attempts to dramatize the complexities of the Palestinian-Israeli situation. It's major character, Don Stevens (Christopher Walken), is an eternally confused American TV correspondent in Beirut. His role is that of a witless witness. In the course of humping his minicam around the burned-out city, Stevens encounters (and sometimes even shoots) episodes of political trickery, political assassination, the bombing of a terrorist headquarters, the massacre of innocents in refugee camps, and continuous street violence in this undeclared war zone.

As Stevens moves through this smoldering wasteland, he repeatedly expresses his confusion. "I just don't know what's goin' on," he says at one juncture. "I can't figure this out," he says at another. His confused stumbling between factions on this terrorist battlefield is emblematic of the confusion embedded in America's foreign policy toward the Middle East and America's inability (as was also the case during the Vietnam War) to either avoid or counter the enemy's political, public relations expertise. The terrorism, whether perpetrated by the PLO or by the Israeli Mossad, that Stevens is trying to both record and understand ultimately has no meaning beyond its public relations potential. Stevens finally gives up and realizes that "its show biz. Hollywood." Both the terrorists and the counterterrorists are primarily concerned with manipulating the media by acts of violence. Words and pictures are valued more highly than people or property.

Like *The Little Drummer Girl* and *Deadline*, *Half Moon Street* (1986) opens with a terrorist act. Dr. Loren Slaughter (Sigourney Weaver), an American anthropologist at the Middle Eastern Institute in London, is jogging past an embassy when a terrorist bomb blows up an official car. Back in her flat, she listens as a TV commentator tells what happened: the "car bombing of yet another Libyan exile in London has underlined the dangerous mood of the unpredictable Arab leader. Because of the rising tide of terrorist violence, Lord Bolbeck, Britain's leading expert in Middle Eastern affairs has stepped up his contacts with Middle Eastern moderate states."

As in *Rollover*, in *Half Moon Street* the international banking community, tied to the Arab oil shieks and their petrodollars and playing both sides of the terrorist/antiterrorist fence, are concerned with Lord Bolbeck's (Michael Caine) attempts to negotiate a treaty between the moderate Middle Eastern nations and the Israelis. Bolbeck's stabilization of Middle Eastern terrorism would cause a destabilization of high oil prices and petrodollar power. Dr. Slaughter (also the title of the Paul Theroux novella from which the film is adapted) becomes an unwitting pawn in the hands of the terrorists who plan to assassinate Lord Bolbeck and thus maintain the profitable if violent status quo. Like the confused cameraman in *Deadline*, Dr. Slaughter does not have a clue that she is going to be used to get to Lord Bolbeck.

Loren Slaughter, in order to supplement her meager academic salary upon which she cannot live in expensive London, becomes an escort service girl with the high brow and discreet Jasmine Agency. One of her first dates is with Karim. "And what is your country?" Loren asks him.

When he answers, "I have no country," she immediately realizes that "you're a Palestinian." As Loren's success as a daytime academic and a nighttime call girl gains momentum, she becomes intimately involved with Lord Bolbeck. Like Charlie in *The Little Drummer Girl*, Loren is pro-Arab and does not realize that she is being used as an actress in a complex terrorist metatheater. Karim is the director of this "theater of the real" as he places Loren in a toney apartment in Half Moon Street appropriate for her assignations with Lord Bolbeck. The film's themes are both political and personal simultaneously. Loren Slaughter represents America selling itself to Arab interests like a prostitute while the rest of the world suffers in the crossfire of terrorist violence, but she also represents, on a personal level, a feminist subtext in which a woman tries and fails to exert control over her own life through sexuality. The reason for her failure lies in the insignificance of the personal in the face of the complexity and international impact of the wide-ranging political theme of terrorism.

Half Moon Street is a love story and a feminist tract, but it is above all a political film of international terrorist metatheater. The characters all become actors whose author is a Petro-conspiracy with terrorism as its catalyst. The human emotions of the characters are subsumed in the impersonal machinations of the terrorists who are pursuing a wider scenario of international monetary manipulation. The rhetoric of terrorism once again is the public text of a much wider conspiracy of public-opinionmaking. Charlie in *The Little Drummer Girl*, Don Stevens in *Deadline* and Loren Slaughter in *Half Moon Street* all become unknowing and confused actors in the terrorist street theater. For them, life truly does become a movie.

While films like *Rollover*, *Nighthawks*, *The Little Drummer Girl*, *Deadline*, and *Half Moon Street* probed the international terrorist psychology and defined the scenario of international conspiracy as orchestrated by terrorist superstars heading up multinational networks, the action film genre of the eighties greedily embraced terrorism as a provider of automatic weapon toting cannon fodder. Just as the "return-to-Vietnam" exploitation films of the mid-eighties (emulating the John Ford/John Wayne Westerns of an earlier era) employed waves of faceless Orientals as targets for Rambo and his ilk, in the late eighties terrorist gangs and even armies begin penetrating the hitherto secure borders of the United States and attacking the institutional cornerstones of American society. Led by a terrorist superstar no longer satisfied with creating isolated international incidents, these cannon-fodder terrorist armies decide to strike at the very symbols of American society. They are putting into effect on a larger scale the "philosophy of bomb throwing" that Joseph Conrad in *The Secret Agent* (1905) so ironically defined. In that novel, Comrade Vladimir insists that terrorism, in order to generate worldwide outrage and the accompanying press coverage, must attack not people or property but universal ideas such as "Science" and "Time." Fittingly, he orders his terrorist pawn Verloc to bomb the Greenwich Observatory.

The Chuck Norris shoot-em-up *Invasion USA* (1985) is perhaps the best example of this action film exploitation of the terrorist scenario. Terrorist superstar Mikhail Rostov (Richard Lynch) in World War II landing craft makes a beachhead on the Florida coast, sends an army of terrorists ashore and packs them into a fleet of rental trucks to disperse them throughout American society. It is not quite the Normandy invasion, but Chuck Norris films tend to operate on a lower budget. "America has not been invaded by a foreign army in over 200 years," Rostov gloats. The terrorists systematically attack every American institution and idea. Naturally, the CIA lures counterterrorist superstar Matt Hunter (Norris) out of retirement to stop Rostov's army. Rostov and Hunter are old adversaries of the terrorism wars. With this rudimentary action plot in place, *Invasion USA* becomes a film about what a terrorist invasion of America would be like and what kinds of targets it would attack.

What is interesting about *Invasion USA* is the symbolic quality of the targets. The invasion takes place during the Christmas season and the first target is a Spielbergian surburban neighborhood of ranch homes. Children are everywhere decorating houses and trees with Christmas lights and playing ball in the street as a terrorist squad pulls up in a pickup truck and rockets houses, cars, boats—opens fire on the American family and the symbols of the American dream. This scene graphically underscores *Rollover*'s warning about "the illusion of safety" and Wulfgar's tense "there's no security" in *Nighthawks*. Subsequently, the terrorists dress up as police and shoot up a Chicano Community Center dance, plant a Christmas present bomb in a shopping mall, wire up with explosives a church where the community has gathered to pray for deliverance from terrorism, open fire on a supermarket, and place a time bomb on a school bus full of children who are ironically singing, "merrily, merrily, merrily, merrily, life is but a dream." When the National Guard is called out to combat this reign of terror, the terrorists dress as guardsmen. This whole daisy chain of confrontations between Hunter and the terrorists has its ironic symbolic side. The terrorists attack the foundations of American life: the family, uniformed authority, community solidarity, shopping, religion, and the childish dream that America is safe from terrorism.

Like Wulfgar in *Nighthawks* and Kahlil in *The Little Drummer Girl*, Rostov is a superstar out to catch the eye of the media. He sits and laughs before a bank of TV sets in his headquarters trailer, as a TV anchorman assures the world that the "three major networks issued a joint statement today denying that television coverage of terrorist activities has in any way compounded their effect." As in all terrorist scenarios, Rostov knows that the only desired effect of international terrorism is media coverage. When he learns that Hunter has been taken to the Governor's Conference in

Atlanta, he marshals his terrorist army for an attack on the symbolic representatives of all of American society. Like the suicide truck speeding into the Marine barracks in Beirut, Rostov's trucks crash into the Governor's Conference compound. The terrorist army floods into the conference center firing at full automatic, but there is no one there. Terrorism does not lend itself to pitched battle with trained armies. Rostov's terrorists have been lured into a trap and the U.S. Army decimates them. Terrorism is designed to function in isolation against the innocent and unsuspecting, not in public confrontation against the experienced.

Invasion USA is not Chuck Norris's only confrontation with terrorists for cannon fodder. In *The Delta Force* (1986) Norris as Major Scott McCoy is called in to rescue the passengers of an airliner hijacked by terrorists. The whole scenario meticulously imitates the 1985 hijacking of TWA Flight 847 right down to its courageous female flight attendant and the throwing of the dead body of a tortured hostage out of the plane onto the tarmac. But Chuck Norris was not the only terrorist-buster operating in the eighties. Charles Bronson in *The Evil That Men Do* (1984) plays a hired assassin taking on a terrorist superstar torturer and his moronic gang in a South American country. In *Iron Eagle* (1986), Lou Gossett, Jr., plays a decorated Air Force pilot who hooks up with the son (Jason Gedrich) of an Air Force pilot being held captive by what appear to be Iranian terrorists in a small Middle East country. The biggest box-office success of all of these cannon-fodder terrorist actioners, however, is *Die Hard*. A combination of *Towering Inferno* (1974) and *Nighthawks*, *Die Hard* pits inventive New York cop John McClane (Bruce Willis) against a gang of international terrorists who have invaded and are holding for ransom a Century City Los Angeles high-rise. Ironically *Die Hard* presents a scenario in which the eighties villain, the terrorist, attacks the seventies villain, the corporation, in this case a Japanese corporation operating in America. It is a disaster movie, but the disaster is no longer caused by a violent eruption of nature. Eighties disasters are man-made and politically motivated while remaining equally unsparing of any human sympathy. In *Die Hard*, terrorism is the equivalent of the fire in *Towering Inferno*. It blazes up, takes a whole microcosm of society captive, then bursts out at each shift in the wind with violent reaction which thwarts all attempts to rationally deal with it.

Like the other terrorists of the films of the eighties, *Die Hard*'s terrorists (in the anti-*Star Trek* mode) are multinational (German, Italian, Oriental) and led by a button-down superstar, Hans Gruber (Alan Rickman). Gruber's first exercise in the rhetoric of terrorism is to claim credit and justify the action: "Due to the Nakatone Corporation's legacy of greed around the globe," Gruber announces, "they are about to be taught a lesson in the *real* use of power."

The L.A. news media are among the first on the scene of the terrorist take-over, and they become the butt of *Die Hard*'s satire. In fact, *Die Hard* is as much a wiseguy action comedy as it is a terrorist disaster thriller. The TV correspondent, Richard Thornburgh (William Atherton), is a pompous clown in the Ted Baxter (of "The Mary Tyler Moore Show") mold. "This is Richard Thornburgh live from Century City," he intones. "Tonight Los Angeles has joined the sad and worldwide fraternity of cities whose only membership requirement is to suffer the anguish of international terrorism." His portentous characterization of the situation becomes a huge joke as the theater audience learns that the supposed terrorists are renegades out for money with little concern for political concessions. In fact, Gruber uses politics as a smokescreen to distract the authorities from his real intention. He employs the rhetoric of terrorism to make extravagant political demands upon the police surrounding the building—

> Attention police . . . This is Hans Gruber . . . I have comrades in arms around the world languishing in prison. The American State Department enjoys rattling its saber for its own and now it can rattle it for me. The following people are to be released from their captors. In northern Ireland, the seven members of the New Provo Front. In Canada, the five imprisoned leaders of the Liberte-de-Quebec. In Sri Lanka, the nine members of the Asian Dawn. (Aside.) I read about them in *Time* magazine.

—then laughs at his own rhetorical ploy. The satire of the media coverage of terrorism becomes a send-up when the network conducts an interview with the author of *Hostage/Terrorist, Terrorist/Hostage: A Study in Duality*. On this airwave exercise in psychobabble, a Professor Hasseldorf recites so much gibberish that it leaves both Hans Gruber and John McClane in stitches. Hasseldorf theorizes:

> by this time the hostages should be going through the early stages of the Helsinki Syndrome. . . . Basically, it's when the hostages and the terrorists go through a sort of psychological transference and a sort of dependency. A strange sort of trust and bond develops. We've had situations where the hostages have even befriended their captors and even corresponded with them in prison.

John McClane does not opt for the Helsinki Syndrome. His personal hardboiled mode of transference is to terrorize the terrorists. He laughs at the pompous FBI agents who try to tell him to back off via walky-talky. Scoffing, he says: "They got the Universal Terrorist playbook and they're running it step by step." McClane realizes that in this terrorist game, there are no rules, no plays, no winners or losers. It is all just an extravaganza being staged for television.

While always an exploitation movie, *Die Hard* is the only terrorist movie with a real sense of humor. Hans Gruber, the superstar, is surpassingly droll and John McClane is wacky in a Yosemite Sam style. But the real comedy of the film lies in its send-up of the news media's ineptitude at covering and complicity in abetting acts of terrorism. Other eighties comedies, such as *Beverly Hills Cop* (1984) and *Ishtar* (1987), employed scenarios of terrorism and arms dealing as backdrops for schtick. One film, *Deal of the Century* (1983), built its comedy exclusively upon the machinations (not nearly as absurd as they seem) of international arms dealers supplying terrorist groups. *Die Hard* is a very savvy film that did its homework on terrorism. It focuses closely (and comically, satirically) upon the fact that terrorism and the media willingly sustain a necessary symbiotic relationship.

The Control Text The rhetoric of political terrorism is conscientiously designed to read well in the mouths of media reporters. Ironically the most frequent protagonists of the second terrorist film text, the control text, which examines death squad governmental terrorism, are journalists (print and TV reporters), who are so often exploited in the classical political text of European and Middle East terrorism. In the films that examine the death squad terrorism text, located most often in Central and South American countries, journalists serve as witnesses to the act of terrorism and unwilling participants or interpreters in the rhetoric of terrorism.

As was the case with the Vietnam War films, the first commentators upon the control terrorism of death squad governments were the novelists. Writers like Graham Greene in *The Honorary Consul* (1973) and Robert Stone in *A Flag for Sunrise* (1981) first rendered the landscape of repression and revolution in South and Central America that would become a major focus of eighties' political films. These films take sides against repressive death squad rule. Most are anti-American in their political message. In 1986, Alex Cox, discussing his project about the life of nineteenth-century adventurer William Walker who became the first American president of Nicaragua, said: "It's just like what's going on now with the United States trying to run Nicaragua and Salvador."[12]

The eighties film industry's fascination with death squad terrorism was a political lesson learned from the Vietnam years. Whereas Hollywood (with the exception of *The Green Berets*) had virtually ignored Vietnam while that war was in session, there was in the eighties a resolve not to miss the opportunity for contemporary political filmmaking, to express insight into social history during the fact rather than after the fact. Even that movie spinoff industry of the rock video participated. The video for The Rolling Stones' "Under Cover of the Night" presented in four minutes a history of totalitarianism in a South American country complete with automatic weapons fire, torture, and executions.

But by far the most popular scenario for the political examinations of control terrorism was the "innocents abroad" plot. In films like *Missing* (1982) and *Under the Volcano* (1984), ordinary American or British citizens hanging out south of the border find themselves enmeshed in death squad government repression. In *The Official Story* (1985), a child's innocence becomes a pawn of fascistic government. But most often the "innocent abroad" is an international journalist or photographer, a recorder of facts, supposedly immune to both the atrocities and the moralities of war, who encounters human oppression and brutality in the world of these death squad government countries. In films like *Under Fire* (1983), *Salvador* (1986), *The Year of Living Dangerously* (1983), and *The Killing Fields*, journalists and photographers find themselves in a situation much like that of Antonioni's photographer in *Blow-Up* (1966). They do their jobs of tracking down, capturing, and recording reality, but they soon realize that under totalitarian governments things are never what they seem, reality is totally manipulable for political purposes, and the only way to fight back is to intentionally falsify reality themselves.

Roger Spottiswoode's *Under Fire* is a major mainstream Hollywood effort that presents the text of control terrorism. It is about seeing, recording, trying to understand, and finally acting against the realities of death squad terrorism. As in Antonioni's *Blow-Up*, the film's central metaphor is photography. The line between shooting pictures and shooting guns ultimately blurs for Russell Price (Nick Nolte). Sharing a prison cell with a priest who supports Raphael, the charismatic leader of this version of the 1979 Sandinista revolution to overthrow Anastasio Somoza in Nicaragua, Price is asked, "Who's side are you on anyway?" He answers naïvely, "I don't take sides. I take pictures." Ironically by the end of the film, his pictures will become death warrants for their subjects, and he will, indeed, take sides by taking propaganda pictures of the already dead Raphael.

While Russell Price is an existential character capable of development and change, perhaps the most symbolic type character is Oates (Ed Harris), the amoral, disengaged, mercenary soldier, who serves as Price's alter ego. The two have been encountering each other in war zones for years, with Oates carrying a gun and Price a camera. Neither is involved in any personal way in the wars being fought around them. At the beginning of *Under Fire* when Price meets Oates in the back of a truckload of soldiers, Oates does not even know which side the soldiers are on. Both men are parasites feeding off the war in Chad, and when they move on to Nicaragua, it is just another assignment.

When Price and Oates meet up again in a church steeple in the middle of a firefight in Nicaragua, Oates is playing dead, supposedly killed by a grenade thrown by a young man with a great arm who idolizes the big league pitcher Dennis Martinez. This ironic juxtaposition of the innocence of throwing baseballs and the reality of throwing grenades parallels the irony of Price's decision involving shooting pictures and shooting guns. Price chooses to not tell the rebels that Oates is playing possum. In turn, as

Price and the young pitcher walk away from the firefight laughing, Oates suddenly shoots the young man in the back. Heeding an institutional impulse to become *engagé* as the young pitcher falls dead, Price drops his camera to the ground and picks up the rifle. It is a symbolic act that Price will be forced to repeat in order to save his own life later in the film.

Michael Herr in *Dispatches* writes:

> We covered each other, an exchange of services that worked alright until one night when I slid over to the wrong end of the story, propped behind some sandbags at an airstrip in Cantho with a .30 caliber automatic in my hands firing cover for a four-man reaction team trying to get back in . . . we were in the Alamo, no place else, and I wasn't a reporter, I was a shooter.[13]

Allusions to Vietnam are peppered throughout *Under Fire*. In one sequence the camera pans over the rooftop bar of the Hotel Continental where the journalists all sit drinking and watching Somoza's plane bombing his own capital. These journalists are spectators to the war, disengaged. What happens to Michael Herr at Cantho, however, is exactly what happens to Russell Price in *Under Fire*. In order to remain human, he must become involved. As with Antonioni's photographer in *Blow-Up*, Coppola's wiretapper in *The Conversation* (1974) and DePalma's sound man in *Blow Out* (1981), it is not good enough for Price to just take pictures. In fact, late in *Under Fire* direct allusion is made to *Blow-Up* as Price breaks into Jazy's house and finds a darkroom with all of Price's pictures of the rebels in their camp pinned to the wall and marked for death with red *X*'s.

Beyond this theme of becoming *engagé*, the motif of photography in *Under Fire* also represents another major theme, that of the elusiveness of reality, that seventies theme of "nothing is ever what it seems." *Under Fire* is a film about "images," not just the photographic images of Price that may be true (in their expressing of the reality of the Chad war or of Alex Grazier's murder by the Guardia) or false (in his propaganda posing of the already dead Rafael) but all the other illusory images that everyone in Nicaragua projects to hide the reality of their roles in the political conflict. In Nicaragua in 1979 everyone has a double role and everyone is a PR-man. The translator whom Price meets at the embassy in Managua turns up later as a rebel. The influential French businessman, Jazy (Jean-Louis Trintagnant), is a spy for both the Somoza government and the CIA. Hub Kittle (Richard Masur) claims to be a PR-man from New York, but everyone knows that he is CIA. Nicaragua in 1979 is a veritable spookfest.

All of these double-identitied characters, not just Kittle, are also PR-men. As is the photographer Price, they are all involved with images, each projecting a false image for the purpose of publicizing a political view. Kittle admits to being a PR-man for Somoza but is really projecting the American CIA line. Jazy is a PR-man for the American interests who support Somoza. Realizing that they are losing the public relations war, the rebels recruit Price to take their PR photograph of the dead Rafael. Even the statue of the dictator in the town square has a double identity; originally it was a statue of Mussolini that Somoza got cheap and put his own head on. The shooting war of death squad terrorism becomes co-equal with the public relations war of false image projection.

From the beginning, the theme of the power and fragility of photographic images of reality is visually stressed. The technique of the sudden freeze-framing switch from motion picture color to still photography black and white is this film's visual trope for the ongoing theme of the difficulty of capturing and interpreting reality. History is not composed of freeze-framed black-and-white facts but involves the photographs of moments of reality that could be true or, just as easily, staged. The first use of this freeze-frame, color-to-black-and-white technique is in Price's dramatic photographs of a helicopter gunship attacking an elephant convoy in the Chad civil war. All through the rest of the film, especially during firefights, this symbolic method of freezing reality is used. At first, Price's photographs are true and unambigious. They are pictures of a war being fought, of refugees fleeing, of individuals dying, of his lover sleeping. Later, however, as he becomes involved with the rebel cause, Price starts taking photographs that alter and manipulate reality. In the rebel village he takes pictures of the dead Rafael that make that leader seem alive and that reinvigorate the revolution. Those photos will be used to convince both the rebels still fighting and the United States, which is trying to decide whether Somoza can win and whether they should send him additional arms, that the rebel leadership is still strong. But Price also takes pictures of the everyday life of the people in that rebel village. Ironically those pastoral pictures taken for Price's own amusement later became death warrants for their objects.

This freeze-frame color switching technique of visual imagery (also used in the brilliant 1988 film about the Russian invasion of Czechoslovakia, *The Unbearable Lightness of Being*) has the effect of allowing the audience to both witness reality and then immediately have the opportunity to interpret that reality. In other words, this technique allows history and criticism to immediately work together.

The one image the control terrorists in the Somoza government, especially Jazy who uses Price's innocent pictures of the rebels to find and kill those people, want to downplay is the death squad terrorist reality of the Guardia's role. It is Price's uneditorialized sequence of pictures of the murder of TV network anchorman Alex Grazier (Gene Hackman) by the Guardia that exposes that ugly image.

Images can tell the truth or lie. False images can be projected and true images can be suppressed. Reality is rarely what it seems because control terrorism involves not only controlling the citizens by terrorizing them but also controlling the images of reality that the outside world receives.

Whereas the political terrorism of Europe and the Middle East is intent upon generating media coverage for its cause, the control terrorism of Central and South America is intent upon suppressing media coverage of its actions and manipulating media coverage toward false positive views of itself. The visual trope of freeze-frame, color-to-black-and-white switching in *Under Fire* underlines the differences between reality and interpretation.

However, in the holographic use of this metaphor of photography to present themes on different levels, *Under Fire* goes further. Through this photography metaphor, it expands its themes from the existential level of Price's need for engagement to the philosophical level of consistent tampering with the nature of reality in a control terrorism situation to a more universal political level. *Under Fire* captures in this trope of photography the confusion not only of the press as to how to deal with Central and South America but of the American public as to who is right and who is wrong south of the border.

Because the images are so conflicting, the contending realities so confusing, in eighties America nobody seems to know who the good guys and the bad guys are in Central and South America. Nobody seems to know the answer to the question of whether the United States government should be interfering in countries like El Salvador, Nicaragua, Panama, Columbia. As was graphically the case in Vietnam, the media are handcuffed by this control terrorist rhetoric of confusion. The press tries to report the facts of these civil wars, but those facts are constantly being doctored before they are made available to the press. The press tries not to editorialize, but the so-called facts beg for interpretation. The goal of the rhetoric of control terrorism is to sustain confusion both in-country and in the international media, to manipulate reality, and if worse comes to worst, to totally obscure reality in favor of a false PR "image."

Over and over in *Under Fire*'s dialogue, this theme of confusion about the nature of reality surfaces. None of the characters, as is also the case in Oliver Stone's *Platoon*, seem able to escape the confusion, to order their world. By the embassy pool on his first day in Nicaragua, Russell Price is initiated into this universal confusion:

PRICE: Who is Rafael?

GRAZIER: Depends on who you ask.

INTERPRETOR: Rafael. Commandante Rafael. He is either a Marxist dupe of Russia and Cuba or the most popular leader of a most popular Democratic revolution. Take your pick.

What she is telling Price is that he is not going to get the answer to his question from anyone but himself, that reality exists only in interpretation.

For the cynical media veterans and the spooks in 1979 Nicaragua this rhetoric of confusion is a too-obvious joke, an ongoing PR game that everyone is playing in the competition to sell their side of the civil war. Seeing straight through each other, yet continuing to play the tongue-in-cheek game, Russell Price and Hub Kittle discuss the Nicaraguan revolution, its confusion, its PR aspects:

KITTLE: Listen Russell, let's grow up. It's very easy to fall in love with the underdog, but there's an upside and a downside to this thing. Just want to remind you that all this stuff about a revolution of poets is crap.

PRICE: It's good PR though (he chuckles), isn't it Hub? So what's the upside?

KITTLE: Simple, and it could happen. Somoza destroys the terrorist insurgents, rebuilds the country, cans the purveyors of excess, stabilizes the cordoba and is finally beloved as the savior of Nicaragua (here Price and Kittle both have a good laugh). Got a smoke?

PRICE: So what's the downside?

KITTLE: Commies take over the world.

The rhetoric of control terrorism feeds on confusion because these death squad governments consistently employ PR imagemaking to hide the reality that the governments themselves, not the insurgents, are the terrorists. Both Price and Kittle are cynical gameplayers laughing at the rhetoric they employ and at themselves for employing it.

One critic desribed *Under Fire* as a film about "love, war and the press in Central America,"[14] but it really is not about any of those things. *Under Fire* is holographically layered with existential, historical, and philosophical themes. It is an existential film about the necessity for personal engagement in the moral struggles of our times. It is a historical film about the methods of control terrorism in Central America. It is a philosophical-ethical film about the illusory nature of reality. Richard Bernstein describes *Under Fire* as a film about journalistic ethics that poses the question: "Can the journalist under any circumstances join forces with those he is supposed to be covering?"[15] But that is too narrow a view. *Under Fire* ultimately is less about journalistic editorializing and ethics and more about the journalist's attempt to find some truth in a rhetoric and confusion of images intended to obscure reality. Once censorship is lifted in a war (as it was in Vietnam) then new modes of manipulating the news must be found. In uncensored wars, the implementing of the rhetoric of control terrorism via PR manipulation became the new form of censorship. If one cannot control reality, one must simply deconstruct reality to the point where no one else can control it either. The result is a universal confusion that works to the benefit of the control terrorist government.

Three years after Roger Spottiswood presented those freeze-framed, color-to-black-and-white switched images in *Under Fire*, Oliver Stone's film *Salvador* (1986), its impact and meaning also based on striking photographic images, appeared. But Stone's images, which feed *Salvador*'s pace and pull together its long passages of political exposition, are different from Spottiswood's in *Under Fire*. Where Spottiswood was reaching for a symbolic depth that needed to be stopped in order to be analysed, Stone is going for the realist shock of being in the middle of unthinkable human aberration. Stone's images do not have to be analysed. They are immediate and shocking: a burning body in the road, the execution by the Guardia of a student in the street (reminiscent of the most famous photo of the Vietnam War), bodies piled on the steps of a cathedral, a dump site for death squad victims that looks like an extermination camp out of the Holocaust, drunken gun-toting jailers standing over the mutilated bodies of tortured prisoners, the assasination of an archbishop at the Communion rail, the broken bodies of children who have been tortured, finally the graphic rape and murder of three nuns and an American worker by a death squad. Each of these images is of unimaginable violence. Each is served neat, its reality undiluted, not editorialized upon or frozen and analyzed. Each is powerful and shocking. The difference between the images of these two films is that Stone's combat photographer, unlike Russell Price in *Under Fire*, does not get the pictures, the stopped images to study. The images that Richard Boyle (James Woods) wants to photograph are so shocking, so sickening, so scary that he cannot shoot them. He wanders dazed amidst the havoc and the bodies trying to hold on to his sanity and survive.

The opening of *Salvador* consciously attempts to out-Costa-Gavras Costa-Gavras. The credits roll over blurry black-and-white slow-motion images (reminiscent of the stop-action black-and-white trope of *Under Fire*) of a massacre by the Guardia of civilians on the steps of a church. The film is dated to 1980–81 and an America TV news anchor intones: "In the wake of the Nicaraguan Revolution, chaos has descended upon tiny El Salvador in Central America. . . . so far in two months over three thousand people have disappeared. Government spokesmen have attributed the murders to the left-wing Marxist terrorists, while left-wing spokesmen point to the right-wing death squads. U.S. government spokesmen will only identify these assailants as . . ." Fittingly that voice leaves everything hanging when it comes to any American evaluation of the situation. Thus *Salvador* starts out by emphasizing that same theme of a rhetoric of confusion necessary to the control terrorist text. Corpses are piled high in town squares and on the hillsides, and nobody seems to know who is doing it.

Ironically the most confused of all is Tom Kelly (Michael Murphy), the American ambassador to El Salvador. Military intelligence in the form of the appropriately named Colonel Hyde (Will MacMillan) and the CIA in the form of yuppie country clubber Jack Morgan (Colby Chester) feed Kelly the Reagan view of the guerrillas and whitewashed view of Mayor Max (Tony Plano), the leader of the death squads and the country's major right-wing political figure. At the same time, Cathy Moore (Cindy Gibb), an American AID worker, and Boyle try to feed him the opposite view, that of the people of Salvador. Kelly never does figure out what is going on. Chaos truly does reign in El Salvador from the highest echelons to the streets. Upon that chaos the control terrorism of the death squads thrives. They offer themselves as a source of order, murderous as it may be, in the midst of this terrible confusion. Kelly clearly defines his confusion and that of the whole American public toward Central America when he sums up the political situation in El Salvador as "a pathological killer on the right, god knows what on the left and a gutless middle."

But the newly elected president of the United States, Ronald Reagan, shows himself on television to be just as confused about El Salvador as Kelly. On TV Reagan stutters that America should try "to halt the infiltration into the Americas by terrorists, by outside interference, and those who are not just aiming at El Salvador, but, I think, are aiming at the whole Central and possibly later South America and I'm sure eventually North America." What Reagan does not realize is that the people whom he is calling terrorist infiltrators have lived in the country they are supposedly terrorizing all of their lives. Dr. Rock (James Belushi), Richard Boyle's sidekick, has the best evaluation of Reagan's confusion. "Can you believe that a straight man to a chimpanzee is going to be the next president?"

The CIA, in the form of Hub Kittle in *Under Fire* and Jack Morgan in *Salvador*, certainly seems to agree with the Reagan view. "Nicaragua was just the beginning, Guatemala and Honduras are targeted next. In five years you're gonna be seeing Cuban tanks on the Rio Grande," Morgan explains to Richard Boyle at an embassy cocktail party just before asking Boyle to spook for the CIA. He wants Boyle to do the same thing Jazy did for Somoza in *Under Fire*; he wants Boyle to pass on any pictures taken of the rebels for Morgan's MI delectation.

When Boyle asks Major Max "it is widely rumored that you are the head of the Death Squads terrorizing this country," Major Max answers with a textbook exercise in control terrorism's rhetoric of confusion: "I really resent that question. Why do you never ask the Communists this? They are not the only victims. We have victims too. They know there are no Death Squads in El Salvador. The outrage of the people against the communists cannot be stopped or organized by one man." He denies the existence of death squads while at the same time acknowledging that there are death squad victims. John Cassady (John Savage), a photographer for *Newsweek*, is the first to cut through the rhetoric of confusion for Boyle. "Nobody cares about this stinking little war," Cassady tells Boyle. "They're not just shootin' Indians. Last week a Mexican TV guy got blown away by their paramilitary groups. They're shootin' at us." In El Salvador, everybody seems to be shooting at everybody, and everyone still standing is spouting a rhetoric of confusion. The ongoing goal of this rhetoric of confusion is to continuously muddy the issue so that the outside world will never find out what is really happening in-country.

Finally, Boyle cannot listen to this rhetoric of confusion any longer. He sits Morgan and Hyde down and talks straight about the origins and political motives of support for death squad government terrorism. This speech confronts the rhetoric of confusion with a passionate directness that is equivalent in words to those shocking realist images of death squad terrorism that have given pattern, pace, and structure to Stone's film:

> BOYLE: C'mon Jack, when are you gonna believe what your eyes see and not what your Military Intelligence tells you to think . . .
>
> HYDE: We've got evidence to prove 10,000 percent that this ain't no civil war but outright Commie agression.
>
> BOYLE: You were the ones who trained Major Max in the Police Academy in Washington. You were the ones who trained Jose Madrano and Rene Chacon. You taught them how to torture and how to kill, and then you sent them here. And what did Chacon give us. He gave us the Mano Blanco. I mean, what are the Death Squads but the brainchild of the CIA? But you'll run with them because they're anti-Moscow. You let them close down the universities. You let them wipe out the best minds in the country. You let them kill whoever they want. You let them wipe out the Catholic Church. You let them do it all because they aren't commies. And that, Colonel is BULL SHIT! You have created Major Frankenstein.

That speech rises to the intensity of a Shakespearean soliloquy in James Woods's delivery (reminiscent of Brando's soliloquy on "Big Oil" in 1980's *Formula*)[16] and attests to the strong consciousness of the holographic nature of social history in eighties film. The speech pinpoints every layer of guilt the U.S. shares in the creation and sustenance of death squad terrorism. It is a high point in the eighties cinema of social history.

In a speech later in *Salvador*, Boyle makes clear how this rhetoric of confusion can spread and corrupt. Once the control terrorist mentality of the death squad takes over a country, its evil infects everyone, even its former victims. Early in the film, a Guardia officer executes a student in the street, gun to kneeling victim's head. Late in the film, during the battle for San Miguel, the guerrillas decide to execute the Guardia prisoners they have taken. When Boyle stumbles upon the prisoners kneeling with arms bound as a female guerrilla with a revolver moves from one to the next firing into the backs of their heads, he screams, "You'll become just like them!"

Once the political blood lust of death squad terrorism takes hold, it becomes near impossible to resist. For all of Richard Boyle's sleaziness of nature, he still cannot believe that human nature can continue to descend to the depths of evil that exists under the control terrorism of the death squad governments. As he condemns both sides in this El Salvador war,

Boyle rejects any political idealism that may have at one time drawn him to the guerrillas and realizes that death squad terrorism descends below the political into the power urges of the individual. Like the Vietnam war films of both the late 1970s and of 1986–87, *Salvador* is a "heavy heart of darkness trip."[17] Unlike *Under Fire* it does not freeze and then step back to analyze its images. *Salvador*'s images are immediate and powerful in their killing realism. *Salvador*'s images are meant to shock, not to carry layers of symbolic meaning.

From Nicaragua in *Under Fire* to *Salvador* to a thinly disguised Chile in Costa-Gavras's *Missing* (1982) to an unspecified South American country in Hector Babenco's *Kiss of the Spider Woman* (1985) to Argentina and Paraguay in *Beyond the Limit* (1983) to 1930s Mexico in John Huston's *Under the Volcano* (1984), the reality and the rhetoric of death squad terrorism vary little. *Missing*, the earliest of these South American control terrorism films presents the same images and the same exposing of a rhetoric of confusion as do *Under Fire* and *Salvador*. Costa-Gavras presents Santiago as a city locked in a "state of seige." It is an armed camp in the days immediately following a military coup and a free fire zone at night after curfew. The coup has been engineered by U.S. Military Intelligence advisers, the same spooks who show up later in *Salvador*. The streets are terrorized by the same Guardia thugs who cold-bloodedly murder Alex Grazier in *Under Fire*. These thugs pull young women out of lines at bus stops and declare "from now on women in this country wear dresses" as they cut their pants off. The same images of dead bodies in the street, bodies floating down rivers, piles of nameless "disappeared" bodies stacked like cordwood, punctuate the film for grim emphasis. These brutal images of control form a visual trope which runs through all of these death squad terrorism films. But the central trope of Costa-Gavras's *Missing* is an audio trope, the constant insistent background sound of gunfire in the streets. As the film's characters move about the city of Santiago, drive, walk, eat their meals, gunfire consistently cracks, and when it does the characters instinctively flinch and the film jumps with signification.

Missing's story is one of the hundreds of thousands of stories of the Latin American "disappeared." Charles Horman (John Shea), however, a free-lance writer working for a leftist newspaper in Santiago, Chile, is not allowed to stay "disappeared" because of the efforts of his wife Beth (Cissy Spacek) and his father, Ed Horman (Jack Lemmon), a conservative Christian Scientist businessman whose change of consciousness is the focal center of the film. What Beth and Ed find out during their efforts to find the missing Charles is that their real enemy is the conspiracy of American spooks who have orchestrated the coup, encouraged the Guardia in their death squad tactics, and are intent on veiling the whole affair in a rhetoric of confusion. "Don't worry, they can't hurt us. We're Americans," Charlie tells Beth the last time he sees her before his disappearance. But his confidence is naïve in a country ruled by death squad terrorism. Later, a young Chilean in hiding laughs at that naïveté: "You Americans. You always assume you have to do something in order to be arrested." When the American Ambassador speculates to Beth and Ed that Charlie may be in hiding, Beth screams, "We all know he's not in hiding. The whole neighborhood saw him picked up by a goon squad." Made early in the eighties, *Missing*'s expose approach to death squad terrorism leans heavily on visual and verbal references to the Vietnam War. One of the American military spooks describes the Guardia's control tactics in the streets of Santiago: "The military are doing search and destroy missions just like in Vietnam. There's bodies everywhere." As helicopters pour fire down into the streets of the city, tourists in cocktail dresses and tuxedos watch the fighting from the balcony of a fancy hotel. Finally, the film focuses upon a single symbolic place, the National Stadium, where all of the prisoners rounded up by the Guardia goon squads are taken for interrogation, internment, and disappearance. Entering the National Stadium is a descent into an underworld, a place of national play transformed into a mass torture chamber. The bodies are piled in underground rooms and corridors. Into this heart of darkness the victims of control terrorism disappear.

For Ed Horman, however, because of his religious belief, the physical evils of death squad terrorism are matched by the spiritual evil of the rhetoric of confusion that this government employs under the benevolent sanction of the United States. Ed's driver from the American embassy asks:

DRIVER: If you don't mind my asking, what's Christian Science about?

ED: It's about faith.

DRIVER: Faith in what?

ED: Faith in truth.

That exchange sums up what these films about journalists and other "innocents abroad" caught in the grip of death squad terrorist governments are all about—individuals trying to cut through the control terrorist rhetoric of confusion to find the truth of what that rhetoric is attempting to hide.

This same desire for truth amidst the rhetoric of confusion is expressed by Dr. Eduardo Plarr (Richard Gere) in *Beyond the Limit*, the Christopher Hampton screen adaptation of Graham Greene's novel *The Honorary Consul*. Eduardo is a doctor in a small city in northern Argentina on the border of Paraguay. He has moved from Buenos Aires to this city in order to pursue information about his father who is a political prisoner in Paraguay. Unlike his father, he is uninvolved in politics but is drawn into a guerrilla scheme by his boyhood friend Leon (Joaquin De Almeida), a former priest who wants to kidnap the visiting American ambassador. Unwilling to become involved, Eduardo is drawn into the kidnapping when the guerrillas promise to exchange the ambassador for his father. Only then does he realize that he has been duped by the rhetoric of confusion of the guerrillas. He expresses the same desire for truth that Ed Horman expressed in *Missing*:

> EDUARDO: You lying bastards. My father died a year ago.
>
> LEON: We had to be sure you'd help us.
>
> EDUARDO: You used me. Did you use my father too. I have to know what happened, the truth.

In the jails, guerrilla camps, and embassies of these Central and South American countries, the truth is an elusive entity that the whole political rhetoric of the hemisphere seems intent upon obscuring.

Dr. Plarr's search for his father and attempts to avoid political involvement are further complicated by his love affair with the former-prostitute wife of the Honorary British Consul to the region, Sir Charles Fortnum (Michael Caine), a whiskey-soaked remnant of the British Empire. This love affair with Clara (Elpidio Carrero) ironically parallels Dr. Plarr's political involvement. He is drawn irresistibly into it just as he is drawn into the guerillas' kidnap scheme. Both the love affair and the politics confuse Plarr, seem built upon illusions. After making love to Clara he asks her not to fake her orgasms as prostitutes do. "I want you to be yourself," he tells her. "I'm not interested in illusions." But illusion is the way of life in this Argentine city. Eduardo holds the illusion that the chief of police, Colonel Perez (Bob Hoskins), is on the side of justice, that the guerrillas can help him find his father who has been "disappeared," that he loves Clara. When Leon asks him if he is being watched, Eduardo answers, "I don't think so. This isn't Paraguay." Leon only laughs at Eduardo's naïveté, "the way things are these days there isn't much difference." The region is wrapped in the rhetoric of confusion.

All of the same images of death squad control terrorism that appeared in the other South American films are also present in *Beyond the Limit*. It opens at a Guardia roadblock after which the everyday life of Dr. Plarr is intercut with scenes of fascistic oppression: students being prodded by rifle butts through the halls of a jail, a Guardia soldier shredding documents, a handcuffed prisoner dripping blood being dragged down a hallway by a policeman, the Guardia running through the halls of a hospital and arresting by force two hundred mentally disturbed patients as political subversives.

These recurrent images of the control terrorism films become much more graphic the deeper Dr. Plarr becomes involved both with Colonel

Perez of the Guardia and with Leon of the guerrillas. Perez brings the bullet-riddled body of a young boy to the hospital for Dr. Plarr to issue a death certificate. Perez insists the boy was shot while trying to escape. "Was he trying to escape backwards?" Plarr asks. Graphic flashback images of a Guardia jail explode in Dr. Plarr's mind as one of the guerrillas describes the music played very loud to mask the screams of the prisoners, the rubber truncheons of the torturers, the bathtub full of shit that they submerge prisoners in. But the one image that echoes throughout *Beyond the Limit* and all the other control terrorism films is the Vietnam War photo image of summary execution in the street. Eduardo's father is executed in this manner when caught trying to escape, and the film ends with the Guardia executing Eduardo Plarr as he lies helpless in the mud.

In *Beyond the Limit*, the exchange when Eduardo Plarr discovers the guerrillas' mistake in kidnapping Charlie Fortnum instead of the American ambassador best defines the irony of death squad terrorism:

EDUARDO: Amatuers!

LEON: We are amatuers. All of us, on our side. It is the police and the Army who are the professionals.

In Latin America, terrorism has become the whip and chair of government rather than the PR tool of isolated political factions.

Hector Babenco's *Kiss of the Spider Woman*, adapted from Argentine Manuel Puig's 1976 novel, also examines the oppressive terrorism of a Fascist government in a thinly disguised Buenos Aires, Argentina, but that examination takes place in a much more restricted, controlled, almost laboratory, environment. *Kiss of the Spider Woman* is a prison movie, 80 percent of which takes place in a cell shared by a flamboyant homosexual, Molina (William Hurt), and a macho intellectual revolutionary, Valentin (Raul Julia). It is through the words of this political prisoner and the prison wardens who exploit and torture everyone that Molina, like Price in *Under Fire*, Boyle in *Salvador*, Plarr in *Beyond the Limit*, realizes that one cannot stay uninvolved in a society governed by death squads.

Like these other films, *Kiss of the Spider Woman* presents its critique of the realities of control terrorism through both the verbal polemics of the political prisoner and the visual images of the acts of torture and death squad murder that occur in the film. When the film opens, Valentin has already been beaten by his jailers during his interrogation. From his cell he sees another prisoner with a black bag pulled over the head being returned from similar interrogation:

VALENTIN: He's really bleeding.

MOLINA: Is he a political prisoner?

VALENTIN: They don't treat you like that for stealing bananas.

This image of a tortured prisoner, his identity and humanity taken away by the bag over his head, is repeated a number of times. Whenever this image of torture occurs, Valentin offers a similar political commentary such as "no crime justifies that kind of punishment!"

As Valentin attempts to justify his life and political involvement to Molina, the necessity of resistance to this death squad terrorism becomes the theme. He tells of his elegant bourgeoise lover, Marta (Sonia Braga), to whom he is attracted even though as a Marxist he detests her lifestyle: "She asked me to leave the movement, but how could I do nothing when my friends were disappearing every day." He tells of changes in his own attitude but realizes that the same government crimes continue: "I no longer believed in violence, but I had to do something. As a journalist I was always hearing about the illegal arrests and secret torture, then leaking this information abroad." Unlike *Salvador* with its powerful unembellished images or *Missing* with its incessant audio (gunfire) punctuation, but quite like *Under Fire*, *Kiss of the Spider Woman* is a more abstract, detached, even symbolic analysis of death squad terrorism. There are images of torture and death, but most of the film is talk. Only at the very end when Molina has been released and decides to become involved with Valentin's movement does the film break from its verbal literariness and present a series of powerful images equal to those of *Salvador*.

Kiss of the Spider Woman ends with yet another execution in the streets. Molina is shot by the revolutionaries he was trying to help but is executed by the police death squad that has had him under surveillance since the moment of his release. The police push his body out of their unmarked car in a garbage dump and forget that he ever existed. This image of human beings dumped like garbage also occurs in *Salvador* and will later be the final image of *Under the Volcano*.

But *Kiss of the Spider Woman* is not only a film of visual and verbal polemic, of abstract theorizing upon social injustice alternated with stark images of torture and death. It also deals in metaphor. In fact, *Kiss of the Spider Woman* is a metamovie, a movie about movies and the relationship of movie illusions to the realities of life. A metamovie is usually a movie about the making of a movie, but in this instance the movie that Molina "tells" to Valentin is the re-creation of a movie for both emotional (to take their minds off their troubles) and symbolic (to complement the film's polemic) reasons. The movie that Molina "tells" to entertain himself and his cellmate is a Nazi propaganda romance in sepia tones. As Molina innocently, romantically, and nonjudgmentally (extremely naïvely) reconstructs each scene, Valentin (who is indeed always entertained) feels compelled to bring Molina back to reality by offering a political critique of the film's motives. As Valentin repeatedly links the actions and emotions of the film to the realities of the political repression of their own time in their own country, the imagined film becomes a metaphor for death squad terrorism. "Your Nazis are about as romantic as the fucking Warden and his torture house," Valentin spits at Molina. As a prisoner is brought back from being tortured, Valentin turns on Molina and screams: "You son of a bitch. They are killing one of my brothers and what am I doing? Listening to your fucking Nazi movie. Don't you know anything? Don't you know what the Nazis did to people? Jews. Marxists. Catholics. Homosexuals." Molina's movie is about Nazis, betrayals, and executions. Though in his naïveté he does not see it, these themes of his imagined movie are all the themes of his life as a tool of the death squad government, of his life as a spy upon Valentin in the prison cell.

The final movie-within-the-movie scene that Molina recounts is not from his Nazi movie but is set on a desert island ruled by the Spider Woman. Molina tells about the terrible dilemma of "a shipwrecked man caught in the huge web of the Spider Woman who cries because she is going to love him and kill him simultaneously." The dual dilemma of this shipwrecked man scene is a metaphor for both Molina's and Valentin's situation in the world of death squad terrorism. Molina is madly in love with Valentin; the "kiss" of the Spider Woman is the curse of anyone who opposes the control terrorism of a death squad government. One opposes out of love for the country, but that country indiscriminately kills those who love it. Death squad governments are black widows who solicit love via the promulgation of death.

Under the Volcano, John Huston's screen adaptation of Malcolm Lowry's 1946 novel, while not as immediate or contemporary or polemic as these other control terrorism films, still bears a close kinship to them. It is no coincidence that a major work of contemporary fiction that has been around for forty years finally was made into a movie in the eighties. Lowry's setting, characters, and themes fit the issues of the eighties in Central and South America perfectly. Set in Mexico, *Under the Volcano* is the story of the last day in the life of a whiskey-soaked British Honorary Consul similar to Graham Greene's Charlie Fortnum. Geoffrey Firmin (Albert Finney), Lowry's and Huston's consul, observes through a drunken haze the political corruption in Mexico and, when he opens his mouth to protest, dies at the hands of a group of equally drunken military Fascisti. As do the victims of the death squad at El Playon in *Salvador*, as does Dr. Plarr in *Beyond the Limit*, as does Molina in *Kiss of the Spider Woman*, Geoffrey Firmin, trapped in a world gone out of control, ends up just another corpse thrown in a garbage dump with the empty bottles and the dead dogs.

The primary text of *Under the Volcano* involves the way in which the chaos of a man's alcoholism as a bar to his moral view of the world mirrors the chaos and loss of moral sense in Mexican society under the spell of fascism. Huston's subtext aligns quite closely with the critiques of other eighties films of contemporary Latin American control governments. Huston presents a moral fable of a man and a country giving up their morality to an intoxicating power. Lowry's *Under the Volcano* was a novel about a drunk with political and moral convictions trying to deal with the onrushing fascism of 1938, but in John Huston's hands it becomes an eighties film about the resurfacing of a similar fascism in Central and South America.

Like *Under the Volcano*, Alex Cox's *Walker* (1988) is a film about an earlier time, Nicaragua in 1855, that serves as a metaphor for the 1980s. Cox's metaphor is about terrorist tactics, not in the hands of a ruling government but rather in the hands of American interventionists' attempts, for economic imperialist purposes, to set up their own control governments on foreign soil. Based on the true story of William Walker, an American adventurer in the pay of Cornelius Vanderbilt, who with an army of mercenaries, Walker's "Immortals," invaded and set himself up as president of Nicaragua in 1855 in order to "stabilize" the country for the furtherance of Vanderbilt's economic schemes, Cox's film becomes a metaphor for American intervention in places like Vietnam, Nicaragua, and El Salvador. Walker's short-lived reign of terror deteriorates into a holocaust of pillage and rape. His "Immortals" become the first functioning death squad in Central America. In one scene Walker (Ed Harris) sends his death squad out to arrest the mayor of Granada whom they execute in the town square. This scene of "arrest and execution" is one of the interchangeable scenes that runs as a motif through all of these control terrorism films.

In a speech to the people of Nicaragua when he declares himself president, Walker threatens:

> You all might think that there will be a day when America will leave Nicaragua alone, but I am here to tell you, flat out, that that day will never happen because it is our destiny to be here. It is our destiny to control you people. So no matter how much you fight or no matter what you think, we will be back again and again.

Walker's heavy-handedness is grounded in that sort of polemic posturing as well as in a wacky anachronistic scrambling of analogic time. In 1855 the "Immortals" talk like a gang of sixties rock-'n'-rollers and are ultimately evacuated from the holocaust they have created by military helicopters. Cox has made a Felliniesque Sam Peckinpah slow-motion blood-spurter that attempts to compress history. Appropriate as his true-story metaphor may be, his handling of it is so idiosyncratic that the result borders on absurdist comedy (or pedantic preaching) rather than political commentary. The same material and the same metaphor were employed to much greater effect in the 1969 film *Burn* in which Marlon Brando played William Walker.

While *Under the Volcano* and *Walker* are different in their metaphoricality from other realistic portrayals of more contemporary control terrorism in

Latin America, *The Official Story* (1985) presents yet another extremely eloquent perspective. Akin to both *Missing* and *Kiss of the Spider Woman* in its primary text of the political awakening to the excess of death squad terrorism of a naïve and innocent bourgeois, *The Official Story* offers an equally powerful subtext examination of the nature of history and its manipulation under fascist rule. *The Official Story* presents no graphic images of death squad terrorism as do *Under Fire, Salvador, Missing*, or *Beyond the Limit*. Rather, it offers a calm, eloquent, detached analysis of the plight of the "*desaparicidos*," the disappeared, in eighties Argentina.

Its text of the discovery of the reality of the *desaparacidos* and its subtext of the shallowness of history in dealing with the realities of death squad terrorism is meticulously revealed through the slow political awakening of Alicia (Norma Aleandro), a bourgeois housewife and mother who works as a high-school history teacher. Alicia and her husband Roberto (Hector Alterio), a successful businessman who works with the Fascist government, have a five-year-old adopted daughter. Alicia first learns of the *desaparacidos* from her girlhood friend Anna (Chunchuna Villafane) when their harmless girl talk one evening departs into Anna's explanation of why she had to go away seven years before. In a long monologue Anna tells Alicia about the Guardia breaking into her house, taking her off to prison, strapping her naked on a table, torturing her with electric prods and submersion in water, and raping her. She ends her monologue by telling Alicia how many people there were in this prison, how pregnant women lost their babies, how prisoners were taken away and never returned, how children were taken from their parents and sold to rich politically connected families. Anna's revelations strike a note of curiosity in Alicia's mind about her own adopted daughter and she begins a personal search for her daughter's parents. "These reports about all those people who are missing," she asks a teaching colleague, "even children . . . are they . . . true?" *The Official Story* is about this bourgeois woman's political awakening to the evil realities of death squad terrorism, but it is also about her awakening to the layered "truth" of history as opposed to the "official story" of history. In this subtext, *The Official Story* may be the ultimate holographic New Historicist film, a film precisely about what Hayden White calls "metahistory."

Early in the film, Alicia naïvely tells her class that "history is the memory of the people." One of her students, however, challenges her and charges that "history is written by assassins." This subtext concerning history is also presented visually, not with graphic images of torture, but with disturbing domestic images of violence. At her daughter's birthday party, little boys with toy guns smash through the door of her daughter's bedroom and frighten the little girl in a parallel to the arrest by the Guardia that Anna described earlier. When Alicia confronts her husband with the facts she has unearthed about their adopted daughter's parents and sees his complicity with the Fascist government that sold them their child, he beats her head against a wall and shuts her hand in a door until it bleeds. This is the history that the children of Argentina are learning and the successful bourgeois are accepting. Roberto orders Alicia to "stop thinking" about who their child's mother is and what happened, but Alicia realizes that she cannot "stop thinking" as the death squad governments and official history dictate. Her search for her child's parents is an attempt to reject the false, one-dimensionality of the official story of history and to explore the holographic layers of true history. Near the end of the film, the plight of the *desaparacidos* is characterized in familiar terms in an angry exchange between Roberto and the radical Anna. "You should all be swept away. Like garbage!" Roberto screams at this woman whose truths he feels have corrupted his wife. Anna calmly replies, "You did that. You swept them away and buried them." All of these films about death squad terrorism ultimately arrive at the mass graves where the victims are dumped like garbage.

All of these overtly political films about control terrorism define the sociohistorical consciousness of who the villains are in the eighties world, but the depth of that consciousness is perhaps best indicated when the tragic themes of death squad terrorism begin appearing in less overtly political films. All of the serious control terrorism films deal with the existential resistance of human beings to oppression and mind control. However, a number of eighties comedies took either a Marx Brothers or a black humor approach to life in a Latin American country ruled by control terrorism.

Moon over Parador (1988), a comedy about both acting and politics, takes the Marx Brothers approach. Like *Tootsie* (1982), *Moon over Parador* is a film about an actor who must change his identity in order to find work. But where *Tootsie* built on an inspired metaphor for feminist politics, a male actor becoming a woman to get parts, *Moon over Parador* involves the less-inspired concept. When the dictator of the tiny Caribbean country of Parador dies unexpectedly of a heart attack, Jack Noah (Richard Drey-fuss) is threatened into taking the dictator's identity by the gangster bankers who control the country.

This Paul Mazursky spoof of eighties control terrorism films has all the same characters and situations as *Under Fire*, *Salvador*, and *Missing*. When Jack Noah assumes the role of dictator of Parador, he finds himself surrounded by murderous gangsters, confronted by an oppressed popu-lace, and being wooed by the American CIA. The only difference is that the death squad thugs of Parador are about as threatening as the Dead End Kids: the revolution is led by a slinky cabaret singer named Madonna (Sonia Braga), and the CIA agent, who has always been the most threaten-ing of the stock figures in the other control terrorism films, is played as a hick moron by Jonathan Winters. For the Eighties, perhaps the idea of an actor becoming the president of a country is not as farfetched as *Moon over Parador* makes it seem.

Romancing the Stone (1984) also generates slapstick in a South American country out of the confrontation of two "innocents abroad" with Colonel Zolo (Alfonso Aran), the mustache-twirling head of the Guardia in Columbia. But, even in lightweight chase comedy like *Romancing the Stone*, the image of the Guardia is brutal and fascistic. In the eighties, the Latin American policeman-torturer has taken over as the villain for the Nazi of the fifties, the fat Southern Sheriff of the sixties and early seventies (in the *Smokey and the Bandit* films), and the corporate executive of the seventies and early eighties.

Much darker in its comedy of control terrorism is Terry Gilliam's *Brazil* (1984) set in a futuristic bureaucratic society in which, sometimes as a result of computer errors, goon squads "disappear" innocent people as in *Salvador*, *Missing*, and *The Official Story*. Notwithstanding its title, Gilliam gives no indication that the computer-governed country in which his black comedy takes place is in South America. However, the film's government calls working people who dare to ask questions "terrorists" and maintains a huge center, called the Ministry of Information Retrieval, where the goon squads deposit those who have been "disappeared." *Brazil* is a lively visual satire of the impersonality of computer technology and the brutality of death squad terrorism. In *Brazil*, Orwell's *1984* is brought up-to-date.

At the opposite end of the spectrum from comedies about death squad terrorism in Central and South America lies the documentary film *The Situation* (1987). Sharing the same protagonists as the fiction films *Under Fire*, *Salvador*, and *Missing*, *The Situation* is a two-year record of a group of free-lance American journalists who cover the death squad terrorism in El Salvador and then are threatened by the control government when the events they film and write about do not correspond to the official version.

But Latin America is not the only venue in which journalists cover the murderous excesses of government control terrorism. These political scenarios were also being played out in Africa, Southeast Asia and Malaysia. Journalists, like those unable to remain disengaged in the Latin American films *Under Fire*, *Salvador*, and *Missing*, learn the same lesson in Southeast Asia, Indonesia, and Africa.

Sydney Schanberg (Sam Waterston) in *The Killing Fields* is another of these globe-trotting journalists eager to get to the center of the action and find the truth or, at least, some version of the truth. Director David Puttnam states that his film is "the story of the results of war. If the film makes one fundamental point, it's the utter unacceptability of conflict because of its effect on those who get dragged into it. . . . Whilst I still may be naive in regarding it as apolitical, it is all too possible that the film will be viewed in a purely political context, as a metaphor for Central America and maybe Lebanon."[18] Though Schanberg chooses to enter the war zone in Cambodia, it is his assistant, Dith Pran (Dr. Haing S. Ngor), who is trapped in the genocidal aftermath of the war. Dith Pran's four-year journey through the famine, beatings, and daily executions of the Khmer Rouge to escape to Thailand is one-half of *The Killing Fields'* counterpointed story. Dith Pran's journey is important because it takes the film out of the Amerocentric point of view and, as will *The Year of Living Dangerously*, gives the perspective of the victims of control government terrorism.

Perhaps the most shocking scene in *The Killing Fields* is that of Dith Pran walking through a valley of corpses, the dumping ground of the Khmer Rouge in Cambodia. It is the same scene as those at El Playon in *Salvador*, in the National Stadium in *Missing*, or Molina's last resting place in *Kiss of the Spider Woman*, but on a genocidal scale. Under the Khmer Rouge, Cambodia has embraced death squad terrorism on a scale approaching that of the Holocaust of World War II.

The Year of Living Dangerously (1982) is also set in a country ready to explode, a country divided by political factions and ruled by a control government intent upon sustaining its own corruption. The two central characters, Guy Hamilton (Mel Gibson), a journalist for the Australian Broadcasting Service, and Billy Kwan (Linda Hunt), a Malaysian dwarf free-lance photographer, have the same relationship as Schanberg and Dith Pran in *The Killing Fields*. They find themselves caught in the middle of events in Djakarta, Indonesia, in 1965 when President Sukarno is attempting to balance the rightist forces of the military against the Communists who are mobilizing a peoples' revolution. On the sidelines watching are the British, the Dutch, the Americans, and, of course, the foreign press corps. This, once again, is a film about the necessity of the press to get involved, to learn the truth, in these death squad terrorism situations.

The primary text of *The Year of Living Dangerously* is a melodramatic love story focused upon Guy Hamilton and Jill Bryant (Sigourney Weaver), a British embassy employee (read "spook"). The political subtext, focused in the character, philosophy, and political action of the sensitive and talented dwarf, Billy Kwan, is the film's real focus. The metaphor upon which this subtext is based is that of the *wayang pulit*, the Japanese shadow puppet play. The puppet master, or *dalang*, moves his puppets so that they cast shadows upon a screen. Each puppet has a mythic identity of either good or evil, black or white, life or death, drawn from the Ramayana or the Mahabarata, the great Hindu epics. In the political/historical metaphor of *The Year of Living Dangerously*, Sukarno is the great *dalang*, or puppet master, and Billy Kwan is a minor *dalang*. Both choreograph their own shadow plays. Billy places Guy Hamilton into a play with Jill Bryant in order for Guy, the objective journalist, to learn how to involve himself with life rather than simply observe it. Simultaneously Billy is trying to involve himself with Djakarta's poor and starving.

Sukarno's shadow play is cast on the screen of the nation of Indonesia. His puppets are the dark forces of the right, the generals who control the military, and the light forces of the left, the Communist PKL that speaks for the starving people of the country. To the side in this shadow play of Third World politics stands the Colonial forces, the British and the Dutch who watch in hopes of protecting their investments. The main problem of Sukarno's shadow play, however, is that the money spent by the puppet master on his personality cult and miltary armaments has led to high inflation, food shortages, and starvation.[19]

Both Sukarno and Billy Kwan lose control of their respective shadow plays. Billy can neither help Djakarta's poor with his involvement nor influence Guy into greater involvement in life. Sukarno loses out to the generals when the PKL peoples' revolt is defeated by the military and the army carries out large-scale executions of PKL sympathizers that estimates place in a range between 80,000 and 500,000 dead. As in *The Killing Fields*, this period of death squad terrorism in Indonesia reached genocidal proportions.

The moral center of *The Year of Living Dangerously* is Billy Kwan. Early he tells Guy Hamilton, "I'll be your eyes." They form a partnership in which Billy is Hamilton's mentor in the need for involvement with the people of Djakarta as well as knowledge of the death squad evils of the government factions who are grappling for the country. "That's what I like about you, Guy," Billy gently taunts his shadow puppet. "You really don't care, do you? Or maybe you just don't see." Guy replies, "We can't get involved," and Billy scoffs: "Typical journalist's answer." Billy shows Guy photographs of the poor and starving. "That's the real Djakarta. Scavenging for a few handfulls of rice to survive. That's the story none of you journalists tell."

Billy Kwan is a true Third World voice in a film about Western naïveté. As a puppet master, he does not commit himself to either of the contending puppets in Sukarno's political historical shadow play. He is committed only to the people who are starving in the background of the play. Billy is ultimately suspicious of any political force who would try to control the people of Indonesia. When Hamilton asks his driver who is PKL, "Can they take over?" the man answers, "Maybe. At least they would give us discipline," and Billy Kwan comments, "Stalin had good discipline. He wiped out ten million." In the world of control politics, death squad terrorism must always be a primary concern.

Both shadow plays end in images of death squad atrocity. When Billy Kwan can no longer stand the starvation and death of his people, when he realizes that the Westerners with whom he associates have no interest in getting involved, he loses the puppet master's control and lashes out. He realizes that Guy Hamilton is a journalist before he is a human being and he screams, "Why can't you learn to love?" At a party, Billy castigates his Western colleagues:

Well, let's drink to that. Whenever the misery is the worst, the press will be there in force . . . You know the people are out there fighting in the streets for rice. . . . Why don't you tell them the true story, gentlemen? Why don't you tell them that Sukarno makes empty speeches and builds monuments to his vanity while his people are starving to death? Why don't you tell them that he tells his people to eat rats?

In the end, Billy unfurls a banner—UKARNO, FEED YOUR PEOPLE— from a seventh floor window of a fancy Western hotel. When caught in this subversive act by a government goon squad, they throw him out the window to die in the street like other victims in other films.

The Year of Living Dangerously is a strange and confused film. In the end, its political/historical subtext overwhelms its love-story primary text. The relationship between Guy Hamilton and Jill Bryant is overshadowed by frightening images of death squad terrorism. The film is not about these two blind Westerners caught in a revolution but about the terrible inhumane things that they choose not to see. During a demonstration, a truck full of army goons armed with automatic weapons repeatedly bangs into the rear of Hamilton's car. When Billy snaps pictures of them, they try to take his camera. Symbolically Billy and Guy find themselves trapped between the right, the military goons, and the left, the demonstrators, as Sukarno's shadow play careens out of control. Near the end of the film as Hamilton attempts to enter the British embassy, which has been taken over by the military, a soldier hits him with a rifle butt, detaching his retina and blinding him. Hamilton's refusal to see has finally been punished.

Like all of the other films about death squad terrorism, *The Year of Living Dangerously* ends with executions in the streets. As Hamilton tries to get to the airport to escape this holocaust, he is driven past lines of poor people on their knees in the streets being mowed down by military machine guns, a death squad in uniform.

Perhaps the earliest film of the eighties to examine the issue of control governments employing death squad terrorism is *The Dogs of War* (1980) adapted from Frederick Forsyth's novel. The film opens with Shannon (Christopher Walken) escaping from "Central America 1980." Like the Oates character in *Under Fire*, Shannon is a mercenary soldier who will fight anywhere for a price. He immediately takes an assignment from a representative of some vintage seventies corporate villains to do a reconnaisance of the political situation in the West African military dictatorship of Zangaro, with an eye to leading a mercenary invasion of that country.

The film is structured in three acts. Act 1 involves Shannon's reconnaisance of Zangaro. Act 2 is the planning and training for the invasion. Act 3 is the invasion itself. Thus *The Dogs of War* is a conventional commando action movie like so many others (*Darby's Rangers*, *The Devil's Brigade*, *The Dirty Dozen*, *The Wild Geese*). Only in its first act, which in some depth examines the control political situation in Zangaro, does *The Dogs of War* differ from these other films. In act 1 of its structure, the film examines three themes: the factionalism of Third World politics, the function of the press in a Third World country controlled by a death squad government, and the rapacity of Western corporate villains in Third World politics.

Shannon goes to Zangaro under the cover of being a photojournalist/naturalist interested in the country's birdlife. In his hotel in Clarence, the capital, he hooks up with North (Colin Blakely) the leader of a British camera crew. North is the film's mouthpiece for political exposition. His first words to Shannon eerily echo that seventies theme line from *Chinatown*: "Nobody knows what's going on here," he says before going on to describe the political history of the young nation of Zangaro. The country is being contended for by three factions: the dictator Kimba who, in the best Death Squad government tradition, "seems content to slaughter his own, and I do mean 'slaughter'"; the dictator in exile, Bubi, who is the puppet of Western corporate interests that have hired Shannon to put him on the throne; and Dr. Acoya, the peoples' political leader who is in prison in Clarence. Shannon's cover, of course, is easily blown. He is severely beaten by Kimba's goon squad and thrown into prison, where he gets to speak to Dr. Acoya who enlightens him on the death squad oppression in the country. After he escapes Zangaro by deportation, Shannon visits Bubi, the pretender to the throne, in London. "Kimba does not do business," Bubi characterizes the Zangaro political situation. "Kimba wants to be God. Bubi wants to be rich."

After this political exposition of act 1, *The Dogs of War* settles down to a rather conventional commando movie until the end. Shannon and his mercenaries take Zangaro, but then Shannon, sick of being owned by these exploiters, becomes a loose cannon on the deck of Third World politics. First, he kills Kimba as the dictator is counting his money in bed. Next, when Bubi arrives to take over the throne in the name of Western economic exploitation, he kills him. Finally, Shannon liberates Dr. Acoya from prison and places him in office. *The Dogs of War* is a simplistic study of the mechanisms of control government, its dependence internally upon death squad terrorism and externally upon Western economic imperialists. But it also offers an interesting character in Shannon, the mercenary with a conscience and the "ultimate in killing technology" who employs violence to manipulate politics back into the hands of the people. As in so many other death squad terrorism films, Shannon chooses to involve himself in the moral issues that he is forced to confront.

What these films, ranging from Central and South America to Southeast Asia and Indonesia to Africa, prove can be summed up in the declaration of Archbishop Desmond Tutu as he was being led off to jail in South Africa in 1989: "I want to say to the world that the terrorists in South Africa are the South African government."[20]

The Commercial Text In an interview on the "Today" television show (21 August 1989) Senator Joseph Biden, discussing the Columbian crackdown on drug cartels stated, "There should be no safe haven for these narco-terrorists." Soon after, Congressman Mickey Edwards, speaking for the congressional delegation, stated, "Noriega's involvement in drug dealing and money laundering, for which he faces indictment before U.S. courts, makes him a premier narco-terrorist." Edwards went on to signal the impact of this narco-terrorism on American society: "From the streets of American cities to the unfolding drama in Panama's neighbor to the south (Columbia), we can see the effects of men like Noriega choosing power and profit over principle."[21] In the late eighties, this term *narco-terrorism* signaled another textual application of the concept of terrorism. Narco-terrorists were drug lords and dealers who employed the same tactics as political (bombings, assassinations) and control (executions, torture, disappearances) terrorists but for commercial purposes; that is, to establish, protect, and expand business territories especially in the international drug trade.

What is alarming to American society about this commercial terrorist text is that it is a form of terrorism that for the first time actively invaded American borders. Viafara Salinas, a federally protected witness, warned a Senate hearing that South American drug dealers would not hesitate to spread terror within the United States: "Some of you may be the victims of attacks and maybe the president of the United States would be a victim of drug traffickers."[22] In the eighties, narco-terrorism had already penetrated American borders in the form of street warfare over drug territories in cities such as Miami, Washington, D.C., New York, and Los Angeles, but in the late eighties the terrorist threat of assassinations of public officials was an escalation of this new form of terrorist activity.

Throughout the decade, a number of films focusing upon strikingly similar characters examined the fragility of America's borders and their vulnerability to penetration. In *Borderline* (1980), Charles Bronson and Bruno Kirby are two Border Patrol officers working to crack a nationwide syndicate of illegal alien smugglers. In *The Border* (1982), Jack Nicholson and Harvey Keitel are two corrupt border patrolmen caught in the crossfire between their two employers, the INS and the illegal alien smuggling syndicate. In *Flashpoint* (1984), Kris Kristofferson and Treat Williams are two inquisitive Texas border patrolmen who in the course of doing their job find themselves involved in a twenty-year-old mystery, the Kennedy Assassination. Though none of these films confronts the issue of narco-terrorism, all demonstrate a movie consciousness of the encroachment upon America's borders of business interests illegally exploiting the rich American market and employing terrorist tactics to accomplish their goals.

The ending of *The Border*, an apocalyptic shootout between the Border Patrol and the illegal alien cartel, is especially pertinent to the theme of terrorist penetration of America's borders. In *Flashpoint*, Federal Agent Corson (Kevin Conway) cynically places in perspective this issue of why America's borders are being assaulted by so many illegal aliens and their exploiters. It is a speech similar to Adam Stiefel's (Marlon Brando) pivotal speech in *The Formula* (1980). The attraction of America to international business cartels, whether they deal in oil or illegal aliens or drugs, is always simply one of supply and demand. America is the world's richest market and international business will employ any and all tactics, including terrorism, to open and protect that American market. In the corporate villainy films of the seventies like *The Formula* the cartels feared political terrorism as a destabilizing force, but the international cartels of the eighties have appropriated terrorist methods as an integral part of business strategies.[23]

Illegally penetrating America's borders has always been an attractive alternative for individuals fleeing either poverty or political oppression. *El Norte* (1983), perhaps better than any other film, chronicles the desire to escape the oppression of control terrorism in Central America via illegal immigration to the United States. In the eighties, however, the penetration of America's borders did not just involve fugitives from death squad governments. Soon the Border Patrol could no longer concentrate on stanching the flow of illegal aliens from the south. Their primary concern became the interdiction of drugs into the country. Their jobs became much more dangerous. Now, instead of dealing with frightened and disoriented illegals, they were dealing with well-organized and heavily armed narco-terrorists.

The incursion of narco-terrorism upon American life is given clear definition in two late eighties action films, *Let's Get Harry* (1986) and *Extreme Prejudice* (1987). In the former, Harry Burke (Mark Harmon), an engineer, is kidnapped by a group of terrorist drug dealers in Bogota, Columbia, for the purpose of blackmailing the Columbian and American governments into releasing their imprisoned drug cartel associates. Harry is just an ordinary guy from a midwestern American background who happens to be at the wrong place at the wrong time. When the Columbian government and Washington show little interest in rescuing Harry, Harry's brother and a group of his construction worker pals from Aurora, Illinois, organize a commando raid. With the help of a burned-out Vietnam vet mercenary (Robert Duvall) and a big-game hunter car dealer (Gary Busey) they set out to rescue Harry. *Let's Get Harry* is *Uncommon Valor* or *Rambo II* for the era of narco-terrorism. It is B-movie action at its most basic, but its whole theme involves the incursion of narco-terrorism into the everyday lives of ordinary midwestern Americans. What *Let's Get Harry's* subtext says is that events in Columbia actually penetrate right to the center of American life, the border war against the narco-terrorists has implications for the heartlands of America as well.

Extreme Prejudice is a more complex and immediate film. Texas Ranger Jack Bentene (Nick Nolte) is a "stone age cowboy" in a high-tech, stoned age. His job is to patrol the nation's southwest border, insulate the country from the intrusion of crime from the outside. The problem is that what seems such a clear and simple task no longer is. In the eighties, border crime has taken on a complete new look and Bentene has to find some way to adapt. He does not, and Walter Hill's (both a writer and an assistant director for Sam Peckinpah) film settles for an inconclusive, apolitical, apocalyptic ending, a shoot-out in a border town that image by image reproduces the final shoot-out in *The Wild Bunch*. What the subtext of *Extreme Prejudice* ultimately says is that America in the form of old-fashioned Gary Cooper cowboy Jack Bentene needs to find some new way to adapt to the high-tech commercial narco-terrorism of the eighties.

The villain of *Extreme Prejudice* is Cash Bailey (Powers Booth), a drug lord who in his ice-cream tropical suit and white helicopter controls the flow of drugs across Jack Bentene's border. Bailey is a former DEA agent gone south who controls his own private army operating into Texas from Mexico. "Ain't nobody can see anythin' clear anymore," one of *Extreme Prejudice*'s hard cases laments, and that line sums up the film's message about what drugs and the terrorism that always accompanies them are doing to the good, old-fashioned values and security that Jack Bentene as an American icon represents. It is a message grounded in Vietnam, Nicaragua, the Iran-*contra*/Ollie North covert fiasco, the Noriega affair, in all of the acts of corruption and violence that debased fundamental American values in the eighties.

This message of how narco-terrorism wipes out the past is metaphorically delivered through the character relationship of Jack Bentene and Cash Bailey. They grew up together, played football together in high school, shared the same women, and yet the terrorist necessities of the border narcotics trade make those long-standing bonds obsolete. When Cash Bailey's army of narco-terrorists are threatened, they have but one option, to open fire.

The movie industry's consciousness of the theme of narco-terrorism (and its attendant bankability) was raised by the tremendous success of the 1985 TV series, "Miami Vice." In vivid images every week, "Miami Vice" presented narco-terrorists as the new villains violently taking over the American landscape. There had been films about narco-terrorism, principally *Scarface* (1983), in production simultaneous to the development of "Miami Vice," but after that TV series became a hit, a plague of narco-terrorist villains descended upon the American action film genres. In reaction to this infestation of drug decade villains, Hollywood came up with a grotesque assortment of antidotes, ranging from Arnold Schwarzenegger as a Russian narc in *Red Heat* (1988) to *Robocop* (1987) in near future Detroit to Jim Belushi and a German shepherd playing narcotics cops in Chicago in *K-9* (1989). Each of these films, however, presents the American urban reality of narco-terrorism. What they say is that it is no longer just a border problem but has made its way north to the streets of Chicago and Detroit in the Midwest as well as the established coastal drug centers. Three films in particular, *Scarface* (1983), *Once Upon a Time in America* (1984), and *Colors* (1988) are specifically about narco-terrorism's incursion upon the American dream.

In the past, films dealing with these sorts of characters, violent business-men in illegal businesses, were simply labeled "Gangster" genre films. However, the reinvestigation of this genre within the sociohistorical con-text of the eighties gives these films an added political significance. In the eighties, the gangsterism in America's urban streets does not involve simply a group of homegrown businessmen protecting their territories. The new narco-terrorism gangsters are either participants in or suppor-ters of a foreign invasion generated by the drug import industry that espouses all of the techniques of international political terrorism. There-fore films that used to be simple Gangster genre movies (such as Brian DePalma's 1987 *The Untouchables*, which makes no pretention to any political or metaphorical significance), take on wider meaning when directed at an eighties audience cognizant of their narco-terrorism con-textuality. As 1987 was the Year of Vietnam at the movies, 1984 could have been called the Year of the Narco-Terrorist.

The 1984 *Scarface* is a remake of a 1932 film starring Paul Muni and modeled upon the career of Al Capone. But this eighties *Scarface* is a Cuban in Miami, a "Marielito," one of the thousands of criminals and mental patients whom Castro deported to the United States from Mariel Harbor in 1980. From the first act of his career in America (a political assassination in the Marielito detention camp), Tony Montana (Al Pacino) is focused on the business of drugs and the terrorist tactics that support that business. Oliver Stone, the writer of the *Scarface* screenplay, tells how the conception of Tony Montana was generated directly out of terrorist sources:

> I was there (Miami) in 1980, 1981, when they had more homicides in one year than they'd had in all of the Seventies. In 1980 you could really draw a parallel between Miami, El Salvador, and Nicaragua. In each place, it heated up. There was more killing, more violence, an orgy of blood. I didn't understand it at first, but six years later the threads are starting to come together because of the connection between coke and the contra trade.[24]

Tony Montana's Miami is a land of opportunity for an ambitious immi-grant lad with a good business sense and the ability to kill. His main motive for commercial terrorism is class and economic impotence. Like the political factions of the Middle East, Tony, the penniless Cuban immigrant, feels shut off from the mainstream of society, cut off from the rewards of social acceptance, cheated out of his right not to a homeland but to the American dream of wealth and status and power.

Early in *Scarface*, when asked what he wants out of life, Tony answers, "Me? Only wan wot's comin' ta me, the worl' an everythin' in it." At a major turning point in the film, on the night that Tony kills his mentor in the coke trade, Frank Lopez (Robert Loggia), and inherits the status symbol of Frank's blonde junkie, Wasp girl friend Elvira (Michelle Pfeiffer), the Goodyear blimp suddenly appears overhead and in acres of blinking lights spells out the film's corrupt American dream theme. "THE WORLD IS YOURS" blinks the blimp. The same words appear on the lighted world globe in the foyer of Tony's mansion later. Unlike the political terrorists in the Middle East or Indonesia or Africa who have been dispossessed of their world by more powerful groups and who try to regain their world with bombs and guns, Tony Montana uses the bombs and guns to gain money with which to buy his world of wealth and power. It is a corrupt American dream world. Tony Montana's motive for the terrorism he spreads through Miami is similar to the suitcase terrorists of *The Little Drummer Girl* except that he is driven not to political action but to the making of money. *Scarface* is a thoughtful movie about the psychopathy of trying to gain identity and keep it in *the* growth business of the eighties, the drug trade.

But there is a real political irony as well to Stone and DePalma's characterization of Tony Montana. Tony claims anticommunism as his motive for any excess or criminality. When he first comes to power, he travels to a meeting in Bolivia with a drug lord who is accompanied by the usual representative from Washington (CIA?). As was *The Godfather* in the seventies, *Scarface* presents a subtext of Tony Montana's career as a metaphor for American political life. Like CIA gangsters masterminding terrorism for the protection of American interests in Nicaragua, El Salvador, and Panama, like the Reagan administration cowboys embracing terrorism in the Iran-*contra* affair, Tony sees violence as his ticket to buying into and sustaining the American way of life in all of its commercial ruthlessness.

The print ads for *Scarface*—"He loved the American Dream . . . with a vengeance"—sold the film on its subtext metaphor of America corrupting itself by embracing worldwide terrorism. The film, more than any other of the decade, explores violence as a way of life, as the only way to do business, as the means to the American dream. Prior to its reedited release, the film was given an X-rating for its heavy violence. As one critic commented on its sociohistorical roots,

ever since Vietnam, the assassinations of the Kennedys and Martin Luther King Jr., the escalating arms race, the various economic recessions and the rise of women's lib, which in itself seems to have spawned an entire cycle of gore films in which women are hideously victimized, there's a lot of anger and frustration out there for filmmakers to exploit.[25]

Tony Montana becomes an icon for terrorism as a reality of American life. He is the bodyguard of the drugs that have penetrated America's borders and permeated American society affecting everyone of every class in every neighborhood. When, at the end of *Scarface*, Tony Montana, riddled with bullets, dies face down in his own foyer fountain, the camera slowly booms up to the garish globe and the motto The World Is Yours. It is a final ironic comment on how, in the eighties, terrorist violence seems to have become the only solution to the world's political and commercial problems.

Another epic-scale Gangster film, Sergio Leone's *Once Upon a Time in America*, also appeared in 1984. Though set in the twenties, thirties, and forties, seemingly possessing little of the sociohistorical eighties contemporaneity of Stone's and DePalma's *Scarface*, still *Once Upon a Time in America* explores, subtextually and metaphorically, as did *Chinatown* for the seventies, the eighties theme of narco-terrorism as commercial necessity. Where *Scarface* deals ultrarealistically with the present, *Once Upon a Time in America* is keyed, in its focus upon the jockeying for illegal liquor territories via violence, to the contextuality of the eighties. Like Coppola's *Godfather*, it denotes how a prior time represents the present. Like Coppola's films about the Vietnam and Watergate-inspired relationship between big business and politics, *Once Upon a Time in America* focuses upon the theme of the drug business and politics.

The tempo of Leone's narrative structure in *Once Upon a Time in America* is based upon the concept of the intertextuality of past, present, and future. The whole film (in its original long version before being reedited by Paramount Studios) is a drug-induced dream memory. The film begins in an opium den and ends there, but it also begins with the song "God Bless America" on the soundtrack and ends with the same ironic anthem. Thus the film announces immediately that it is about time, memory, and American history. Leone's narrative of the rise and fall of a gang of New York Jewish bootleggers is in four acts. Three of those four acts take place in the teens and twenties culminating in the repeal of prohibition, but the final act brings down the curtain in the sixties. The primary text is about friendship, love, betrayal, and memory within the context of the American dream. The subtext, however, is an eighties analogue, a fable parallel to that of DePalma's *Scarface* about the nature of American business and how it works via terrorism.

Near the end of *Once Upon a Time in America*, Deborah (Elizabeth McGovern) describes the U.S. Secretary of the Treasury Christopher Bailey, who is also Max Bercovitch (James Woods), a gangster supposedly killed by the New York Police the week that Prohibition was repealed, as "a rich businessman. He came to the United States as a poor immigrant and made a lot of money." She could well be describing Tony Montana. Like *Scarface*, *Once Upon a Time in America* chronicles the rise of an extremely successful criminal business via terrorism.

Act 1 recalls the childhoods of Max, Noodles (Robert DeNiro), Patsy (James Haydn), Cockeye (William Forsythe), and Fat Moe (Larry Rapp) when they first gain their business territory. Like the drug smugglers of the eighties, the gang first establishes itself by protecting shipments. Noodles invents a salt float that allows them to salvage shipments of booze that otherwise would be lost to Coast Guard interdiction. But as was the case with Tony Montana and Frank Lopez, the only way they can ever attain and keep their own territory is by killing the rival gang leader. Noodles knifes him in the street. That street murder is the act that makes it all work. Noodles goes to jail, but six years later when he gets out business is booming.

Act 2 of Leone's narrative as analogue to the eighties deals with the forming of a cartel. Everything hinges on a test set up by the reigning crime lord, Frankie Minoldi (Joe Pesci). When the gang completes Frankie's job, which is a combination jewelry heist and assassination, they pass the test and gain entry into the cartel.

Act 3 defines what any drug cartel must ultimately do in order to survive when operating across national boundaries; that is, it must insulate itself politically. Jimmy O'Donnell (Treat Williams) is a young Union organizer who the politicians (aligned with the factory owners thus paralleling the Republican administrations of the eighties) want to stop. They hire a rival gang who put O'Donnell in a bathtub of gasoline and start lighting matches. "Listen to me you socialist asshole," this death squad terrorist threatens O'Donnell. "We don't give a good fart about the socialist workers and their movements. We just want you oughta the factories so we can get the furnaces workin' again." When Noodles and Max rescue O'Donnell from these control terrorists, the film's most telling exchange on the analogic contextual relationship between the time of the film and the eighties occurs:

O'DONNELL: We don't want you in with us. Our fight's got nothing to do with liquor and prostitution and dope.

MAX: You better get used to the idea, pal. This country is still growing up. Certain diseases it's better to have when you're still young.

O'DONNELL: You boys aren't a mild case of measles. You're the plague. Bastards like him (pointing to the politician who had paid to have him put in the tub of gasoline) are immune. That's the difference between us and them.

NOODLES: The difference is that they're always gonna win, and you're gonna keep gettin' it up the ass.

As analogue to the eighties, *Once Upon a Time in America* is a mirror not just of the rise and fall of Tony Montana in DePalma's film released only months earlier, but of the pattern of terrorist development of the eighties drug cartels. In order to establish their territories in American cities such as Miami, those drug cartels employ street warfare. In order to form their cartels on an international scale, they consolidate their interests by terrorist violence against those who resist incorporation. In order to protect their territories against political interference or law and order crackdowns, they employ both political extortion and assassination. For example, in the period 1987 to 1990, more than 60 percent of the South American country of Columbia's judges were assassinated by the Medellin Drug Cartel. *Once Upon a Time in America* is a superb period piece, but it is also a cogent analogue to the narco-terrorist eighties in America.

By the end of their rise to power, Max begins to bear an eerie resemblance to Tony Montana. Money, the full attainment of the American dream, corrupts Max just as it did Tony Montana. Like Tony in his swimming-pool-sized tub in his Miami mansion, Max buys a seventeenth-century pope's throne to sit on. Money drives both Tony and Max to the betrayal of their best friend. *Scarface* and *Once Upon a Time in America* are much the same film. Though set in different time periods, both are about narco-terrorism in America in the eighties.

Leone uses the same storyteller's invocation in the titles of three of his films — *Once Upon a Time in America* was preceded by *Once Upon a Time in the West* (1969) and *Once Upon a Time in the Revolution* (1972), which was released as *Duck You Sucker!* in the United States — his films are not about a particular time and place but about both then and now simultaneously, a memory of the past while also a fable for our time. *Chinatown*, in the seventies, possessed the same temporal intercontextuality. Set in the thirties, *Chinatown* nonetheless was about Vietnam and Watergate and the corporate conspiracies of the seventies. Set in the twenties, *Once Upon a Time in America* is about the drug cartels and the narco-terrorism of the eighties that have made America's cities too dangerous to inhabit.

By the eighties, the street gangs that grew into the syndicates of the twenties and thirties were still following the same developmental process but with more sophistication, quicker and bigger rewards, and much more impressive firepower. The production notes for *Colors* (1988) quote this description of the Los Angeles street gang scene:

> Fifteen minutes from the manicured lawns of Beverly Hills, kids as young as 15 years old roam the streets toting Uzi submachine guns and Soviet-made AK-47 assault rifles. Last year, police tallied more than 5,000 gang-related violent crimes in the city and county of Los Angeles. The authorities blame the trouble on youth gangs that make millions of dollars a year selling crack.
>
> The Crips and the Bloods used to fight over turf, "West Side Story" style. Now, they battle for market share.[26]

Another newspaper story spotlights the terrorist tactics of the Los Angeles street gangs: "During lunch, right over there, under these fences—ganglord style—they held the kid and shot him in the head," a high-school football coach told the *Los Angeles Times* (23 June 1987). "My fullback was killed the following weekend because they said he was seen talking to a policeman." In Los Angeles in the late eighties the great majority of the gang-related street violence can be attributed to the drug trade. In the L.A. area there are 600 street gangs with more than 700,000 members, and in 1987 there were 387 gang-related killings in L.A. County. It is the drug trade that brings these street gangs into existence and fuels their terrorist violence. *Colors* is a film lifted right out of the social history and the headlines of the late eighties. It is a realistic buddy-cop film focused upon American urban narco-terrorism.

In the crack cocaine markets of the inner cities, there is lethal competition for drug profits among the retailers, the urban street gangs. The most frequently employed competition stopper is a commercial version of the political terrorist car bomb, the "drive-by" shooting. But oftentimes the terrorism of a gang is more premeditated: "In some gangs, taking out a policeman is a mark of distinction, like landing a big account in the business world."[27] What *Colors* examines is the helplessness of the police to regulate the terrorist tactics of this lethal commercial competition.

Colors' two main characters, street cops Danny McGavin (Sean Penn) and Bob Hodges (Robert Duvall), represent the two methods of dealing with street gang violence—with the nightstick and the gun or with negotiation. The issue that McGavin and Hodges are constantly arguing is: Do you solve the problem short term or long range? McGavin is a hard-nose who will take any risk, use any strong-arm tactic, to intimidate street gang terrorists. He acquires the nickname "PacMan" for his reputation for gobbling up drug dealers. Hodges believes in taking things slower, establishing debts and ties with the gangs, trying to negotiate. These two squad car partners form an antiterrorist dialectic that, unfortunately, never reaches any synthesis. *Colors* is a naturalistic film that shows how far gone to the narco-terrorists America's inner cities really are. Neither PacMan's nor Hodges's counterterrorist methods work. The apocalyptic automatic weapons shootout is always going to come. Innocent bystanders are always going to get caught in the crossfire. *Colors'* almost documentary theme is simply the realistic presentation of the fact of widespread narco-terrorism in the cities. It is a sociohistorically accurate and relevent film, but it is not a analytic or perceptive film. Because it opts for action over resolution, it ends up a conventional buddy-cop shoot-em-up that for a while pretends to social consciousness but finally offers no direction, no solution to the problem. *Colors* tells it like it is but does not dig very deeply into what it means. Unlike more complex films of the eighties, *Colors* surface realistic exposition is all there is. No subtext lies beneath that surface. Its primary text, however, that of the clear and present danger of narco-terrorism on America's urban streets makes a powerful statement in itself.

In the films of the eighties, the texts of terrorism not only are fully defined but are meticulously analyzed in all of their sociohistorical variations and implications. Terrorism, in its varied forms, became a commonplace of eighties life, and the films of the decade acknowledged its widespread influence by making it the predominant source of villainy. Eighties films also clearly defined a coherent rhetoric of terrorism and a representational "tropics of terrorism." This rhetoric and these textual tropes placed the motives and methods of terrorism into clear perspective. "Terrorism is everywhere in eighties life," these films assert. Terrorism emanates from oppressed political factions, from oppressive governments, from greedy business groups. In the films of the eighties, terrorism becomes the most prominent trope for the frightening loss of stability and erosion of security characteristic of life in this decade.

The eighties version of the
Vietnam War. From
Casualties of War (1989).

The survivor guilt, "bring 'em back alive" fantasy of post-Vietnam America. From *Braddock: Missing In Action III* (1987).

The face of international
terrorism. Mike Shelton
editorial cartoon from the
Orange County Register
(1983). Reprinted with
special permission of King
Features Syndicate, Inc.

The face of resistance to
government control
terrorism. From *Brazil*
(1985).

The faces of urban
terrorism. From *Colors*
(1988).

One antidote to urban
terrorism. From *Robocop*
(1987).

An Amero-Russian cold
warrior. From *No Way Out*
(1987).

A Russian E.T. cast adrift
in American society. From
Russkies (1987).

Mother and daughter
neoconservative Southern
feminists. From *Steel
Magnolias* (1989).

Matriarchal feminism.
From *Gorillas in the Mist*
(1988).

A yuppie confronts his
angst. From *Bright Lights,
Big City* (1988).

The wilderness girls on
Rodeo Drive, the ultimate
shopping movie. From
Troop Beverly Hills (1988).

One of the yuppie
battlefields. From *The 'burbs*
(1988).

Babies invade the yuppie
workplace. From *Baby Boom*
(1987).

5

The Nuclear War Film Texts

ARRY MCGUIRE'S 1969 folk song "Eve of Destruction" bemoans one side of the nuclear issue in its description of the most basic "cold war" fear, while Colonel Whitacre's (John Heard) speech in the 1989 film *The Package* counters with the opposite view: "Why do you think we've had peace with Russia for 40 years?" Whitacre barks. "Nuclear weapons, that's why!"

The doomsday fear of nuclear Armageddon expressed in "Eve of Destruction" has been around since the reality of world annihilation was first created by the Manhattan project and demonstrated incontrovertably at Hiroshima and Nagasaki in the forties. In the fifties, sixties, and seventies, important films like *On the Beach* (1959), *Dr. Strangelove* (1964), *Fail-Safe* (1964) and *Twilight's Last Gleaming* (1977) plus less important films like *The World, the Flesh and the Devil* (1959) and *Damnation Alley* (1977) examined this threat of nuclear war. All are involved with the button pushing and the death of the world that "Eve of Destruction" announces. Near the end of the eighties, in Steven Spielberg's *Empire of the Sun* (1988), the dropping of the atomic bombs on Hiroshima and Nagasaki actually becomes a religious symbol, the creation of a powerful new technological sun to replace God's sun and the rising sun on the sides of the swift Japanese fighter planes that Spielberg's young hero so admires. In another 1988 film, *Bull Durham*, a young pitcher with an overpowering arm, an explosive fastball, and no control is ironically nicknamed "Nuke." In most of these films, nuclear holocaust has been tonally treated in terms of threat and fear, but if we are insane enough to believe Whitacre in *The Package* or Spielberg in *Empire of the Sun*, nuclear war could possibly be our only salvation.

The eighties, like the three preceding decades, always had the nuclear war issue in the forefront of its social history, but the Eighties version added a new, ecological dimension to its doomsday threat. Americans, while never flinching in their nuclear standoff with the Russians, also had to look to a new nuclear threat in their own backyards. *The China Syndrome* (1979) predicted this econuclear threat. Released a short two weeks before the Three Mile Island nuclear leak and exploring a scenario much like what would actually occur at the Chernobyl nuclear power plant in Russia years later, *The China Syndrome* signaled that the nuclear threat does not only take the form of bombs and missiles but can also cause death as an invisible pollutant of the air, water and waste dumping grounds of America. In *Tootsie* (1982), an out-of-work playwright and a group of out-of-work actors want to mount an original play titled *Return to Love Canal*. Curiously, ten years after the pollution of Love Canal was discovered and the residents evacuated, a headline trumpeted "Commissioner Approves Return to Love Canal" (Associated Press, 28 October 1988). In the wake of the near disaster of Three Mile Island and the real disaster of Chernobyl, expensive half-completed nuclear power plants in Indiana and California were abandoned in a backlash of nuclear fear. Thus nuclear destruction and nuclear contamination posed a dual threat.

On 16 July 1985, the atomic bomb celebrated its fortieth birthday. First exploded in the New Mexico desert in 1945, it redefined the concepts of both "war" and "peace," started an arms race, sent shockwaves of paranoia through the four subsequent decades, and generated the covert intelligence activity that has come to be known as the "cold war." Ever since, the president of the United States has never been out of sight of an omnipresent black bag, dubbed "the football," that contains the nuclear strike codes. Ever since, one of the three flying nuclear attack headquarters, dubbed "Looking Glass," has never been out of the air. Throughout the eighties, while science was expanding the perceptions of the ecodangers of nuclear contamination, and the military and the politicians were escalating the nuclear arms race, a wide range of media—poetry, fiction, television, film—were also consistently focusing upon these nuclear issues.

Novelists like Don DeLillo in *End Zone*, Tim O'Brien in *The Nuclear Age*, Whitley Strieber and James Kunetka in *War Day*, Walter Miller, Jr., in *A Canticle for Liebowitz* and Pat Frank in *Alas, Babylon* all dealt with preholocaust and postholocaust realities and exposed the political and economic causes that could precipitate a nuclear war. On television, films like *The Day After* (1983) and miniseries like *World War III* (1981) created scenarios for nuclear disaster. They built upon *The War Game* (1967), a BBC documentary that dramatized life in the aftermath of a nuclear war. Finally, films like *The Manhattan Project* (1986), *War Games* (1983) and *Fat Man and Little Boy* (1989) looked at the issue both hysterically and historically. *Silkwood* (1983) looked at the issue ecologically. *Testament* (1983) looked at the issue psychologically. The Mad Max movies looked at the issue existentially and metaphorically.

Tim O'Brien in *The Nuclear Age* questions the metaphoricality of nuclear war. His hero carries a sign that reads "The Bombs Are Real" and raves internally:

Nuclear war, nuclear war, just a metaphor. Fission, fusion, critical mass . . . The world, I realize, is drugged on metaphor, the opiate of our age. Nobody's scared. Nobody's digging . . . Nuclear war. It's no symbol. Nuclear war—is it embarassing? Too prosaic? Too blunt? Listen—nuclear war—those stiff, brash, trite, everyday syllables. I want to scream it: Nuclear war! Where's the terror in this world? Scream it: Nuclear war! Take a stand and keep screaming: Nuclear war! Nuclear war!"[1]

Don DeLillo's hero in *End Zone* is also fascinated by nuclear war:

It started with a book, an immense volume about the possibilities of nuclear war—assigned reading for a course I was taking in modes of disaster technology. The problem was simple and terrible: I enjoyed the book. I liked reading about the deaths of tens of millions of people. I liked dwelling on the destruction of great cities . . . I liked to think of huge buildings toppling, of firestorms, of bridges collapsing, survivors roaming the charred countryside. Carbon 14 and Strontium 90. Escalation ladder and sub-crisis situation. Titan, Spartan, Poseidon. People burned and unable to breathe . . . People diseased and starving. Two hundred thousand bodies decomposing on the roads outside Chicago. I read several chapters twice . . . I became fascinated by words and phrases like thermal hurricane, overkill, circular error probability, post-attack environment, stark deterrance, dose-rate contours, spasm war. Pleasure in these words. They were extremely effective, I thought, whispering shyly of cycles of destruction so great that the language of past world wars became laughable.[2]

For both O'Brien and DeLillo, the real irony of the nuclear issue is that the world since 1945 has developed an immunity to its reality. The possibility and ensuing envisioned reality of nuclear war has become merely words, metaphors, when it should be starkly real. What O'Brien and DeLillo and the films of the eighties intend is to reestablish that realist view and deconstruct the language illusions that have been erected around the nuclear war threat.

The increase in nuclear war consciousness in the eighties coincided with Ronald Reagan's ascent to the presidency and his eight years of hawkish saber rattling and arms racing. "Nuclear holocaust is not a subject calculated to bring audiences pouring into the theaters, and the studios have generally stayed away from it, at least since the cycle of early Sixties nuclear war films (*On the Beach, Fail Safe, Dr. Strangelove, The Bedford Incident*). Now that too is changing," writes an anonymous editor introducing a 1982 special section of *American Film* magazine titled "How Hollywood Learned to Start Worrying and Hate The Bomb."[3] In this special section, voice after voice affirms that this renewed interest in the nuclear issue is occasioned by Jonathan Schell's startling book *The Fate of the Earth* as well as the renewed saber rattling of the Reagan administration. For actress Jill Clayburgh, the Schell book made clear "that doing something about the threat of nuclear war is the only thing that really matters."[4] In the early eighties, as Clarke Taylor describes, "increasingly, actors in the film and television industry are stepping out from behind their characters and involving themselves in the nuclear disarmament issue. And so are the writers, directors, producers, agents and others."[5] Meetings of anti-nuclear Hollywood creative people were organized in which "small groups considered how they might translate their concerns into projects for the screen."[6] Stephen Farber notes how quickly Hollywood picked up on the nuclear war issue despite the fact that "when tackling a topical social or political issue, Hollywood habitually follows, not leads," and how "these films will break a long silence in Hollywood about nuclear war."[7] Edward Hume, the scriptwriter of *The Day After*, realizes that the effects of movies are hard to guage, yet he argues "most people have no sense of the enormity of these weapons and just how suicidal they are. My aim is to provide information that will add to any dialogue on the subject of nuclear arms."[8] That is exactly what Hollywood set out to do in its portrayal of the two major texts of the nuclear issue, to stimulate a dialogue which examines the insanity of the arms race.

But the politics of Hollywood are never one-dimensional, and Hollywood often has a way of contradicting itself. While real projects presenting an antinuke message arose out of Schell's book and the Reagan committment to the Star Wars or SDI (Strategic Defense Initiative) system, still other films, beginning with Rambo and continuing with *Firefox* (1982), *The Right Stuff* (1983), and *Top Gun* (1986), uphold the jingoistic militarist attitude of the Reagan administration as well as the American romance with military technology that got us into Vietnam and failed so miserably there.

Interviewed on the set of *Top Gun*, a navy pilot nicknamed "Flex," when asked if he thinks about war, answered, "We have to. It's part of our job. People say 'Are you warmongers?' and I say, 'No, for the most part, we're not.' On the other hand, we're on a football team that's always practicing, but never gets to play. We work hard to be able to do something we don't want to do. But there is that frustration, because you want to test yourself."[9] Flex's ambivalence is exactly the reason that, first, the nuclear freeze movement of the early eighties and, then, the nuclear disarmament movement of the late eighties (which gained momentum from the ascension to power of Premier Gorbachev in Russia rather than from either the Reagan or Bush administrations in America) pushed so hard. The worry was that Flex's frustration at being on a team that never got to play would ultimately overcome any stated desire for peace and take unilateral action to get the game on.

Nevertheless, in answer to the new cycle of antinuke films in the early eighties, films of peacetime military competitiveness arose, with *Top Gun* being the most spectacularly successful. Its makers vehemently denied any such political motive. "The film has nothing to do with *Rambo* or Reagan or war fever," actor Tom Cruise of *Top Gun* assures. "I'm not interested in making a propaganda film."[10] Nevertheless, after the spectacular box-office success of *Top Gun*, military recruitment also rose spectacularly. Thus in the films of the eighties, there is a definite political confrontation between the right and the left, the promilitary and the antinuclear agendas. No film, however, had the temerity to take a pronuclear war stance.

Star Wars (1977) is, perhaps, the clearest precursor to the heightened nuclear awareness of the eighties. Not only did it give a show-biz name to the Reagan administration's space-based laser cure-all for the nuclear threat (SDI), but it also trivialized the idea of the world being blown apart in a nuclear war. Both *Star Wars* and *Return of the Jedi* (1983) end in pyrotechnic nuclear explosions. Pauline Kael chastises the latter for this trivialization: "There's no blood in the killings in 'Jedi,' but is killing without blood really preferable? The picture is indecently affectless: it ends with the triumph of the good guys and the grand celebration of a bloodless nuclear explosion—with no worry, no aftermath, no fallout."[11]

Kael's concerns about *Return of the Jedi* are the same concerns that define the two major nuclear film texts of the eighties. Nuclear fission poses two major kinds of threat. One, that of a nuclear holocaust, is evident and immediately fatal to the world. The other, that of the nuclear contamination of individuals and the environment, is invisible and slowly insidious (though, as in the Chernobyl disaster, it too can reach the level of minor holocaust). A variety of different kinds of eighties films took aim at these two nuclear threat texts, set out to expose and explore by means of popular dramatization the threats and the potential effects of what Jonathan Schell in *The Fate of the Earth* warned was near to getting out of hand.

The Econuclear Text

In 1982, *If You Love This Planet*, a Canadian-made, Academy Award-winning antinuclear documentary, was labeled "political propaganda" by the U.S. Department of Justice of the Reagan administration. Also in 1982, another documentary, *The Atomic Cafe*, hilariously compiled 1950s U.S. government and educational media propaganda of the "duck and cover" sort into a goofy send-up of pronuclear attitudes. In terms of goofiness and the antinuclear issue, nothing surpasses *Fletch Lives* (1989). The McGuffin of this slapstick detective movie turns out to be a radiation-contaminated Southern-fried plantation that stands at the center of a huge real estate fraud being perpetrated by a crooked politician and a Jim Bakker-like televangelist. The range between those award-winning antinuclear documentaries and the radiation bubbling up under Chevy Chase's sneakers in *Fletch Lives* attests to the variety of the antinuclear discourse in the films of the eighties. Besides the two primary texts, the econuclear text and the nuclear war text, within each primary text lies a wide range of approaches to the nuclear issue. In the econuclear text, the discourse ranges from the documentary to the slapstick (in *Fletch Lives*) to the metaphorical to the exploitative to the overtly sociohistorical (in a film like *Silkwood*).

Dune (1984) is an example of a metaphorical approach not just to the econuclear issue but to the ecological spectrum of issues of the eighties. Adapted from Frank Herbert's popular series of science fiction novels, David Lynch's *Dune* is one of the most frequently misread films of the decade. While most critics read *Dune* as futuristic fantasy set in a medievalist world or as a post-Genesis myth populated with giant worms who rule an arid postlapsarian paradise longing to be reborn or as a theological fable about the need for Messiahs, Frank Herbert's original *Dune* was an extended metaphor of ecological Darwinism. In Herbert's book and in this movie, the planet Dune is an ecometaphor dealing with the need to conserve our resources and available goods and not to pollute our shrinking, increasingly hostile environment.

Dune is a desert planet of the year 10,191 populated by the most ecoconscious race ever conceived by man. Instead of a militarist sci-fi film emphasizing the destructive power of technology (like *Star Wars*), *Dune* is a humanist sci-fi film that emphasizes how free men must always be conscious of the scarcity of the natural elements that allow them to live. *Dune* is a book and film about water and how valuable it is for the survival and adaptation of our planet. When young King Paul Atreides (Kyle MacLachlan) moves to the planet Dune, he finds an arid desert world peopled by the Fremen, a tribe of desert survivors whose "still suits" are an ecoparody of the military flight suits that *Top Gun*'s Maverick (Tom Cruise) and *Star War*'s Luke Skywalker (Mark Hamill) climb into before mounting their metal monsters to wreak technological havoc. In his still suit, Paul Atreides mounts the great worms that supply the life-force of this futuristic universe.

As a message movie, *Dune* posits that the deteriorating ecology of our universe cannot be saved by technology (as the pronuclear power argument implies) but is actually being caused by technology. In its wasteland aridity, the planet Dune itself serves as a metaphor for a postholocaust, postapocalypse world. *Dune*'s subtext beneath the action and messianic posturing is a plea for men to value the precious resources of our planet, not to waste and pollute them.

Star Trek IV: The Voyage Home (1986), the most interesting of this series of eighties sequels to the cult-successful TV series of the sixties, summons a similar ecometaphor to that of *Dune*. *Star Trek IV: The Voyage Home* is about saving the whales, preserving a valuable species. Superficially, this film seems just another time-travel movie, a curious fascination of the eighties. In *Time After Time* (1980), Jack the Ripper time-travels from Victorian London to eighties San Francisco. In *Somewhere in Time* (1981), a young man (Christopher Reeve) returns to the Grande Hotel on Mackinac Island at the turn of the century to search for his lost love. In *The Terminator* (1984), a lethal Cyborg (Arnold Schwarzenegger) comes back from a post-nuclear-holocaust future to attempt to change the past in order to influence the future. Ironically this mechanical monster has no interest in preventing nuclear Armageddon but simply wants to kill one woman in order to prevent the birth of one man who will become a destabilizing force in the postholocaust world. Also in 1984, the first of three *Back to the Future* (also 1989, 1990) films posited this same time travel solution to future problems though much less violently than *The Terminator*. Finally, Francis Coppola's *Peggy Sue Got Married* (1986) took the most sophisticated view of this time-travel trend. The decade, in its nostalgia and its sequelmania, expressed a longing for the simplicity of the past (especially the fifties) and a fear for a future that is consistently being mortgaged by the cavalier deficit spending of the arms-happy Reagan government. Of all of these time-travel films, however, *Star Trek IV: The Voyage Home* is the only one that explores ecohistory, the influence of the sins of the ecological past upon the precarious future.

As in *Dune*, the focus of its theme is upon the fragility of the planet and the need for a new ecoconsciousness to replace the consumption frenzy of eighties life. An alien space probe that is draining power via water evaporation from twenty-third-century Earth can only be communicated with by humpbacked whales that had been commercially hunted into extinction in the late twentieth century. Thus the crew of the *Starship Enterprise* must go back in time to right this ecowrong and save the future world. Though director Leonard Nimoy asserts, "I did not set out to make a cause film. It's a piece of entertainment in which there are some ideas" (Associated Press, 8 December 1986), the ecomessage is unmistakable. It is not an antinuclear message, but it confronts the possibility of the death of the world because of eighties ecoirresponsibility.

The Terminator, however, is an overtly nuclear parable. Its opening future sequences portray a postnuclear holocaust world of totalitarian repression, troglodytic life, and graphic high-tech violence. After the time-travel premise is executed, the film portrays an eighties world of innocence and incredulity in the face of the nuclear threat. The relentlessness of the terminator Cyborg is a metaphor for the relentless approach of nuclear disaster upon an unsuspecting world. There is an irony built into the Cyborg villain that declares it is our technology that will turn upon us and ultimately destroy us.

Other sci-fi horror movies of the eighties, Ridley Scott's *Alien* (1979) and James Cameron's (also the director of *The Terminator*) *Aliens* (1986), carry a similar message. Both films, as is *The Terminator*, are about survival. In the first, Junior Officer Ripley (Sigourney Weaver) survives because she is quicker and reacts better than the alien, but in the sequel Ripley (again Weaver) survives because she goes on the offensive, exercises her determination not to let her child (the next generation) be destroyed by forces larger than herself. Cameron talks about the antitechnological subtext of *Aliens*. Describing the detachment of space marines sent to discover the fate of a human colony gone suddenly silent, he says: "Their training and technology are inappropriate for the specifics, and that can be seen as analogous to the inability of superior American firepower to conquer the unseen enemy in Viet Nam: a lot of firepower and very little wisdom, and it didn't work."[12] In the original *Alien*, all of the humans except Ripley were lost because "the company," a conglomerate set up for the commercial exploitation of outer space, wanted the alien taken alive for use in their weapons division. In both films, as in *The Terminator*, the embodiments of evil are nonhuman. Military weapons have little or no effect upon them. Both films opt for humanity over hardware, footraces over arms races.

The technometaphor for ecothreat to life on our planet takes yet another form in John Boorman's *Emerald Forest* (1985). Its imagery of a huge dam being built in the green world of the Amazon rain forest strikes a direct confrontation between technothreat and a fragile natural world. In this film, man's technological advances are often obscurely as well as directly corruptive, such as when the captured women of one tribe are sold into the brothels that have grown up around the damsite. *The Emerald Forest* is about two kinds of technoinduced holocausts: the destruction of the Amazon rain forest and the destruction of the tribal civilization living upon that fragile ecosystem. Like *Star Trek IV: The Voyage Home*, *The Emerald Forest* is an ecological fable couched in the genre of a jungle adventure, a Tarzan movie.

A similar film is *Iceman* (1984), directed by Fred Schepisi, which places a forty-thousand-year-old Neanderthal, who is also very much a human being, up against the technological lust for information and the experimental laboratory rapaciousness of modern science. This confrontation between scientific progress and humanism comes to a grisly impasse when the scientists begin performing vivisectionist experiments upon the iceman when he is unconscious. They take sections of flesh and samples of blood for analysis, yet never acknowledge that he is, to use Conrad's phrase, "one of us." As in both *Alien* and *Aliens*, the scientific establishment is characterized as irresponsible, self-serving, technocratic, ecologically unconcerned buccaneers plundering the planet and its atmospheres that they sail.

Of all the films of the eighties that explore the econuclear text of social history, the most realistic is Mike Nichols's *Silkwood* (1983). "It was not our intention to make some kind of political, anti-establishment film, to blast Kerr-McGee or to try and solve the case," *Silkwood*'s executive producer, Larry Cano, insists. "We were extremely naive about it. This was before the days of nuclear consciousness raising, and the more we researched the subject, the more it seemed to us a frightening case of runaway technology."[13] That theme of "runaway technology" is one constant in all of these ecothreat movies. Everyone involved with *Silkwood* was aware of the film as a sociohistorical document. "I think everything has a social message," says Meryl Streep who plays Karen Silkwood.[14] Producer Cano agrees with Streep's conception of film as a contribution to social history: "I saw that film lends itself to affecting the way people think of the world around them."[15] *Silkwood*, based on real events and people, produced with an acute sense of accuracy and history, yet clearly politicized, set an example for the eighties of the possibilities for big-screen docudrama in the same way that *All The President's Men* set that example in the previous decade.

Ironically (some would say intentionally on the part of the Kerr-McGee Corporation and the United States government) the facts upon which the film is based are as muddled as its central character, Karen Silkwood. Karen is many different people. She is a complex blue-collar plutonium-plant worker being pulled in different directions before her mysterious death in 1974. On the night of her death, she was on her way to meet a *New York Times* reporter purportedly to give him documentary evidence not only of the poor safety conditions in the Kerr-McGee factory that made plutonium rods for nuclear weapons but also of the secret diversion of plutonium from that plant. William Taylor, the chief investigator of the Silkwood family's civil suit against Kerr-McGee, feels that the evidence Karen was supposed to possess pointed to something much bigger than simply a safety regulations cover-up. For Taylor, Karen Silkwood "unknowingly stumbled across a sophisticated, government-sanctioned plan to supply plutonium to selected allies of the United States such as Israel, Iran, South Africa and Brazil." Because the Nuclear Non-Proliferation Treaty bans the supply of weapons-grade nuclear materials to other countries, Taylor contends that Karen Silkwood "was a target not only of Kerr-McGee but also of the U.S. government" who, when the Silkwood legal team began probing the missing Kerr-McGee plutonium in the courtroom, stepped in and under the seal of "national security" stopped further questioning.[16] This conspiracy theory was debated once again when the film appeared in 1983. Reed Irvine, chairman of the right-wing Accuracy in Media Inc., called *Silkwood* "another left-wing message movie,"[17] while film critic Michael Burkett, analyzing Mike Nichols's docu-direction of the film, argued:

> his refusal to let political or moral stands become more important than his people, and his unremitting efforts to make his film historically accurate.
> Such a sense of responsibility is rare in the motion picture industry. It is particularly pleasing to note, therefore, that it has resulted in one of the finest films of the year—and possibly of the decade.[18]

Finally, one of the real-life principals, attorney Steve Wodka, whose character is called Paul Stone (Ron Silver) in the film, felt that it should have had more of a "serious Costa-Gavras documentary" quality because the conditions at the Kerr-McGee plant were actually far worse than they were depicted in the film.[19]

Despite all of this controversy, over both the screen depiction and the facts, *Silkwood* is a complex multitextual film about just how dangerous the "runaway technology" of the nuclear age has become. It carefully dissects different aspects of the econuclear threat. Those aspects range from the dangers in the nuclear workplace to the indisposability of radioactive waste (or accidentally contaminated materials) to the lackluster enforcement of on-site and government safety standards to the clear and present danger for both the environment and people of proximity to radioactive nuclear materials to the possibility of illegal nuclear arms proliferation.

The primary text theme of *Silkwood* is straightforwardly blue-collar. Before anything else, it is a film about nuclear factory life and its incumbent dangers. The Kerr-McGee Corporation is a company right out of that old Tennessee Ernie Ford social consciousness folk song "16 Tons." In the eighties, the "company store" workers are still getting "another day older and deeper in debt" except that they are no longer working for the coal industry. Now the nuclear power industry presents all sorts of new threats to their health. Angela (Diana Scarwid), Dolly Pelliker's (Cher) lesbian lover and a beautician who works for a funeral home, says it best: "You know . . . I can always tell when a dead person I beautified worked for Kerr-McGee. Because they all looked like they died before they died."

Silkwood opens with an almost documentary unfolding of a day's work in a plutonium rod plant. The workers, the machines, the procedures, the dangers, are observed directly. In one sense, *Silkwood* is a corporate villain exposé reminiscent of seventies films like *The China Syndrome* (1979) or *Network* (1976) rather than a full-blown nuclear warning like *Testament* (1983). Yet the problems of this nuclear workplace are more threatening than those of the anticorporate films of the seventies. In some ways, *Silkwood* is a film like the midwestern farm crisis movies of 1984, because it shows the desperation of people in small American towns who need jobs and are forced to risk their lives to literally trade future years of health for a present living. The lack of concern for the lives of its workers by the Kerr-McGee Corporation as portrayed in *Silkwood* is numbing.

Angela the beautician, a sort of realist chorus figure, best expresses this hostile corporate theme: "Karen, you ever been downtown? There's two big streets. One's called Kerr, one's called McGee. And that's how I see it. They own this state. They own everybody in this state." The structure of the film is dialogic. The personal lives and coming to consciousness of the econuclear threat of Karen, Dolly, and Drew (Kurt Russell) alternates with scenes at the plutonium plant. The danger of working life and its impingement upon personal life accrues in scene after scene of blue-collar realism. In bed one night, Karen asks, "Drew, do you feel different about me since I got cooked?" Earlier, Drew had given his resigned answer. "You just wakin' up to this?" he taunts Karen. "Whattaya think we're workin' with over there? Puffed wheat?" One of the central symbolic motifs of the film is an audio effect, the terrible sound of the contamination alarm screaming that a person has been cooked and must be dragged off to the decontamination ordeal, a process that visually echoes images of the gas chambers of the Holocaust. When the contamination alarm shrieks, it is like a bomb going off in the midst of everyday life. What the film leads up to is Karen Silkwood's ultimate realization of her own naïveté: "All that stuff about acceptable levels is all bull shit."

But the effects of Kerr-McGee's lax safety procedures radiates outside of the workplace as well. It is not only the workers whose lives are put in jeopardy by this negligent nuclear power industry, but the whole society. Early in *Silkwood*, a truck gets "cooked" (contaminated by radiation), and it becomes a lurking image in the film. In the plant lunchroom, the workers talk about the accident:

WORKER: Where they gonna park a contaminated truck that's gonna stay that way for 25,000 years?

DREW: Put it in space.

WORKER: Hell, put it in orbit.

DREW: Put it on the moon.

KAREN: What's goin' on?

WORKER: They cooked a truck. There was a leak in one o' the barrels.

Later that evening, while waiting in the plant parking lot for her ride home, Karen hears the electric crackle of cutting torches and sees the fluorescent arcs of acetylene in a fenced-in area next to the plant. Before she is told to "move on out" by the security guard, she gets a glimpse of the bizarre scene of a gang of men cutting up a truck. "We did a job out there the other night," one of Karen's co-workers brags, "buried a truck." Karen scoffs, "Sure you did." But the man is serious: "Yeah, we had a hot truck. We chopped it up, put it in these little baggies and sent it off to be buried." The econuclear problem is not simply one of safety but of disposal of radioactive waste as well. This image of the cooked truck is a grotesque hyperbole that captures the threat of this disposal problem.

The second half of *Silkwood*, however, switches to a focus upon yet a third aspect of the nuclear problem. By insinuation and the laying out of circumstantial evidence, the film implies a government conspiracy not only aimed at the cover-up of Kerr-McGee's safety procedures laxity but perhaps involving something even more sinister. The closest the film actually comes to accusing the American government of conspiracy in the Silkwood affair is when, in frustration, Dolly Pelliker complains, "Goddam government fucks you comin' and goin'!" Pauline Kael perceptively argues that "Mike Nichols has made a passive advocacy film—it raises suspicions of many kinds of nuclear-age foul play."[20] *Silkwood* examines the perniciousness of this econuclear threat. Radiation, invisible, invades the safety of the workplace, contaminates the environment for the next 25,000 years, and corrupts the political life of the nation.

All of these films that make up the econuclear text point to the volatility of peacetime nuclear energy and its danger, not just to everyday life but to the future of the environment. Radiation is not like a human lung or a hole in the ozone layer that can cure and regenerate itself when the cause of the irritation is taken away. Radiation stays around for centuries and these films question whether its utility in any way justifies its tremendous risk. Chernobyl remains the graphic proof of the validity of this econuclear text.

The Nuclear War Text

The real nuclear fear of the eighties, however, was not for the 25,000 years of half-life of a contaminated environment but for the clear and present danger of an all-out nuclear war between the United States and Russia. The political posturing of the decade between these two superpowers was predicated upon the realities of first strike capability and space-based nuclear defense systems. This doomsday nuclear text took a four-pronged shape in the films of the eighties. One group of preapocalypse films, dealing mainly with the making of the atomic bomb and the cold war maneuverings to disperse its secrets, examines the motives and political philosophies that brought the threat of nuclear apocalypse into existence. A second group of films, of the spy thriller genre, deal with cold war attempts to forestall apocalypse. A third, and by far the most important, group presents actual images of nuclear war. These are the next generation of disaster films, the most popular subgenre of the seventies. Most meticulously avoid overtones of science fiction and claim speculative realism. Finally, a fourth group of nuclear war films, dealing with the postapocalyptic world, present a future so bleak, a wasteland so arid, that it makes T. S. Eliot's vision of the twentieth century seem almost utopian.

A number of eighties films chronicled the building of the bomb and its subsequent development. Two television miniseries and the end of the decade's *Fat Man and Little Boy* (1989) focused directly upon a purely historical attempt at re-creation of the methods and motives surrounding the building of the bomb at the end of World War II. *Desert Bloom* (1985), from a *Silkwood*-like blue-collar point of view, zeroes in on the era of nuclear testing. Set in Las Vegas in the fifties, it examines the effect of the bomb upon the people who were closest to it when it was being developed. *The Manhattan Project* (1986) looks at the reality of building atom bombs from a comical perspective. As a gentle satire and an emotional warning, yet done realistically and believably (unlike the somewhat similar *War Games*), *The Manhattan Project* is about a brilliant young student who manages to build an atom bomb in his basement and transport it to his high school science fair in the trunk of his girl friend's car. Despite the seeming outrageousness of its premise, the film raises some political points about the possibilities for, and the government participation in, nuclear arms proliferation. Sidney Lumet's *Daniel* (1983), adapted from E. L. Doctorow's novel *The Book of Daniel*, examines the Julius and Ethel Rosenberg nuclear spy case of the early fifties. Both book and film are more about Jewish family life and the madness of the McCarthy era than about the bomb itself as a totem of power to be possessed, yet the bomb as the major cause of the cold war madness is clearly defined.

The machinations of that cold war world first in quest of, and then in the attempt to forestall the actual use of, nuclear weapons are the subject of a second group of eighties films. In these spy thrillers, the surfacing of a nuclear threat usually accompanied by some form of international blackmail sets the plot in motion. That plot characteristically takes the form of a cold war knight's quest for, and disarming of, this explosive grail. A number of James Bond films, particularly *Dr. No* (1961), *Thunderball* (1965) and its remake *Never Say Never Again* (1983), and *Moonraker* (1979), all employ nuclear McGuffins for Agent 007 to pursue. *Doctor No* ends with an apocalyptic explosion of a heavy water plant; *Thunderball* and *Never Say Never Again* both involve the hijacking of nuclear warheads; and *Moonraker* is an SDI movie, loaded with space-based nuclear hardware. Both *The Fourth Protocol* (1987) and *The Package* (1989) build their suspense plots on frantic attempts by Western agents to keep Russian agents from either detonating nuclear devices or tipping the balance of power via assassination so that nuclear disarmament will not occur.

A number of other films dealt, in comic ways, with the issue of nuclear arms proliferation. In *Real Genius* (1985), the issue is a space-based laser much in the SDI mode so accurate that it can eliminate people on the ground. Despite its antimilitary themes, the basic premise of the Star Wars nuclear defense system is consistently affirmed. In *Deal of the Century* (1983), Chevy Chase and Gregory Hines play two wiggy international arms dealers who could care less if they are selling the tools to start a WW III that could destroy the world.

But the most important nuclear war film texts of the eighties constitute a third grouping. These films portray in realistic terms a nuclear war and its aftermath. This third group consists of two major texts, both originally made for TV, *Testament* (1983), which was originally released in movie theaters, and *The Day After* (1983), which after its startling success on television was released for videotape sale as a feature film.

Testament is the most direct, disciplined, and powerful message movie of the eighties. Its message is one of clear emotional realism, of how a nuclear war would affect individual lives, of how a nuclear war makes it extremely difficult for human beings to remain human. What keeps the focused emotional realism of *Testament* from becoming sentimental, however, is the film's consistent irony, its underlining of the fragility of concepts such as "love" and "home" and "the future." Director Lynn Littman and screen-writer John Sacret Young, on a small budget by Hollywood standards and using actors who committed essentially to work for free because of the political and emotional message of the film, created a text that powerfully proclaims: *We Must Not Let This Happen! Testament* takes a microfocus upon one close family and what it must endure in the wake of a nuclear war. It re-lentlessly chronicles the family's physical deprivations, but it also sensitively observes the family's emotional tribulations. Strangely, the microfocus upon a single family universalizes the impact of its message much more than does the wider social vision of *The Day After*. Also, in *Testament*, Jane Alexander may play the strongest woman character in any eighties film. She is a mother continuing to function under the worst possible circumstances, yet still struggling to love. She embodies the complexity of *Testament*'s message: that though nuclear war will threaten our lives, our future, our climate, our food supply, what it really threatens is our humanity.

Testament begins ironically as if it were another Steven Spielberg paeon to suburbia. The first sound is an aerobics class on the radio exhorting the listening audience to get healthy for the future. The earliest images are of the father, Tom Wetherly (William Devane), and his son, Brad (Ross Harris), bicycling to get in shape. As their morning ride takes them past the cemetary, they talk about the future. When Brad once again fails to make it up the Sisyphean hill on their run, his father says, "You'll get it next time." At the village gas station, Tom makes plans to take the owner's mentally handicapped son fishing the following Sunday. Mary Liz Wether-ly (Roxanna Zal), meanwhile, is practicing her piano for future recitals. In bed that evening, before making love, Tom and Carol Wetherly (Jane Alexander) make plans for their children's upcoming birthdays. All of this future consciousness becomes ironic when the nuclear strike occurs and both past and future are obliterated in bright searing seconds. All the plans seem so frivolous in the face of knowing that there no longer is a future for the world.

Testament is *E.T.: The Extra-Terrestrial* (1982) with an unhappy ending and no "home" to go to. It is *Poltergeist* (1982) with a real, more powerful, monster suddenly arising to threaten the All-American family. *Testament*'s small Spielbergian town is Hamlin, California, about two hours from San Francisco. The opening scenes become even more ironic as the myth of "The Pied Piper of Hamelin" is superimposed upon them. That is the play the elementary-school children are rehearsing. "They won't come back until you've proved you deserve the children," the Pied Piper, who has turned the small mythical town of Hamelin to desolation, tells the village elders in the play. This fairy-tale myth about how decisions in the present can exacerbate the fragility of the future underlines the irony of *Testament*'s Spielbergian opening. The myth is symbolic in political terms as well. Since the forties, the everpresent Pied Piper of international relations has been the threat of nuclear attack. Both the U.S. and Russia (and other countries as well) have threatened that "if you don't deal with me I have the Pied Piper power to take your children away." The final scene of the film has Carol and Brad and their adopted Hiroshi lighting candles at the empty dining room table:

BRAD: What do we do now?

CAROL: Make a wish.

BRAD: What will we wish for, Mom?

CAROL: That we remember it all. The good and the awful. The way we finally lived. That we never gave up. That we were last to be here, to deserve the children.

Testament is exactly that, a testament to the ways in which adults are threatening the future, are, like the foolish elders of fairy-tale Hamelin, placing in jeopardy their children's lives.

The film is structured in three parts. At the end of this first Spielbergian introductory section, the TV set goes to static fuzz just as it did in *Poltergeist*. Immediately this loss of the ultimate symbol of American suburban normality is followed by the bright light of the nuclear explosion.

Part two of *Testament* is a frighteningly realistic postnuclear war checklist that dispenses information on what the survivors of a nuclear attack would have to face. The checklist notes how communications are lost, utilities are lost, looting begins, the citizenry arms, gas lines form, food lines form, disease begins. In its checklist approach, *Testament* is like the popular disaster movies of the seventies in which communities of survivors struggled to overcome the obstacles to their journey to safety. Unfortunately in a nuclear disaster film, there is no safety to journey toward. The major purpose of this checklist section of *Testament* is didactic, intent on dispensing information about the nature of the postnuclear age:

TOWNSPERSON: Are you people crazy? You're talking like this is an earthquake or a hurricane. Well, it's not! Bernie, you're a doctor. Why don't you tell these good people what they've got to look forward to here.

DOCTOR: We don't know yet. We really have no equipment available for accurately measuring radiation fallout. If the rads dosage reaches 40 or 50 per hour and remains there long, there will be illness and that can lead to dizziness, gastroenteritis, vomiting, skin sores, hair loss.

YOUNG MOTHER: Doctor, my baby wouldn't take my milk this morning.

TOWNSPERSON: You people make me laugh. Bombs, hundreds of bombs are leveling cities. It's throwing debris miles into the sky.

What this second section isolates is the enormity of both the destruction and the change that a nuclear attack would cause. The world as we know it would literally cease to exist, and unlike the fires, earthquakes and tidal waves of the disaster movies of the seventies, a nuclear attack is simply not something that can be survived.

Testament's final section is a depressingly positive exercise in Sisyphean futility and human endurance. Knowing that her efforts can never work, Carol Wetherly tries to make life go on as usual for her family. It is clear to everyone involved, including the theater audience, that her efforts are a futile illusion. This third section comprises a series of scenes in which the members of the family struggle to preserve their humanity and their ability to love in an increasingly hostile, utterly hopeless world. Mother and daughter talk about what it is like to make love, something that the daughter will never experience. The son rides his bike through the rubble of the town carrying messages. The daughter continues her piano lessons. The mother rocks her youngest son in her arms as he dies. Mother and son dance to a Beatles song. The mother sews her daughter's shroud. *Testament* becomes a film about man's struggle to remain human in a world that has de-evolved, gone back to the caveman, animalic, ages.

In the penultimate scene of *Testament*, Carol sits Brad and Hiroshi in the family car, closes the garage door, and turns on the ignition. It is a scene out of the fifties nuclear war film *On the Beach*, but with one difference. Carol cannot go through with this suicide. She is too human. In existential terms, she opts for the Sisyphean struggle over the suicide. Of all the eighties films, *Testament* drives to the very crux of the major threat to the social history of the world. In its directness and its incontrovertability, it is a paradigm of what socially conscious films should do.

"The important difference between the modest *Testament* and the massive ABC-TV movie *The Day After* is how you are left feeling afterwards," Sheila Benson writes. "I left *Testament* shattered but with the feeling that now I must move on from 'private feelings' to useful action. I left *The Day After* determined that I would have on hand a way to die, along with my family, should we be in that marginal band to survive the initial nuclear blasts." Benson acknowledges that both films have tremendous impact, yet she valorizes *Testament*'s impact in aesthetic terms:

> But I wonder about bad art in the service of a good cause. For all its intentions and its graphic educational value, the screenplay of *The Day After* gives us so many characters so thinly sketched that it almost wards off what it most desperately needs, our most intimate identification with its doomed Kansans. . . . No one can deny the impact, even on small screens, of the film's four-minute holocaust sequence . . . [but] the strength of *Testament* is that its horror occurs almost entirely in our imagination, and it proceeds from a beautifully written and decently constructed script. . . . Littman and

her screenwriter, John Sacret Young, aimed for a climate of loss, and you cannot mourn the loss of people you do not know.[21]

Barry Koltnow does not agree. "You haven't seen this on television before," he writes of *The Day After* (1983).

In fact, you don't always see this in your neighborhood theater. The critically acclaimed *Testament*, a film on the same topic presently making the rounds of movie houses, fails to deliver for the very reason *The Day After* succeeds. Unlike its television counterpart, *Testament* does involve itself in plot and you do care about the characters. But it's too easy, too clean. Littman didn't want to turn people off with the ugly details of nuclear war. . . . That's where her movie loses its effectiveness. In *The Day After*, we see it all and the message therefore is not lost in the act.

Despite what seems a clear critical disagreement, both Benson and Koltnow are right. Both films are powerful in their own way and on their own terms.

Whereas *Testament* is a before-and-after portrait of the emotional ravages of nuclear war upon the individual, *The Day After* gives a powerful sense of what it would be like during a nuclear attack. In *Testament*, the explosion of a nuclear device over San Francisco takes place offstage and is presented representationally by a bright light. In *The Day After*, however, the chilling launching of nuclear missiles, the nuclear explosions, the vaporization of human bodies, the firestorms, the panic in the streets, the mushroom clouds, are all seen via some stunning special effects and editing techniques. *The Day After*'s real strength is in this apocalyptic sequence that is the single thing *Testament* does not provide. Without question, *The Day After* is more dispersed, superficial, lacks the intense character focus of *Testament*, but, argues Koltnow, "the situation itself is so powerful and overwhelming that it overshadows any superficiality in character or skimpiness of plot."[22]

But *The Day After* also differs from *Testament* in its physical, rather than psychological, emphasis in presenting the grisly aftermath of a nuclear war. *The Day After* emphasizes the graphic physical toll, first, in the immediate images of devastation (huge cities turned to rubble) and, second, in the graphic physical detailing of the effects of radiation upon the human body in the form of lesions, tumors, hair loss, skin rash, and the mounds of the dead. *The Day After* has more of a documentary, journalistic focus, whereas *Testament* brilliantly offers a moving psychological perception. "The film will tell you quite simply what will happen in the event of a nuclear war," *The Day After*'s director, Nicholas Meyer, explains, "and the answer is that everybody will die. I felt a moral obligation to make this as a gigantic public service announcement."[23] If *The Day After* tells what happens, then *Testament* studies the psychological effect of what happens upon people with whom the audience identifies very closely. Marcel Ophuls congratulates Meyer on that service success of *The Day After*:

> What we are shown is the scrupulous result of competent teamwork, a fundamentally honest and sober vision of nuclear horror, a universal nightmare sanitized through the filter of corporate responsibility. No festering sores, no calcinated corpses, no slow agonies caused by radioactive fallout are ever presented in gratuitous close-ups. Whatever monstrosities we are shown are part of the demonstration, part of the dire, cruel, but necessary warning. It all serves a purpose, a decent, respectable, and generous one.[24]

The Day After delivers its message powerfully, though perhaps not as indelibly as does the haunting and painful *Testament*. *The Day After* shocks one into recognition, while *Testament* haunts one with the personal consequences of reckless public policy, argues eloquently even as *The Day After* bludgeons home the facts.

This comparison of the two films and reaction to *The Day After*, however, only points to the impact that *most watched* of any TV show had upon the society of its time. Whatever its success or lack thereof as art, its message is powerful and clear. It is the same message that *Testament* delivers: that *we must not let this happen!* Early in *The Day After*, a man and wife lie in bed listening to the news of an escalating international crisis:

> WIFE: My god, it's 1962 all over again. The Cuban Missile Crisis. Do you remember Kennedy on television? Telling Khrushchev to turn the boats around.
>
> DOCTOR OAKES: Full Retaliatory Response. He didn't bat an eye. . . . We got up and went to the window and looked for the bombs.
>
> WIFE: Didn't happen. It's not gonna happen now.
>
> DOCTOR OAKES: Naw. People are crazy, but not that crazy.

As it turns out, in *The Day After* people are every bit "that crazy," and the false sense of security, based in a misguided trust in political wisdom, must be dispelled. The film aims at revealing the insanity of even considering the feasibility of a nuclear war:

> 1ST DOCTOR: You heard the latest. There is a rumor they are evacuating Moscow. Yeah, there are even people leaving Kansas City because of the missile fields. Now I ask you, where does one go from Kansas City? To the Yukon? To Tahiti? We are not talking about Hiroshima anymore. Hiroshima was peanuts.
>
> DOCTOR OAKES: What's going on? Do you understand what's going on in this world?
>
> 1ST DOCTOR: Yeah, stupidity. Has a habit of getting its way.
>
> DOCTOR OAKES: Nah, if that was true we wouldn't be mending peoples'

hearts, we'd be back in caves eating them. If that were true. . . . why bother doing anything?

Whether it be insanity or stupidity or simply the naïveté of believing that a nuclear holocaust could never happen, from its earliest frames *The Day After* sets out to remove the blinders from an uninvolved American populace.

The film opens in a more generalized yet quite similar way to the opening of *Testament*. The credits roll over a montage of images of midwestern Americana from the amber waves of the food chain farms to the dairies and cattle pens to the baseball fields and football stadiums. The camera pans over all of the comfortable symbols of the pastoral normality of life in "the heart of the heart of the country" as preparation for the reality of destroying all those valued things in a few violent minutes. The opening, like that of *Testament*, is consciously ironic because beneath that pastoral facade in missile silos under the fields wait the machines, the technology of destruction. The opening of the film laughs at the naïveté of superficial American life. Though radios and TVs repeatedly report on an escalating international crisis, no one pays any attention. Everyone keeps making plans for the future as if this life in all its normality is going to go on forever. In this early ironic emphasis upon the normality of everyday life and the naïve confidence in the future, *The Day After* begins almost exactly as did *Testament*. But whereas *Testament* is a film of closeups, *The Day After* is a film of montages. *Testament* focused in upon the individual emotions of its characters, but *The Day After* scans over the landscape, over a wider range of characters, collects series of images that illustrate what is happening in quick visual bursts, simply presented and unanalyzed.

The most powerful montage of *The Day After* is the four-minute bombardment of images of the actual events of a nuclear war. Edited with a chilling, uneditorialized, progression of realistic events, the images take on a symbolic life of their own so powerful that they demand to be read as a frightening horror text. The montage begins with images of buttons being pushed, missiles beginning to fire, huge bombers taking off, panicked crowds stampeding through supermarkets for food, families provisioning their basements and underground shelters, a view across a peaceful rural landscape as a colt jumps in a field just as a missile silo suddenly spurts forth its flaming bullet out of that peaceful rural earth. This startling image is followed by images of everyone looking to the sky, riveted upon the contrails of the hundreds of missiles being simultaneously launched. The accumulating power of the montage is broken for a brief moment by a human voice, a guy named Joe in that center of midwestern society, a barbershop:

> JOE: Those are Minuteman missiles. They're on their way to Russia. They take about thirty minutes to reach their target.
>
> STUDENT: So do theirs, right?

The montage resumes with scenes of panic in the streets and huge traffic jams that are suddenly enveloped in a searing bright light, and EVERY-THING STOPS as the mushroom clouds bloom on the horizon. Next, scenes of horror, holocaust, and apocalypse bombard the screen: fire-storms, concussive winds, explosions, human beings vaporized to their skeletons. When the montage mercifully stops, nothing is left but a smoking wasteland. The green prewar Kansas world has turned completely gray. The success of *The Day After* lies in the eloquent visual effect of this single montage sequence. Script, characters, acting, direction, be damned; this apocalyptic montage is so frightening that its message is unmistakeable.

As was the first section of *The Day After*, the third postwar section is also quite similar (if more graphic) in its thematic emphasis to the concluding section of *Testament*. Both films emphasize didacticism and the loss of basic conceptions of humanity. The sources of these two themes in *The Day After* are Doctor Oakes (Jason Robards) and a university scientist, Joe Huxley (John Lithgow). One didactic exchange almost exactly echoes a similar exchange in *Testament* except that it leaves no margin for hope:

> JOE: We're getting 50 rads an hour. I would have thought it would have diminished by now. . . .
>
> DOCTOR OAKES: When will it be safe to move people to other buildings?
>
> JOE: It'll never be safe.

After the president of the United States finally establishes contact by shortwave radio and ludicrously declares that "America has survived," Joe Huxley grimly lectures, "You know what Einstein said about World War III? He said he didn't know how they were going to fight World War III, but he knew how they would fight World War IV, with sticks and stones." The concluding scenes of *The Day After* support Einstein's prediction. The survivors (if that is what they can be called) revert to barbarism to survive the deprivations of postnuclear fallout.

The film clinically examines the onset of nuclear winter as ashen snow falls on roads clogged with trudging refugees. Desperate people storm the locked doors of the one remaining hospital. Fights break out in a line at a lone water pump. Roving bands with guns kill people for food. The university basketball arena, the scene of such animation and excitement before the war, now is filled with the silent, motionless stretchers of the dead and dying. When Oakes returns to his home in Kansas City, he finds little more than a rock-strewn desert. And the green world of the opening credits has turned completely gray. The second major strength of *The Day After* is its refusal to ameliorate the devastation of nuclear war. When the film ends, the only possible message that the text delivers is that nuclear war will utterly destroy all life as human beings have known it, that if anyone above the species of cockroach chances to survive they will de-evolve to an animalic level of existence.

Because *The Day After* was the most widely watched television program of all time, the reactions to it were many and varied. "Basically, I think everyone feels this is the largest social issue of our time," one viewer speculated. "I think people feel powerless when they watch something like this and they don't know what to do about it."[25] Arguing that "no topic has ever been more important and timely than this one," the *Los Angeles Times* predicted that "nuclear policy will be a hot issue in the coming presidential campaign. Hence, both sides in the emotional nuclear debate have been vocal about *The Day After* with 'freeze' advocates seeing it as a cause to rally around and opponents targeting it for criticism."[26] In many ways, that prediction proved true as the second half of the eighties decade was marked by stepped up nuclear 'freeze' protests followed by 'disarmament' talks between America and Russia and, ultimately, at the end of the decade, with the succession of Mikhail Gorbachev to power in Russia, an actual reduction in the expensive nuclear arsenals of both countries.

Though they were the most widely seen and discussed nuclear war texts of the decade, *Testament* and *The Day After* were not the only films to directly confront the realities of nuclear war and its terrible aftermath. *Threads* (1984), originally produced for British television before being released to theaters as were *Testament* and *The Day After* in America, is very much like both of those films. Set in the factory town of Sheffield, England, it has all of the unrelenting graphic detail and violence of *The Day After*, but it also has a strong focus on two families whose futures are about to be connected by a wedding but are connected very differently by Armageddon. The French film *Le Dernier Combat* (1986) is also a bleak journey through the nuclear rubble. It is peopled by lost souls whose larynges have been paralyzed by the concussion of the blast and thus can only grunt like cavemen. They struggle to stay alive in a world where there is nothing to live for. *Night of the Comet* (1984) is *The World, the Flesh and the Devil* (1959) campily updated to the eighties. As a result of the doomsday flyby of a radioactive comet, Los Angeles is completely depopulated except for a group of inexplicable survivors.

If *Testament* and *The Day After* explore the nuclear war scenario in realistic terms, and these other films do variations upon those primary texts, *War Games* (1983) goes in yet a different direction. It simulates the nuclear war scenario as a result of the same runaway technology that was at issue in *Silkwood*. It examines how the eighties love affair with computers could possibly run amok and destroy the world. The harshly realistic terms of these other nuclear war scenarios is transformed in *War Games* into a uniquely eighties metaphor, that of reality as an elaborate videogame.

Early in the film, NORAD computer specialist McKittrick (Dabney Coleman) successfully suggests to the president's closest civilian defense adviser, "We should take the men out of the loop." He is suggesting that the button-pushing responsibilities in America's missile silos be taken out of human hands and given to electronic relays controlled from the massive, multivideo-screened war room of the NORAD computer center that electronically tracks every military movement of the Soviet Union. By taking the "men out of the loop," the basic theme of *War Games* is generated. If human morality and judgment are removed from the process of nuclear war decision making, is it not possible that an apocalyptic holocaust could be started by a computer error? A similar theme questioning the new age overconfidence in computers was being explored as far back as *2001: A Space Odyssey* (1968). The run-amok computer HAL of Stanley Kubrick's film has engendered WOPR (nicknamed "Whopper"), aka "Joshua," which controls all of the computer simulations of "Global Thermonuclear War" that when he (WOPR) takes over appear as a real Soviet nuclear attack on the huge video screens of the NORAD tracking center. What *Testament* and *The Day After* clearly set out to realistically demonstrate is that "Global Thermonuclear War" is not a game. The cautionary metaphor of *War Games* is ironic yet similar. This film emphasizes the danger in the mindset that could actually believe the planning of a war that could destroy the world and civilization as we know it is really a game. In *War Games*, the idea that nuclear weapons can be used as board pieces in a complex strategy game is ironically exposed as scary beyond anyone's limited conception of danger or horror. What *War Games* warns is that the threat of nuclear war lies in men's minds as well as in the extant missiles. If men's minds create a concept that argues the feasibility of nuclear war, then that war could actually occur.

Though *War Games* seems a mere trifle, a teenage high jinks movie like *American Graffiti* (1973), *Risky Business* (1983), or the *Porky's* series (1981, 1983, 1985), in its high-tech way it explores exactly the same issues, presents exactly the same philosophical discussions of nuclear war that the other starkly realistic, more "serious," nuclear war films do. In Platonic terms, by combining the teenage subgenre with a nuclear age social consciousness, *War Games* succeeds because it both entertains and instructs. Its plot—about an amoral teenage computer hacker named Lightner (Matthew Broderick) who manages to break into the NORAD computer and by accident begins a "Global Thermonuclear War" simulation that the war room generals mistake for the real thing and, thinking that Russia is initiating a preemptory missile strike, move to retaliate—is, indeed, a trifle. However, the dialogue of awakening to nuclear reality and the images of technology run amok are striking. *War Games* succeeds not on what it does (its predictable action) but on how it does it. It is a better, more serious, more socially conscious film than it seems because, though its plot offers little, its style equals its meaning. While the trivial plot escalates from a high school student using his computer to change his grades to a battalion of moronic military types believing what they are watching on television, that triviality is initially backgrounded and then paralleled by frightening images of technology taking over and the world approaching doomsday. Those images are also interspersed with perceptive dialogue exchanges that echo the discussions of the same issues in *Testament* and *The Day After*.

The technological images of the film's opening are imposing and complex. The camera gives a tour of the computer war room of the United States as McKittrick explains his theory of a computerized national missile system and declares that we can "take the men out of the loop" and replace them with electronic relays in two weeks' time. At this point, the film's duality becomes apparent as it crosscuts to David Lightner cutting up in his high school class. His goofy Jerry Lewis imitation provides an interesting counterpoint to the serious issues of the war room. Ironically when Lightner realizes that it was probably he who initiated the computer simulation that almost started World War III, he is only worried about his own neck, never even considers what might have happened. He laughs off the whole affair and only stops laughing when the WOPR computer calls him back on the phone and tells him that the game of "Global Thermonuclear War" is still on and it is thirty-eight hours to doomsday. In the war room, McKittrick sums up Lightner's amorality best:

BUREAUCRAT: Why would a bright boy like this jeopardize the lives of millions?

COMPUTER EXPERT: He says he does these things for fun.

MCKITTRICK: I wanna talk to this little prick.

When the computer calls Lightner back, it signals that the men are "out of the loop" and the rest of the film follows the efforts of McKittrick, Lightner, and WOPR's mysterious original programmer, Falken (Barry Corbin), to get man back into the loop before the world is destroyed.

The imagery of the second half of the film is almost completely that of the video screen and the computer terminal. On the huge video screens in the war room the Soviet submarines flash bright red completely surrounding the United States, and the rainbow arcs of the airborne missiles incoming out of Russia form a tight lattice over America. On the smaller screens of the computer terminals, WOPR prints out the "death kill ratios" and "damage percentages" in terrifying numbers: 72,000,000 dead, 90 percent of hospitals destroyed. This is *War Games*' version of the didacticism of those speeches by doctors and scientists in *Testament* and *The Day After* taken to a purely visual, statistical limit. Complementing the didacticism of that visual imagery are the didactic speeches of the philosophical Falken. His "bedtime story" for Lightner and Jennifer (Ally Sheedy) begins with the same caveman and dinosaur allusion that was also employed in *Testament* and *The Day After* then moves to the "horror of survival." When Lightner accuses him of starting all of this madness, Falken replies:

FALKEN: My fault! The whole point was to practice nuclear war without destroying ourselves. . . . Did you ever play Tic/Tac/Toe?

JENNIFER: Yes.

FALKEN: But you don't anymore?

JENNIFER: No.

FALKEN: Why?

JENNIFER: Because it's a boring game. It's always a tie.

FALKEN: Exactly. There's no way to win. The game is pointless. But back at the war room, they believe you can win a nuclear war, there can be acceptable losses.

That speech pinpoints the "runaway technology" mindset that *War Games* is warning against.

War Games ends with "the big game," only this time the final game is played for the life of the world. In the final game, the players actually watch the world blow up on the video screens. The bombs bloom all over the map of America, but by doing nothing, by not pushing their buttons, by realizing that it is only a game and not worth risking the real lives of 72,000,000 people, the generals put "the men back into the loop."

War Games is both a paean to, and a warning against, hardware, a warning not heeded in the case of Vietnam. It is a cautionary fable about technological overconfidence couched in the terms of one of the eighties favorite subgenres, the teenage movie. Its vehicle is perhaps trivial, but its message (delivered in the images and numbers that come up on the video screens) is every bit as scary in its austerity as the terrible visceral images in those more realistic films. A seventies film, *Capricorn One* (1978), first advanced the premise that the global village was rapidlly becoming a big TV show, and *War Games* simply pushes that premise to its outer limits.

The last of the four nuclear war film texts is the very text that Falken in *War Games* warns against anyone even considering, the unthinkable post-apocalypse text that assumes human civilization can survive a nuclear war and work toward an improbable rebirth. This postapocalypse text is most clearly delineated in the Mad Max movies of George Miller. Set in a blasted desert world, these films are acutely aware of the history that brought civilization to this pass. Their reaction to that history is the valorization of a new code of honor, a new existential hero clothed in black silence, and a new eloquence of action. The language of the Mad Max films is a discourse of the body, of motion, of physical survival. But the Mad Max movies did not spring up full-blown from dragon's teeth. They are direct descendants of L. Q. Jones's cult postapocalypse favorite of the seventies, *A Boy and His Dog* (1975). In fact, unpretentious as the hot rod/biker action of the Mad Max trilogy may seem, next to *A Boy and His Dog*, the Mad Max movies are a pretentious mythic extension of that film's wacky "Mr. Ed" and *Francis the Talking Mule* version of the post-nuclear world. Albert (Don Johnson), the horny hero of *A Boy and His Dog* and the precursor of Mad Max, is little more than a feckless scavenger who wanders the world of postbombs Phoenix, Arizona, looking for food and sex.

The opening newsreel footage images of both *A Boy and His Dog* and *The Road Warrior* (1981), the second film of the Mad Max trilogy, are identical. Both begin with the bombs going off, with the blooming of mushroom clouds. "World War IV lasted five days" the first banner on the screen in *A Boy and His Dog* announces. The second banner, however, initiates the film's black comedy: "Politicians had finally solved the problem of urban blight." The worlds of both films are identical, blasted wastelands infested with roving gangs of rapacious scavengers. Both *The Road Warrior* and *A Boy and His Dog* are also immediately conscious of history. Blood (Tiger), Albert's dog, recounts the recent history of the world starting in 1953 and moving through nuclear World War IV to the film's present in 2024. *The Road Warrior* also begins with an omniscient narrator's voice-over recounting of the wars over oil which formed this wasteland world. *A Boy and His Dog* in its postapocalypse, Walt Disney style prefigures the world of the Mad Max trilogy in a wacky, adolescent way. George Miller's three eighties movies bring those undeveloped ideas to a mythic fruition.

Mad Max (1979), the first film of the trilogy, is a strange conglomeration of seventies film plots and fifties ideas. As revenge tragedy, it follows and draws from films like *The Outlaw Josey Wales* (1976) and *Death Wish* (1974), with allusions to *Straw Dogs* (1971), *The Wild One* (1954), and the biker movies of Roger Corman. The film repeatedly offers images of apocalypse in the form of vehicles blowing up and burning out of control and corpses burned to lumps of black charcoal as they would be in a nuclear war. There is, however, no direct allusion to the postapocalyptic nature of this future world. In its revenge tragedy simplicity, *Mad Max* is a throwaway movie remarkable only for its action sequences and the mythic memorableness of its dark paladin title character. The second Mad Max film, *The Road Warrior* (1981), cannot be dismissed so easily. It builds on the action and simplicity of the original *Mad Max* for the purpose of elaborating a nuclear age political metaphor.

By means of newsreel footage, *The Road Warrior* begins with the Third World War followed by a series of clips from *Mad Max* that chronicle Max's losses and Max's revenge. "He wandered out into the wasteland and here he relearned amid the dark wreckage that the fire that burns in the heart of man will endure. Hope survives," the narrator announces as the newsreel footage and film clips end. Thus is announced that *The Road Warrior* is about survival:

    a. The survival of the world from a nuclear holocaust
    b. The survival of hope in a wasteland world ruled by roving biker gangs
    c. The survival of myth in a hero like Max

As the narrator announces, hope catalyzes the survival metaphor, but that philosophical metaphor parallels a political metaphor based in the "dark wreckage" of *The Road Warrior*'s wasteland world.

The world of *The Road Warrior* is a desert wasteland of blasted trees and scrub vegetation, a windblown, dust-fogged, burned-out world whose roads are strewn with wrecked, charred, cannibalized cars. Gasoline has become the most valuable social commodity in this retrogressive world. It provides energy, mobility, power, and survival. A community of survivors has actually refurbished an oil refinery out in the desert and are filling up a huge tanker truck with gas. This refinery community is, however, under siege by the outlaw biker gangs who want the gas. The world of the community of the refinery is medieval and fights with bows and arrows, knives and boomerangs. It is a primitive world in every detail except their cars and gasoline. Yet it is nowhere near a realistic postapocalypse world if *Testament* and *The Day After* are to be believed. It is a desert, but it is nowhere near being utterly burned out. There are a few mutants and evolutionary throwbacks like the Feral Boy (Emil Minty), who along with Max's cur is probably a direct allusion to *A Boy and His Dog*, but there is no radiation disease and no sense that the human race is facing extinction.

What the conception of the oil refinery community completely surrounded by hostile armies, who keep it under siege, offers is a metaphor for the energy greed of the eighties focused mainly in Persian Gulf oil. In the late seventies and early eighties, that oil was the occasion for all sorts of saber rattling on the parts of Iran, Iraq, Israel, and the United States. This oil siege that drives the plot of *The Road Warrior* mirrors the eighties Middle East volatility until Max arrives to lead this lost tribe to its promised land.

As was emphasized near the end of both *Testament* and *The Day After*, the difference between the lost tribe members of the refinery community and the besieging bikers of the wasteland is the difference between humanity and an animal existence. When Mad Max initially refuses to help the tribal community, the leader accuses him of being like the bikers: "You're a scavenger, Max, a maggot, livin' off the corpse of the old world." In *The Road Warrior*, the grand finale is Max's breakout in the huge tanker truck, his running of the postapocalypse gauntlet. As he makes his break, the refinery, the "corpse of the old world," is abandoned and then blown up in a mushroom cloud behind him while the barrels of precious gas (unbeknownest to Max his tanker is full of sand) are driven to safety to provide the energy for the building of a new society.

Mad Max Beyond Thunderdome (1985), the last film of the trilogy, is more of the same, another parable about energy, only this time it is methane gas produced by a troglodytic race from pig offal. It is the same wasteland world populated by the same mixture of human beings, nuclear mutants and postapocalyptic outlaw barbarians. Throughout the trilogy, the imagery of this world and the theme of survival operating on a number of different levels has remained consistent. Other films going all the way back to the *Planet of the Apes* series (1968) and including *Escape to New York* (1981), *Moonlighting* (1982), and *The Last Chase* (1981) have, in much less perceptive ways, also set their action against this backdrop of post-apocalyptic survival.

The Mad Max trilogy, however, is a natural coda to the nuclear war text. They are basically silent films. They signal the failure of language in the face of the realities of a nuclear holocaust. Not only can words not express the horror and devastation of nuclear war, but, realistically, words will not even exist after the human race, like the dinosaurs, is bombed into extinction. As the earth will be silent after a nuclear war, the Mad Max films return to the silence of film history's stone age. All of the major nuclear film texts—*Silkwood*, *Testament*, *The Day After*, *The Road Warrior*—are ultimately rendered speechless, end in the silence of desolation.

6

From the "Evil Empire" to Glasnost

NEVER AVERSE EITHER to the symbolic gesture or to using movie references to make historical points, when Ronald Reagan went to the Moscow Summit in 1988 he took a print of a single American film to present to his hosts, the Gorbachevs. That film was William Wyler's *Friendly Persuasion* (1956) about pacifism in the Civil War. That symbolic gesture of conciliation near the end of Reagan's almost decade-long tenure in the American presidency was, however, a far cry from the Reagan rhetoric of Russian-American relations of the earlier years of the decade. In 1983, employing one of the many references to *Star Wars* that peppered the rhetoric of his administration's international relations, Reagan characterized the Soviet Union as the "evil empire." In 1985, Reagan invited Sylvester Stallone to the White House in another symbolic, anti-Russian gesture. Stallone at that time was dominating the American box office with unremittingly anti-Russian fare. In *Rocky IV*, he had beaten a Soviet Superman into submission, and in *Rambo II*, he had cut a lethal swath through the Soviet-backed Vietnamese army in retribution for America's defeat in Vietnam. Draped in the American flag and crushing the hammer and sickle underfoot, Stallone had become an exploitable symbol for a presidency that had spent the decade expressing itself in the language of the movies.

The history of America's relations with Russia during the eighties was like both a mirror and a gradually brightening lamp. The United States and Russia mirrored each other in Olympics boycotts, unwinnable wars, Summit meetings, shot down civilian airliners, and natural and unnatural disasters. In 1980 and 1984, both countries exchanged letters of political protest via the Summer Olympics. Russia's decade-long war in Afghanistan mirrored America's fascination with its own ten-year mistake in Vietnam. America hosted the pivotal Summit Meeting in Geneva in 1985 that lit the lamp of understanding, and Moscow hosted the historic Summit of 1988 that steadied and magnified that light.

But even in the light of détente, other strange mirrorings marked the similarities of these two mammoths of the Eastern and Western hemispheres. In 1983 Russia shot down a Korean Air Lines plane that had wandered into its air space, and in 1988 America shot down an Iranian airliner mistaken for an attacking military plane. Russia's Chernobyl nuclear disaster in 1986 was a graphic demonstration of what almost happened at Three Mile Island in 1978. The earthquake that wracked Soviet Armenia in 1988 mirrored the devastation that Hurricane Hugo of the summer and the San Francisco earthquake of the fall would wreak in America in 1989. In the eighties, America and Russia observed their striking historical similarities through these both orchestrated and coincidental mirrorings and generated the light of a new understanding. If there is one thing the Reagan administration should be proud of it is the change in its own rhetorical stance toward Russia, the shift from antagonism and suspicion to friendship and negotiation accomplished over the course of its decade in office.

A marvelous movie irony projects across the imagemaking of the decade. From the dominance of the American Cowboy movie star personality cult of Ronald Reagan in the early eighties, the world audience shifted its allegiance to the gradual rise to stardom of the Russian personality cult of Gorbachev in the late eighties. The bureaucrat took a lesson in imagemaking from the movie star and became a star himself. From the "evil empire" to *glasnost* and *perestroika* was partly a case of Gorbachev looking in the mirror of America and lighting the lamp in order to study that image more closely.

In a symmetry of belligerence turning to enlightenment, the films of the eighties that dealt with American/Russian affairs demonstrated this evolution of the relationship between these two previously antagonistic superpowers. Early in the decade, and as late as 1986 when *Top Gun* was such a summer hit, that antagonism was still evident, but it was being moderated by other voices and a change in rhetoric.

Since the end of World War II, the primary historical text of Amero-Russian relations has been a cold war text of suspicion, wariness and competition on a series of levels (militarist, intelligence, economic, political). In the eighties, that historical cold war text held until the Geneva Summit of 1985, where something extraordinary happened: the rhetoric of the previous three and a half decades suddenly shifted and was jettisoned. After the Geneva and then the Moscow summits, both Ronald Reagan and Garry Trudeau, the satirist of the *Doonesbury* comic strip, publicly declared an end to the cold war. The decade's rhetoric of international relations had miraculously transformed itself from the distrust and belligerence of the cold war years of 1980–85 to the unlikely mediating spirit of cooperation in the years 1985–90.

While this rhetorical change certainly had something to do with the personal popularities of both Reagan and Gorbachev, the accelerated rhetorical evolution was perhaps most strongly attributable to Russia's domestic economy problems, to the burgeoning American deficit due mainly to defense spending, to the expense of Third World standoffs (both military and political), and to the economic threat of Japan. Through the personality cult fascination of the media for Reagan and Gorbachev, the nuances and evolution of this Amero-Russian rhetoric was much on the collective minds of the peoples of both countries. When Gorby sneezed in Moscow, Ronnie said, "Gesundheit!" in Washington, and the whole world knew about it. When the "evil empire" evolved into "friendly persuasion," the world listened in on that tonal modulation, including Hollywood. The films of the eighties that dealt with American-Russian relations tailored their themes and characterizations directly to the evolution of this Amero-Russian cold war rhetoric.

The fascination of eighties American films with Russian themes closely followed the contour of the historical rhetoric of Amero-Russian relations. Early, films like *Red Dawn* and the TV miniseries *Amerika* examined the differences between the societies and ideologies, their potentials for brutality toward each other. By mid-decade, films like *Rocky IV* and *White Nights* had taken up the Reagan "evil empire" patriotic jingoism that emphasized the differences between the two societies, especially the dehumanized power of the totalitarian Soviet State. But after the 1985 Geneva Summit, Hollywood had to scramble to accommodate the sudden change in the rhetoric of Amero-Russian relations. The resultant softening of characterizations and minimizing of cultural differences in films like *Little Nikita*, *Russkies*, and *Red Heat* underlined that rhetorical shift.

In fact, in the shock of that rhetorical shift at the 1985 Geneva Summit, Hollywood got caught by surprise and was criticized for the inappropriate rhetoric of films like *White Nights* and *Rocky IV*. Both films portrayed heavy-handed Soviet villains, and Hollywood was roundly criticized by the Soviet government newspaper *Izvestia* for fostering anti-Soviet feelings in a post-Geneva time of thawing cold war sentiment. Charles Z. Wick, director of the U.S. Information Agency and a former Hollywood producer, answered *Izvestia* in a surprisingly ill-informed way. He could have defended Hollywood by arguing that *White Nights* and *Rambo IV* had been more than two years in development and had gotten caught in the backwash of an uncharacteristically rapid rhetorical shift. Instead, he evidenced no sense that such a rhetorical shift had even occurred: "The Soviet Union should worry not about whether the movies are leading public opinion, but to what extent is it reflecting public opinion."[1] However, many people in both Washington and Hollywood, whose ears were better attuned to the rhetorical shift in superpower politics, listened to the complaints made by the Soviet deputy culture minister Georgi Ivanov in 1986 denouncing films like *Red Dawn*, *Rocky IV*, and *Rambo II* as "anti-Soviet" propaganda. ABC-TV certainly listened when Russia protested the TV miniseries *Amerika* and temporarily halted its production by threatening to expel ABC's news bureau from Moscow.[2]

Hollywood and the rest of America adjusted rather quickly to this rhetorical shift, so that by the end of the decade American culture was expressing a strong fascination for things Russian. The two most popular novels of the summer of 1989 in America, Martin Cruz Smith's *Polar Star* and John Le Carre's *Russia House*, were set in Russia and had Russian heroes and heroines. Due to the effects of the rhetorical shift of 1985, wrote one commentator, Americans no longer needed "to dehumanize Russians but are ready to be interested in them as people."[3] The new rhetoric of Amero-Russian relations by the end of the eighties had made visible inroads upon American xenophobia.

Those same inroads were visible in Amero-Russian film relations. After the *Rocky IV/White Nights* faux pas of bad timing in 1985, the American and Russian film communities quickly adjusted to the rhetorical shift. In 1988 the Soviet state film agency hosted Moscow's first American film festival. One of the films screened was *King's Row* (1942), which gave the Russian people the chance to see Ronald Reagan in his other job. The American sponsors of the festival, Film and Theater Diplomacy, in their name signaled how far Hollywood had heeded the rhetorical shift.[4]

One of the most charming and visionary metaphoric films of the eighties, Steven Spielberg's *E.T.: The Extra-Terrestrial* (1982), metaphorically dramatized the need for understanding and the eventual thaw in relations between these two wary nations. *E.T.: The Extra-Terrestrial* actually served as a metaphoric template for films later in the decade that portrayed Russians attempting to understand and adapt to the American way of life. The Amero-Russian film history in the eighties employed four distinct conceptual strategies in its representation of the rhetorical evolution of the two cultures' relationship. Each of these texts had its own subrhetoric of historically conversant ideology. The four texts that make up this Amero-Russian film history in the order of their mirroring of the rhetorical shift are the *rightist militarist* text, the *cold war spy* text, the *E.T.* text, and the *leftist freedom under totalitarianism* text.

One of the earliest predictors of the change in American-Russian relations in the eighties were the sixties creators of the fabulously successful James Bond spy films. Alexander Cockburn writes that

> from the start the films were pro-detente—in marked contrast to the books. The only bad Russians are those renegades who sow distrust between the great powers. . . . starting with *Dr. No* "looking at the very, very long-range future, United Artists did not want the Russians to be out-and-out villains. That was really done for reasons of motion picture distribution, thinking that someday Bond might go to Russia."[5]

American films of the eighties certainly went to Russia for their settings, characters, stories, and themes. In the process, those films served as popular culture barometers of the state of Amero-Russian relations.

Their four subtexts also served as an evolutionary map of the drastic shift in the rhetoric of Amero-Russian relations.

The Rightist Militarist Cowboy Text and the Russian Machine

In 1986, J. Hoberman wrote: "Not since the Nixon-era cop-and-vigilante cycle has the action film become so blatant an arena for political wish fulfillment."[6] But in 1989, Sylvester Stallone complained about how drastically things had changed:

> Berlin. *Rambo III* was done and Stallone, on the road plugging it, was getting pilloried for its content. Too many people were sick of Rambo's blood lust and his sadistic one-liners. *Glasnost* was in its first flower and an anti-Communist film about Russia in Afghanistan had become an instant anachronism. "Everything was going fine," says Stallone, "until Gorbachev's wife kissed Reagan on the cheek and blew my film. God—the heat I caught! People said, 'Why are you making the Russians look bad?' I said, '*Look* bad! They kill two million fucking Afghans—they take children and bake them on a spit—and I'm cruel?'"[7]

If *Rambo II* portrayed Russian advisers as the Mephisophelean figures behind the Vietnamese army and was criticised because it got caught in the backwash of the speed of the Amero-Russian rhetoric shift post-Geneva Summit, *Rambo III* (1988) in which the Russian army ran head-on into the Rambo juggernaut in Afghanistan should have known better. The rhetoric shift had long since been perceived and *glasnost* was in full bloom, but Rambo and his producers did not heed the sociohistorical signs of the times. Or else, as Buzz Feitshans (producer of *Red Dawn*, *Uncommon Valor*, *Rambo*) intimates, they did not want to heed them:

> I like *Red Dawn* and *Uncommon Valor* and *Rambo*. I like what they say. . . . *Red Dawn* says, Watch out: there are a group of people out there called the Russians that really do want to take away your freedom, to enslave you, and make no bones about it, and it's only people living in a dreamworld who will sit there and say they're really not too bad—we should try to coexist with them. To coexist with them is fine, but you must coexist with a club in your hand because the minute you drop the club they're gonna hit you.[8]

By the time that *Rambo III* appeared, the cycle of the rightist militarist fantasy had seized up and the shift to the left in films like *Platoon* and *Born on the Fourth of July* (1989) was under way. But the rightist militarist fantasies of the first six Reagan years did not seize up without a struggle. John Milius was the prime mover behind this new version of the American Cowboy conquest fantasy. Milius first turned to comic book violence in *Conan the Barbarian* (1982) and then began the anti-Russian cycle of rightist militarist fantasies with *Red Dawn* (1984).

The virulently anti-Soviet *Red Dawn* was an instant box office success when released during the Soviet-boycotted Olympics in Los Angeles in 1984. It is a "What if" fantasy that poses the question: What if all of America were invaded by the Russians? Milius's answer is that it would be like the bloodthirsty descent of the Mongol hordes upon Eastern Europe under the command of the great Khan. The invaders would be rapists and monsters who would line up civilians and mow them down as the Nazis did during the Holocaust. The film establishes these historical metaphors visually and depends upon them throughout, but it begins with a verbal historical text. The ominous opening shot of *Red Dawn* is from a helicopter skimming at low level over the American landscape, "from the mountains to the valleys to the prairies." Superimposed over this view from the speeding chopper is the historical text of the causes of World War III and the invasion of America:

> Soviet Union suffers worst wheat harvest in 55 years. Labor and food riots in Eastern Europe. Cuba and Nicaragua reach full military strength of 500,000. Revolution in Mexico. Nato dissolves. United States stands alone.

That treetop-skimming chopper finally hovers over the prairie farmland and the main street of small-town USA, Calumet, Colorado, at the foot of the "purple mountains' majesty." Shots follow of the mountains, the prairie farms, this small one-street town, the neighborhoods waking up, kids going to school past the statue of the old Roughrider, Teddy Roosevelt, in front of the courthouse. There is an intentional clichéd Americanness about this landscape.

At the high school on this sunny prairie morning a teacher is lecturing on the Mongol hordes' descent, led by Genghis Khan, upon Europe from the steppes of Russia. As he describes this barbarian invasion, black parachutes suddenly float down into the schoolyard, descend like dark spiders over the landscape. Soldiers in camouflage suits harvest their guns, kill the teacher wordlessly, shatter the school with automatic weapons fire, rocket the cars in the parking lot.

Subtle the film's opening words and images are not, but ideologically effective they are. In the first five minutes, the political stance of *Red Dawn*—barbarian Russian hordes descending upon small-town America—is quickly and cleanly proclaimed. As the film unfolds, this simplistic metaphor gets even simpler. When Colonel Andrew Tanner USAF (Powers Boothe) joins a group of young guerrillas, led by Jed (Patrick Swayze), who have armed themselves against the Russians, he explains the start of World War III so simplistically that even Jed, the dim, former football player, questions the oversimplification:

JED: What started it?

TANNER: I don't know. Two toughest kids on the block I guess. Sooner or later they're gonna fight.

JED: That simple?

TANNER: Maybe somebody just forgot what it was like. . . . In Denver the pyres for the dead light up the sky. It's medieval.

The Russian invaders are the Mongol hordes, while America is a medieval city under siege.

After this metaphoric opening, *Red Dawn* settles into a crosscutting structure between the band of young guerrillas in the mountains, who call themselves the "Wolverines," and the occupation by the combined Russian/Cuban forces of the small town of Calumet. A ring of tanks circles the town. Barbed wire segments the streets. The people are silent, afraid. The stores are open, but soldiers are stationed in the aisles. Russian troops burn books on the street corner. The drive-in movie has been circled by a chain-link fence and turned into a combination concentration camp and reeducation facility. Propaganda movies run continuously on its screen. "It's all gone," Jed's father mourns the American way of life. What is left is only war, for the Wolverine guerrillas, for the Cuban/Russian occupying army, for the rural villagers who will be systematically executed in their own main street. Director Milius has laced his simplistic militarist fantasy with allusions to every war ever fought, from the Mongol invasions to medieval sieges to Nazi executions to the Hungarian and Czechoslovakian uprisings to the Vietcong guerrillas in Vietnam to the Cuban commander's fond memories of his own guerrilla partisanhood in Cuba, El Salvador, Chile, Nicaragua, and Mexico, while his Soviet army counterpart talks of the Afghanistan War. All of these specific historical allusions to past wars are visual, and they spread a patina of historical accuracy over a shamelessly rightist ideological text. This history is exploited to demonstrate that war is the only solution available to the Amero-Russian standoff of the mid-twentieth century. *Red Dawn* advocated World War III as a valuable opportunity for America to prove its mettle, assert its racial purity over the invading barbarians, reearn the right to live in the greatest country in the world. Milius is selling a comic book fantasy and the film's box-office success indicated that there were a great many buyers of his patriotic, early Reagan-era, Teddy Roosevelt, cowboy militarism.

What Milius's total commitment to his barbarian/Russian metaphor, his All-American imagery and his militarist ideology obscures, or at least camouflages, is the unbelievability of the fantasy, the one-sidedness of the racial stereotyping. At times that stereotyping actually becomes comic, especially when the tall Cuban commander who looks suspiciously like Che Guevara and the short Russian commander who looks suspiciously like Adolph Hitler are together. Only one moment of real perception breaks through. Late in the guerrilla war, Jed must decide whether to execute one of their own who has betrayed them. His brother Matt (Charlie Sheen) challenges this execution with a perceptive question:

MATT: Tell me, what's the difference . . . between us and them?

JED: Because we live here!

It is a good question, but one that *Red Dawn* never really considers, just as Jed never really answers. *Red Dawn*, because it never humanizes the Russians, can only exist as an overt exercise in ideological propaganda. It would play well on the drive-in movie screen of an American reeducation center if the tables were turned.

Red Dawn sets an eighties standard for the portrayal of the Russians. It dehumanizes them into, first, barbarians and, second, machines. It portrays their society as silent, lifeless, and imprisoned. It calls for America to take up arms against this Russian enemy. It was one of the most short-sighted and simplistic films of the decade, yet it was, as was the Reagan administration, heartily embraced by the American public.

Ironically though American foreign policy toward Russia changed drastically after the Geneva Summit of 1985, turning the rightist stereotyping of *Red Dawn* into an anachronism, those "evil empire" sentiments did not die easily. *Rambo III* (1988) presented the same images of the barbarian Russian hordes and the genocidal Nazi-like tactics of Russia's Vietnam, the war in Afghanistan. The Russian hordes in Afghanistan in *Rambo III* (as in *Red Dawn*) are portrayed as sadistic torturers and faceless machines. Rambo's major antagonist is a Russian helicopter that proves his only worthy opponent after he cuts a swath through the faceless Russian army. He faces the helicopter "mano-a-machino" and defeats it. The similar imaging of the Russian character in *Red Dawn* and *Rambo III*—in which Mongol-mustachiod torturers torment Colonel Trautman (Richard Crenna) and faceless soldiers machine-gun Afghan villagers—attests to one strain of American jingoism that longs to sustain Reagan's "evil empire" characterization as a proof of American moral righteousness even in the face of the late-eighties ideological softening of the Reagan administration's stance toward the Soviet Union.

Another set of rightist militarist films—*Firefox* (1982), *Top Gun* (1986), *Iron Eagle* (1988)—also portrayed Amero-Russian relations as an ongoing battle between men (the Americans) and machines (the Russians). These films sent out the same anti-Soviet message despite the mid-decade rhetorical shift, but the conflict was in the sky and the machines were jet warplanes. All three films had to overcome the cloying problem (for rightist militarist ideology) of how to justify combat between American and Russian pilots in a cold war situation, how to ignore the mid-decade rhetorical shift in Amero-Russian relations. Both *Red Dawn* and *Rambo III* had the luxury of locating their anti-Soviet hate messages in real wars. These three films, however, must, of cold war necessity, contrive situations where Amero-Russian face-offs can occur.

Like the fantasy unbelievability of *Red Dawn* and *Rambo III*, the premise of *Firefox* stretches the range of credibility—or does it? If sixteen-year-old Matthias Rust can fly a small private plane from West Germany, under Russian radar, and land it in the middle of Moscow's Red Square, is it so farfetched to fantasize that a rightist militarist cowboy like Clint Eastwood could make his way into the heart of Russia and steal the fastest and most sophisticated warplane ever conceived? *Firefox* has some of the plot characteristics of a cold war spy movie, but its primary text involves the impatience of the American rightist militarist establishment with their own cold war inactivity, their need for a cold war war. The very existence of the "Firefox," a supersophisticated Russian warplane that flies at 100,000 feet at Mach V and has a thought-controlled weapons system, becomes an excuse for taking the hot war hardware out of mothballs and playing with it a little bit.

Firefox, *Top Gun*, *Iron Eagle II*, and *The Hunt for Red October* (1990), which is about a nuclear submarine rather than jet airplanes, are hardware films—films in which the war machines that have been forced into dormancy are given the opportunity to get a little exercise. All are films in which the machines are much more important than the men. Beneath this manifest text of cold war hardware lie a number of subtextual themes that focus upon Amero-Russian sociohistorical relations in the eighties.

On a political level, *Firefox* portrays the cold war attitude—that of hardware superiority, aka SDI or Star Wars—of the Reagan administration (as symbolically represented by Vietnam-weakened cowboy Mitchell Gant trying to get it back together) toward Russia. Gant, in his weakened condition post-Vietnam, represents America at the beginning of the Reagan eighties. On a social level, *Firefox* portrays the repressive nature of the Russian government toward its people. On a mythic level, *Firefox* again turns to the metaphor of the machine to symbolize the dehumanization that the Russian military impose upon their soldiers and the Russian government upon their people. On this level of interpretation that primary hardware text takes on symbolic signification as is similarly represented by the tanks in *Red Dawn*, the helicopter in *Rambo III*, and the computerized Goliath characterization later in the decade of Russian boxer Ivan Drago in *Rocky IV* (1985). These subtextual themes coupled with the actual setting of *Firefox* inside Russia (as opposed to *Top Gun* and *Iron Eagle II* that are set in the neutral medium of "the air") make this film a more substantial sociohistorical document than those other two "hardware" films.

Firefox begins with the sinister image of a helicopter descending (reminiscent of the ominous parachutes in the opening sequence of *Red Dawn* and the dark helicopter in *Rambo III*) to intrude upon Mitchell Gant's (Clint Eastwood) isolationist cold war life. Gant, a Vietnam War flying ace, is whisked off to a military briefing room in the Pentagon. In each of these hardware films, the briefing room becomes the venue for the verbal exposition of the rightist militarist anti-Soviet party line. In *Firefox* a group of men in uniform (with a few civilians sprinkled in) sit around a large conference table consulting a handy movie screen for visual affirmation and coldly state their motives for anti-Russian action. This is the boardroom of the rightist militarist establishment of the Reagan eighties. In *Firefox* the subject of this boardroom discussion is a Russian warplane that with its thought-controlled weapons system has succeeded (to use a phrase from *War Games*) in taking "the men out of the loop." "If the Soviets can mass produce it, it could change the structure of our world," declares a ranking uniformed member of the rightist militarist board of directors. This boardroom scene presents the fidgetiness of the military mired in the stasis of a cold war. They are hungry for any action even if it is only some silly intelligence game.

The second thematic section of *Firefox* deals with a detailed examination of the nature of Soviet society. Mitchell Gant goes to Moscow and experiences the day-to-day repression of Soviet life. His baggage is searched at the airport. His hotel room is bugged and equipped with a two-way mirror. Soldiers with weapons march in the streets outside his window. He is followed everywhere by KGB agents. In fact, the intelligence plan of which Gant is a part is specifically designed to exploit the closed nature of Russian society. "Because of its very size," Gant's control officer tells him, "the KGB is sometimes slow to awaken. It is like a monster. If you walk by carefully enough, it might just sniff at you. But if you awaken it!" Following the structure of Dostoevsky's *Crime and Punishment* and similar to the structure of *White Nights* (1985), Gant's movements through Russian society in this middle section are crosscut with a KGB security plot of a detective trying to find out who Gant is and why he is in Russia.

The emphasis throughout this section is a familiar one: the repressive and closed nature of Russian society coupled with the barbaric inhumanity of the Russian military establishment. One scene, in a Moscow subway station, unfolds in a Hitchcock-like way as this familiar place becomes a threatening prison. In mere seconds the KGB can shut down a society. As in both *Red Dawn* and *Rambo III*, the Russian military (and the KGB) in *Firefox* are portrayed as barbarians. In one scene a prisoner is beaten to death in an interrogation. One Russian citizen characterizes the moral effect of this repressive government upon those who resist: "I have a wife. . . . She is a Jew. She is educated. Still she married me. She has been in prison for twelve years for demonstrating against the invasion of Czechoslovakia. They do not treat her well in prison. I have spent the last twelve years trying to be worthy of her." As is the case in the government control terrorism text, in this portrayal of Russian society repression breeds resistence that ultimately breeds revolution.

This second section of the film finally focuses upon the difference between Russian and American society. Mitchell Gant, with a grin, teases his Russian contact: "What is it with you Jews anyway? Don't you ever get tired of fighting city hall?" His contact grins back but quickly turns serious: "Fighting city hall, as you say Mr. Gant, is a freedom we don't enjoy." Freedom is the key word, the difference between the two societies:

GANT: Supposing I get to Liftoff and everything works well. What happens to you?

SCIENTIST: It doesn't matter.

GANT: What do you mean it doesn't matter? I don't understand why you all are so willing to die.

SCIENTIST: I don't expect you to understand.

GANT: Don't you resent the men in London who order you to do all this?

SCIENTIST: Mr. Gant, you are an American. You're a free man. I am not. There is a big difference. If I resent the men in London who are ordering me to die, then it is a small thing compared to my resentment of the KGB.

In the simplification of the rightist militarist view, freedom is the only important difference between the two societies. It is the difference that the United States has always stressed in its worldwide public relations, its spreading of a Western rightist militarist gospel to the rest of the world. Inherent in that gospel is the necessity of martyrdom, this willingness to die for American-style freedom. Since the mid-forties, American movies have consistently preached this gospel of the religious sacramentality of a communion of the free always attained through militarist violence. It is a startlingly illogical rightist exploitation of Christian history.

In the final section of *Firefox*, the primary text, the hardware, takes over. *Firefox*, as will *Top Gun* and *Iron Eagle II*, ends in an Amero-Russian cold-war war, a high-tech dogfight in the wild blue yonder that proves the superiority of American man over Russian machine. The final confrontations of these films simply confirm the added advantage that the free American individual has over the restricted, machinelike (and thus indecisive) Russian. The moral of the story is that you must become like us in order to compete with us. If the events in Eastern Europe in 1989–90 are any indication, Russia at the end of the eighties decade was beginning to heed that message.

Top Gun and *Iron Eagle II* are essentially the same film. Neither is as complex as *Firefox*. Both are more interested in hardware and less interested in people. Whereas in *Firefox* the Russian characters and society were given rather detailed portrayal, in these films the Russian characters are faceless appendages to their hardware (in *Top Gun*), straight men for Maverick's (Tom Cruise) airborne antics, or (in *Iron Eagle II*) stereotypical stick figures who carry little ideological weight. Russian society is never portrayed in either of these films.

Top Gun is a rightist militarist masturbatory fantasy. It begins with two U.S. Navy jets off a carrier in the Indian Ocean flirting with two Russian

MiGs. Because it is peacetime, the aircraft carrier wing commander forbids engagement or intercourse between the American planes and the Russian MiGs. "Do not fire until you are fired upon," he barks. Both the Russian pilots and the American pilots know that it is just a game, that they are airborne cowboys working out their horses. Maverick (Tom Cruise) says, "I can't shoot this guy so lets see if we can have a little fun with him" and reverses himself upside down at Mach 1 over his Russian partner in this cold war foreplay. This opening sequence featuring the potency of high-powered hardware frustrated by cold war circumstances sets the whole masturbatory metaphor of the film. The camera just loves these jet fighter planes. It always has since World War II. They hang in the air like exquisite pieces of sculpture, yet they are the ultimate in speed and firepower. They are incredibly sexy and they need to engage, to exercise their potency. But in peacetime they do not get that chance.

After that opening sequence of interrupted foreplay, the scene shifts to the Top Gun pilot training school in Miramar, California. In this masturbatory section, the flyboys play with themselves in cold war frustration.

The film ends, however, in a typical cold-war war, a contrived Amero-Russian confrontation over the Indian Ocean, another simulated sex act, an excuse to test the equipment. When an anonymous rescue operation arises, a disabled American ship that has floated into Russian territory, the seductive possibility is too much for the Top Gun pilots to resist. Once again, the rightist militarist gospel is preached in a formal briefing room: "There are MiGs in the area. Tensions are high. If you witness a hostile act, you will return fire. Those MiGs carry the Exocet antiship missile. They can fire that missile from 100 miles away. Gentlemen, this is the real thing. This is what you've been trained for. You are America's best. Make us proud." It is truly a case of a group of teenage jerk-offs being turned loose in a whorehouse. The problem with these cold-war wars, however, is that they are so contrived and ultimately so unsatisfying, so impersonal. As in *Firefox*, the Russian pilots, the love objects, are faceless parts of their machines (they actually wear opaque black visors, whereas the American pilots' faces are uncovered and their names are on their helmets). As the dogfights unfold, the Russian jets are presented only in long shot, while the American pilots are continuously humanized in closeups. In line with the central cliché of this rightist militarist film text, in *Top Gun* it is American man against Russian machine.

The only progress in *Iron Eagle II*, the last of these militarist hardware films is that because of the post-Geneva Summit rhetorical shift a bow is made to détente. American and Russian pilots masturbate together in an "airobics" class identical to that in *Top Gun*.

Because of détente the rightist militarist establishments of both America and Russia can no longer work out against each other, so in *Iron Eagle II*, they join forces, find a hostile, anonymous, nationless missile base in the

Middle East and do their cold war workout together. In the first *Iron Eagle* film, the mission was the rescue of a young pilot's father from terrorists, but in the sequel the rhetoric shift to détente in Amero-Russian relations is being exploited as a means of contriving yet another cold-war war. The beauty of this scenario is that all of the American rightist militarist hostility toward the Russians can still be expressed even though they have ostensibly become partners in this joint operation. Thus the rightist militarist doubts—Can Americans and Russians work together? Can Americans trust the Russians? Should Americans share their secrets and expertise with the Russians?—are expressed under the guise of an adherence to a nervous détente.

The most important hardware movie of the decade, however, was *The Right Stuff* (1983), which in its colonialist subtext of beating the Russians to the moon, indirectly participates in this body of Amero-Russian films. *The Right Stuff* as a historical document, a history of America's space programs, never really gave free rein to the rightist militarist anti-Soviet fantasies of these other films. *The Right Stuff* was more about how men related to hardware than about how two nations' hardware tested out against each other. It was a hardware film but (at the time) the hardware was not either military or offensive. There is competition with the Russians lurking in the background of *The Right Stuff*, but unlike the final confrontations of other hardware films it never gets a militarist foregrounding.

Of all of the films of the eighties that explore the text of Amero-Russian relations, *Rocky IV* (1985) is the most direct in its iconographic representation of the man vs. machine cliché of Amero-Russian confrontation. More simplistically than any other film, it exploits the Reagan era "evil empire" rhetoric of East-West confrontation even while giving lip service at the end to the post-Geneva shift in that chauvinistic rhetorical stance. Though Robert Chartoff, co-producer of the *Rocky* series, mightily protests that "it was never our intention that 'Rocky IV' should be viewed as anti-Russian,"[9] one would have to be politically neutered not to react to the film's simplistic polemic. Jack Kroll, describing an interview with Sylvester Stallone, laughs at Chartoff's attempt to depoliticize the Stallone persona:

> He (Stallone) is also able to vent his political views, which manage to be right wing without being in tune with the times—unless the times you're talking about are the 1950's. "The Russians" is a phrase that re-occurs in his conversations. They are masters of surveillance, he says—sly psychological manipulators. Their boxing champion in "Rocky IV" is a totally unlikeable lab rat, pumped up with steroids and computer programmed to handle every ring situation. But the one thing the Russians couldn't account for, it seems, is the American spirit.[10]

In a later essay, Kroll reasserts the overt political intention of Stallone's Rocky/Rambo canon: "Fast running out of viable opponents, Rocky clearly had to take on a whole society—the evil empire itself—if he was to remain our champ."[11] Despite one producer's denial of political intention, *Rocky IV*, as Jack Curry so clearly asserts, is the most strident piece of anti-Soviet propaganda of the decade. While it is not an overtly militarist hardware film like the others, it employs all of the icons and structures of those other right-wing militarist fantasies: the imagery of machines, the briefing room propagandizing, the need for cold war confrontation.

Rocky IV begins with a comical machine image. Rocky's (Sylvester Stallone) birthday present to his cigar-chomping brother-in-law corner-man, Paulie (Burt Young), is a household robot. Ironically the major contender for Rocky's title, who turns up soon after, is also a robot of sorts. Ivan Drago (Dolf Lundgren), the Russian amatuer boxing champion who has come to the States to challenge America's best, is a man molded on robotic technology, a Russian fighting machine.

Rocky IV's cold war iconography virtually trumpets from the screen. A motif of American magazine covers acts as a transitional bridge between scenes. A *Time* cover blares "Russians Invade U.S. Sports." A *Ring Magazine* cover takes up the challenge, "Red Star vs. Old Glory." These magazine covers jingoistically sing out the cold war exhileration of this simulated East-West confrontation. The usual David and Goliath mythology of the *Rocky* series is unceremoniously superceded in *Rocky IV* by the cold war politics and the man vs. machine iconography. Whereas Rocky has always been a David figure fighting against the odds, in *Rocky IV* he (as writer) has raised himself (as character) to the level of a patriotic American political icon.

Russia as relentless, emotionless machine is clearly symbolized in the iconographic characterization of Ivan Drago. He is an utterly nonverbal robot. His wife, Ludmilla (Brigitte Neilsen), and his manager speak for him. He is visually connected only to machines. He wears a military uniform, yet, seemingly, is not supposed to represent a militarist view. Iconographically he is supposed to represent the faceless, mechanicalness of Russian society, a concept proved ludicrous upon the crumbling of the Berlin Wall in 1989. The Russian people are not machines programmed by the state, therefore Ivan Drago is just another militarist fantasy. With the two antagonists set as political icons, one a patriotic chauvinist, the other a silent machine, this *Rocky* sequel moves through its typical three-act structure.

Every *Rocky* movie except the first has followed a plot development from antagonism to preparation to ultimate confrontation. What is added to *Rocky IV* is the political overtext (it cannot be a subtext because it is too strident and obvious) that punctuates each of the film's sections. Act 1, set in Las Vegas, turns the prefight hype between, first, Drago and Apollo Creed and then, Drago and Rocky, into a full-blown cold war rhetorical shouting match. Act 2, composed of the standard training montages (though set this time in the Ural Mountains of Russia) develops the polemic metaphor of the human spirit of America vs. the Russian machine. In act 3, the fight, all of the previous iconography breaks down as did the rightist militarist cold war rhetoric of Amero-Russian relations after the Geneva Summit in 1985.

In act 1, Apollo Creed (Carl Weathers) verbalizes the frustration of the cold war warrior. Rocky, comfortable in his family life, says to Apollo: "We're changin'. We're, like, turnin' into regular people." That sets Apollo off on a tirade of cold war frustration: "You and me, we don't even have a choice. See, we're born with a killer instinct that you can't just turn on and off like some, some radio. We *have* to be right in the middle of the action because we're the warriors. And without some challenge, without some damn war to fight, then the warrior might as well be dead, Stallion." Apollo comes right out and states the cold war militarist frustration of not having "some damn war to fight." He argues the need for some sort of war simulation to keep up their warriorness. "Let's make them look bad for a change," Apollo says of the Russians, but in his bravado he fails to recognize the seriousness of this simulation. Rocky sees it as merely a cold war simulation—"It's just some kind of exhibition fight. This don't mean nothin'"—but Apollo sees it as a political clash—"No. You're wrong. This is not just some exhibition fight. It is us against them." Apollo as militarist will simply not accept the stasis of the cold war. He longs for the real thing and gets it. Drago kills Apollo in what was supposed to be a simulation.

All of the posturing that surrounds the first fight is blatantly jingoistic. Apollo dresses up like Uncle Sam, the Stars and Stripes are the motif of the arena, and James Brown welcomes Apollo to the ring with the song "I Live in America." Before the fight begins, Ludmilla Drago turns to Mrs. Creed and says, "Good Luck. I hope after we can be friends. Of course, they are sportsmen, not soldiers." But if all the rhetoric and jingoistic iconography that has led up to this fight is to be believed, they certainly are soldiers. Perhaps then it is fitting that the only way this fight can end is in Apollo's death.

After the funeral of Apollo Creed, this first act of *Rocky IV* ends with a press conference. In the militarist hardware films like *Top Gun* and *Firefox*, the briefing room was the staging area for the rhetoric of the cold war. In *Rocky IV*, that briefing room has been replaced by the press conference, but the same rhetoric still governs the exchange between East and West:

PRESS: How much are you making for this fight?

ROCKY: No money. This is not about money.

PRESS: Has the fight date been set yet?

ROCKY: December 25th.

PRESS: Why Christmas?

ROCKY: That's what I've been told.

PRESS: Where?

ROCKY: It's in Russia.

PAULIE (TO ROCKY): Are you nuts?

PRESS: Rocky, why did you agree to this?

DRAGO'S MANAGER: We fight in Soviet Union or we fight nowhere. Why don't you ask Drago's wife why she is afraid? Tell them please.

LUDMILLA: I am afraid for my husband's life. We have threats of violence everywhere. We are not politics? All I want is for my husband to be safe. To be treated fairly. You call him a killer. He is a professional fighter, not a killer. You have this belief that this country is so very good and we are so very bad. You have this belief that you are so fair and we are so very cruel.

DRAGO'S MANAGER: (interrupts) It's all lies and false propoganda to support this antagonistic and violent government.

PAULIE: Who? Violent? Hey, we don't keep our people behind the wall with machine guns.

DRAGO'S MANAGER: Who are you?

PAULIE: Who am I? I'm . . . the unsilent majority, big mouth.

DRAGO'S MANAGER: Good, insult us. Perhaps this simple defeat of this little so-called champion will be a perfect example of how pathetically weak your society has become.

This press conference begins with a series of cold war points. This fight is "not about money." It lets Rocky reject the capitalist decadence of Las Vegas and purify his political motives. The fight will be fought on Christmas day in Russia, thus punctuating the godlessness of atheistic Russia and the Christ-like sacrifice of Rocky. At this point, Drago's wife, Ludmilla, delivers the central speech of cold war rhetoric on American "belief": that America is better, morally superior, fairer than Russia. She claims that she and her husband "are not politics," yet her speech is overtly political. Compared, however, with Drago's manager's speech, Ludmilla's speech is innocent. The manager's speech is the bluntest political rhetoric, and Paulie answers him with the image of the Berlin Wall (which will come down before the end of the decade) to which he has no answer. Paulie's invocation of this long-standing symbol of the cold war difference between East and West drives the Russian to admit that everything has been simply the orchestration of a cold-war war, "a perfect example of how pathetically weak your society has become," just another flexing of muscles that the cold war has allowed to atrophy.

After this press conference parody of the rhetoric of the cold war, *Rocky IV* essentially shuts up, deverbalizes, returns to the imagery and iconography that gives it visual (if not intellectual) vitality. Act 2 of the film, the extended training montage, crosscuts between the training regimen of Rocky as man and Drago as machine. Rocky runs in the snow, while Drago runs on a computerized treadmill. Rocky chops wood and drags sleds, while Drago strains against computerized stress machines. Rocky fells trees outdoors, while Drago fells sparring partners indoors. Rocky runs to the top of a mountain for his famous two-hands-in-the-air victory pose, while Drago gets high on steroids injected into his body. Again as in act 1, the differences between the two countries have been emphasized. But in act 3, heeding the post-Geneva Summit rhetorical shift, all of that changes. Instead of emphasizing the differences between Rocky and Drago, the film suddenly turns on itself and starts emphasizing their similarities.

Ridiculously in mid-fight, Drago, who has been a silent robot all through the film, is suddenly converted to the American rugged individualism that Rocky has represented throughout. Drago turns to the Soviet crowd and screams, "I win . . . for me!" Even more ridiculously, after he wins, Rocky delivers a speech that goes directly against the grain of all the previous cold war chauvinism of the film: "In here there were two guys killin' each other and I guess that's better than twenty million. What I'm sayin' is that if I can change, you can change, everybody can change." The film, after that earlier press conference, had dropped the rhetoric of the cold war for visual iconography, but at the end it returns to speech. Incongruously Rocky's final speech, draped in an American flag in a Moscow arena, is an incoherent repudiation of all that cold war rhetoric of the film's first act. This final speech is a last-ditch attempt to palliate what is the most overt American propaganda film of the eighties.

The Spy Thriller Text of Cold War Desperation

In lieu of the orchestration of cold war wars (the rightist militarist choice), America and Russia always had the more conventional cold war amusements. The secret infiltration and undermining of the opposing society has always been an accepted form of political game playing. "If we can't shoot each other, at least we can steal each other's valuable secrets," goes the rationale for this cold war game. Pushing the game one step further: "if we can't shoot each other, perhaps we can embarrass each other into an act of war which will make everything right again." In effect, spies often are used as tools by the rightist militarists to push enemy nations into war.

In films, the text of Amero-Russian relations has always been tied to the spy thriller genre. The East, as represented by Russia's KGB, and the West, as represented by the American CIA or its ally the British MI-6, have been playing their intelligence games since the end of World War II. In the eighties, however, the film machinations of the intelligence establishments have been more internal than external, more concerned with justifying their own existence and methods in an extended period of détente and then *glasnost* ("openness" being the greatest threat to secret intelligence networks). For movie spies in the eighties, it was not a case of America/Britain and Russia not being able to trust each other as it was a case of neither the Eastern nor the Western intelligence agencies being able to trust themselves. Most of these films involve renegade cells or agents within either the Eastern or the Western spy networks (and sometimes both, as in *The Fourth Protocol*) working out internal bureaucratic feuds. As the decade progressed, and the East and West moved closer to understanding and cooperation, the spies (like the militarists) became more and more desperate for something to do, for justification of their own existence.

The Fourth Protocol (1987), adapted from a novel by Frederick Forsyth, is an excellent example of this desperation within the spy establishments. Forsyth's title refers to the four protocols of the 1968 NATO nuclear disarmament treaty with Russia, only one of which, the fourth, remains unviolated. That fourth protocol prohibits the explosion of a nuclear device within the borders of any of the signees countries by the agents of any other signee country. The film is about a KGB attempt to violate the fourth protocol by exploding a small atomic bomb on an American NATO airbase in England.

In Russia, a power-hungry KGB bureaucrat unilaterally sends his best covert operations field agent, Petrofsky (Pierce Brosnan), to England to build and detonate the bomb. In England, an out-of-favor but adept British Intelligence agent, John Preston (Michael Caine), gets wind of the plot. Meanwhile back in Russia, the good guys in the KGB, Karpov (Roy McAnally) and Borisov (Ned Beatty), suspect their superior's renegade operation. Back in London, Preston's pursuit of the saboteur is hindered by his own knighthood-hungry Director (Hugh Glover). With its plot set in two locations (London and Moscow) and playing on two levels (field agents and self-serving bureaucrats), the film is a complex set of interfacing relationships.

It is mostly composed of scenes of "tradecraft," as John Le Carre would call it. This is the spy genre's version of the war film's obsession with hardware. But sometimes the plotting bureaucrats stop to contemplate the purposes and effects of all of this "tradecraft" upon East-West relations: "If an atomic bomb explodes on an American base," Karpov, the KGB second-in-command speculates, "they'll be blamed for a nuclear accident and the British will kick them out. That will destroy NATO. But if Petrofsky is caught with those components, then Russia will be blamed for breaking the Fourth Protocol and Givorshin will have forced us back into the cold war." Just as the rightist militarist hardware fantasists long for cold-war wars, the spook types in America, Britain, and Russia long to prolong the cold war so that they can continue to play their tradecraft games.

The Fourth Protocol is set against a backdrop of antinuclear demonstrations that exacerbates the uncertainty within both spy establishments. The most ironic revelation comes early and is reasserted at the end. A British diplomat who has been passing "top secret" information to South African intelligence confesses: "for years now I have taken the attitude that there was only one struggle on this planet worth a damn, the fight against world Communism." When he learns that his supposedly anti-Communist South African contact is really a Soviet double agent, he is visibly shaken. The end of the film, however, reveals that the seconds-in-command of both the KGB and MI-6 are allies, working together to protect their bureaucracies and further their careers. In the spook world, all bedfellows are strange.

Besides presenting this utterly cynical view of cold war spook politics in which bureaucracies are undermining themselves, *The Fourth Protocol* also presents a stereotypical view of the difference between the Western good guys and the ruthless Russian bad guys. Petrofsky and Preston, the players of their superiors' bureaucratic games, are portrayed as opposites. Petrofsky is humorless and deadly, programmed to follow every order. He even murders a female contact immediately after making love to her. Preston, however, is a comical fellow, a maverick. The Russians kill ruthlessly, while the British try to avoid bloodbaths. This difference in humanity between East and West is driven home by one symbolic scene. The KGB Director sits in front of his document shredder and feeds the whole operation, culminating in field agent Petrofsky's picture, through the machine. In this parallel to the machine imagery of the rightist militarist hardware text (as in *Rocky IV*), the KGB is shown to feed people into the shredding machine of international politics as if they were infinitely disposable.

Two other spy thrillers portray the motives and methods of the KGB in the East vs. West conspiracy game in similar terms. *Just Another Secret* (1989), also adapted from a Frederick Forsythe novel, and *The Package* (1989) both begin at official meetings where public politics mask private intrigue. In *Just Another Secret*, a Communist Politburo meeting is being addressed by Chairman Gorbachev giving a speech on *Glasnost* while simultaneously an American CIA cell in East Berlin is being assassinated. In *The Package*, terrorist violence explodes during an East-West nuclear arms negotiation conference. In both films, the target of the spy plot is the assassination of Chairman Gorbachev by renegade factions within his own spy establishment. Why do they want to kill their own leader? Because they view him as too soft on the West, too willing to stabilize relations with America and negate the need for both an intelligence and a military establishment. As in *The Fourth Protocol*, the major motive is again that of bureaucrats protecting their cold war jobs.

Jack Grant (Beau Bridges) in *Just Another Secret* and John Gallagher (Gene Hackman) in *The Package* find themselves in the "strange bedfellows" situation of trying to prevent the assassination on Western soil of Mikhail Gorbachev. Grant actually takes Gorbachev's place, while Gallagher kills the would-be assassin with a second to spare. Both films are paradigms of an American version of détente. In both, the Russian renegade spooks are the villains, while the Americans enter the lists to protect the good Russians from their own.

Each film also portrays the ruthlessness of both the Russian and American intelligence bureaucracies in trying to sustain the Amero-Russian cold war. When Jack Grant realizes that the target of the KGB plot is Gorbachev, he sees its motive immediately:

JACK: It could send the cold war right back to the Ice Age.

BRITISH AGENT: Could start a hot war.

JACK: In just an hour, renegade KGB's are gonna try to turn the clock back to the days of good ol' Joe Stalin.

And when John Gallagher confronts his superior, Colonel Whitacre (John Heard), who has been working with the KGB all along, that lead spook asserts his fondness for the cold war in rightist militarist hardware terms. "Why do you think we've had peace with Russia for forty years?" Whitacre poses his rhetorical question. "Nuclear weapons, that's why."

Both *Just Another Secret* and *The Package*, like *The Fourth Protocol*, are ultimately détente films that stress the need for cooperation between East and West. Actually all of these films go beyond the détente era into the dawnings of *glasnost*. *Glasnost* means "openness," and the one thing spies (whether CIA, KGB or even spookier military intelligence types) do not function well in is the open. The question these films pose is, What would happen if the U.S. and Russia established enough of a verifiable "openness" that there was no longer any need for spies? According to these films, the spies would still find a way to make themselves useful.

The plots of all of these spy movies are right out of the eighties headlines, but none moreso than *No Way Out* (1987). Set in the late eighties in Washington, D.C., it follows the career of a brilliant young naval commander, Tom Farrell (Kevin Costner), who gets, first, sexually and, then, emotionally involved with a gorgeous party girl, Susan Atwell (Sean Young), who just happens to be the mistress of the secretary of defense, David Brice (Gene Hackman), for whom Farrell just happens to work on a Pentagon operation so "top secret" that the secretary of defense does not want anybody, not the president, the CIA, certainly not the Congress, to know about it. Sound familiar? Not only is *No Way Out* another one of these "internal-conspiracy-within-the-larger-intelligence-establishment" films, like *The Fourth Protocol* and *The Package*, but it is timely in some other, more vulgar ways. Susan Atwell is an obvious Donna Rice clone. Brice reminds of John Poindexter, and Farrell is both an incipient Ollie North and an echo of the John Walker (also a naval officer) spy scandal.

But the real monkey wrench in the plot of *No Way Out*, which is adapted from Kenneth Fearing's novel *The Big Clock*, is that all along Farrell is really a Russian deep-cover spy and the secret operation he is running for Brice is to catch himself. Brice is the bureaucrat employing his own intelligence community to cover up his personal sexual indiscretion, while Farrell is a Russian agent trying to function in the face of his emotional attachment to the murder victim. Real cold war objectives take a back seat to the solving of internal personal and personnel problems within the spy establishment.

If *No Way Out* brought deep-cover KGB plots to Washington and the basement of the Pentagon, two other spy thrillers, *The Osterman Weekend* (1983) and *Little Nikita* (1988) go even deeper to the heart of the Russian infiltration of American life. In both, the KGB invades American suburbia for its cold war version of the backyard barbecue. Like so many other eighties films—*Poltergeist* (1982), *E.T.* (1982), *Testament*, *Halloween* et al., *Blue Velvet* (1986), *Running on Empty* (1988)—*The Osterman Weekend* and *Little Nikita* portray suburbia under fire. The government spy scenarios of America and Russia intrude upon the placidity, even interrupt the TV-viewing habits, of seemingly normal middle-class Americans. But as John Fasset (John Hurt), another intelligence renegade gone berserk because his own agency has murdered his wife, says in *The Osterman Weekend*: "In this world that you have entered, things are rarely what they seem." He is right. In these films, suburbia is not a placid yuppie world of weekend swimming parties and teenage romance. It becomes, in *The Osterman Weekend*, a battleground and, in *Little Nikita*, a testing ground for Amero-Russian relations as represented by face-offs between the CIA and KGB.

In *The Osterman Weekend*, Fasset, a top CIA agent, has uncovered "OMEGA," a Soviet spy network in America, but in the course of that discovery his wife was killed. CIA chief Maxwell Danforth (Burt Lancaster) blames the Russians and turns Fasset loose, equipped with the most sophisticated closed-circuit TV surveillance gear, upon a cell of Soviet spies operating in New York. What Danforth does not know is that Fasset knows that Danforth ordered the death of his wife. Thus another double game begins as the American agent uses the Russian agents to bring down the American spymaster. Fasset's link to the cell of Soviet sleeper agents is John Tanner (Rutgar Hauer), a New York talk show personality whose media access and clout Fasset uses to expose Danforth and the CIA. The setting for this confrontation between American and Russian spies is a weekend house party at Tanner's Westchester estate, where the KGB agents—Bernie Osterman (Craig T. Nelson), Richard Tremaine (Dennis Hopper), Joe Cardone (Chris Sarandon), all college classmates of Tanner—meet annually.

The Osterman Weekend, Sam Peckinpah's last movie, is about two things: cold war intrigue and the Big Brother power of the media. When Danforth pressures Tanner into helping the CIA entrap the three classmate spies, he argues for the use of surveillance cameras: "The Russians don't suffer from the restraints of our system." The central thematic focus of the film is upon television, its potential for the invasion of privacy and the controlling of truth and freedom in society. Like *The Anderson Tapes* of the seventies, it is a movie about surveillance and how TV distorts reality, edits its significance. Fasset coordinates and monitors the assault on Tanner's suburban house from a TV truck. He watches the life-and-death spy struggle as if it were a TV show that he was producing. He speaks to the spies he has trapped in the house over their TV monitors. "We're in prime killing time," he announces. "All it took was to have my wife murdered while my employers watched it on closed-circuit TV. It's just another episode in this whole snuff soap opera we're all in." Robert Ludlum, from whose novel *The Osterman Weekend* is adapted, and Peckinpah take the cornerstone of suburbia, the TV set, and show how it participates in cold war terrorism. If America and Russia cannot have a shooting war this film says, then their cold war scenarists must be content with making international snuff movies. Television and Amero-Russian relations go together because both deal in smoothly edited lies. KGB agent Bernie Osterman (a TV writer) sums up the eighties best: "The truth is a lie that hasn't been found out. . . . These are strange times Amigo. We can only survive them." That is, in these spy genre films, the cold war goal of both the Russian and American spy communities.

Whereas *The Osterman Weekend* shows all the agents to be utterly ruthless and cynical, *Little Nikita* humanizes both Russian and American agents by showing them, first, in internal disagreement with their spymasters and, then in the striking of personal détente. Again, a renegade operation within the Russian network typifies the confusion about the goals and methods of cold war confrontation. The KGB spy in *Little Nikita* is worn out, bored with the game, questioning of the inability of his superiors to see the shift away from cold war confrontation to détente. In fact, *Little Nikita* only masquerades as a bloody spy thriller. It is really a movie of suburban family life into which cold war politics just happen to intrude.

Little Nikita focuses upon Jeff Grant (River Phoenix), a cool, seventeen-year-old in love who is about to go to the Air Force Academy to college. Everything seems perfect and normal for Jeff on the Fourth of July in suburban Fountain Grove, California. However, in the Russian embassy in Mexico City, veteran KGB hand Karpov (Richard Bradford) is assigned to track down and interdict renegade double agent Scuba (Richard Lynch) who is systematically killing each member of a network of Russian sleeper agents put in place by Moscow in California twenty years before. By computer coincidence, veteran FBI agent Roy Parmenter (Sidney Poitier), while running a security check on young Jeff Grant's Air Force Academy application, discovers that Jeff's parents just "don't compute" and connects them to Scuba and Karpov twenty years earlier.

The America vs. Russia cold war provides a vehicle for what *Little Nikita* is really about: how a seventeen-year-old feels when he finds out that his parents are Russian spies who have lied to him all his life. Setting the collision of cold war politics and coming of age dilemma in the Spielbergian placidity of suburbia presents even more powerfully the idea of how fragile are American innocence and openness. Yet despite the symbolic reverberation of Jeff's discovery that his life as an American has been a twenty-year lie, *Little Nikita* looks for a solution to this cold war dilemma and finds it in a late rhetorical shift that directly mirrors the rhetorical shift of eighties Amero-Russian relations. One of the more eloquent détente scenes of all of these Amero-Russian film texts occurs at the end of *Little Nikita* as Parmenter and Karpov face each other with guns drawn and young Jeff Grant directly in the line of fire. It is Karpov who lowers his weapon saying, "Russians are not monsters. We do not shoot children." His characterization is evidence of the post-Geneva Summit rhetorical shift. This movie argues, as none of the other spy thriller or rightist militarist fantasies do, that underneath their cheap spy suits and bushy eyebrows Russians are also normal people. This is a theme that will form the third Amero-Russian text, the *E.T.* films.

The light side of cold war intrigue proved sporadically funny in Dan Aykroyd and Chevy Chase's *Spies Like Us* (1985). In this parody, the plots of *The Fourth Protocol* and *The Package* are combined and played for laughs. Emmet Fitz-Hume (Chevy Chase) is a lazy Washington bureaucrat, while Austin Millbarge (Dan Aykroyd) is a nerdy Pentagon computer jock. As was the case in the real cold war thrillers, these two morons are set up as expendable fall guys in a secret pentagon plot to start a hot war by triggering a Soviet ICBM. By the time the generals have dropped these two idiots in the desert to carry out their mission, the cold war humor that has poked fun at both Ronald Reagan and the KGB goes stale. A funnier, though certainly not a comedy, tour of the cold war world of Amero-Russian relations appears in *The Falcon and the Snowman* (1985) based on the true story of Daulton Lee (Sean Penn) and Christopher Boyce (Timothy Hutton).

Near the end of *The Falcon and the Snowman*, Chris Boyce tells Daulton Lee, his co-conspirator in the selling of U.S. government secrets to the Soviets, of the despair he feels: "I'm gonna be lookin' over my shoulder the rest of my life, and for what? There's never gonna be any reconciliation. They're just as paranoid and dangerous as we are." The tone is one of frustration and hopelessness. *The Falcon and the Snowman* is an accurate guage of the pre-Geneva Summit paranoia and belligerence between America and Russia. What is most striking about John Schlesinger's film is that it does not portray Boyce and Lee as villains, as traitors to America. They are a money-hungry drug addict and a conscience-stricken former seminarian, two altar boys gone awry. The film was criticized for its failure to vilify them. What went unnoticed, however, was the reasoned critique of the Nixon government's (in real time) and Reagan government's (in metaphoric time) orchestration of illegal covert operations some three years before Iran-*contra*. In 1985 this film expresses a desperation for the direction Amero-Russian relations have taken under the Nixon and Reagan administrations and a fear that the CIA's cold war cowboying really could lead to World War III:

INTERROGATOR: Who did you receive your instructions from?

CHRIS: My conscience. I know a few things about predatory behavior (cut-away to his falcon hunting) and what was once a legitimate intelligence gathering agency is now being misused to prey on weaker governments. I appreciate fear. A chance to face it. There's nothing more exhilerating than confronting your fears.

INTERROGATOR: What are you afraid of?

CHRIS: Of people who can imagine and create sophisticated weapons, and a government that can't be trusted with it. We're the only nation on earth to ever use atomic weapons on other human beings. We are capable of it.

The Falcon and the Snowman, based on a true story, chose not to be just another cold war thriller, chose not to rely upon gunfights and assassination plots for its suspense. Instead, it chose to focus upon character and political motive, why two American suburbanites chose to betray their country, because their country was betraying them. "Manipulations of foreign press, political parties, whole economies," Chris Boyce marvels, "it's incredible. I had no idea the extent of the lie, the level of the deception." For Christopher Boyce, the state of the Union circa 1975 (the real time) and 1985 (the film's time), whether it be under a criminal Nixon or a saber-rattling Reagan, is hopeless. Something desperate has to be done in opposition to these American government-sponsored illegalites and lies.

This whole film is about why two young Americans would betray their country. Their motive is that both the American and Russian governments are wrong. The film's refusal to take the patriotic highground endemic to the rightist militarist fantasies is attributable to the choice of English director John Schlesinger. As did Louis Malle in *Alamo Bay* and Alan Parker in *Mississippi Burning*, a foreign director can sometimes give a different view of American society. This was the case with *The Falcon and the Snowman*. It comments less on the crime and more on the sorry state of Amero-Russian relations that motivated the crime.

Late in the film, a drugged-out Daulton Lee bemoans the hopelessness of the cold war. "I don't know who my friends are anymore," he says. "I don't know who to trust." In the Amero-Russian dilemma of the mid-eighties (the time of the film's release not the time of its real events), nobody can trust anyone, and Schlesinger's film clearly states that the situation must change. Ironically the situation does change soon after with the rhetorical shift in Amero-Russian relations at the Geneva Summit. David Ansen agrees that Schlesinger's choices for presenting "the ambiguities of this tale are more stimulating than the certainties of many more conventional movies."[12] What most of the critics of *The Falcon and the Snowman* in their praise of Sean Penn's performance and their disdain for Schlesinger's cool unsuspenseful approach to the factual material missed, however, is the strong political subtext of the film.

The Falcon and the Snowman is very much about cold war suspicion between America and Russia, but it is also about the closed aspects of American society that justify that suspicion, especially the covert intelligence operations of the CIA. The central visual metaphor of the film, Chris Boyce's falcon, eloquently represents how the vaunted freedom and openness of American society, its long-standing Western version of *glasnost*, is tied down, like a tethered and hooded falcon, because it is a lie, an illusion. The American CIA in its illegal manipulations is no different from the Russian KGB. Both are the hoods over the eyes of the American and Russian people who long to fly free but are kept in check by political establishments and strategies that they do not even know about, much less understand. Alex (David Suchet), Boyce and Lee's KGB contact in the Russian embassy in Mexico City, describes the closedness of the two societies:

> ALEX: Leaving RTX and going to college is a very good idea. You should consider majoring in Russian studies. History, language, political affairs. And then think very seriously about applying for a job in the State Department or the CIA.
>
> CHRIS: Absolutely not!
>
> ALEX: You know Christopher. We are not unlike, you and I. Oh, I too have my doubts. I know what it does to a person. I know how hard it is. I know what you are feeling.
>
> CHRIS: What are you talking about. I'm not a professional at this, like you. This isn't a career for me. This was impulsive. . . . I'm not like you. . . . You want a mole in the CIA, find someone else. I have a life apart from all this, unlike you. . . .
>
> ALEX: Whether you realize it or not, you are a professional. You can't leave here tonight free of it all anymore than I can. Did you really think that you could. It's not over, Chris. It's just beginning.

Alex expresses the illusion of American idealism, the illusion that somehow Americans are more moral, more right, more free than the closed societies of the world. Chris Boyce is a walking symbol of that illusion. He names his falcon after Guy Fawkes: "He was seventeenth-century England. Tried to blow up Parliament. He failed." He sees nobility and freedom in the resistance to the illusion of American openness. But in reality, Chris is still a spy, a traitor, and Alex emphasizes that he must face that fact and subsume it beneath the catchword of a new immoral morality, "professionalism." But if Chris Boyce represents the need for America to replace its illusions with professionalism, then Daulton Lee gives that professionalism a bad name.

Another important subtext of *The Falcon and the Snowman* is its journalistic exposé of the slapstick looseness of both the American and Russian professional intelligence industries. In this spook world, the hardware of spying may be the highest of tech and infallible, but the humans in the loop are comically inept. At TRX Chris Boyce works in the "Black Vault," a room full of wire machines and document shredders that collect and pass on coded intelligence data for the CIA. "The Black Vault is a code name for a family of covert surveillance satellites conceived by the defense department and manufactured and maintained by RTX and used by a company you may have heard of in Langley, Virginia," the head of security tells Chris. "Circling the earth," the man goes on in a paean to the hardware of the cold war,

> each carrying high resolution cameras, microwave antennas, heat sensors, they rather significantly brighten the workload of human spies. When Brezhnev chats with his mistress over his supposedly clean phone, the birds listen in. When he takes his dog for a walk in the park, the birds take a picture of it pissing on the shrubbery. When he tests his latest warhead underground in Siberia and claims he hasn't, the birds know he's lying.

These mechanical birds and their all-too-human handlers also contrast to that idealistic image of the falcon. In the Black Vault at TRX a loose party atmosphere prevails. The men and women in this intelligence loop drink margaritas, grow marijuana plants, dance, play board games, and smoke cigarettes while the intelligence machines click away. Finally, in the spirit of this decadent ambiance, one of the men in the loop starts selling secrets to the Russians.

The real parody of the Amero-Russian spy establishments, however, is the comic characterization of "Daulton Lee, Superspy." He bumbles through the tradecraft like a combination of Pee Wee Herman and Chevy Chase. He walks openly into the Russian embassy in Mexico City. He forgets the streets set for meets. He tries to pick up girls by telling them that he sells American secrets to the KGB. He even tries to convince the KGB to help him smuggle drugs out of Peru in Soviet diplomatic pouches. He keeps himself flying on cocaine and heroine. "He who dies with the most toys wins," is his capitalist philosophy. The irony of Daulton's characterization is its fallibility in comparison with those clicking CIA machines in the Black Vault and the arrogant professionalism of the KGB agents. As did the nuclear war film *War Games*, this film reifies the presence of the men in the loop. Daulton Lee is inept, yet for a while he defeats the spy hardware.

The Falcon and the Snowman juxtaposes the illusion of the openess of American life and the idealization of American morality to the businesslike professionalism of Russian bureaucracy and finds both wanting. It captures the suspicion and frustration of the cold war, pre-détente, pre-Geneva Summit rhetorical shift, pre-*glasnost* world of Amero-Russian relations, but it also signals the precise need for greater openness that America and Russia ultimately took in the second half of the eighties decade. In all of these Amero-Russian genre spy films, the one constant is that no one is any better than the other. The CIA and its NATO allies are just as bad as the KGB, just as ruthless, venal, lying, and self-serving. Of the four film texts of Amero-Russian relations in the eighties, the spy genre representation is the most evenhanded and the least chauvinistic.

The E.T. Text of Russians in Western Society

The first two Amero-Russian film texts deal with the two nations in confrontation either on the battlefield or in the cold war shadows. Both texts tend to portray Russia as the "evil empire." Some of the films that make up those texts portray both America and Russia as less-than-admirable empires. The third text, however, is a more optimistic, cooperative text, which portrays Russians and Americans working together for common goals. In almost every case, the plot, characters, and détente/*glasnost* tone of these films is similar to the most famous film of the decade, Steven Spielberg's *E.T.: The Extra-Terrestrial*.

E.T. is a fable for international cooperation, a warning that people cannot continue to react violently toward those who are different from them. *E.T.*'s tone is one of love, friendship, and understanding replacing suspicion, fear, prejudice, and belligerence as the style of dealing with those unlike us who enter our supposedly free and open society. A series of eighties films based upon the premise of a Russian E.T. attempting to live in Western society not only questioned that vaunted openness of American society but also commented upon that which is good in Russia's closed society. These films that embraced the *E.T.* fable stressed the necessity for communication between East and West. Most often, that theme was embodied in a Russian E.T. entering American society and partnering with one or more American stereotypes who proceed to guide him through the pitfalls of capitalism and freedom. Actually the model for this particular eighties film text was *The Russians Are Coming, The Russians Are Coming* (1966), which exploited American cold war paranoia toward the Soviet Union. In this third Amero-Russian film text, the tone moves away from rightist militarist bellicosity and cold war competitive paranoia toward comic sentiment, cultural exchange, and even zany slapstick.

An early tentative piercing of the iron curtain between East and West came in Jerzy Skolimowski's *Moonlighting* (1984). The story of an illegal work crew of Polish carpenters sent to London to remodel their boss's townhouse turns on all sorts of East-West ironies. The rich man who sends them is a Communist who is really a capitalist. Nowak (Jeremy Irons), the leader of the remodeling crew, is the only one who can speak English, thus is responsible for speaking "for all his men." Instead, he lies to them, conceals historic events from them, oppresses them to the point of slavery. Nowak even breaks their watches so that Amero-Russian films such as *Gorky Park* (1983), *Moscow on the Hudson* (1984), and *Russkies* (1987) are. Its central character, its E.T., ends up alienated by his experience, defeated by the struggle to survive in another country. London society has not even noticed his existence. He has tried to communicate but has failed. This tentative foray into East-West relations is an ironic critique of both the East and the West. This is not the case in the most visible of the subsequent Amero-Russian E.T films.

Paul Mazursky's *Moscow on the Hudson* is like an advertisement for a weight-loss clinic. It is a before-and-after film that pictures the life of a Russian on both sides of a defection to America. The after picture is more attractive, but there is clear evidence that something substantial has been lost. Ironically the images of the two societies are directly opposite of those before-and-after pictures advertising diet regimens. The beginning of *Moscow on the Hudson* pictures the sparseness, the grayness of Russian society prior to Vladimir Ivanoff's (Robin Williams) defection to America, while the second half pictures the fullness of material possibility in American society. The same before-and-after contrast parallels, in spiritual terms, the changes in Vladimir's soul, his relishing of that thin spiritual concept of freedom in Russia and his questioning of it once he possesses it in all of its substance in America. Each time that doubts about his being a stranger in a strange land or paranoia about being followed or the threat of living in a free society begin to trouble Vlad, freedom raises its beneficent head to comfort him. Mazursky's film is not a simplistic before-and-after contrast of Russian society to American society. Flaws in both societies are vividly represented, but freedom ultimately tips the scale in America's favor. The film opts not for nationalist, political comparisons but for human advantages. In the end, it is simply easier to fulfill one's humanity in America; it is easier in America to bring to perfection the music of the soul as imaged in Ivanoff's love for jazz saxophone.

Like Spielberg's E.T., Vladimir is a gentle and friendly creature, a hairy, dancing Russian bear, both a comical and loving animal and an introspective man, capable of love and abhorence of violence. In Russia, he is a stoic, standing in endless lines to buy toilet paper, toadying to his KGB overseers, and playing the jazz for which he lives only for caged circus animals. In America he learns to laugh, falls in love, learns to hustle in the best capitalist style. Mazursky's film even looks like E.T., especially in its middle section when Vladimir is defecting in Bloomingdale's. He runs down the aisles and crawls like a child under the counters like E.T. trying to hide himself from the adults who just are not ready to understand. Bloomingdale's is a wonderful symbolic place for Vladimir's defection. While it symbolizes all of the opulence and excess of American society, it is also a kind of neutral country where the whole world speaks a common language, that of shopping. In fact, the American obsession with shopping and consumer goods forms an evocative symbolic motif in *Moscow on the Hudson*. After living his whole life in the gray snowy sparseness of Moscow, standing in endless lines to buy strictly rationed and poor quality merchandise and food, Vlad's first trip to an American grocery store is overwhelming. When he enters the supermarket he first asks where the lines are and then faints in the coffee aisle from the overstimulation of abundance and availability. Freedom for Vladimir is not at all political but purely physical. It is a liberation from "endless lines," from total lack of privacy (he must borrow a friend's apartment in order to make love in Moscow), from harassment for simply expressing human emotions.

Moscow on the Hudson is a cleverly structured tale of two cities. The opening Moscow section is captured in one striking image, a high overhead shot of a little man walking to the end of an endless line along a cold, gray, snowy street to buy toilet paper. He is so small and the line is so long and the city is so glum and the faces of the people are so dead and the toilet paper is so rough. Later in New York, after being mugged, this same Chaplinesque little fellow questions New York society but is brought up short by another Russian immigrant who reminds him: "He tells me now if I want law and order I should go back to Moscow and stand in line for bread . . . stale bread." This scene, in an all-night diner, is right out of "The Legend of the Grand Inquisitor" section of Dostoevsky's *Brothers Karamasov* in which the Inquisitor argues that human beings want bread not freedom. This scene gives that Inquisitor's argument the lie and ends in a diner full of immigrants reciting the Declaration of Independence as firecrackers go off to celebrate America's Independence Day.

The most basic human needs, such as making love, are always restricted in the Moscow world. On the way to a friend's apartment, borrowed in order to be alone, Vlad's girl friend nags him: "Before we marry, you should join the party. It would help us get a good apartment." Vlad gives her a romantic present, a roll of toilet paper. "You really know how to get to a girl's heart," she smiles sadly. "It isn't for your heart. It's for your soft, rosy bottom," he laughs. As they make love in these stilted circumstances, they talk of the politically indoctrinated image of America. "I would like to see it with my own eyes . . . the decadence . . . the crime . . . the poverty," she muses.

Vladimir will get this opportunity. He will be playing in the Moscow circus band on a trip to New York City. But before the circus departs, the

KGB must reinforce the Russian image of American life:

> KGB OFFICER: When you arrive in New York, you must understand that you are representing the Nation of the Revolution. Many people will take perverse pleasure in tempting you with American decadence . . . see you as targets for seduction. Like whores, they want you to share their disease, their immorality. And stay away from places like the subway, Times Square, Greenwich Village, Rockefeller Center.

Ironically when Vlad gets to New York, this image of American life is partially true. The seductions are there, but the disease is not nearly as acute. Most evident is the similarity to Moscow life, tempered by one major difference, freedom. Hence the title, *Moscow on the Hudson*. The two cities are populated with people pursuing the same dreams, except that in Moscow those dreams are less available. In New York, Vladimir finds that life, in many ways, is much the same as it was in Moscow. When he defects, he is helped by a black Bloomingdale's security guard, Lionel (Cleavant Derricks). His first American residence is a small Brooklyn apartment where he lives with Lionel's family, just as his family lived in a one-room apartment in Moscow. Vlad's first American joke is at the expense of both his countries:

> LIONEL: Must be pretty bad in Russia.
>
> VLAD: It's not human, but there are many beautiful people.
>
> LIONEL: Sounds like Alabama.
>
> VLAD: I read about slavery.
>
> LIONEL: Yeah, well slavery, at least the work was steady.
>
> VLAD: Sounds like Russia.

As a tale of two cities for the eighties, *Moscow on the Hudson* is evenhanded. It does not fall into the trap of making everything about America good. At Lucia's (Mary Conchita Alonzo) naturalization ceremony, the judge declares: "Today you will become citizens of America. No longer are you an Englishman, Italian, or Pole or whatever." But the judge is wrong. All of these immigrants are still "whatever" they are. As Vlad tells Lucia: "Everybody I meet is from somewhere else." She simply shrugs: "Is America." Though Vlad has taken up residence on the Hudson, and glories in America, he is still a Muscovite. As he takes the locks and bars off of his door to let in a fellow immigrant, he apologizes, "that's New York." Both societies have problems, both have strong attractions, but America has one difference that, in chorus, the immigrants of all nationalities recite in the all-night diner at midnight on Independence Day: "All men— are created equal—and endowed with the inalienable rights—to life— liberty—(all together) and the pursuit of happiness."

The montage imagery of *Moscow on the Hudson* is lyrical in its representation of the freedom of America as seen through the eyes of an expectant immigrant. Just before he defects, through the windows of a Liberty Lines bus, Vlad, wide-eyed, watches the panorama of America pass before him, just out of reach on the other side of the glass. All races and nationalities of people, street bands, breakdancers, punks with Mohawk haircuts, Orthodox Jews, smiling children of all colors, huge Times Square billboards, classic movie posters, porno theater marquees, all passing by in brilliant sunshine of the sort never seen in wintry Moscow, make Vlad's eyes go wide and make his friend print with his finger the word "freedom" on the steamed-up window pane. After Vlad defects in Bloomingdale's, an FBI agent questions him:

> FBI: Mr. Ivanoff, can you tell us why you want to defect?
>
> VLAD: Freedom.
>
> FBI: Political or Artistic?
>
> VLAD: Freedom.

For Vladimir, that is the one difference in this tale of two cities and it is everything. As Pauline Kael points out, the beauty of *Moscow on the Hudson* is that it is "a one-world circus."[14]

Other E.T.'s who find themselves wandering in the "one-world circus" include Mischa (Whip Hubley), a Soviet sailor shipwrecked off Key West, Florida, in *Russkies* (1987), and Danko (Arnold Schwarzenegger), a Russian police officer sent to track down a drug dealer in Chicago in *Red Heat* (1988). Both films pair up their Russian E.T.'s with American interpreters, not so much of the language, but of the whole culture.

Russkies is an eighties updating of that earlier comedy of a shipwrecked Russian submarine looking for help in an invasion-panicked New England coastal town, *The Russians Are Coming, The Russians Are Coming* (1966). But whereas the whole crew of the disabled submarine constitutes the quizzical invasion force in that earlier film and the Americans are afraid of their sudden appearance on their soil, in *Russkies* the invasion consists of one forlorn Russian sailor, an E.T. utterly lost in the complexity of American society. When Mischa, the Soviet sailor, is found by three American boys, their first inclination is to turn him over to local military authorities. A burgeoning friendship, however, forestalls this political first response, and the sharing of the Russian and American points of view makes for a running commentary upon the stereotypical fear of the other and the political wariness of the enemy that is central to these Amero-Russian E.T. film texts.

Red Heat is a genre conventional film, and its E.T., Captain Danko (Arnold Schwarzenegger), holds the distinction of being by far the biggest and most violent of these E.T.'s. If Vladimir in *Moscow on the Hudson* is a cuddly Russian bear and Mischa in *Russkies* is a forlorn and disoriented seabird, then Danko is a lumbering Russian bull in an urban china shop. *Red Heat*, like *Moscow on the Hudson*, begins in Russia, thus somewhat participating in the tale of two cities motif. But it is not as interested in Soviet society as is that earlier film. *Red Heat* begins with a nude fistfight in a Russian steambath by which Captain Danko of the Moscow-Militia gets the information leads him to pulverize a squalid Moscow bar in search of a Soviet cocaine dealer. In the course of this mayhem, Danko's police partner gets killed and the drug dealer escapes miraculously to the south side of Chicago, where he allies himself with Big Bad Leroy Brown and a street gang called "the cleanheads," who in their bigness and baldness all look like Kareem Abdul Jabbar with shotguns. Danko, of course, is dispatched from Moscow in pursuit of the drug dealer/cop killer. The film spends no time or perception on its Moscow sections and offers zero insight into Russian society. The plot focuses upon Danko as an oversized E.T. fighting the Chicago thugs.

When he arrives in Chicago, Danko is partnered with an unconventional police detective named Ridzik (Jim Belushi). What has been generated in *Red Heat* is an international superpower buddy-cop movie, the main point of which seems to be that Danko has more freedom to blast away at bad guys in a closed Russian society then Ridzik has in a *Miranda*-ized American society. Danko looks at Ridzik as a wimp because he does not break down doors and blast away at will. The sociohistorical statement in this cop movie actually tilts toward Danko's Moscow rules version of justice. In the best shoot-em-up tradition, the film affirms the society that puts the most firepower in the hands of the police good guys. This particular E.T. does not turn on his heartlight; instead, Danko turns on his headlights and drives right over (in a bus) the criminals he has come to America to kill.

A much better, more human, version of the international superpower buddy-cop movie, which also predicts the tale-of-two-cities structure of *Moscow on the Hudson*, appeared earlier in the decade in *Gorky Park* (1983). Whereas in *Red Heat* the tale of two cities is heavily overbalanced in Chicago's favor and in *Moscow on the Hudson* the balance is even, in *Gorky Park* the balance is tipped heavily in Moscow's direction. "Never before has the cold, bleak life in Russia today been so graphically depicted," one reviewer declared.[15]

That critic's emphasis upon the portrayal of "Russia today" is important because the first film of the eighties to go inside Russia was Warren Beatty's epic (in the political epic tradition of *Dr. Zhivago*) *Reds* (1981). Where *Reds* sent an American into a past Russia and relayed his reactions through the conduit of a love story, the totalitarianism film text of the eighties enters a present Russia and exposes the repressions and rewards of that society.

Gorky Park was the first major curtain piercer of the eighties. As had Martin Cruz Smith's enormously popular best-selling novel from which

Gorky Park is adapted, the film satisfies an American desire to look inside Russia and see if there really is any basis for the world's most discussed cultural clash. Masquerading as a police procedural, *Gorky Park* first anatomizes the closedness of Russian society, then chronicles the collision of the Russian and American social experience.

In the gray depths of Russian winter, three frozen bodies, their faces and fingertips completely torn off, are found in Gorky Park only short blocks from the Kremlin. These bodies are ironically symbolic. They are, for Arkady Renko (William Hurt), the cynical police detective assigned to the case, symbols of an almost universal Russian loss of identity, of a whole nation—faceless, identityless—locked in an existential deep freeze. But not all Russians are frozen in anonymous existential death like those corpses in the park. Arkady finds identity in doing his job well, and while interviewing possible witnesses, he meets Irina (Joanna Pacula), a struggling actress who embodies another point of view toward the existential chill of Russian society. In contrast to Arkady's cynical work-ethic stoicism, Irina only wants out, longs to escape the artistic repression of Soviet society. But in the course of his investigation, Arkady encounters yet a third strategy for dealing with Russian facelessness. That third strategy is corruption and greed. "Are you sure we should investigate this?" Renko asks the chief prosecutor (Ian Bannon). "Who knows where it will lead to?" Renko suspects that it will lead directly to the KGB, but what he does not suspect is that these are not political murders, but that the case is one of greed operating on all levels of Russian society instigated by—who else?—an American capitalist businessman, Jack Osborne (Lee Marvin). Arkady discovers within Russian society this multidimensional acknowledgment of, and struggle against, existential facelessness. His stoicism, Irina's longing to escape, his superiors' corruption, are all necessary strategies for survival in this closed society.

But parallel to this interior culture clash is the East-West culture clash that ignites when New York City homicide detective William Kirwell (Brian Dennehy) arrives in Moscow looking for his kid brother who has disappeared and is probably one of the faceless corpses found in the park. Renko and Kirwell buddy up just as Vladimir and Lionel do in *Moscow on the Hudson* and Danko and Ridzik do in *Red Heat*. Their culture clash, however, is appropriate to the police procedural pace of the film. It is a clash over methods, over how murders get solved. Renko goes about his detecting methodically, intellectually, while Kirwell comes through the iron curtain shooting from the hip like any self-respecting American cowboy. Renko and Kirwell are walking allegories of their countries' cultures. Thus the cultural clashes of *Gorky Park* operate on all of the film's thematic levels. On one level, American capitalism corrupts Russian communism. Osborne wants to smuggle live Russian sables, bred only in Siberia and thus constituting a world monopoly, to the United States. In symbolic terms, this is a scheme to steal an integral part of the Russian character, to Westernize and cheapen it. On another level, American agressiveness fuels Russian taciturnity and produces results out of a détente. Kirwell's cowboying gets Renko moving.

But perhaps the greatest irony of *Gorky Park* is that Arkady Renko finds himself an E.T. in his own land. Near the end of the film, he goes to America to tie up the loose ends in the case. When the three KGB men who accompany Arkady are killed by Osborne in the Staten Island snow, Arkady is offered a chance to stay in America, to defect, but he refuses and returns to Moscow, losing Irina in his decision. Arkady's decision takes into account the degree of E.T.-ness of his existence. In Russia, in his dedication to his job of opening up mysteries in a closed society, Arkady is an exception. But in the freewheeling, ultraviolent world of America, he is truly a stranger in a strange land. Like *Moonlighting* and *Moscow on the Hudson*, of the E.T. movies of cultural contrast, *Gorky Park* gives a full view both of Russian society and of the nature of the Russian people, who do not want to leave their society but want that society to be more open. In *Gorky Park*, when E.T. Arkady Renko gets the chance to "go home," it is to the society in which everyone is an E.T. like him.

Coping with Totalitarianism

While the E.T. films chronicle a series of flights to freedom out of the closed Russian society and set up elaborate tale-of-two-cities contrasts between East and West, the fourth Amero-Russian film text focuses upon life inside Russia (or countries like Russia) for those who may long for American openness but must cope with their Russian reality on a daily basis. These are films about people chafing at the yoke of totalitarianism, adapting and existing despite the restraints of their society. In the majority, America is but a gauzy ideal of freedom that these people behind the iron curtain long for.

In the first half of the decade, an old Russian-baiter, *1984* (1984), and an imaginative new black comedy about totalitarianism, Terry Gilliam's *Brazil* (1985), presented two visions, different visually yet similar ideologically, of life in a totalitarian state. The greatest irony of the newest version of George Orwell's *1984* is that it is no longer a futuristic political fantasy but a grotesque reality of contemporary life. The dark urban rubble of Michael Rudford's *1984* is as contemporary as downtown Beirut or Russian tanks rumbling into Hungary in 1958, Czechoslovakia in 1968, Afghanistan in 1979, or Lithuania in 1990. Rudford's *1984* is a gloomy, too realistic, fantasy of life in a totalitarian state in which the KGB has become Big Brother and the thought police have not learned much subtlety. Neither *1984* nor *Brazil* is set in Russia but rather in nonexistent fantasy states. Yet the grayness and gloominess of the urban landscape in *1984* and the black humoresque of the city's inhabitants in *Brazil* both echo consistent representations of Moscow life in the other films of the decade.

Brazil especially captures in satire the absurdity of Russian life with its food shortages, bureaucratic foul-ups, police mindlessness and insane resistance to government through individual action. In *Brazil*, one major rebel against the totalitarian state is Harry Tuttle (Robert De Niro), a renegade heating-and-cooling repairman who converts people to the ideology of rebellion against the state by fixing their ductwork. While *1984* focuses upon the physical oppression of the totalitarian state and *Brazil* satirizes the bureaucratic excesses of the totalitarian state, both highlight the reasons why people want out, why Russians like Vladimir in *Moscow on the Hudson* choose to defect. Both, however, were pre-Geneva Summit, pre-*glasnost* and *perestroika*, pre-Gorbachev, prior to the rhetorical shift in East-West superpower relations.

Later in the decade, other films also looked at the reasons for fleeing Eastern Europe and Russia but balanced their treatment with arguments for staying. One such was Philip Kaufman's *Unbearable Lightness of Being* (1988), and, as did *Moscow Does Not Believe in Tears* (1980) and the first halves of both *Moscow on the Hudson* and *Gorky Park*, it meticulously and stylishly explores the compensatory strategies that the Russians concoct for finding freedom in their everyday lives. The two main strategies are those of sex and of art.

The style of *The Unbearable Lightness of Being* is that of Georges Rouault—clear bright strokes combined with textures layered on with a palate knife. Set in Prague in 1968 at the time known as "Prague Spring," which was a brief flowering of freedom of speech and artistic expression—a so-called "socialism with a human face"—before the Soviet tanks closed everything down as they had done in Hungary a decade earlier, and like Roualt's paintings, the coarse textures of the city in the first third of the film contrast to the romantic gossamer of the provincial forests in the final third. These two sections are composed as paintings, while the middle third of film, the Russian invasion of Czechoslovakia and the flight of the major characters from that repression to Geneva, captures the violence of the political conflict in stark black-and-white terms. Two mediums, the painterly medium of romance and the realistic medium of photography, represent how sexuality and imagination, love and art, must struggle constantly against the weight of political oppression.

The three major characters—Tomas (Daniel Day Lewis), a brilliant young surgeon; Tereza (Juliette Brioche), his wife and a photographer; Sabina (Lena Olin), his mistress and an artist—all enjoy the freedom of Prague Spring, all flee from the Russian invasion, but Tomas and Tereza return to Czechoslovakia, give up their passports in order to live in love with each other. Sabina, opting for the freedom of art, flees to California. It is a film that emphasizes both universal themes and political themes.

Making love, laughing, and expressing oneself in works of art are the only weapons these characters have against the oppressions of their society.

When the Russian tanks invade Czechoslovakia, winter descends upon "Prague Spring" and these three young people are trapped in a world that stifles the lightness of their being. Sabina's gay mirror paintings had dominated the first "Prague Spring" section, but in section two, as the tanks rumble down the streets, Tereza's stark and violent photographs (at one point she shoots her camera fearlessly directly into the barrel of a gun) supersede Sabina's mirror paintings. This middle photographic section is reminiscent of the similar symbolic use of photography in both *Blow-Up* (1966) and *Under Fire* (1984).

In the aftermath of the invasion, these three flee to Geneva to try to regain the freedom and power of sensual laughter, but they become exiles: from their country, from each other. "Life is light for you," Tereza tells Tomas. "For me it is very heavy. I cannot bear your lightness. You are strong. I am weak. I'm going back to the country of the weak." What Tereza is saying is that she cannot bear to live in exile uncommitted to the reality of the Russian occupation of Czechoslovakia. What Tomas learns is that he cannot bear to live without Tereza. Sabina can run away from every problem, every relationship, into her art, but Tereza and Tomas cannot. Though Czechoslovakia has become a prison, Tereza and Tomas, like Meursault in the second half of *The Stranger*, have learned how to be free even though imprisoned.

America is present in *The Unbearable Lightness of Being* only as one possible refuge from Russian oppression and only one of the three central characters chooses it. Perhaps more than any other film of the decade, *The Unbearable Lightness of Being* denies the faceless dehumanization of the rightist militarist films and affirms the humanity of the real people who live behind the iron curtain. In her teasing way, Sabina asks Tomas, "Are you only seeking for pleasure or is every woman a new land that you wish to explore?" In eighties film, the new land that Americans wished to explore was Russia, and *The Unbearable Lightness of Being* was the most humanistic and least sensational of explorations.

White Nights, however, was a rather different story. One critic called it "a Reagan-era movie after all" and "shamelessly manipulative,"[16] while another discussed its "built-in dialectic" between a defector from Russian artistic oppression and a defector from American racism and Vietnam War disenchantment as "transparently opportunistic."[17] Its director, Taylor Hackford, defended it by arguing "*White Nights* is a film about the need for artistic and individual freedom. I didn't set out to make a Cold War movie."[18] Despite his protestations, *White Nights* gives terminal punctuation to all of these Amero-Russian film texts because it is the most verbally ideological film of the decade concerning the differences between American and Russian society. The whole thematic focus of *White Nights* is upon getting out of Russia. Released soon after the 1985 Geneva Summit that initiated the drastic rhetorical shift in Amero-Russian relations, it not only failed to acknowledge that shift, but it regressed to a cold war rhetoric more appropriate to the fifties than the eighties. As one critic wryly noted: "There'll have to be a lot of Genevas before this one's booked into the Leningrad Bijou I and II."[19]

White Nights is a set piece propaganda film that verbally and visually represents the ideological clash between white knight America and "the evil empire" of Reagan's spin-doctors. Its set piece structure alternates long ideological speeches about the loss of freedom with brilliantly choreographed dance sequences that express the freedom which has been lost. The film's title is from Dostoevsky and the opening dance sequence, Roland Petit's "Le Jeune Homme et la Mort," captures the underground-man tenor of the rest of the film. Both Nicolai Rodchenko (Mikhail Baryshinikov) and Raymond Greenwood (Gregory Hines) are on the outside looking in upon their doubled societies. Both are both American and Russian. Both have strong, yet painfully ambivalent, feelings about both of their societies. In the longest set piece of *White Nights*, Ray tells Nic why he defected to Russia:

RAY: You used to be Russian.

NICOLAI: I'm still Russian. I'm just not Soviet.

RAY: You're Amerikans now. I forgot. . . .

NICOLAI: It's a wonderful country.

RAY: What the hell do you know about America? Answer me, you ever been to Harlem? Like on your way to the airport or something? You ever look inside? You ever dance at the Apollo? Huh? You go on your tippy toes to the White House.

NICOLAI: Tell me, why did you come here?

RAY: I'm surprised you never heard of me . . . I was a star. Not as a tap dancer, of course.

NICOLAI: You're a defector.

RAY: I'm a selector, not a defector. . . . You know the funny thing about me? . . . I used to feel the way you do about America. I was a patriot. Greatest country in the world. I was always a tap dancer which for a black person is not that unusual. . . . I loved to dance. And I got work. I was a . . . cute little colored kid tappin' away. . . . By the time I grew up it was a different story. He's an adult black man now. I wasn't cute . . . Uncle Sam wanted me. He wanted the whole ghetto. Uncle Sam said, "I want you all, get in here." I said, "Ma, this is it. I'm gonna git myself a real career. Electronics. Become a communications expert, defend my country against Communism." Wherever. But when they made me the offer, nobody said you were gonna become a murderer, gonna become a rapist, gonna maim and rob people. I kept sayin' to myself this war's gotta be about somethin'. Can't just be hired killers. It's not possible. We're Americans. Little voice in my head it said, "Ray, you've been used. They're tryin' to kill ya. They don't even think you're human and they want you to die for 'em. . . ."

NICOLAI: It's still a better place than this.

This first major ideological speech seems to strike a balance between the two societies, intimates that both have their weaknesses. But immediately that balance tilts and Russia becomes "the evil empire," while America rides in as the white knight. Ray's speech makes it clear that he is describing a past America, a racist and exploitative America of the Vietnam years of the sixties. But *White Nights* is really about the totalitarian Russia of the eighties. The implication is that America has changed, but Russia remains a prison. Ray's speech presents a negative panorama of American society twenty years past, but the film never makes another negative comment on America. The dialectic overbalances toward a critique of Russian society.

Russian society is portrayed in *White Nights* as a prison, certainly of the body in terms of mobility but also of the spirit in terms of one's possibilities for self-expression. Both Nic and Raymond are imprisoned. "Am I under arrest," Nicolai asks Raymond. "No, you're not under arrest. You're free as a bird," he answers, but immediately cuts off Nic's phone call to the U.S. embassy. Later, KGB Colonel Chaiko (Jerzy Skolimowski) demonstrates Raymond's imprisonment in a simple choice of backdrop. Chaiko takes Raymond to a Siberian mine for a chat. He wants Raymond to help the KGB convince Nic to dance in the opening gala of the Kirov Ballet. Chaiko employs intimidation by landscape. He never threatens or gets angry with Raymond, but the whole conversation is framed by images of little tiny men working the mine. Chaiko's mine game is but one of the mind games played by the KGB. *White Nights* is a tale of two cultures vying for these two artistic men. Ideology once again invades the buddy movie.

Where Raymond is torn between the two societies, Nicolai has no doubts. Though nostalgic for his past, especially as he does a solo turn on an empty stage to the silent seats of the great Kirov Theater, he knows that he can never be free in the prison of Russian society. The whole film is a prison break. The society's mind games place mind-forged manacles on the Russian people. "Everyone drinks too much here," Nic says. "It helps." In a sense, *White Nights* portrays Russian history as a chronicle of people escaping from the prison of society. Chaiko tries to use history to convince Nicolai to dance:

CHAIKO: The Kirov Ballet. This is where Pavlova, Nijinski, Balanchine were taught. Oh yes, Nicolai Rodchenko shouldn't be forgotten. All of them danced here at the Kirov.

NICOLAI: And all of them left here.

As his former dance partner, Galina (Helen Mirren), tries to convince him to go along with the KGB and dance, the stage is set for another set piece ideological speech:

> GALINA: But why are we speaking in Russian? You are no longer Russian, are you?
>
> NICOLAI: I had to go. I had to do it . . . I was choking here.

Galina answers him with an extended description of the prison of Russian society:

> When I came back from London, I had to defend myself to the KGB. They wouldn't believe that you stayed in the West without a word to me. I couldn't believe it myself. They took away my passport. For four years I wasn't allowed to travel. And for three years I was taken every week to the big house where I had to answer their questions. Every week their same stupid questions. . . . Yes, I rebuilt my life. I was supposed to give up everything so that you can live in Disneyland?

The irony of this prison house of society in Russia lies in the KGB's elaborate attempts to cover up the closed society realities.

The salient subtext of *White Nights* involves the intricacies of superpower public relations. When Nicolai's publicist, Ann Wyatt (Geraldine Page) threatens to take the story of his detention to the international press, a U.S. state department spokesperson argues against it: "No, right now they're taking credit for saving 250 lives. Soviet PR has never been better." Colonel Chaiko of the KGB is not a sinister, brutal thug or a leather-coated Nazi like the KGB agents in past films. Instead, he is a slick, charming spin-doctor, an orchestrator of the symbolic event. At the end, after Nicolai and Darya (Isabella Rossellini), Raymond's wife, have escaped from their detention site and made it into an American embassy car, they are cut off by Chaiko within sight of the embassy gate. Public relations provides for their escape. Ann Wyatt rushes out of the embassy with a battalion of news cameramen and unaligned nation diplomats. Chaiko cannot forcefully detain Nicolai and Darya under the white lights of the TV cameras.

Win Scott (John Glover), an American CIA spook, knows exactly how this PR game is played. "Oh stop all this cloak and dagger bull shit and do something," Ann Wyatt demands. But Scott knows that direct action does not get results in the game of image dueling. "This guy Chaiko," Win Scott answers, "has put together something fantastic here . . . if you were to jeopardize their sweet-smelling position with world opinion, they just might try to protect themselves. They could fly the man to Siberia, give him an overdose of drugs, and say he died of his injuries . . . I don't want you to kid yourself about a press conference. That sort of thing just doesn't fly over here."

At one point, in exasperation at Chaiko, Ray Greenwood says, "for Christ's sake, he's only a dancer." *Rocky IV* and *White Nights* were "only" movies, but what political and sociohistorical art has a tendency to do is catch the attention of the world. These two films certainly caught the attention of the Soviet Union. Through *Isvestia*, Russia lodged a protest in the international press against these two films. Thus the movies were recognized as participating in and constituting a public relations arm of the post-Geneva Summit rhetorical shift and the subsequent thaw in East-West relations.

7

The Feminist Farm Crisis and Other Neoconservative Feminist Texts

I N W. P. KINSELLA'S novel *Shoeless Joe* (1982), an Iowa family farmer goes into debt to build a baseball diamond in his cornfield. His baseball dream, however, is frontally assaulted by an agribusiness corporation that wants to install "computer farming" on his land and that of all the other family farmers in the county:

> I can visualize what they want to do. You don't need fences around corn. Farmhands will roll the barbed wire up on giant wooden spools. . . . The houses and outbuildings will all be torn down—bulldozed and hauled away, making the plains as flat and silent and lifeless as they were 150 years ago. The farm will be run from one concrete bunker the size of an electrical-transformer station. One man will sit in bluish light in front of a television screen that every fifteen minutes provides updated information about market prices, weather forecasts, legislative happenings, planting, spray and harvest advisories, USDA news, and dozens of other topics—data fed into the computer on a continuing basis. . . . At a command from the single pale figure, posed vulturelike over the computer screen, battalions of combines can be unleashed to gobble up the crops and spew them into trucks to be wheeled to market—all neat and clean and sterile and heartless.[1]

Shoeless Joe is the novel from which *Field of Dreams* (1989) was adapted, and this futuristic vision of the demise of the family farm is never more than a sociopolitical subtext in either the book or the resulting film. Both novel and film are about the power of imagination and the necessity of dreams. Nevertheless, the theme of what Ray Kinsella (W. P. Kinsella's central character played by Kevin Costner in the film) calls "the tyranny of the powerful over the powerless"(7) is a clear-sighted analysis of the American farm crisis of the early eighties, a crisis that saw wholesale foreclosures upon family farms in every region of the nation, saw the generation of a grassroots survival politics (whereby powerless farmers banded together), saw the formation of FarmAid (a national fund-raising movement to help the family farmer), and finally in 1984, spawned a cluster of films focused

246

directly upon this "tyranny of the powerful over the powerless" on the American family farm.

The films *Places in the Heart, Country,* and *The River,* all released between September and December 1984, dealt with the threat to the family farm in America. All three confronted the farm crisis issue in terms of a similar textual discourse. All took an anticorporate or antigovernment stance, and all argued from a feminist perspective. "Back to basics" was a strident cry in the schools and the legislatures that funded those schools in the eighties, and the same "back to basics" sentiment held true in the films. *Places in the Heart, Country,* and *The River* are films about simple, basic Americans trying to understand the complexity and heartless impersonality of computerized eighties life. They all present the contrast between country life, where human beings (in these three films, women) are in touch with the land, and urban life, where people move constantly within the control of a machine.

The Feminist Farm Crisis Films

Harking back to the thirties, the movies of the eighties rediscovered mid-America and the rural dream of its peoples' direct relationship with the land. In 1985, commenting on the new patriotic jingoism of the *Rocky/Rambo* double whammy, social theorist Robert Reich also looked back at the three farm crisis films of the previous year: "Last year's farm movies— *Country, The River* and *Places in the Heart*—fit into the new nationalism as much as Rocky. They're about purity, hard work and the sense of community that's very much a part of our American consciousness."[2] While the farm crisis film texts of 1984 are about the rediscovery of America in terms of a rearguard action against the mechanizing and malling of American life, and the grassroots political movement of the powerless to gain power, all three are also about women, *their* strength, and *their* movement from powerlessness to power.

The farm crisis films of 1984 were a continual tribute to the character of Ma Joad (Jane Darwell) in John Ford's *Grapes of Wrath* (1940). While these latter-day Ma Joad's were all thinner, prettier, and softer-spoken, they were no less enduring and hopeful and willing to roll up their sleeves to sustain their own families and to maintain a sense of community no matter how dismal the circumstances. The farm crisis films, however, were formed not only out of past mythic images but out of contemporary headlines as well. All through the eighties, from the spate of small farm foreclosures by the FHA early in the decade to the impassioned criticism of Reagan administration farm policies to the devastating drought of 1988 that forced another wave of family farmers to sell out, the farm crisis was a sustained social issue, a threat to two basic American institutions: the family and the individual ownership of land. Sometimes this intense focus led to violence as in 1985 when James Lee Jenkins and his son Steven ambushed and killed two officials from the bank that had foreclosed on the family's ten-acre Rushton, Minnesota, farm.[3] But more often it led to social action (as in the FarmAid movement) and to political debate (as in 1985 when Jessica Lange, Sissy Spacek, and Jane Fonda, all stars of farm crisis films, went to Washington to lobby Congress to help farmers).

Congressman Tony Coelho, in answer to criticism of the three actresses' visit to Congress, said: "Yes, we want publicity. We knew that when they came forward, everyone would pay attention."[4] Congressman Thomas Daschle, chairman of the House of Representatives farm task force also admitted that the 1984 farm crisis films and the appearance of these three actresses before Congress was "the Hollywoodization of a very serious issue," but he went on to assert that the movies and the actresses' speaking out had succeeded in attracting the national attention that individual farmers could not. Speaking directly about Jessica Lange's film *Country* on the occasion of the actress's congressional appearance, Anne Kanten, Minnesota's deputy agriculture commissioner, said: "It raises all the issues, the economics of what is happening in agriculture; it shows what is happening in the stress between spouses, between parents and children, between neighbors; and it speaks very strongly to the role of the women in it all."[5] For all of these different spokespersons, the farm crisis was more than simply a political or economic problem; it was a threat to the American way of life, the family farm.

The farm crisis films of 1984 were certainly a case of political Holly-woodization, but they were also an affirmation of the "back to basics" impulse loose in America. Those films were not just about farms; they were about women on farms and their importance at the heart of American life.

No political or critical theory has blown more fitfully on the winds of social change than has feminism in its evolution from the radical sixties to the neoconservative eighties. The combination of farm politics and feminism was a logical extension of the feminist politics of the radical sixties and the feminist economics of the urban-anchored, upwardly mobile seventies. In the eighties, in tune with a Reaganite neoconservatism, feminism turned to its grassroots in the American family, a constituency that had been generally ignored in the feminist targeting of both the sixties and the seventies. The acronym WIFE (Women Involved in Farm Economics) symbolically comments upon both the evolution and the conservatizing of the eighties feminist vision as represented in the 1984 farm crisis films.

This newly discovered grassroots feminist consciousness had a prehistory in films like Robert Altman's *3 Women* (1977) and Sissy Spacek's earlier role as the *Coal Miner's Daughter* (1980), a quite socially conscious, feminist-aimed, biopic of country singer Loretta Lynn. But the 1984 trio of farmwife roles earned Academy Award nominations for all three actresses, an unprecedented legitimization of not only the quality of those films and their acting but of the manner in which that single role, that of the determined farmwife under duress, had caught the imagination and social consciousness of the American people. Sally Field won the Academy Award for Best Actress that year for her role in Robert Benton's *Places in the Heart*, the first of the 1984 farm crisis texts to be released.

Of the three farm crisis films of 1984, *Places in the Heart* is the least polemic, the most metaphoric, and the furthest removed from the realities of the eighties farm crisis. Set in the thirties in rural Texas, *Places in the Heart* could well be a second coming of a pint-sized Ma Joad. Yet despite its temporal separation from contemporary social and political issues, *Places in the Heart* still metaphorically represents the pertinent issues of the eighties farm crisis. Exactly as the heroines of the other farm films will later, depression-era single parent Edna Spalding (Sally Field), to meet the payment on her farm loan, must survive the weather (a tornado), the buck-passing bankers, and the rigors of running a farm without a man around. But even while facing down those obstacles, Edna, in the best Ma Joad tradition, forms a viable community of outcasts, a new family made up of her fatherless children, of Mose (Danny Glover), a black sharecropper cast adrift by the Great Depression, and of Will (John Malkovich), a blind boarder foisted upon her by the so-called pillar of the community, the banker, who threatens to take her farm away. *Places in the Heart* is a metaphorical reclamation project about people reclaiming their land and their dignity. It is a story of hard times, but the hard times of the thirties, not the more complex hard times of the eighties, which both *Country* and *The River* confront.

Country came second. Of these farm crisis films, it is the most polemic and politically accurate, the most contemporaneous in its dissection of the problem. Jessica Lange, who both produced and starred in *Country*, got the idea from a newspaper photo of an Ohio farm family forced to sell all their belongings in a foreclosure auction. Of these three films, *Country* is the most overtly a sociohistorical document, a checklist film that item by item—FHA foreclosures, Reagan farm policy, foreign grain sale embargoes leading to low domestic grain prices, family breakups, suicides, foreclosure auctions—explores the causes and results of the powerless situation of so many family farmers in the eighties.

As did John Ford's *Grapes of Wrath* in places, at times *Country*'s polemic turns it into a somewhat blatant propaganda piece. Like the "coming home" films about the post-Vietnam era, like the nuclear war films, *Country* has its moments of "getting out the message," informing the audience of the sociohistorical and political facts of this Reagan-era farm crisis. One such moment occurs when a drunken Gil Ivey (Sam Shepard) confronts a local FHA agent who has foreclosed on the Ivey family farm:

What are you tryin' to do to us, McMullin? Wasn't it you who was givin' all those great speeches here a few years back about how we're gonna feed the world, we're gonna expand, plant fence post to fence post. Wasn't that you? Then here goes the government puttin' embargoes on foreign sales. Leaves all us poor fools out here in the landscape with all this grain and no place to get a fair price for it.

Another such propagandistic moment occurs when a federal bureaucrat tells the local FHA agent the political facts:

FORDYCE: We gotta get tougher Tom.

MC MULLIN: Tougher? God, this family's barely hangin' on as it is, farm prices bein' what they are.

FORDYCE: The point is we gotta cut our losses, get what we can before these people are in so deep there's nothin' left to get.

MC MULLIN: You're tellin' me to go ahead and foreclose these people out?

FORDYCE: 40 percent of your accounts are delinquent. There's not much future in the FHA for someone with somethin' like that on their record. Just show they can't make it farmin' anymore. They'll go.

Without question, in *Country* the FHA and the Reagan farm policies are the villains, but *Country* is much more than a propagandistic polemic.

Through its gritty realism, its solid characterization of a true farm family, *Country* rises above purely political message-mongering and delivers a more powerful message about a larger crisis at the heart of the American way of life. Jewel Ivey (Jessica Lange) and her family become struggling survivors of the shipwreck of the American dream in a changing mid-America where the old values seem to be breaking up on the rocks of a shortsighted materialism. Gil Ivey tells the FHA loan officer: "I don't understand this. Here we been dealin' with you people here for six, seven years. You know what farmin's like. I mean, we may have a couple of rough years, but it always comes back around. You can't look on this thing short term. Hell, it's a way of life!" To which, the FHA banker answers, "No Gil, it's a business. Farming is a business." Talking to a private banker 400 who has turned him down for a loan, Gil protests weakly, "I remember when this bank used to loan money on the man not the numbers." This shortsighted materialism on the part of the government and the banks is an active threat to the American way of life, to the land itself. Jewel momentarily panics when the FHA, without warning, calls in all of their loans: "Where do they think we're gonna get that kind of money in one lump. We'd have to sell everything, even the land. They wouldn't make us do that, would they Gil? We're not gonna sell the land. This land's been in my family for over a hundred years." *Country* is not about the selling out of a single farm family, or of the American family farmer, but about the story of the selling out of the American way of life, the land itself upon which that original American dream was based.

But Jewel Ivey is not content to sit back and watch the passing of this American way of life. She goes back to basics, turns to the grassroots to reclaim the land, stop this materialist erosion of an elemental way of life, restore viability to a buffeted American dream. In *Country*, the Ivey's financial, social, and domestic disaster comes upon them as unexpectedly as the natural disaster of the tornado early in the film. "Your dad and me," Jewel tells her children after she has exiled Gil from the farm, "we're caught in the middle of somethin' we never saw comin'." The only way to survive in this whirlwind is to get close to the ground, put your trust in the land, and fight to hold on. That is exactly what Jewel Ivey does. She organizes a grassroots resistance against the FHA foreclosure tactic. As in the central image of the Juggernaut Caterpillar tractors in *The Grapes of Wrath*, Jewel decides to place obstacles in the way of the FHA Juggernaut that is trying to bulldoze these family farmers out of business. Jewel personally, her baby in her arms, by dirt road mail boxes, in feed lots and pig pens, in the snow in front of isolated farmhouses, talks to every farmer in the county, pleads with them to come to the foreclosure auction at the Ivey farm. "Your bein' there would help," she tells them. "If we were all together. If enough of us could get together, maybe we could kick up a little dust." She is an eighties feminist version of Steinbeck's Jim Casy.

The climactic scene of this political text of *Country* is the foreclosure auction during which the Ivey's neighbors refuse to buy. The crowd's chant—"No sale! No sale!"—becomes a symbolic rallying cry for the film, interpretable on a number of levels. That "no sale" refers immediately to the Ivey's belongings and land, but it also refers to the refusal to sell out the midwestern farmer's way of life, to the refusal to sell out the American dream itself.

Yet co-equal with the sociohistorical political text of *Country* is its feminist text. Jewel Ivey is an equal partner with her husband Gil in the operation of their farm and family. When the tornado hits, she is out in the fields with Gil, her son, Carlisle, and her father, Otis (Wilford Brimley), working on the harvest, threatened by the danger. Under duress from the FHA, Jewel's part in the partnership is further underscored. She keeps the books while Gil works the fields. When the pressure of the FHA drives the Iveys inexorably toward selling out, it is Gil who gives up, seeks relief in a bottle, while Jewel carries on the fight. As was Ma Joad, Jewel is the strength that not only keeps the family together but brings the community together in political resistance to the government sellout. One symbolic, Sisyphean scene captures the elemental strength of Jewel Ivey. When the FHA comes with a livestock truck to impound the sheep of the Ivey's neighbor Arlen, who later commits suicide, Jewel runs back and forth in the pasture waving her arms, competing with the sheepdog, until she cannot run or breathe anymore. The dog wins, but this scene signals her determination to fight to the last ditch no matter how powerless one's situation may seem. In *Country*, the feminist theme is a powerful, if somewhat stacked, statement that women are both the brains and the stamina that will get America through the crisis at its grassroots.

Mae Garvey (Sissy Spacek) in *The River* is a woman similar to Jewel Ivey, though her personal situation is different. All three women in this 1984 cluster of farm crisis films find themselves alone with the responsibility of keeping family and farm together. But whereas Edna Spalding's husband was killed and Jewel Ivey's was off seeking solace in a bottle, Mae's husband, Tom Garvey (Mel Gibson), is forced to leave the farm to do scab labor in a city. In Tom's absence, Mae faces not only the economic forays against her farm but sexual forays against her person. Hers is a touchier feminist characterization than the maternal toughness of Lange's Jewel Ivey. Spacek is quite aware of the eighties neoconservative feminist overtones of her Mae Garvey character: "I've always been drawn to roles of being either a wife or mother. I never wanted to be *the girl*. You know what I mean, that kind of part where you kind of roll alongside the guy as his sidekick? I am attracted to strong characters who have never heard of the feminist movement."[6] This is one of the clearer statements of the nature of the neoconservative feminist consciousness.

These films are all about feminist assimilation, the necessity of bringing into the sisterhood those women whom the radicalism of the sixties and the careerism of the seventies had overlooked. While Mae Garvey is a strong feminist figure equal to Jewel Ivey, *The River* is not the same movie as either *Places in the Heart* or *Country*. Though it is almost identical in plot and characters right down to its natural disaster, its separation of husband and wife, its moustache-twirling corporate villain, and its farm foreclosure auction, it does not have the sociopolitical edge of *Country*. There is always the sense in *Country* that the story, the characters, and the dialogue are part of a lobbying effort, an attempt of art to talk to the nation. *The River* is more personal, melodramatic, in its tone. It asks us to care about some people. In *Country* we are asked to care about a vanishing way of life, the basis of the concept "America."

Also in 1984, in fact preceding these three farm crisis films by five months, was the exquisite television production of *The Dollmaker*. This story of Gertie Nevels (Jane Fonda) is both a story of country people forced out of their element into urban-displaced personhood and a neoconservative feminist fable of the possibilities of a woman's artistic and maternal commitments coinciding. At the center of *The Dollmaker* arrives an ironic symbol. Gertie's husband brings home a jigsaw that he thinks will help her to turn out mass-produced dolls. But Gertie never touches this industrial tool. Like Jewel Ivey, she realizes that the hand-carving of each of her dolls is more than just an aesthetic or existential act, it is the perpetuation of an American way of life.

After the frenzy of farm films in 1984, Hollywood took a hiatus from what was clearly an overdone issue. In the backwash of this cluster of farm films, *The Milagro Bean Field War*, originally scheduled for 1985, did not get made and released until 1988. *Milagro* means "miracle" in Spanish, and in a sense, miracles are what all of these farm crisis films are about. Each chronicles the miracle of "the powerless" holding off "the powerful," of the poor outmaneuvering the rich. All explore the dynamics of these kinds of miracles, but Robert Redford's *Milagro Bean Field War* explores this modern miracle of community action to save the farmer's way of life with a gentle realism and a subtle humor. Even Sally Field's perkiness got lost in the hardships and nostalgia of *Places in the Heart*. What little humor was present in the early scenes of *Country* was quickly submerged in that film's polemic. *The River* early embraced an unrelievedly grim tone. But *The Milagro Bean Field War* chronicles the bumbling, comic, flawed natures of these farmers trying to make their miracle.

The Milagro Bean Field War is not about old-style miracles like walking on water or multiplying loaves and fishes or raising men from the dead but rather about modern miracles like watering a bean field, multiplying one man into a community, or bringing a town back from the dead. The film is a sentimental ensemble story of flawed people looking to maintain lives of quiet dignity. Milagro is a tiny, dying, dusty town in a New Mexico valley populated by three generations of Latino farmers who cannot get water to grow their crops. Because of these hard times, Ladd Devine (Richard Bradford) is buying up all the small family farms in the valley to build a condo community and golf course. The film's early images of tractors bulldozing the land are clearly reminiscent of similar images of the rape of America in John Ford's *Grapes of Wrath*.

When, by mistake, one farmer, Joe Mondragon (Chick Vennara), opens up a government water channel and floods his beanfield, suddenly the powerless begin to acquire a little power. The whole town admires Joe's unintended courage, and led by Ruby (Sonia Braga), the local auto mechanic, and Charlie (John Heard), a disenchanted activist lawyer and newspaper editor, they turn Joe into a hero against the tyranny of the land development company. Meanwhile, Herbie Platt (Daniel Stern), a nerdy sociology professor from the East, shows up to do research, and Kyril Montana (Christopher Walken) shows up to break this incipient revolution via violence. Through it all, trying to defuse the confrontation, walks Sheriff Montoya (Ruben Blades). *The Milagro Bean Field War*, like *Country*, is about ordinary people coming together to form a human community to solve their problems. Like the farm crisis films of 1984, like the subtexted "computer farming" theme of *Shoeless Joe* (and *Field of Dreams*), this film raises the issue of the people vs. the commercial rape of the American landscape. Yet layered above this political theme in *The Milagro Bean Field War*, as it was layered below the overt politics of *Country*, is the theme of a religious humanistic faith that keeps these ordinary people going even in the face of seemingly insurmountable obstacles, like FHA foreclosure auctions and land developers' bulldozers.

Though perhaps one of the most short-lived sociohistorical issues in eighties film history, lasting for only five months in 1984, the farm crisis films made two lasting impressions upon American social consciousness. First, they contributed to the heated discussions and revisions of the Reagan farm policy and gave impetus to other highly visible social movements, such as FarmAid, which continued throughout the rest of the decade. But second, though the farm crisis issue faded rather quickly from Hollywood's social consciousness, the way in which these three farm crisis films were presented served as a neoconservative feminist template for other women's issue films of the eighties. This feminist text had been referenced earlier in the decade in existential films like *The French Lieutenant's Woman* (1981) and gender films like *Tootsie* (1982), but the farm crisis films as well as films like *Silkwood* (1983) and *Cross Creek* (1983) and *Testament* (1983) gave a neoconservative cast to the eighties feminist text, presented a clear-sighted pragmatic feminism as an essential part of the American social landscape.

Neoconservative Feminism

What the Reagan economists had hoped would happen to the nation's economy, actually did happen in the neoconservatizing of feminism in the films of the eighties. Feminist targeting and sisterhood inclusion began to "trickle down" to farmwives, to married women (mothers and homemakers), to blue-collar working women. This neoconservative shift in feminist film consciousness really started with the box-office success of two female buddy movies released in 1977: *Julia*, which chronicled the friendship of two women in the highly charged political situation of Germany in the late thirties (adapted from Lillian Hellman's memoirs); and *The Turning Point*, which revealed the friendship of two women despite both their artistic (in the world of ballet) and maternal competitiveness. These women's films of the late seventies, however, including such political statement films as *Coming Home* (1978) and *An Unmarried Woman* (1978), were still tentative and exploratory about the roles of ordinary women—wives and mothers, not career women or ballerinas or writers—in American society. In the eighties, as exemplified by the farm crisis films, these ordinary women began to jettison their powerlessness and find their paths to power.

Feminist neoconservatizing in eighties films portrayed women who were not previously active in sexual politics finding their voices, becoming more adventurous, realizing their political and moral potential. Meryl Streep, who would become *the* dominant actress of her generation, described her early roles in *The Deer Hunter* (1978), *Still of the Night* (1982), and *Sophie's Choice* (1982) as "mauled, maimed or martyred."[7] But by the mid-eighties, while some of that mauling, maiming, and martyring was still going on (especially in highly controversial films like *The Accused* and *A Cry in the Dark*), it was most often presented in service to a clear political statement on a particular feminist issue. In fact, films clustered (as had the farm crisis films in 1984) around clearly defined feminist issues: rape, abortion, adoption and motherhood, divorce rights, gender identity, and just plain independence (from men, from sexual and gender stereotypes, from social discrimination). While focusing upon these issues, the feminist films introduced a new rhetorical tone to the old genre forms of what had historically been women's films—biopics, weepies, female ensemble pieces—while also providing women entrée into what had been traditionally male movie roles—the investigative reporter (as in 1979's *China Syndrome*), the political activist (as in *Silkwood* and *Norma Rae*), the detective (as in *Mike's Murder* and *Black Widow*).

These changes in theme and tone of eighties films also made this decade rival the forties—the heydey of the film noir and the weepy—in the availability of interesting and challenging female roles and the attendant ascension of a rather large contingent of extremely talented and eventually powerful actresses (and, for the first time, female directors). The actresses of the eighties—Lange, Streep, Glenn Close, Debra Winger, Cher, Susan Sarandon, Sigourney Weaver, Michelle Pfeiffer, and the throwback sexpot, Kathleen Turner—and seventies actresses revivified by eighties roles that fit their feminist politics—Jane Fonda, Shirley Mac-Laine, Barbra Streisand—as well as the historic breakthroughs of female directors in the "boys town" of Hollywood—Martha Coolidge, Susan Seidelman, Gillian Armstrong, Amy Heckerling, Donna Deitch, Joyce Chopra, Randa Haines—and older pros reborn as directors—Streisand, Lee Grant, Joan Micklin Silver, and Elaine May—signaled an accelerating feminist consciousness in an industry unparalleled in its history of male domination both on the screen and behind the cameras.[8] As one eighties industry watcher observed: "Hoping to hit the middle-aged woman, studios develop a prestige line of films, more often than not with classy roles for serious actresses. . . . Hollywood in the Eighties is making more silly pictures than serious ones, but it's making more Oscar-worthy films with women than with men."[9]

Traditional Forms of Sexual Exploitation

The old themes and sexual stereotypes were not abandoned, but oftentimes the old portrayals of female stereotypes were overlayed by this blossoming feminist consciousness. For example, a number of Pygmalion films were made in the eighties culminating in *Pretty Woman* (1990), but in each case bows were made to the rejection of that stereotyped dominance/submission relationship. In *Atlantic City* (1980), an old gangster (Burt Lancaster) helps an ambitious but uneducated young woman (Susan Sarandon) to grow and survive in a brutally exploitative world. In *Personal Best* (1983), the relationship of two highly talented female athletes confronts each of their individual relationships to their ruthlessly dominating coach. The coach (Scott Glenn) uses the feminist ideal of the pursuit of excellence to co-opt a competing feminist ideal of sisterhood. *Star 80* goes over the edge of the Pygmalionesque into the dark region of Svengali. It is the story of Paul Snider (Eric Roberts) turning Dorothy Stratton (Mariel Hemingway) first into a *Playboy* magazine centerfold and then into a movie star for the eighties. What intervenes in Snider's Pygmalion plan, however, is Dorothy's growth out from under his Svengali-like influence toward selfhood. When Snider sees that he is losing his meal ticket and chance for power, he murders Dorothy. Of all these Pygmalion films, *Educating Rita* (1983) is the most perceptive in offering the neoconservative feminist accommodation necessary in the eighties. Rita (Julie Walters), an uneducated working-class woman who wants to escape both the social and sexual subservience of her life, enters a mentoring relationship with her English professor (Michael Caine). Quickly, however, the roles of student and teacher become ironically reversed, and Rita brings her drunken mentor back into the mainstream of life even as he teaches her all he knows about literature and manners.

But films of less intellectual, more overt sexual exploitation were also made in the eighties. Many, such as *Angel* (1984) and its *Avenging Angel* (1985) sequel—"High School Honor Student by day. Hollywood hooker by night."—were cast in the same mold as decades of sexploitation B-movies. Angel was not the only working girl in the films of the eighties. A number exploited the hooker's world and glamorized it from a male perspective. *Sharky's Machine* (1981), *Some Kind of Hero* (1981), *The Best Little Whorehouse in Texas* (1982), *Night Shift* (1982), *Risky Business* (1983), *Trading Places* (1983) present the worn-out stereotype of the hooker with the heart of gold. Sheila Benson writes of these exercises in sexploitation:

> I've always fought off the assumption that one or another sex had the patent on empathy or compassion or social realism. After all, *Klute*, the American high-water mark so far in the psychology of a prostitute, was written by Andy and Dave Lewis and directed by Alan Pakula. But this gush of sentimental contemporary fantasy about the lives of hookers makes me wonder if we will ever glimpse the truth from a director who is not a woman.[10]

The true social realism of prostitution was briefly captured in films like *Fort Apache, The Bronx* (1981), and *Street Smart* (1987). The ultimate eighties symbol of old-fashioned Hollywood sexploitation, however, was Bo Derek who in the aftermath of her success in *10* (1979) was Svengalied by her husband into making *Tarzan the Ape Man* (1981) and *Bolero* (1984). Jamie Lee Curtis, daughter of Janet Leigh, Hitchcock's breakthrough symbol of female brutalization in *Psycho* (1960), starred in *Perfect* (1985), while Christopher Atkins starred in *A Night in Heaven* (1983), films that exploited the eighties body culture and prefigured the most grotesque sexploitation film of the decade, *Pumping Iron II: The Women*, a documentary combining sweat, grease, and the human body but offering no philosophical rationale as had Arnold Schwarzenegger in its predecessor. Finally, Kathleen Turner reigned as the sexploitation queen of eighties films. Compared to the other serious actresses of her decade, she is a throwback to the forties. Alternating between film noir like *Body Heat* (1980) and screwball comedies like *Switching Channels* (1988) and *Romancing the Stone*, she never escapes the past genre demands upon her characters. All of these films indulge in sexual exploitation without ever really exploring it.

A few films, however, while not explicitly exploring issues such as rape or abortion, nonetheless examined the general topic of sexual exploitation in some fresh ways. *Dangerous Liaisons* (1988), for example, presents a situation in which both female sisterhood and even motherhood are betrayed in the service of sexual exploitation. Despite its eighteenth-century period setting and costumes, *Dangerous Liaisons* is very much a late-twentieth-century film, and one aspect of its metaphorical contemporaneousness is its feminist critique. If Machiavelli had been interested in sex rather than politics, he might have written Laclos's *Liaisons Dangereuses* (from which the film is adapted) rather than *The Prince. Dangerous Liaisons* is a ruthless Machiavellian film of sexual politics in which the Marquise de Merteuil (Glenn Close) and her creature, the Vicomte de Valmont (John Malkovich), play what Pauline Kael calls "erotic power games" with the women who become their victims. In order to gain revenge against a former lover, the Marquise commissions Valmont to deflower the former lover's new love. To prove his power of seduction, Valmont vows to seduce the most virtuous woman in the kingdom.

Both the Marquise and Valmont view women as objects. For the Marquise, the women upon whom she sets Valmont are tools for her revenge against the men who have jilted her and against the gender of victims into which she was regrettably born. Pauline Kael writes:

> There are times when the Marquise—a happy widow—sounds much like a modern, "liberated" woman . . . the Marquise is actually the opposite of liberated: She is one of the most formidable examples of hell-hath-no-fury-like-a-woman-scorned in all literature. . . . She's a power-hungry, castrating female as conceived by an eighteenth-century male writer.[11]

For Valmont, the women whom he seduces are no more than toys or objects of furniture in his priapic games. In one scene, lying in bed, he writes a letter to one lover using the naked derriere of another lover for a desk. In *Dangerous Liaisons*, sexploitation is an exercise of power, but irony accrues when one woman is exerting exploitative power over other women. It is a betrayal of sisterhood. Women should not use other women as objects in their power games. Later, the same theme will occur in *Working Girl* (1989).

Sexual exploitation of a different yet equally complex sort occurs in Gillian Armstrong's *Mrs. Soffel* (1984). Like *Dangerous Liaisons*, *Mrs. Soffel* is set in a different time, yet is extremely contemporary in theme. It is ostensibly about a woman's liberation, but that liberation occurs through her submission to a seduction, to a planned act of sexual exploitation. Jack Mathews signals the ambivalence of this feminist theme when he writes that "*Mrs. Soffel* is not a feminist film—or if it is, it undermines itself—but it is hard to imagine the central relationship being as effectively developed by a male director."[12] The story of a neurotic, emotionally imprisoned, prison warden's wife who falls in love with a condemned criminal, helps him and his brother escape, then throws over her whole life—home, marriage, children—to flee with them might be one of sexual exploitation if Kate Soffel (Diane Keaton) were not such a clear-sighted character. She is well aware that Biddle's (Mel Gibson) seduction is a desperate attempt to save his own and his brother's life, yet she allows it to happen because his exploitation is better than the airless, dark life she leads with her insensitive husband in their prison quarters. "No less imprisoned—at least from a contemporary feminist view—" writes Jack Kroll, "was the warden's wife."[13] Both Ed Biddle and Kate Soffel are breaking out of prison, and both are aware that they are exploiting the other to do it. The romantic part is that they do it nonetheless. The feminist moral has an interesting parallel to the plight of the female director in male-owned hollywood. What *Mrs. Soffel* says is that a woman's first concern is freeing herself from the confinements of her society, and the means she uses are less important than the attainment of the desired end result.

A Room with a View (1986), adapted from E. M. Forster's 1908 novel, makes much the same point. It is a feminist dilemma when Lucy Honeychurch (Helena Bonham Carter), a turn-of-the-century young lady, must decide between the man who arouses her passions and the rich suitor who demands that his wife accept him as her master. Lucy's liberation, her breaking out in search of a room with a view, is similar to Kate Soffel's breaking out of that dark, grim prison where her husband kept her locked up right along with the prisoners.

A somewhat different feminist breakout is attempted and brutally stifled in *Against All Odds* (1984), a contemporary thriller that does not have nearly the impact in its feminist theme as these metaphoric period films. In *Against All Odds*, Jessie Wyler (Rachel Ward) is a young woman trying to escape a variety of exploitations in her upscale Beverly Hills/

Hollywood lifestyle. She runs to hide in Mexico, but a broken-down former football player, Terry Brogan (Jeff Bridges), is sent to find her. She convinces him to hide her instead. But *Against All Odds* is such a morally adrift film, so confused in its characterization, especially of Jessie's motives in trying to escape, that no theme, whether feminist or otherwise, ever gets established.

But while these sexploitation films, some of which actually acknowledged a feminist point of view if only to undermine it, were appearing throughout the decade, other films were also being released that confronted major feminist issues head on.

Rape

One of the most controversial films of the decade, *The Accused* (1988), dissects one single feminist issue, rape, by examining its social acceptance and its effects upon the victims. However, *The Accused* also demonstrates an ambivalence toward its subject matter. Is it a film with a feminist social conscience? Or is it a voyeuristic faction that capitalizes upon the fringe pornographic mentality of a *National Enquirer* America? *The Accused*, actually, is both. As a feminist social consciousness film, it presents a strong and thoughtful critique of the American judicial system's treatment of rape victims and of the public's cavalier perception of the crime. On the other hand, because of the extended presentation of its central scene, a brutal gang rape in a crowded bar with onlookers cheering, *The Accused* could itself be accused of sexploitation.

Perhaps the real question is, Why will people go to see *The Accused*? To understand why rape is such a terrible crime and to analyze how badly America deals with it? Or to be voyeuristically entertained by a graphic rape scene that is self-reflexively about the act of an audience vicariously participating in the crime of rape? In the real-life case from which *The Accused* was adapted, both the rapists and the cheering onlookers were prosecuted. Perhaps one justification for the extended and graphically edited rape scene being saved for the end of the film is to demonstrate to the audience the potential in their own heart of darkness to participate in the same criminal voyeurism of the cheering onlookers in the bar. Whether this participatory art theme was Hollywood's motive for presenting the extended gang rape scene the way it did is questionable, yet possible. The theater audience does sense what was happening in the minds of those present at the real event.

But despite the controversy over the scene itself, *The Accused* does offer an informed feminist social consciousness that makes clear points about how women are treated by American society. Sarah Tobias (Jodie Foster) is a drunk, a doper, an attractive and aggressive foulmouthed free spirit who drives a sexy Camaro with a sexy license plate and wears sexy miniskirts and halter tops. She is definitely not the girl next door. But the negative characterization of Sarah Tobias underscores the film's feminist theme: a woman's lifestyle, or her personality, or her mode of dress does not give a man (or men) the right to totally dehumanize her, forcibly rape her. Conversely, Kathryn Murphy (Kelly McGillis) is, indeed, the girl next door. She is a naïve yuppie prosecuting attorney tottering on the tightrope between political expediency and a dawning feminist consciousness. She is smart, ambitious, highly moral, a winner; everything that Sarah Tobias is not. *The Accused* tracks the relationship between these two as they overcome their distrust for each other as social entities and gain respect for each other as women in a brutally exploitative male world.

The Accused was not the first time in either her art or life that Jodie Foster has portrayed or lived the object of criminally obsessive love. In *Taxi Driver* (1976) she was exploited as a child prostitute. She was raped in *The Hotel New Hampshire* (1984) and stalked by a rapist in *Five Corners* (1988). But her closest experience with obsessive love came in John Hinckley, Jr., who attempted to assassinate President Reagan to get her attention. "I was doing two weekends of a play," Foster tells her version in a way that casts her own experience in the same mold as that of Sarah Tobias in *The Accused*, "one weekend happened and then . . . Reagan got shot. And then I had to go back and do the next weekend's [performance]. It was, uh, standing room only. The odds were against anybody getting the play . . . that's not why they were watching."[14] How different were the voyeurs in Foster's Yale theater audience from those cheering onlookers to the rape in *The Accused*? Other eighties films, such as *Extremities* (1986), adapted from William Mastrosimone's Broadway play, examined the psychological effects of rape, but more often than not, American films such as Charles Bronson's *Death Wish* series (1974, 1982, 1985, 1987) and Clint Eastwood's *Sudden Impact* (1983) in which a woman sets out to avenge her rape (reprising the 1976 *Lipstick*) exploited rape for its felicitous box-office coupling of sex and violence.

Abortion

A second issue, that of abortion and a woman's right to choose, surfaced in some unexpected places in eighties films. In *Criminal Law* (1989), Martin Thiel (Kevin Bacon) is a smiling, soft-spoken, rich, yuppie serial killer who rapes, kills, mutilates, and burns young women. His motive? All of his victims have recently had abortions. The criminal psychology of this film is textbook Freud updated to the eighties. Martin's violence against women is motivated by his childhood trauma of perceiving his doctor-mother as a killer of babies. *Criminal Law* combines the genre characteristics of a psychological thriller with the moral exploration of the social issues of abortion, the victimization of women, and (as in *The Accused*) the injustice of the American justice system. The issue of abortion arises in a completely different context in *Agnes of God* (1985) as the issue of child murder becomes a theological as well as social issue. During the second half of the eighties decade, the abortion issue became the battle line drawn between religious institutions, especially the Catholic church, and the feminist prochoice movement.

Motherhood and Adoption

The alternative to abortion is motherhood or adoption for those unable to have children. One of the major tensions of feminism in the eighties existed between the neoconservatizing of the movement that reached to include married women and religious working-class women and the movement's stance on abortion. Two films, released within weeks of one another in 1988, looked closely at the obstacles that society places between a woman's maintaining of her own existential identity and her commitment to being a mother. In *The Good Mother*, Anna (Diane Keaton), the divorced mother of a six-year-old girl, enters a passionate sexual relationship to which her former husband reacts with a custody suit alleging unfit motherhood and sexual misconduct toward the child. In the trial, it is made clear that Anna either can fulfill her desire to be a passionate sexual woman or can be a good mother, but society will not allow her to be both.

Pauline Kael brilliantly analyzes the feminist text of *The Good Mother*:

> Nimoy (director) and Bortman (writer) ask us to see Anna as a victim of generations of patriarchal domination . . . her grandfather (Ralph Bellamy) bullying her sweet grandmother (Teresa Wright) and crushing her defiant red-haired aunt (Tracy Griffith). The family pattern of men mistreating women seems to be laid out for us.

But Kael, who would have liked to have seen a happier, more triumphant, Hollywood ending to the film, criticizes the realistic ending as a feminist letdown:

> Anna just goes limp on us; she rolls with the punches. . . . it's a disturbing let-down for the audience—especially, perhaps, for feminists, who may see it as a betrayal. The movie wants to be about the way the patriarchal system can batter women to a pulp. . . . But since this is the story of Anna's defeat . . . women can feel it's saying, "That's how it is folks. Resign youselves."[15]

Kael, however, overstates the film's negativity. What the film also is about is the manner in which the feminist movement, in its neoconservatizing, must not lose sight of its essential philosophy of women's rights in the face of both personal and social patriarchy.

A Cry in the Dark also subjects a mother's love to courtroom scrutiny, as in *The Good Mother*, and also punishes its mother for her honesty, her insistence upon being herself. *A Cry in the Dark* is the story of Lindy

Chamberlain (Meryl Streep) who was tried for the murder of her infant child and convicted by an Australian court that rejected her defense that a dingo (a wild dog) dragged off her baby while the family was on a camping trip in the Outback in 1980. Director Schepisi's film and actress Streep's performance form a strong polemic against both the sensationalistic media and the appearances-stereotypes-biased justice system. Lindy Chamberlain became the most reviled woman in Australia during her trial because she neither looked nor acted the way that female trial defendants and grieving mothers were supposed to look and act. The media and the public demanded that Lindy be someone she was not and then punished her for refusing to buckle to their stereotype.

But Lindy Chamberlain was not punished nearly as severely as was Ruth Ellis (Miranda Richardson), the last woman executed for murder in England in 1955. Ellis's story is told in *Dance with a Stranger* (1985), and like *A Cry in the Dark*, the film is a feminist exposé of the double standard in the English court system. Because of her wild lifestyle, Ellis never gets the chance to declare the reasons for shooting her abusive boyfriend in order to save herself from the gallows. Like Lindy Chamberlain in *A Cry in the Dark*, the media and the court system portray Ruth Ellis as both a whore and an unfit mother and thus secure the death penalty. The film reminds of the illogical legal arguments in Albert Camus's *Stranger*.

One of the more insightful films about motherhood was *Immediate Family* (1989), a weepy for the yuppie eighties about a childless couple who want to adopt a baby. It is about the frustration of infertility and the agonies of adoption for both the natural and the adopting mother. Its characterizations of Lucy (Mary Stuart Masterson) and Julie (Glenn Close) are touching, neoconservative feminist portraits. They are two women trying to find themselves and their maternal ethics in a confusing eighties society. The film is full of telling moments in which women face their own emotions and identities. In one, Julie sits alone, getting drunk, dialing her busy, married-with-kids, thirtysomething friends on the day she learns that her artificial insemination did not work. In another, Lucy stands looking out of the nursery window of Julie's house imagining what the baby she is giving away will see as it grows up. But the real feminist subtext of *Immediate Family* arises out of the sisterhood in motherhood that these two women build to the point where Julie would like to be a mother to Lucy as well as the unborn baby. This neoconservative affirmation of sisterhood in traditional female roles is a strong component of eighties feminism.

One film deeply concerned with the complexities of eighties motherhood was *Terms of Endearment* (1983), the decade's champion weepy. Yet no one would call this illogical tearjerker a feminist film. One critic had this to say about Emma (Debra Winger), the younger of the two mothers in the film:

Why is she so passive? Why does she seem so untouched by feminine ideals? . . . And why does Brooks try to create sympathy by putting her in a room with a group of bitchy career women who react to Emma (who all her life has wanted nothing more than to be a good wife and mother) as if she were distributing herpes virus? What is Brooks saying here? That wimpy passivity is the normal state of things? That a career makes a woman into a castrating bitch?[16]

What Brooks is saying is what so many other films of the eighties are saying, that feminism must include people like Emma, must neoconservatize the movement so that women's rights will trickle down to the rest of the gender's constituency.

But if feminism includes Emma, it has to include her mother, Aurora (Shirley MacLaine), too, which is harder because Aurora is an unimaginably painful person who only becomes human when her only daughter comes down with cancer. All of Emma's life, Aurora has been doomsaying and Emma has resisted her mother's predictions. Aurora predicts that Flap (Jeff Daniels) will be a lousy husband, but Emma counters by being a great wife and fulfilled mother. If Emma is a neoconservative heroine, then Aurora is a throwback to the eccentric, situation-controlled women of the forties weepies, the Irene Dunnes and Greer Garsons to whom Pauline Kael compares her.[17] In an eccentric way, *Terms of Endearment* is about mothers and daughters coming to terms with each other. Their motivations and characterizations, however, seem extremely stilted when examined from a neoconservative feminist perspective.

Divorce and Betrayal of Sisterhood

Another feminist issue frequently considered in eighties films is that of the rights of a divorced woman. Once again Hollywood demonstrates an ambivalent feminist understanding. In many films divorces are caused by competition between women and a betrayal of sisterhood. *Honeysuckle Rose* (1980) is a good example. Viv (Dyan Cannon) is country singer Buck Bonham's (Willie Nelson) wife who stays home on the ranch with their son while Buck is on the road with his band. Viv is forty and feisty and faithful, but Buck has to go out on the road, and as a mother, she no longer wants to go out with him. When Buck's backup guitar player, Garland (Slim Pickens), also decides that he is getting too old to go "on the road again," Viv suggests that Buck take Garland's daughter, Lily (Amy Irving), along as his backup for the summer. Twenty-year-old Lily has worshiped forty-year-old Viv's husband Buck from afar since she was a child, and when she gets out on the road with Buck, her worshipful fantasizing beams at him like the light on an approaching train. "I've gone to bed with a song of yours since I was nine years old," Lily tells Buck, thus setting the classic competition of movie adultery. But *Honeysuckle Rose* is different in the strength that Viv generates as she competes against this younger woman, not just for her man but for her self-respect as a wife and mother.

In *Falling in Love* (1984), the competition is much less classical, as if keyed to the commuter train rhythm and the randomness of eighties urban life. Frank (Robert De Niro) is a Manhattan contractor whose wife, Ann (Jane Kaczmarek), is attractive, intelligent, and a wonderful mother. Yet when Frank meets Molly (Meryl Streep), a housewife like his wife, on a commuter train and later in a bookstore, that same competition is drawn. This film, however, gives the wife no chance. Ann gets one hurt speech and then drops out of sight as if a trapdoor had suddenly opened.

Both of these films recognize that the competition between women for married men exists, but neither pursues any clear feminist resolution as the seventies film *Diary of a Mad Housewife* (1970) had or the middle-aged wife's angry speech to her adulterous husband in *Network* (1976) had expressed. What eighties film realized in characters like Viv in *Honeysuckle Rose* and the two wives, Molly and Ann, in *Falling in Love* is that this competition between women is unhealthy and the neoconservative thrust of eighties feminism presses to eliminate this competition between different types of working women (read career women vs. housewives), different classes of women, different geographically located women, and different maritally aligned women (read single vs. married vs. divorced).

One film, however, *Twice in a Lifetime* (1986), works all the way through in a realistic and thoughtful way the ravages of a divorce upon everyone involved. When on his fiftieth birthday Harry (Gene Hackman), a steel-worker, meets the new barmaid Audrey (Ann-Margret), it is the beginning of the end of his thirty-year marriage to Kate (Ellen Burstyn). There are no villains in this film; all the characters are losers to begin with. Harry is bored comatose. Kate's biggest thrill is watching "The Price Is Right" on TV. Audrey is an aging barmaid forced to take harassment from men she does not know. But these losers try to make adjustments in their lives, and in the end, all come out winners. Harry convinces himself that he can still love. Kate becomes more independent. And Audrey finds a man who loves her. But despite these little victories, the reality of women in competition with each other is written all over the film. Perhaps the most symbolic competition in *Twice in a Lifetime* is between older daughter, Sunny (Amy Madigan), and younger daughter, Helen (Ally Sheedy), about their father Harry's behavior. Sunny is enraged. Helen is more understanding and forgiving of her father's adultery. The film is an ensemble study of how women react to the reality of divorce, and it includes all of the necessary components: betrayed wife, competitive mistress, confused children. It carefully examines all sides of this volatile feminist issue.

Perhaps the most controversial of all the eighties films about deteriorating families, *Fatal Attraction* (1987) is not nearly as careful. It is a film of troubling feminist undertones and confusing subtexts. Upon its release and instant box-office success, the American media put *Fatal Attraction* under a microscope to isolate the components that had made it such a work of fascination for American audiences. One of those components was its neoconservative feminist backlash elements in which good and faithful wife rises up and triumphs over aggressive, liberated careerwoman. Upheld in this feminist backlash scenario is the age-old double standard as the unfaithful husband walks away from the competition between women unscathed. But *Fatal Attraction* was not always a feminist backlash film. It was originally conceived as a much darker, more evenhanded representation of the wages of sex. In an interview (*American Film*, Nov.– Dec. 1991) Glenn Close talks about the original ending of *Fatal Attraction*:

> The original script . . . was a beautiful, seamless *film noir*. In that . . . you saw me at the opera watching Madame Butterfly kill herself. In the original, after we have that terrible fight, he takes the knife from me and puts it down. It ends with me committing suicide—like Madame Butterfly, a ritualistic slitting of my throat. And then the police come to his house and say that I'm dead, and they take him away because his fingerprints are on the knife. And that was it.
>
> But Hollywood is very uncomfortable with unhappy endings, especially if your wife is gorgeous Anne Archer and there is a sweet little child. They want the hope that they'll be happy again. When we were making the movie, we didn't realize how emotionally involved people would get and how they would scream for my blood. So they gave them my blood. But it wasn't psychologically right. I mean, that character basically was suicidal. She was not a psychopath.

Close accuses the producers of *Fatal Attraction* of a conventional Hollywoodization of the film, but the changes in that ending were motivated by more complex social attitudes than simply a long-standing fetish for happy (or happier) endings. In this case, the ultimate ending fit more closely the neoconservative mood of the feminist direction of the eighties. The resolution of this competition between women in favor of the model wife and the villainizing of the liberated careerwoman certainly signaled a feminist backlash and a predictable reaffirmation of the double standard, but it also affirmed, as the farm films of the decade already had, the power of the wife and mother to protect and preserve her domain. As a feminist text for the eighties, the final version of *Fatal Attraction* is fatally at odds with itself and ultimately confused. As one of the most widely seen films of the decade, it sends out—in its feminist subtext—a set of rather unfortunate mixed signals.

Two other, less social, more philosophical, existential issues examined in the feminist film texts of the eighties are the nature of gender itself (Are men and women so different? What qualities and aspirations do they share?) and the possibilities for female independence (How far can a woman go in a man's world?).

Gender

Tootsie (1982) is a perceptive Hollywood gender study. When New York actor Michael Dorsey (Dustin Hoffman) becomes a woman to get a part in a TV soap opera, he learns a lot more about gender than just how to wear a dress, shave one's legs, and fight off unsolicited sexual advances. He learns how women are patronized by males in American society. When the female character that Michael creates first encounters the arrogant chauvinism of Ron (Dabney Coleman), the soap opera director, he/she coins a catchword that continued to define this sort of personality throughout the decade. In a ladylike voice but with an unladylike emphasis, she calls him a "macho shithead!"

Michael Dorsey also learns about how ordinary women who watch TV soap operas — the neoconservative silent majority — long for strong female voices to emulate. Dorothy Michaels, the "tootsie" of the title, becomes a household word because of her forcefulness on camera. The housewives of America unite behind her.

Finally, Michael Dorsey learns about the female and the feminist side of himself. In the final scene, Michael meets Julie (Jessica Lange) outside the stage door and admits: "Look, you don't know me from Adam, but I was a better man with you as a woman than I ever was with a woman as a man. You know what I mean? I just got to learn to do it without the dress." Michael's confession is one of the most confused and eloquent gender statements of the decade.

Barbara Streisand's *Yentl* (1983) is the same film as *Tootsie*, based on the same gender reversal premise. Where Michael Dorsey the actor turned into a woman to get a job and in the process became human, Streisand's *yentl* becomes a man in order to qualify for an education. Both films, in witty ways, examine the neoconservative necessity for gender understanding.

Independence

But by far the biggest cluster of all of these feminist-issue films focused upon the text of female independence. These are stories about women who want to be just plain free and are willing to take whatever means necessary to gain their independence from both male and social domination. The first major eighties film about a woman's hunger for independence amidst the starvation of social barriers upon women's freedom was *The French Lieutenant's Woman* (1981). Adapted brilliantly by Harold Pinter from a novel by John Fowles, it parallels the plight of women in the Victorian age and women in the seemingly liberated yet no less restricted eighties.

The French Lieutenant's Woman opens with a stunning visual of a woman alone asserting her independence and a conventional overprotective man's inability to resist intruding upon that independence. On the gray, bleak, south coast of England, a woman stands at the end of an ancient quay as the stormy seas crash around her. A Victorian gentleman walking with his betrothed sees this solitary female figure defying the storm-tossed waves and feels compelled to warn her of her danger. He approaches, cries out his warning, and she fixes him with a long devastating look of defiance, vulnerability, and mystery. The gentleman is stopped dead by that look and retreats from its existential authenticity. In the Victorian age, a woman simply does not look a man directly in the face and assert her independence with her penetrating eyes. Sarah Woodruff (Meryl Streep) does, yet the image of her independence in this opening scene belies the reality of her socially imprisoned situation. Yet despite reality, the look that Sarah casts upon young Charles Smithson (Jeremy Irons) defines her hunger for freedom so defiantly that he cannot dispel it from his mind. He becomes fascinated by this woman who disdains his male protection for her own quiet strength. The film is a disconnected dance in which Charles moves toward Sarah and she alternately attracts and moves away from him. David Ansen captures this enigmatic ambivalence as he writes of "the elusive figure of Sarah, whose stubborn, possibly deranged concept of freedom sets her apart from her times. Temptress, deceiver, harbinger of the New Woman, she is a kind of beacon forcing Charles to emerge from his nineteenth-century mist. . . . she is both the archetypal male fantasy, the Woman as Mystery, and a feminist rebuke to male fantasies."[18]

That feminist rebuke takes the form of Sarah Woodruff claiming a sexual freedom not open to Victorian women accompanied by a rejection of male possession. Both are forms of independence that Anna (Meryl Streep), the film actress in Pinter's metaworld, his film within the film, has already claimed and is exercising upon Mike (Jeremy Irons) in the parallel twentieth-century world. In a later scene, lured by a surreptitious note, Charles meets Sarah in a graveyard, where she describes her situation as an independent Victorian woman: "If I went to London I know what I would become, what some have already called me." For a woman alone in the nineteenth century the choices are narrow and the temptation to sell oneself to a man (either on the street or in the marriage market) overwhelming.

Throughout the film, however, this duel of dominance between the male and the female is visually choreographed by means of camera angles. In their second meeting in the Undercliff, Sarah begins to tell Charles the story of her ruin in a deep-focus two-shot. Charles stands above her in the background looking down as she stands among thick phallic trees in the foreground. As she tells of her sexual adventure with the French Lieutenant, Sarah moves above Charles and undoes her hair. She has taken control of the scene, and the shot goes to a low angle on Sarah underscoring her dominance. Out of nervousness, Charles walks until he is again above Sarah, has reasserted his superiority. At this point, the camera returns to a low angle on Charles. When the scene ends and the temporal cut to the twentieth-century film shoot is made, the shot is a closeup of Anna on top of Mike kissing down on him as they picnic on the rocky Dorset beach. In the twentieth century, Anna easily siezes the position of superiority that Sarah is so tentative about claiming and holding.

This use of high- and low-angle shots to assert sexual dominance occurs again in Charles and Sarah's next meeting in the ruined barn in the Undercliff. Anna is sleeping in the hay as Charles enters and stands above her. The camera alternates an extremely low angle on the dominant Charles with an extremely high angle on the vulnerable, sleeping Sarah. When Charles takes her hand, she rises into his arms and they kiss passionately only to be interrupted by the giggling servants. When Charles gives Sarah money to escape to Exeter, her silent look says that the money makes her feel like a whore. "You are a remarkable person, Miss Woodruff," Charles reassures her. "Yes, I am a remarkable person," Sarah agrees. Sarah answers as a twentieth-century woman, and her use of the word "person" is more feminist-informed than Charles's use of that same word.

Meanwhile, back on the twentieth-century film set, Mike is trying to assert a similar possessiveness upon Anna. She announces that since her scenes in Lyme Regis are done, she is going up to London:

ANNA: David's flying in tonight.

MIKE: How nice for you. Will I see you in London?

ANNA: That would be very difficult.

MIKE: I *must* see you.

Mike is a nineteenth-century romantic, whereas Anna is an utterly twentieth-century woman. Mike cannot untangle his real life and his Victorian movie life. Anna, at this moment, begins her flight from Mike's Victorian possessiveness.

The contrast between the artificiality and captivity of the Victorian woman and the independence of the New Woman is underscored by the imagery of gardens and flowers. In the opening series of shots establishing the setting and characters, Charles's servant is carrying a bouquet of cut flowers to Ernestina (Lynsey Baxter), Charles's fiancée. Throughout the film, Ernestina and Charles meet either amidst the artificial hanging baskets and greenhouse plants of the mansion's solarium or in the formal garden where Ernestina practices her archery. Sarah, however, is always amidst the wild foliage of her employer's untended garden or in the wilds of the Undercliff. Both Charles and Dr. Grogan (Leo McKern) spy on women with telescopes. When Charles catches Grogan, Charles admits that he too is studying "one of your local *flora*." When Charles addresses

Ernestina in her artificial garden as she shoots her arrows at her stationary target, he says: "The true charm of this world resides in this garden." But he is more attracted to pursuing the wild *flora* of the Undercliff.

When Charles finally pursues Sarah to Exeter and goes to the cheap hotel where she has taken rooms, it is the first time that they have ever been alone indoors. Always before, their trysts had been outdoors—on the cobb, in the graveyard, in the Undercliff, in the ruins of the barn—but now they are behind closed doors with only the faded artificial flowers on the wallpaper to remind them of the garden from which they have fled to commit this, for the Victorian age, quite original sin.

This climactic sexual scene is also shot in terms of alternating high and low camera angles accentuating the lovers' dance of dominance and submission. Low angles on Charles as he undresses and descends to Sarah are alternated with high angles of Sarah waiting on the bed. After they make love and Charles realizes that Sarah is a virgin, she tries to explain in a strikingly composed deep-focus shot. Charles stands angry in the foreground while Sarah sits on the bed in the middleground and a candle burns behind her in the background. It is a shot much like the "summer hat" scene in *Chinatown*[19] in which an object comments upon the relationship of the two characters who occupy the other planes of the frame. In this case, the candle represents both the fiery sword that has escorted them out of their romantic garden of Eden and the burning truth that each has been exploiting the other in their fire dance of dominance and submission.

Back in the twentieth-century world of *The French Lieutenant's Woman*, the cast attends a luncheon at the home of Mike and his wife. "They have a lovely garden, don't they, so serene?" an older actress says to Anna. "What a lovely garden, who takes care of it for you?" Anna asks Mike's wife, who answers, "I do." Anna is taken aback and stammers, "I really envy you" and when the wife asks "why" answers, "for being able to create such a lovely garden." The wife's answer to Anna's distracted envy is an ironic and wry comment upon this whole dalliance upon forbidden fruit and lovely gardens. The imprisonment of marriage or imprisonment within Victorian social stereotypes is not a female state to be envied. The independence of a Victorian Sarah or a twentieth-century Anna is a more enviable position.

In the final Victorian scene of the film, in that sunny romantic room overlooking the lake at Windermere, Charles pours out the frustration of his three-year search for Sarah, and she simply says: "It has taken me this time to find my own life. It has taken me this time to find my freedom." The film is about that journey to freedom that all of the Sarah Woodruffs and Jane Eyres and Becky Sharps and Estellas and Sue Brideheads took and that the Annas of the twentieth century have inherited. Sarah left Exeter and Charles behind in order to find her freedom. Anna flees from

Mike at the end of the film in order to keep hers. *The French Lieutenant's Woman* is both a history and a demonstration of woman's possibilities for freedom from both social imposition and male possession. It is adapted from a novel with three endings, is a film with two endings, and is both a novel and a film composed of multiple texts. Its text of feminist independence is one of its strongest and most complex. When Mike, in their very last moment, cries "Sarah" after the fleeing Anna, his mistake is a male longing for a return to Victorian femininity that no twentieth-century feminist can accept.

Though the novel *The French Lieutenant's Woman* was written by a man and the film was written and directed by men, it presented a positive feminist text that did not buckle to the old clichés. Unfortunately *Working Girl*, directed by Mike Nichols, did. Rather than being the feminist film that it might have been, it is an embarassingly transparent feminist backlash film that makes absolutely the wrong case throughout its female independence text.

The opening shot of *Working Girl* is a 360-degree aerial closeup of the Statue of Liberty. In one sense, this opening image is appropriate. Tess McGill's (Melanie Griffiths) story is an immigrant's journey, not from the Old World to the New, but from the downscale working-class world of Staten Island to the upscale class-conscious world of fast-lane Wall Street yuppiedom. The second image of *Working Girl*, the Staten Island ferry, becomes a symbol of passage that supports the immigrant's journey theme. These opening images signal that this is a Dick Whittington or Horatio Alger story in the best rags-to-riches tradition. But wait! The opening image of Lady Liberty holding the torch of freedom can also be read ironically from a feminist perspective. She proclaims the right to freedom to all who enter America, yet *Working Girl*, like its predecessor *9 to 5* (1980), is also a movie that (admittedly with confusion) examines the continuing exploitation of women in American society and especially in the business world. Thus those opening images are thematically deceptive because what *Working Girl* purports to be is a progress report upon the feminization of the American workplace. The film tries hard to make a sociohistorical statement on where women stand or sit in America twenty years into the feminist movement, and it fails miserably because it is made by insensitive men, director Nichols and writer Kevin Wade.

The opening images, then, do double duty. They signal the nature of the story as a rite of passage, but they simultaneously and ironically question whether the same possibilities that were open to the Dick Whittingtons and Horatio Algers have ever been open to their sisters. Tess McGill's story of moving out of the invisibility of secretarydom and into the executive suite seems a neat little feminist fable. Whatever feminist possibilities this film might have had, however, somehow got badly bent. How can a film make a feminist statement if it is consistently negative and patronizing toward women, not to mention blatantly sexist in its camera work? Pauline Kael notices this problem that begins with the film's "double entendre title" and proceeds to the camera's consistent catching of Tess "in black garter belt, push-up bra, and bikini panties."[20]

But even more problematic than the camera's obsession with Melanie Griffiths's and Sigourney Weaver's underwear are the characterizations of Katherine Parker (Weaver) and Tess McGill. The social statement that their characterizations push is that the way for women to succeed in the American workplace is, first, to become like men and, second, to betray other women. It is no coincidence that men and women keep invading each others' bathrooms in *Working Girl*. It is no coincidence that at a crucial point in a big business deal Jack Trainor (Harrison Ford) turns to his partner, Tess, and declares, "She's your man!" It is no coincidence that the major villain of the movie is a woman who exploits and betrays other women for her own profit. In D. H. Lawrence's *Sons and Lovers*, the central character wishes, "If I were a man." Katherine Parker, the female villain of *Working Girl* (who is a mirror image of the boss role created by Dabney Coleman in *9 to 5*), seems to have gotten that wish, and her characterization proves that it is not really much toward which to aspire. In no other film of the decade is the betrayal of sisterhood more ruthlessly drawn.

Another set of working girls are featured in *Swing Shift* (1984). They serve as a forties metaphor for the working women of the eighties. In fact, these forties wives, pressed into service in defense plants while their husbands are off fighting World War II, are an apposite historical paradigm for the feminist neoconservatizing of wives and working-class women in films like the farm crisis cluster as well as *9 to 5*, *Working Girl*, *Norma Rae*, and *Silkwood*. The story of Kay (Goldie Hawn) and Hazel (Christine Lahti) doing a "man's job" as riveters during the war identifies them as working-class ancestors of the feminist era of the seventies and eighties. The theme of *Swing Shift* is, once again, freedom. These women realistically handle the freedom that only men enjoyed up until the war years gave women the opportunity to work for their own living. These women make their own decisions, both financial and sexual. *Swing Shift* is a historical metaphor for neoconservative feminism, just as *Walker* is a historical metaphor for American interventionism in Latin America and *The Godfather* films were a historical metaphor for the corporate takeover of America.

One by-product of this neoconservative feminist consciousness in eighties films was that individual actresses across the decade built whole bodies of work out of feminist portrayals. *Swing Shift*'s Goldie Hawn and Christine Lahti are good examples. Besides *Swing Shift*, Hawn played women discovering their own independence in *Private Benjamin* (1980), *Protocol* (1984), and *Overboard* (1987). *Swing Shift*, for which she was nominated for a Best Supporting Actress Academy Award, was Lahti's breakthrough film, but she complemented it with strong portrayals of neoconservative women in *The Executioner's Song* (1982) on television and in *Running on Empty* (1988). Other prominent eighties actresses who built significant bodies of work upon neoconservative feminist portrayals were Cher, Debra Winger, Susan Sarandon, and, of course, Meryl Streep.

In the late sixties, Cher was the ticket to stardom of her husband, Sonny Bono, and their big pop hit "I Got You Babe" summed up the gold mine that her dusky voice and exotic looks were for him. In the seventies, he mined that gold in a TV show premised completely upon Cher's wise-cracks and wild wardrobe. But Sonny and Cher divorced in 1975, and since then, as one of her friends put it, "she's always been the man in her life."[21] In the eighties, Cher turned to film acting. Given her first acting role by Robert Altman in his Broadway production of *Come Back to the 5 & Dime, Jimmy Dean, Jimmy Dean* (1982), Cher later reprised the role in Altman's film version. What followed was a steady progression of neoconservative feminist film roles. She was nominated for a Best Supporting Actress Academy Award for her portrayal of lesbian nuclear plant worker Dollie Pelliker in *Silkwood* (1983), followed by her strongest role as drug-dependent biker and loving mother Rusty Dennis in *Mask* (1985). She finished out the decade as the blue-jeaned artist in *The Witches of Eastwick* (1987), as the Brooklyn accountant trapped in her Italian family in *Moonstruck* (1987), and as the overworked public defender in *Suspect* (1988). All of her roles were of lower- or middle-class working women, all new participants in the expanded feminism of the eighties. Comparable (to Cher's Dollie Pelliker and Rusty Dennis) neoconservative working-class portrayals were also turned in by Susan Sarandon as a clam-bar attendant in *Atlantic City* (1980), longing to get rich quick, and as the magnificent, intellectual, minor-league baseball bimbo Annie Savoy in *Bull Durham* (1988).

Debra Winger's feminist canon got its impetus from two working-class roles, that of the bull-riding urban cowgirl in *Urban Cowboy* (1980) and that of Paula Pokrifki, a Seattle paper-mill worker, in *An Officer and a Gentleman* (1982), but then her portrayals went in a different feminist direction. She was a bank teller forced to become an amateur detective in *Mike's Murder* (1984), a loving daughter, wife, and mother in *Terms of Endearment* (1983), a yuppie lawyer in *Legal Eagles* (1986), and an FBI agent in *Black Widow* (1986). In every film she asserts not only the independent values of her characters but also their honest sexual enthusiasm. But if Debra Winger broke new ground in *Mike's Murder, Black Widow,* and *Betrayed* (1988) as a female detective, Sigourney Weaver in her character, Ripley, in *Alien* (1979) and *Aliens* (1986) went further than any actress had ever gone in portraying a woman in what was formerly a man's job. After *Alien*, the media took to calling Weaver "Rambolina." But in *Aliens*, a film driven equally by its action genre primary text and its subgenre feminist text of matriarchal violence, Ripley combines the roles of warrior and mother. These *Alien* films proved to be actress Weaver's feminist text preparation for her central role of the decade, that of Dian Fossey in the feminist biopic *Gorillas in the Mist* (1988).

Other actresses—Jessica Lange in *Frances* (1982), then *Country* (1984), then *Sweet Dreams* (1985); Sally Field in *Norma Rae* (1979), then *Places in the Heart* (1984), then *Murphy's Romance* (1985), then *Stand-up* (1989); or Sissy Spacek in *The River* (1984), then *Marie* (1985), then *The Long Walk Home* (1990)—played neoconservative feminist characters, but always setting the standard with each new feminist character she created was Meryl Streep. From her debut as a working-class steel-town girl in *The Deer Hunter* (1978) to a divorced mother in *Kramer vs. Kramer* (1979) to the ultimate displaced person in *Sophie's Choice* (1982) to *Silkwood* (1983) to a confused wife in *Falling in Love* (1984) to the betrayed wife and mother in *Heartburn* (1986) to a homeless street bum in *Ironweed* (1987) to a mother on trial in *A Cry in the Dark* (1988) to a silly writer of romance novels in *She Devil* (1989), Streep has focused her career upon feminist statements. Perhaps her strongest feminist statement was made in one of her least-seen films, *Plenty* (1985), in which she plays Susan Traherne, a woman who will not allow herself to be molded to fit into English society after World War II. In the French Resistance during the war, Susan is a true heroine; the intensity of her war experiences, her heroic independence, make the rest of her life anticlimactic. Returning to postwar English society, Susan becomes a mad housewife desperate in her attempts to regain her passionate wartime identity and destructive in her outbursts against the patriarchal society that will not allow her to do so. Next to *Silkwood*, *Plenty* is Streep's most pointed sociopolitical portrayal.

But younger actresses also portrayed the neoconservative feminist quest for independence. *Desperately Seeking Susan* (1985) is about a bored housewife, Roberta (Rosanna Arquette), who creates a fantasy life out of watching a set of sexy personal ads that two New York punk rockers use to set up love trysts. Armed with this fantasy that the free-spirit Susan (Madonna) possesses the independence and passion she would like to have, Roberta sets out to spy on the punk lovers. Through a series of screwball mishaps, Roberta's fantasy of independence and sexual excitement actually comes true as she changes identities with Susan. Directed by Susan Siedelman, the film is a fast-paced feminist metaphor for conservative women grasping the opportunity to fulfill their identities and escape the patriarchal cages of eighties society. *Splash* (1984) pushes this metaphor of a woman finding her new identity into the alternative world of fantasy. In this film about a mermaid, the idea of becoming a woman functions on the level of pure metaphor, a movement out of male-authored myth into female reality. *Splash* is a metaphor for women escaping men's fantasies and finding their own footing (and feet) on solid ground. *She's Gotta Have It* (1986), Spike Lee's debut film, reveals the struggle for feminist independence in yet another alternative world, that of black women. Pauline Kael describes this alternate world as Lee's "tapping a whole new subject matter. Whites don't exist in this world. . . . It's a screwball comedy of sexual manners set in a world that's parallel with the white world."[22] Nola Darling (Tracy Camila Johns) is a black artist living in Brooklyn who blithely juggles three lovers. She is perfectly content keeping all of these balls in the air until each of her lovers starts placing restrictions upon her freewheeling love life. Lee has created a marvelously original feminist character: a black woman, a professional woman, a sexual woman, a free woman. His targets are the black males who try to restrict Nola's spontaneity and the society at large that sees her promiscuity as a threat. *She's Gotta Have It* exuberantly throws open the doors to one room that patriarchal society has always kept jealously locked, the bedroom where a sexual woman dares to dominate. The double standard has always allowed men their sexual independence but in *She's Gotta Have It* a black woman claims that same independence.

The Feminist Biopics

Even while the neoconservative "trickle down" effect of focusing upon ordinary working and mothering women was strong in the fiction films of the eighties, parallel to that trend was the increase in nonfiction feminist biopics. The main purpose of biopics (and of the biographics from which they spring) always has been to hold the overachievers of history and society up to scrutiny as examples of the themes that their lives embody. Prior to the eighties, the epic biopics—*Lawrence of Arabia* (1962), *Patton* (1970), *MacArthur* (1977)—had usually been of men. Into the eighties, there were still epic biopics of men being made, biographies of the imagination like *Amadeus* (1984), of the spirit like *Chariots of Fire* (1981) and *Ghandi* (1982), of courage like *Cry Freedom* (1987) and *Never Cry Wolf* (1983), and of political mavericks like *Walker* (1988) and *Blaze* (1989). Still, the largest cluster of biopics during the decade focused upon extraordinary women and made powerful feminist statements.

A number of feminist biopics chronicled the lives of real women who, often in small ways, resisted and made a difference. *Eleni* (1984) is just such an epic film about a small resistance. Adapted from *New York Times* reporter Nicholas Gage's book, it tells the story of his mother, the title character, a peasant woman who in 1948 during the Greek Civil War was executed for sending her children away from the war in which the Communists were conscripting children to send to reeducation camps. Even in its epic scope, the neoconservatizing impulse of eighties feminism still shows through in *Eleni*. It is the story of a mother taking care of her children. As she stands in a line of men before a firing squad, she throws her fists up in the air in triumph and screams, "my children!"

Marie (1985) is the story of Marie Ragghianti. In 1976 she was appointed to head the Tennessee Board of Pardons and Paroles. While working at that job, she discovered that an old-boy network of state officials was actually selling pardons. Refusing to be a yes-woman for this corrupt administration, she exposed the irregularities and was in turn publicly fired by the governor on television. She sued the state of Tennessee and ultimately her suit brought down the administration of Governor Ray Blanton. *Marie* is the story of a lone woman fighting to survive in a corrupt world of men. From the moment she leaves her abusive husband in 1968 to the public firing on television by a grandstanding Governor Blanton, Marie Ragghianti refuses to be victimized by men. Hers is a real survival story of a woman who first made a difference in her own life by leaving her abusive husband, working her way through college as a cocktail waitress, through sheer competence and hard work rising quickly through a number of state government jobs, and then made a political difference through her courage in standing up and ultimately toppling a crooked state government. Like so many of the feminist biopics of the eighties, *Marie* takes the form of a near-documentary profile in courage.

Pauline Kael characterized another profile in courage, *Gorillas in the Mist* (1988), somewhat ambivalently. At one point it is the story of "an activist heroine—a woman who made a difference," while at another "it's a feminist version of 'King Kong'—now it's the gorillas who do the scream-ing."[23] Of all the feminist biopics of the decade, *Gorillas in the Mist* is the most holographically sociopolitical in its themes. It can be interpreted upon ascending levels of sexual politics, of Third World politics, and of a global politics of ecology.

Gorillas in the Mist is the story of Dian Fossey (Sigourney Weaver), who spent her adult life studying, living with, communicating with, and protecting the mountain gorillas of Africa, which were an endangered species when she first entered the field, but who, thanks to her determina-tion (some would surely say "unhealthy obsession"), no longer are. Dian Fossey's story begins in a university lecture hall where she convinces the legendary Dr. Louis Leakey that she is the one to take the census of the mountain gorillas of Kenya. Hers is the story of an extremely courageous and determined woman who in experiencing hardship, isolation, destruc-tion of her research by a civil war, the killing of her research subjects by ruthless poachers, and government opposition to her very presence be-comes the most knowledgeable authority in the world on the African gorilla and that species' most outspoken and controversial advocate.

But the years of living with "her" gorillas and her advocacy do take their toll. In the end her anger drives her to escalating violence and the terrible frustration and fear of a threatened matriarch. This becomes a film about motherhood (much as 1986's *Aliens* did). In one of the most striking scenes in *Gorillas in the Mist*, Fossey, cradling a baby gorilla in her arms, invades a fancy hotel restaurant in an African town and confronts a Dutch zoo importer in front of all of his friends. She reads him the riot act, curses him for murdering and kidnapping helpless animals, literally for breaking up her family, all the while holding one of her surrogate children in her arms. It is a powerful scene built upon the distinct imagery of threatened matriarchy.

Gorillas in the Mist offers gorgeous vistas of the mountains of Africa and spectacular footage of the gorillas at play in the wild, but the film is far from being just a *National Geographic* documentary special. It is a highly political film that might well be characterized, in both its sexual and its ecological politics, in terms of the ominous warning of Bambi's mother: "MAN IS IN THE FOREST!" Fossey, at one point, has a romantic affair with Bob Campbell (Bryan Brown), the photographer who comes to her mountain to take her and her gorillas to the rest of the world through the pages of *National Geographic*. But she cannot give up even a portion of the time with her gorilla family, and finally she banishes Campbell from her mountain for being trivial in wanting to maintain some touch with civilization. But the other men in the forest, the poachers, she cannot banish so easily, and they are much more dangerous. As time goes on, Dian circles her matriarchal wagons and hisses like her female antagonist in *Aliens* at anyone who even approaches her brood. Perhaps the actress who plays Dian Fossey best captured the feminist nature of her character: "Usually women in films have had to carry the burden of sympathy, only coming to life when man enters. Doesn't everyone know that women are incredibly strong?"[24]

Gorillas in the Mist displays its feminism, the affirmation of women's courage and determination and ethical strength, but it also neoconservatizes that feminism by once again tying it to the power of a strong maternal instinct. Dian Fossey actually becomes the matriarch of her gorilla family, and the final symbolic image of the film, taken from that fiery pillar of nineteenth-century romanticism *Wuthering Heights*, is of the barrier between her and her favorite gorilla, which separated them in life, being removed in death. Finally, *Gorillas in the Mist* succeeds as biopic due to its "warts and all" approach. Dian Fossey is never a saint in this film, but she is an extremely dedicated and strong woman.

While Eleni and Marie Ragghianti and Dian Fossey were heroic women who made a difference politically in their world, eighties biopics also spotlighted talented women who overcame social obstacles to fulfill their talents, women forced to depart from the patterns of American life in order to pursue personal dreams. *Coal Miner's Daughter* (1980) and *Sweet Dreams* (1985) were similar in their chronicling of the tortuous rise out of poverty and personal tragedy of country singers Loretta Lynn and Patsy Cline. But these two music biopics were also very different. *Coal Miner's Daughter* gave a much stronger sense of a woman having to overcome her birthright on the outer fringes of American society, the dirt-poor hollows of backwoods Appalachia. *Sweet Dreams'* Patsy Cline's talent was pretty obvious to everyone from the beginning, but her story takes on tragic proportions as she must overcome a series of personal disasters—a near-fatal car accident, a stormy marriage—in order to exercise her god-given talent, only to die in a plane crash at age thirty at the apex of her professional success and popularity.

Shirley "Cha Cha" Muldowney rose to the top of a profession more dangerous than country singing. *Heart Like a Wheel* (1983) is the story of her career in professional auto racing. Pauline Kael describes it as "a feminist movie about a working class woman who was fighting men on their own turf" and as about "what happens to a woman who bucks a sexist society."[25] Like other rags-to-riches biopics, *Heart Like a Wheel* is an American dream movie unusual only in the combination of its setting, the world of professional auto racing, and its subject, a woman. Though the most documentary of these feminist biopics, the real events of Shirley Muldowney's life, flatly presented, still vibrate with feminist significance. In her rise through the ranks of the racers, Shirley loses her first husband to male insecurity and jealousy of her success, exploits a male fandom with a "hot pants" persona, and loses the second man in her life because of her single-minded pursuit of excellence. Of the eighties biopics, *Heart Like a Wheel* is the least neoconservatized. Though it focuses upon a working-class subject, it is about a woman facing off against men on male ground.

But country singers and race car drivers were not the only professions chronicled in the feminist biopics of the eighties. Two writers, Marjorie Kinnan Rawlings (Mary Steenburgen) and Isak Dinesen (Meryl Streep), were given eloquent film biographies. *Cross Creek* (1983), the story of Rawlings's retreat into the Florida swamps to find her identity as a writer and a self-sufficient woman is a quiet film. Set in a rural backwoods world of hard scrabble families and a need for community in order to survive, it is a classic neoconservative biopic. *Out of Africa* (1986), however, was one of the decade's biggest productions and most popular films. It romanticized the feminist impulse to identity and independence. In director Sydney Pollock's feminist style (as demonstrated earlier in *Tootsie*), *Out of Africa's* feminist message was delivered with wit and understanding of the common ground that men must learn to share with the new woman.

When Karen Blixen (Meryl Streep), aka Isak Dinesen, later when she writes her haunting stories, first arrives in Kenya in 1913, she commits a glaring faux pas. She intrudes into the men's bar of the British Club to ask directions, draws the icy stares of this all-male enclave, and is escorted out. At the end of her stay in Africa, as she is departing from the same club, the men invite her into their bar for a farewell drink. They all raise their glasses to her in a toast of earned respect. Another male-female barrier has fallen. The film is based on exactly that premise of Karen Blixen daring to go where only men were permitted.

The pivotal sequence in which Karen earns her spurs occurs when her husband gets into "a silly argument between two spoiled countries," World War I, and the British troops with whom he is fighting are cut off without supplies. Karen leads a pack train on a brutal cross-Africa trek under threat of attack from the Germans, the Masai, and roving bands of lions, to relieve her husband and the British troops. As she rides into camp through the army of aghast men, she looks like holy hell but is smiling bravely, and is greeted by the funniest line of the film:

DE LA MERE: Hello Karen.

KAREN: Hello De. Hello Bror. I've brought you some things.

BLIXEN: You've changed your hair.

Later, in their tent, Blixen scolds Karen: "You were lucky to get through. It was foolish." Beaming confidently, she answers, "but I did get through . . . and it was fun!" *Out of Africa* delivers its feminist message with wit and a *joie de vivre* that escapes many of the other, less deft, feminist biopics of the decade.

The Ensemble Weepy

One final vehicle for expressing a neoconservative feminism was the old-fashioned, so-called woman's picture, the weepy. *Terms of Endearment* might fit this category if it were not contaminated by a number of strong male presences. The best examples, however, are *Beaches* (1988) and *Steel Magnolias* (1989). The latter may be the quintessential woman's film. Set in a beauty parlor and spanning three generations of female friends and including every possible approach to feminism, *Steel Magnolias* is never tainted by even the shadow of a male character. It is, unabashedly, a movie about women and how they come together to help and take care of each other. *Beaches*, on the other hand, like *Rich and Famous*, is a film about sisterhood, about no matter how far apart sisters may drift, they still remain sisters and are responsible for each other.

Perhaps the one film that served as a beacon to the eighties direction of neoconservative feminism was Woody Allen's *Hannah and Her Sisters* (1986). It has all of the neoconservative specifications—it is about family, stresses sisterhood, interweaves working women with housewives and mothers—except that it is set in Manhattan rather than in a rural small town. At the heart of the film, however, is the sense that communication—between men and women, women and women, the generations—is a very sensitive and tentative thing yet the key to any freedom or relationship no matter what gender is involved. The final coda to the neoconservative trend in feminist film in the eighties came, ironically, in the form of a black humor blockbuster, *The War of the Roses* (1989). This version of the eighties battle of the sexes ended on the sick and hilarious note of a husband and wife literally killing each other over their house. Though this film offered a violent ending to the feminist debates of the decade, overall the films of the eighties that dealt with feminist issues took the path of lesser resistance and reached for a neoconservative accommodation to a wider inclusion of wives, mothers, rural women, and lower-class working women, which the women's movement had not actively courted in the past.

8

The Yuppie Texts

I N   T H E   A C T I O N   comedy *Burglar* (1987), Whoopie Goldberg and Bob Goldthwaite steel themselves to enter a crowded fern bar to gather information, when Goldthwaite panics and babble-screams: "I can't go in there! I can't go in there! It's full of crazed yuppies from hell!" While the Hell's Angels of the biker films of the fifties and early sixties have not really been replaced by the Hell's yuppies of the eighties, Goldthwaite's terror at the spector of America's cities being taken over by roving gangs of young urban professionals wearing three-piece suits, driving Volvos, BMWs, and Mercedes, and flaunting their Gold Card wealth in an orgy of material acquisitiveness certainly seemed the case in the films of the eighties.

Residing at the opposite end of the spectrum from the Mid-American, rural, feminism of the farm crisis films, the text of urban yuppie materialism also exhibited a neoconservative style fostered by Reagonomics. The yuppie drives to make large amounts of money quickly, to succeed in a ruthless competitive world, to acquire the most expensive material goods, to spend rather than save, to party extremely hard as a reward for working extremely hard, to sacrifice (especially human relationships) for one's job, mirrored the Reagan administration's deficit spending policies and hi-tech defense system acquisitions. Eighties yuppies saw their ruthless competitive work ethic and their consumptive materialism as hedges and buffers against an increasingly unstable terrorist- and nuclear- and deficit-threatened world. Yuppieness became a form of protective coloration against the economic and status threats from ethnic minorities and the poor, from a questionable national economy, from an increasingly competitive world. Yuppies saw themselves as a uniformed cavalry circling the wagons around what was left of the American dream, that dream's material icons: the job with a chance for advancement, the house (in its new condo form), the car, the status goods, perhaps even a controlled and economically justified family. The films of the eighties were acutely aware not only of the stereotypes and accoutrements of the yuppie lifestyle but also of the insecurity of the dying American dream.

For example, in the eighties, the heroes of films were less likely to be cowboys or spacemen with the right stuff or loner cops like Dirty Harry Callahan (Clint Eastwood) than they were businessmen or marketing executives or advertising geniuses. In films like *Kramer vs. Kramer* (1979), *Nothing in Common* (1986), *Baby Boom* (1986), *Planes, Trains and Automobiles* (1987), *The Secret of My Success* (1987), *Parenthood* (1989), *When Harry Met Sally*, and *Crazy People* (1990), the central characters are all advertising executives, while in *Wall Street* (1987), *Dad* (1989), and *Rollover* (1981), the central characters are all aggressive urban money men.

"So what are all those work-obsessed, amoral advertising and marketing men doing in today's movies?" one industry observer asks. "'Studio executives relate to them,' insists a marketing executive who requests anonymity. 'It's a high-pressure, brutally competitive environment that mirrors the style and workings of making movies.'"[1] Yuppie filmmakers like Steven Spielberg, George Lucas, and Ron Howard reached their positions of power in eighties Hollywood, according to industry analyst Tony Hoffman, because "they're going to make commercial hits . . . movies that gross over $100 million."[2] The demographic definition of the yuppie lifestyle would seem to support this industry view. A report based on twenty years of polling data on six million college freshmen noted a sharp rise in conservatism, in an interest in material success, and in business majors, as opposed to a steady decrease in people interested in developing a philosophy of life or pursuing English, math, and science majors.[3] By the end of the eighties decade, yuppies were so prominent and accepted as part of the American landscape that none of the reticence of TV critic Harry F. Waters, writing about a new show at mid-decade, any longer existed: "Its creators are reportedly touting 'Sara,' a sitcom about a career woman working in a San Francisco law office, as 'The Mary Tyler Moore Show' of the Eighties. The difference between Mary and Sara is that the latter is—let's come right out and say it—a yuppie."[4] By the end of the eighties yuppies were accepted, not without some contempt but with lessening ridicule and caricature, as the movers and go-getters of American society, and their image—the way they dressed, the cars they drove, the things they valued (or did not)—had itself become a recognizable uniform. Perhaps the most symbolic precursor of the eighties yuppie films was *Urban Cowboy* (1980). In a highly ironic myth, the film chronicles how the Old West of cowboys and bucking bronchos has been replaced by a new yuppie West of designer-dressed cowboys riding mechanical bulls. *Urban Cowboy* is the death knell of the Western, of an American mythology that has been superceded by a new species of Wall Street gunslingers. The yuppie films of the eighties all explore the contours and the effects of the new myth of the American dream and measure it against the old.

The eighties yuppie film text took two separate forms. The first, the yuppie angst text, portrayed and critiqued the yuppie lifestyle from a skeptical perspective, focusing upon its flaws, excesses, and failures. Yuppie angst was seen as a direct result of job stress, the obsession with success and the rejection of spiritual fulfillment for material acquisitiveness. It was most often occasioned by the insecurity of maintaining their position in society and their fast-lane lifestyle as well as by their own doubts and dissatisfactions with the superficiality of their existence. The second yuppie text, much like the feminist-issue texts, confronted a spectrum of yuppie issues from sex to babies to sports to houses. In eighties films, the characters were more likely to inhabit the milieu and the economic strata of the yuppie than any other segment of the American public.

Yuppie Angst

The major eighties document, in both its novel and film forms, of yuppie angst was Jay McInerney's 1984 best seller and film adaptation *Bright Lights, Big City* (1988). Early in the film, Alex Hardy (Jason Robards), a drunken writer-editor at *Gotham* magazine tipsily counsels Jamie Conway (Michael J. Fox) over a three-martini lunch:

ALEX: Have you ever considered getting an MBA?

JAMIE: Absolutely not.

ALEX: Well, I'm not necessarily saying go into business. No, no, but write about it. That's the stuff now. The guys that understand business are writing the new literature. Money is poetry now.

JAMIE: I don't wanna believe that. It may be true, but I don't wanna believe that.

ALEX: Don't be seduced by all that crap about writing in a garret like I was. Write about money.

In the eighties the yuppie moneymongers not only are taking over literature but are insinuating their acquisitive lifestyle into every corner of American society. *Bright Lights, Big City* is a sewer guide to the underside of the yuppie American dream. Almost clinically it dissects the angst attached to the eighties. Lust for money, fame, social acceptance; how the yuppie's social struggle, because it pursues purely material goals, causes a gradual disintegration, or at least disorientation, of the existential self.

Bright Lights, Big City is a declawed eighties version of *Dr. Jekyll and Mr. Hyde*. See cute little conservative materialistic Alex Keaton (also Michael J. Fox) of the long-running eighties TV sitcom "Family Ties" turn into guilty, confused cokehead and undersized playboy of the New York disco scene. Jamie's friend Ted Allegash (Kiefer Sutherland) describes their dark yuppie Hyde-like quest: "Into the heart of the night. Wherever there are dances to be danced, drugs to be hoovered, girls to be Allegashed."

As in the *Dr. Jekyll and Mr. Hyde* original, one central stream of imagery in *Bright Lights, Big City* is that of mirrors. Jamie spends much of his time either snorting coke off of them or trying to find his lost self in them.

Much of the film, in fact, is spent in unisex disco restrooms where men and women share their coke in the stalls and then check out their noses in the mirrors before returning to the yuppie fray. But at other times, Jamie looks into bathroom mirrors in hopes of finding a self that the coke, the loss of his wife, his mother, his job, have all blurred. In fact, much of the film, its night scenes, are shot in a yellow neon blur, a drug blur that sends Jamie off into memory flashbacks and *National Enquirer* hallucinations of "coma babies" (the film's embarassingly obvious controlling metaphor) refusing to come out of a drug womb. The film's visual blurring of reality is ironically paralleled by Jamie's job as a fact-checker at *Gotham* magazine. The coke, the late nights, the guilt, and insecurity of his yuppie lifestyle are all blurring his ability to see the facts both on the job and in his own life. In his job performance, Jamie becomes a close parallel to Buddy Fox (Charlie Sheen) in *Wall Street* (1987). Both deceive themselves in thinking that they can get away with the shortcuts of their fast-lane lifestyles.

But *Bright Lights, Big City* also provides a checklist of the yuppie image. It defines the uniform—button-down shirt, tie, three-piece suit—or more casually—shirt, tie, sports jacket, jeans—and, of course, no self-respecting yuppie ever sleeps in anything but an Ivy League T-shirt—Jamie is a Dartmouth grad. The yuppie uniform is this confused mix of the formal and the casual; Dustin Hoffman wore it in *Kramer vs. Kramer* (1979), Michael Murphy in *Manhattan* (1979), and Steve Martin in *Roxanne* (1987). Drugs serve as the anaesthetic to the confusion of this life; they create the illusion that all of this imagery means something.

One other early eighties film, Lawrence Kasdan's *Big Chill* (1983) presented the same sort of angst-burdened blueprint of the yuppie lifestyle. Late in that film, Meg's (Mary Kay Place) best friend, Sarah (Glenn Close), in an act of generosity has just sent her husband, Harold (Kevin Kline), in to impregnate Meg with the baby Meg so wants. Despite her delight at this turn of events, Meg confesses "I feel like I just got a great deal on a used car!" Meg's feeling could serve as a metaphor for the yuppie eighties. The decade seems to be a nostalgic attempt to regain the innocent acquisitive joy of the American dream of the fifties and the passion of the sixties while simultaneously realizing that the dream is rusted out and has too many miles on it. All of the characters in *The Big Chill* have pretty much gotten the deal they wanted but it has not worked out.

The film begins at Alex's funeral. A member of a close-knit group of friends who all went to college at Michigan in the late sixties, Alex has committed suicide. During the funeral, the preacher ironically asks the film's thematic question: "Where did Alex's hope go?" But the question applies to this whole generation who in the years since the fiery radicalism of their college days have chilled out.

Like *Bright Lights, Big City, The Big Chill* is a checklist film for the yuppie generation, but it carries the extra baggage of comparing the eighties yuppies to their past sixties selves before the big chill set in. That change, from a passionate and involved sixties generation to the cool and aloof yuppie generation, is endlessly dissected in a weekend of soul-searching triggered by Alex's suicide. His death, the first of their generation going to the big sleep because of the big chill of the mindless acquisitive Reagan eighties, is an intrusion upon all of these people's nice safe yuppie lives.

Perhaps the most ironic symbol of their yuppieness is the running shoes, an essential part of the uniform. Harold owns a string of athletic shoe stores, ironically named "Running Dog," and each member of the house party finds his or her pair on the kitchen table in the morning. They lace on their yuppie uniform, then try to figure out why it is so comfortable.

Meg is, perhaps, the ultimate young urban professional of the group. A lawyer who began her career as a public defender in Detroit and realized that all of her murderer and rapist clients were guilty, she explains what happened to chill out her life: "And then I left. I had this friend from law school who was with a firm in Atlanta doing real estate law, so I went to see them. The offices were very clean, and the clients were only raping the land, and then, of course, there was the money. El greedo strikes again."

In the sixties garden of Eden, alluded to in the song "I Know Something about Love" on the soundtrack, the serpent who gets them driven out of the garden into the postlapsarian yuppie world of the eighties is money. "Who would've thought we'd both make so much bread, two revolutionaries?" Sam (Tom Berenger), a TV star, tells Harold, who answers: "Good thing it isn't important to us." And in another exchange, Michael (Jeff Goldblum), a pop magazine journalist, asks:

MICHAEL: Hey remember senior year? We were all gonna get together and buy that land near Saginaw. Hey, what happened to that?

HAROLD: We didn't have any money.

MICHAEL: Oh yes, that's when property was a crime.

Even Nick (William Hurt), wounded Vietnam vet and present-day drug dealer, knows that he has committed the original sin of greed like everyone else. As he interviews himself in front of a VCR camera, his monologue is a confession: "What are you doing now, or I should say, what have you evolved into now? I'm in sales." All of them have, literally, sold out. They have followed the serpent of money into the real world of yuppie greed and acquisitiveness and, like their running shoes, have found a comfortable fit.

Despite these conflicts between the generations, the basic sources of yuppie angst—the competitiveness of their jobs, the turning to drugs as an anesthetic, the guilt over their greed and meaningless acquisitiveness—still nag at all of the characters in the yuppie film texts of the eighties. The reigning *auteur* of yuppie angst, in fact of all varieties of urban angst, during the eighties was Woody Allen. He made two kinds of films during the decade: marvelous period pieces like *Radio Days* (1987), *Broadway Danny Rose* (1984), and *The Purple Rose of Cairo* (1986); and his yuppie angst films, *Hannah and Her Sisters* (1986) and *Crimes and Misdemeanors* (1989). The yuppie angst text of Woody Allen stalks big ideas through small groups of people (usually families). His movies alternate philosophy with slapstick, social history with comic hysteria. Though Woody Allen is undeniably Jewish, utterly New York, shamelessly literary, and unabashedly existential, in the eighties his New York Jewish literate self-seekers were also yuppies. In *Hannah and Her Sisters*, Allen's yuppie angst takes the form of guilt over bad marriages, bad relationships with one's parents, bad relationships with men, and a terrible relationship with death. But all this guilt is set against a contending background: Hannah's familial stability vs. the superficiality and fenzied materialism of yuppie society. Allen sees the family as literally under attack from this eighties cynicism.

Crimes and Misdemeanors, like *Hannah and Her Sisters*, is about an extended family (actually three families) that is coming apart because of sexual problems: infidelity, loneliness, lack of love. As Allen juggles his three different family groups, he examines some large philosophical dualities: reality vs. dreams, truth vs. belief, nihilism vs. optimism, the past and its hold on the present, life vs. Hollywood movies, blindness vs. seeing, and the ultimate Jewish yuppie question, chicken soup vs. white wine? Eighties wrestling with all of these dualities ultimately, for the Allen character, ends in either a crime or a misdemeanor and everyone is guilty. But which are crimes and which are misdemeanors? Does a crime like murder really cause more pain than a lover's rejection? Is a lie a crime when truth is so elusive? *Crimes and Misdemeanors* is a philosophical dialogue set in the monied world of yuppie angst. The largest irony of the film is that its most acquisitive, phony yuppie character, Lester (Alan Alda), a wonderfully corrupt filmmaker, ultimately gets the girl, success, the yuppie dream, because only he is qualified for it, only he chooses not to heed his angst.

Bright Lights, Big City, *The Big Chill*, and Woody Allen's contemporary films are all checklists of yuppie angst. They plot the landscape, define the uniform, and reveal the anxieties and guilts of people who have allowed themselves to become Yuppies. But how did they come to this pass?

The Job Battle Most often, the workplace became the yuppie battlefield. Their jobs took precedence over all other areas of their lives: self, relationships, family, morality. The competition for success, power, status, money, in the workplace and in society became an unhealthy obsession. Whereas young Jamie Conway in *Bright Lights, Big City* looks at the Manhattan skyline at the end and vows to fight his way back, in *Wall Street* young Huckleberry Fox (Charlie Sheen) cannot just wipe the slate clean with a firm purpose of amendment as he stands on the balcony of his million-dollar condo overlooking the Manhattan skyline. Rather, Bud Fox has participated in the criminal defrauding of thousands of people and must pay in loss of reputation, in court, and in prison. In both films, these innocents are abroad in the fast-lane world of their jobs and are not able to handle the pressure.

Broadcast News (1988) and *Switching Channels* (1988) both went behind the scenes in the world of TV news to study the job-generated yuppie angst of the high-pressure media world, while *Street Smart* (1987) examined the loss of ethics of a yuppie print journalist. In all three, the pressure, the competition, and the frantic pace of the news-gathering profession force the characters caught in this vortex to take shortcuts, sacrifice their ethics for the scoop, the exclusive. Unfortunately the sacrifice of their ethics seems to come fairly easy to these characters and the rewards for their dishonesty are huge in terms of young urban professional success.

Right up there next to the media as a favorite yuppie profession in film texts of the eighties were the legal profession and Wall Street. In *Legal Eagles* (1986), *Suspect* (1987), and *The Accused* (1988), yuppie lawyers plied their trade. These lawyers, most of them women, wear the three-piece yuppie uniform and carry their briefcases with grace and assertiveness. *Legal Eagles* especially highlights the yuppie accoutrements. Set amidst the high-rent rehabs of Greenwich Village and the Tribeca area of Manhattan, it wanders through the expensive world of the New York art gallery scene as well as the trendy world of performance artists. Both the TV news people and these lawyers work hard at their jobs and are remunerated well, but not nearly as well as the kamikaze kids of Wall Street, the brokers, the junk bond salesmen, the investment bankers and the corporate raiders, the Ivan Boeskys and the Michael Milkens and the Boone Pickens who made the megabucks and catapulted the yuppie lifestyle into the materialist stratosphere.

Wall Street (1987) is the ultimate film text of the workplace battlefield. It inventories the ammunition that loads up the yuppie dream, tracks the quick and easy money that fires that dream off. In *Wall Street*, Gordon Gekko (Michael Douglas), microphone in hand and working the room like a rock star, addresses a corporate stockholders' meeting and delivers the Gettysburg Address of the yuppie philosophy:

> Well, ladies and gentlemen, we're not here to indulge in fantasy, but in political and economic reality. America, America has become a second rate power. Its trade deficit and its fiscal deficit are at nightmare proportions. . . . Today, management has no stake in the company. . . . *You* own the company and you are being royally screwed over. . . . Well in my book you either do it right or you get eliminated. In the last seven deals that I have been involved with, there were 2.5 million stockholders who have made a

pre-tax profit of 12 billion dollars. [applause] Thank you. I am not a destroyer of companies; I am a liberator of them. The point is, ladies and gentlemen, that greed, for lack of a better word, greed is good. Greed is right. Greed works. Greed clarifies, cuts through and captures the essence of the evolutionary spirit. Greed, in all its forms, greed for life, for money, for love, for knowledge, has marked the upward surge of mankind and, greed, you mark my words, will not only save Teldar Paper, but that other malfunctioning corporation called the USA. Thank you very much.

Gekko's speech, his preposterous paean to greed, rings with a kind of evangelistic fervor. It is delivered in a setting similar to the UBS stockholders' meeting in *Network* presided over by the snakelike Frank Hackett (Robert Duvall) and the charismatic corporate evangelist Diana Christiansen (Faye Dunaway).[5] In his address, Gekko offers an absolution to all the yuppies in the audience who are suffering guilt over their materialism. Though addressing the shareholders of Teldar Paper, a corporation he is raiding, Gekko begins his Sermon on the Mount by defining how the American dream has turned into a nightmare due to bad management. For Gordon Gekko, America is no longer an idea, it is merely another large corporation being mismanaged by bureaucrats and suffering from cash flow problems. Gekko uses the nation as a macrocosmic metaphor for Teldar and offers his panacea for the problems of both troubled corporations, greed. Greed, one of the Seven Deadly Sins, takes on moral stature (it is "good" and "right"), pragmatic efficiency (it "works"), rhetorical power (it "clarifies" and "cuts through and captures the essence"), and progressive force (it marks "the upward surge of mankind"). Greed, literally, becomes a savior for both Teldar Paper and for the USA, and Gekko's speech becomes a fervent absolution of the yuppie angst that clouds the hardhearted decision making of corporate raiding.

Wall Street is the ultimate yuppie nightmare. It portrays the crash of the yuppie ideal of money, power, and status. The dialogue of *Wall Street* is a constant rollercoaster of buying and selling. The film's most prominent icons are cellular phones and computer terminals. Much of the action takes place at desks. The film issues a backstage pass to America's longest running economic repertory theater where comedy and tragedy alternate on a daily basis.

Buddy Fox (Charlie Sheen) is an American innocent from Queens who has worked his way into the inner circle of stock brokerage trading, hostile takeover deals, and the Manhattan yuppie ratrace. It is no wonder that his father Carl (Martin Sheen), the representative of an airplane mechanic's union, has nicknamed him Huckleberry. By a lot of toadying, Buddy becomes the protégé and soon-to-be fall guy for Gordon Gekko, the most ruthless of the *Wall Street* corporate raiders. To use the metaphoric language of actual corporate raiding, the plot of Wall Street is like a medieval joust. Gekko, the black knight, and Sir Laurence Wildman

(Terence Stamp), the white knight, fight it out with telephones mounted on stretch limos attended by their squires who are either Brooks Brothers lawyers or innocent young stockbrokers like Fox.

The plot of *Wall Street*, however, is much less engaging than the momentum that the film's language creates, its fast-paced rhetoric of the art of the deal featuring two recurring metaphors: of war and of sex. The rhetoric of Gordon Gekko's deal making is violent and bloodthirsty and seems to emanate more appropriately from the grunts in director Oliver Stone's previous film *Platoon* than from a suspendered, manicured, and slicked-back businessman talking on the phone in an upholstered office overlooking Manhattan. Gordon Gekko's office is the computerized control center of a battlefield. He barks the macho language of war on his speaker phones as he triggers his deals:

> I loved it at 40, it's an insult at 50. Their analysts, they don't know preferred stock from livestock. See, wait'll they head south and then we'll raise the sperm count on the deal. Get back at ya. [Hangs up phone. Turns to Bud Fox.] This is the kid. Calls me 59 days in a row. Wants to be a player. Oughta be a picture of you in the dictionary under "PERSISTENCE," kid. [Phone rings. He picks up and swivels away from Bud.] Listen Jerry, all I want is negative control. No more than 30–35 percent. Just enough to blow anyone else's merger plans and find out from the inside if the books are cooked. If it looks good as on paper, we're in the kill zone, pal, lock and load. Lunch? What, are you kiddin'? Lunch is for wimps.

His rapid-fire patter toys momentarily with a macho sexual metaphor—"we'll raise the sperm count on the deal"—but quickly drops that for a more violent rhetoric of war. In the steam room after destroying Bud at racquetball, Gekko returns to his war metaphor to define the tactics of the yuppie battlefield:

> GEKKO: The most valuable commodity I know of is information, wouldn't you agree?
>
> BUD: Yea.
>
> GEKKO: The public's out there throwing darts at a board, sport. I don't throw darts at a board. Read Sun Soo, *The Art of War*. Every battle is won before it's fought.

Later, Bud Fox quotes Sun Soo word for word back to Gekko as evidence that he is man enough to join the battle. In the eighties, Oliver Stone made his reputation portraying the decade's battlefields. From *Salvador* to *Platoon* to *Wall Street* to *Talk Radio* (1989) he moved from the terrorist war of Central America to the shooting war of Vietnam to the yuppie battlefields of the stockbrokers and the media stars.

Gordon Gekko relishes his macho battle rhetoric, but Bud Fox is defined in terms of a more human metaphor, that of sex. In the world of *Wall Street*, the human emotions of love and the excitement and release of sexuality are overshadowed by the making of money. Making money becomes a twisted form of sex, an almost orgasmic thrill. After buying a painting for $2.5 million, Gekko invites Darien (Darryl Hannah), Bud's upscale decorator girl friend, to share a room at the Carlyle Hotel for the afternoon. "You and I are the same, Darien," Gekko argues. "We are smart enough not to buy into the oldest myth running, love—a fiction created by people to keep them from jumping out of windows." Darien laughs off his proposition with "you know, sometimes I miss you Gordon. You're really twisted." That is what this yuppie drive for money and power and status does to natural human emotions, twists them into deformity. The yuppie dream replaces the human with the purely material, sexuality with money and power. "See that building over there," Gekko brags to Bud Fox. "It was my first real estate deal. I bought it eight years ago. Two years later I sold it for an $800,000 profit. It was better than sex."

But while *Wall Street* (by means of these rhetorical flights) captures the violence and excitement of the yuppie battlefield of the workplace, the film also visually (by means of montages, multiple split screens, and quick-cutting) captures the frenetic pace and the intense pressure of the broker's work life. In fact, *Wall Street, The Secret of My Success,* and *Working Girl* open with exactly the same montage of aerials of the Manhattan skyline and morning rush New York street scenes. In each film this stylized urban montage sets the competitive pace of urban professional life. Getting ready to place his phone call to Gordon Gekko for the fifty-ninth straight day in a row, Buddy plugs the numbers into the dream: "47 million on the Melcort deal, 23 on the Imperial deal. The guy makes twenty times what Dave Winfield does in a year." It is the numbers that fascinate Bud Fox, that render the yuppie dream, give it the color of money.

Like *The Big Chill* and *Bright Lights, Big City* did, *Wall Street* stresses the importance of the yuppie uniform, the dress-for-success ethic. When his father questions his yuppie lifestyle, Buddy crunches the numbers that it takes to be a player in the game, to wear the uniform:

BUD: Dad, I'm not a salesman. I'm an account executive. Pretty soon I'm moving to the Investment Banking side of it.

CARL: You get on the phones and ask strangers for money. You're a salesman.

BUD: Dad, it takes time. I'm building a client list. I can make more money in one year as a broker than I could in five years at this airline.

CARL: I don't get it kid. You borrow money to go to NYU. The first year out you make 35 grand. You make 50 grand last year, and you still can't pay off your loans. Where does it all go?

BUD: 50K does not get you to first base in the big apple. 40% goes to taxes. 15 grand for rent. I got school loans, car loans, food. Park my car, that's three bills a month. I need good suits at $400 a pop.

Buddy Fox has just itemized the price of the yuppie uniform. The yuppie dream is based solely upon making money and owning things, on wearing the uniform at a young age while it still fits. The only problem is that when they attain the dream they find it empty. That is why, after a perfect dinner cooked with the help of every possible yuppie kitchen appliance in his perfect apartment, and after perfect sex with a perfect woman, Bud Fox finds himself out on his balcony looking at the city skyline and asking, "Who am I?" The ultimate nightmare of the yuppie dream is that one must give up all that they are to attain it.

If *Wall Street* is a deadly serious Monopoly game in which Bud Fox goes directly to jail, *The Secret of My Succe$s* is the same game played for laughs. It is no coincidence that in the print advertising for this film the penultimate *s* in the last word of the title is represented by a dollar sign. The film's primary text, as was that of *Wall Street*, is that anything goes as long as there is money to be made. The film is a yuppie version of the Dick Whittington story sans cat. Its plot chronicles the step-by-step acquiring of the yuppie uniform — business degree, three-piece suit, executive position in the corporation, corner office with secretary, boss's wife and mistress, finally the corporation itself — by its "yupwardly" bound young protagonist. Michael J. Fox, himself a yuppie icon, plays Brantley Foster from Kansas who gets a job in the mailroom at Prescott Industries, presided over by his ruthless Uncle Howard (Richard Jordan), a cross between Gordon Gekko and Mister Magoo. Uncle Howard is so incredibly shortsighted to everything but himself that he allows his nephew to sleep his way out of the mailroom and into the Executive Suite. Pauline Kael identifies this farcical flip side of *Wall Street* as a lighthearted exploration of yuppie angst. After describing the film as "the adventures of a polite yuppie hustler," she characterizes a female corporate executive as "deadeningly fatuous. . . . And maybe that's why when this executive was hurt and began to weep the audience laughed. Besides, we don't want to be reminded that Yuppie robots have feelings."[6] In a farce like *The Secret of My Succe$s*, the surfacing of yuppie angst cannot be taken too seriously because the uniform that hides it is too sleek.

Another set of films dealt with the job stresses of those who must police the excesses of the yuppie world. In a number of films, the old cops and robbers antagonism shifted to a cops and yuppies game. *No Man's Land* (1987) points to the reality that once a cop goes undercover he must fight to survive in a no-man's-land between the good guys and the bad. The only problem is that once you get used to living in the middle there is a chance of forgetting who the good guys are, especially if the bad guys live in the yuppie high-rent district of Beverly Hills. In *No Man's Land*, Benjy Taylor (D. B. Sweeney), a rookie cop, is put undercover as a mechanic in a Porsche garage using the name Billy Eyles. Billy is supposed to gather information on Ted Varrick (Charlie Sheen), the mastermind of a stolen Porsche operation. Varrick is a Beverly Hills yuppie in full possession of the uniform, who has chosen his life of crime as a way of striking out at his rich parents who have neglected he and his sister Ann (Lara Harris). Enter the twist. Billy and Ted become good friends. Billy and Ann become lovers. Billy gets a taste of the yuppie lifestyle and really likes it. Ultimately he must choose between his duty as a cop and his duty as a friend and lover.

In *Someone to Watch Over Me* (1987), Mike Keegan (Tom Berenger), a young NYPD detective who lives happily in Queens with his former-cop wife and eight-year-old son, is assigned to provide protective custody for a rich yuppie princess, Claire (Mimi Rogers), who has witnessed a murder and can identify the killer. Slowly drawn into the glitter of Manhattan's high society discos, art galleries, and elegant Park Avenue apartments, Keegan falls in love with Claire and her world. His attraction to the yuppie uniform is symbolized by his neckties. Early in the film when he is just a cop protecting his yuppie charge, Keegan wears atrocious neckties and Claire will not be seen in public with him when he has them on. She buys him an expensive silk tie to wear when he escorts her out, and he is hooked.

The same premise of downscale cops working undercover in the upscale world of yuppie glitz functions in the *Beverly Hills Cop* films (1984, 1987) and in William Friedkin's *To Live and Die in L.A.* (1985). Eddie Murphy's hip Detroit cop, Axel Foley, exudes so much protective coloration, changes identities so fast, that he fits into any setting, even that of a black man at home on Rodeo Drive. Axel Foley parodies the yuppie style at every turn and carries it off with a panache that leaves the real yuppies open-mouthed in awe.

To Live and Die in L.A. is a completely different story, however. The villain in this film, Eric Masters (Willem Dafoe), is a brutal counterfeiter who is both living and living off of the excesses of the yuppie lifestyle. In order to catch him, two Secret Service agents, Chance (William Peterson) and Vukovich (John Pankow), must adopt both the uniform and the lifestyle of the villain's upscale world. But more interesting is that *To Live and Die in L.A.* is literally a film about money. In a long and detailed montage, the filmgoer sees the process of Ric Masters' counterfeiting genius. What that montage signals, however, is the controlling metaphor not just of this film but of all the yuppie films of the decade. Making money in whatever way one can is the driving force behind the plotting and the characterization of all the films that make up the yuppie text.

The Religion of Acquisition If the yuppie characters of films like *Wall Street* and *The Secret of My Success* are obsessed with making money, they are equally driven to spend it. Acquiring the most expensive components of the uniform, whether it be clothes or cars or homes or art or power over others, became a sole form of nonworking-hours entertainment pursued with an almost religious zeal. Second only to their love of working is the yuppies' love of shopping. This religion of acquisition's Rome is Fifth Avenue in New York and its Mecca is Rodeo Drive in L.A., and all its parishes and sects are located in the malls and designer specialty shops and luxury car dealers all across America.

Characters in these films typically were already or suddenly possessed of vast sums of money (as was Bud Fox in *Wall Street*), and their function was to spend it. One excellent example is the sixth remaking of *Brewster's Millions* (1985) in which Montgomery Brewster (Richard Pryor) must spend $30 million in thirty days in order to inherit $300 million. It can hardly be called a yuppie movie, as its protagonist is an aging black semipro baseball player, but it certainly strikes to the heart of the fantasy of the American dream, possessing and spending unlimited amounts of money. Monty Brewster, when he inherits all that money and must spend it suddenly, finds himself surrounded by greedy yuppies, especially his accountant and his lawyer.

But if *Brewster's Millions* is the ultimate eighties film about spending money, *Troop Beverly Hills* is the ultimate shopping film. Rich Beverly Hills housewife Phyllis Nefler (Shelley Long) possesses the yuppie uniform—a pink mansion hung with priceless art, a Rolls Royce with driver, a walk-in closet stocked with the most bizarre couturier gowns, and a charge account in every store on Rodeo Drive—with a vengeance, but as a way of proving to her husband that she is not simply a lightweight yuppie dilettante, she becomes the leader of her daughter's Wilderness Girls troop. "I'm sure it's very helpful to know how to live in the forest and eat bark," Phyllis tells her troop at their first meeting, "but I'm going to teach you girls to survive in the wilds of Beverly Hills." Noting that the *Wilderness Girls Handbook* allows for individual troops to design the specifications for their own merit badges, Phyllis has her chauffeur take the girls to salons for manicures and pedicures in order to earn a "Grooming Badge," to Cartier's on Rodeo Drive to earn a "Jewelry Appraisal Patch," to divorce court for a Beverly Hills "Marriage Badge." Her idea of camping out is toasting hot dogs in the fireplace of a Beverly Hills Hotel bungalow. Phyllis Nefler is intent upon teaching her Wilderness Girls all of the metaphysical and existential satisfactions of shopping.

Down and Out in Beverly Hills (1986) uses the same ploy to caricature the yuppie, Beverly Hills lifestyle: a common, well-known agent—such as girl-scouting or a street-smart Detroit cop like Axel Foley or, in this case, a homeless derelict—is suddenly parachuted into the middle of the yuppie excesses of Beverly Hills where he can go shopping. Jerry Baskin (Nick Nolte) begins *Down and Out in Beverly Hills* pushing a shopping cart piled high with the refuse of suburbia that he has scavenged out of garbage cans. Even the homeless know the value of shopping, and when by a fluke of suicide Jerry gets taken into the Beverly Hills yuppie establishment of wire hanger magnate Dave Whiteman (Richard Dreyfuss) and his pampered wife, Barbara (Bette Midler), who are clones of the Neflers of *Troop Beverly Hills*, he abandons his shopping cart and goes shopping in a much classier set of garbage cans. Added to the yuppie uniform in *Down and Out in Beverly Hills* are such accessories as a dog psychiatrist and the necessity of keeping the gardener on a retainer. When Jerry realizes that he has been given carte blanche for shopping in Beverly Hills, not only does he get an expensive haircut and starts wearing Armani jackets, but he manages to shop around in the bedroom of wife Barbara, daughter Jenny (Tracy Nelson), and the Whiteman maid. "Who says that clothes don't make the man?" this film seems to be saying. Pauline Kael says of *Down and Out in Beverly Hills* that it presents "a vision of the sensuousness of money" and goes on to declare, "I don't think conspicuous consumption has ever been made so integral to a way of life."[7]

Trading Places (1983) operates on the same principles (as *Down and Out in Beverly Hills* and *Beverly Hills Cop*) doubled. In it, a street-smart black conman (Eddie Murphy) and a rich yuppie Wall Street broker (Dan Aykroyd) are forced to switch lives. When the conman enters the yuppie world, his point of view triggers instant satire of that world, but when the yuppie enters the world of down-and-out everyday life, it is also his former lifestyle that, in its inappropriateness for day-to-day existence, is being caricatured. Thus no matter which world the film is focusing upon, the yuppie lifestyle is being critiqued.

Bette Midler returns as another pampered yuppie housewife who gets kidnapped by real people from a poorer world in *Ruthless People* (1986). When her rich husband refuses to ransom her, and the kidnappers actually mark her down, she feels like a designer line that has gone out of style, relegated to yuppie hell: "I've been kidnapped by K-mart!"

What all of these films have in common is the emphasis upon clothes and property as status symbols, whether it be neckties (in *Someone to Watch Over Me*) or running shoes (in *The Big Chill*) or designer scout uniforms (in *Troop Beverly Hills*) or the perfect house in *The War of the Roses* (1989), the yuppie uniform comprises the vestments of these priests of the religion of acquisition. In many of these films, the silliness of acquisitive obsession with the yuppie uniform is punctuated by viewing it from a black person's perspective. Axel Foley's hilarious manipulation of yuppie pretention in *Beverly Hills Cop*, the black con man's acquisition of the yuppie uniform in *Trading Places*, and Little Richard's manic characterization of the Beverly Hills nextdoor neighbor to the "Whitemans" in *Down and Out in Beverly Hills* are all social comments upon the racial exclusivity of the yuppie lifestyle. No film title better captures the "minorities need not apply" reality of yuppie America than that of Martin Mull's satire of suburbia, *The History of White People in America* (1987).

Another film title that has the yuppie religion of acquisition written all over it is Martin Scorsese's *Color of Money* (1986). Masquerading as a sequel to Robert Rossen's cynical film noir *The Hustler* (1961), Scorcese's eighties updating turns Fast Eddie Felson (Paul Newman) into a yuppie salesman and gives him a flaky yuppie protégé named Vincent (Tom Cruise) whom Eddie is supposedly going to teach how to acquire money ala pool hustling. In so many ways—its mentor-protégé relationship, its deification of moneymaking, its emphasis on hustling—*The Color of Money*, set in a world of eighties pool halls, is much the same film as *Wall Street*, set in the telephone hustles of the financial district. *The Color of Money*'s primary settings point to its yuppieness. No longer does Fast Eddie hang out in the dirty, smoky pool halls of the black-and-white fifties. Now, his hustles go down in the plush, full-color, pool palaces of Atlantic City to the soundtrack accompaniment of religious processionals. But the religion the soundtrack pushes is the religion of acquisition that for the eighties can be churched in a pool palace, a Wall Street office, or any shop on Rodeo Drive.

Another group of films, not satisfied with satirizing this yuppie religion of acquisition, examined the consequences of the obsession with money. In *Prizzi's Honor* (1985), money wins out over love as husband and wife hitpersons choose to accept contracts on each other rather than give up either their money or their earned status. Charlie Partanna (Jack Nicholson) is a corporate executive in one of America's most profitable companies, organized crime. Irene Walker (Kathleen Turner) is a freelance broker, a cold, accountantlike hitwoman who wears the yuppie uniform from her Excalibur car to her designer clothes to her upscale California home. The clear passion that these two feel for each other, however, cannot compete with their tenacity for holding their money and status. This yuppie irony of love turning to violence over possessions surfaces again in *The War of the Roses* (1989).

Another plot that explores the consequences arising from the religion of acquisition is the "sins of the fathers." This plot motivates action in both *The Breakfast Club* (1985) and *Say Anything* (1989), two of the more serious of the hundreds of teen problem films of the eighties. *The Breakfast Club* dissects the defenses that an encounter group of teenagers in a suburban high school, all of whom have yuppie parents more interested in money and acquisition than in them, have built up around themselves in order to cope with a world that seems to have opted for a strict caste system based upon money and style. *Say Anything* is an offbeat teenage love story in which Lloyd Dobler (John Cusack), an extremely ordinary young man, pursues and actually wins Diane Cort (Ione Skye), who is not only gorgeous but is also the class valedictorian and has won the most prestigious college scholarship in America. In its teen love plot, *Say Anything* is an utterly conventional film, but its subplot concerning Diane's nice yuppie father embezzling hundreds of thousands of dollars from his nursing home patients is what proves the major obstacle to Lloyd and Diane's love relationship.

This linking of the yuppie lifestyle and its acquisitive obsessions with violence found its terminal punctuation in two end-of-the-decade yuppie revenge tragedies, *She-Devil* (1989) and *The War of the Roses* (1989). In these black comedies, yuppies actually go to war over their most valued possessions. Ruth Patchett (Roseanne Barr), the vengeful wife in *She-Devil*, actually makes a list of the assets of her unfaithful husband's yuppie lifestyle—(1) home (2) family, (3) career, (4) freedom—and then sets out to destroy them one by one. Burning down their house and forcing him to take over maintenance of their obnoxious kids are easy, but destroying his career as an accountant and getting him thrown in jail for his creative bookkeeping take a bit more ingenuity and an actual transformation of her slovenly housewife self into an agressive young urban professional. The moral seems to be that it takes a yuppie to get revenge on another yuppie. If the characterization of Ruth Patchett is deadly serious, the characterization of romance novelist Mary Fisher (Meryl Streep) is broad yuppie caricature. Wearing her hot pink couturier dresses in her hot pink palace by the sea, where she works on her hot pink word processor and takes hot pink bubble baths, Mary Fisher is the epitome of acquisitive excess. Her sexual relationship with Ruth's crooked accountant of a husband begins when he convinces her that he can make her more money. In gratitude, she treats him to a night of erotic game playing. In this film money begets sex begets violence.

But if the workplace was the yuppie battlefield in films like *Wall Street* and *The Secret of My Success*, another war zone lay within the yuppie version of the institution of marriage with its prenuptial agreements, its disposable affections, its vicious possessiveness of the acquired things of the union such as houses, cars, and children. No other film of the eighties portrayed this particular yuppie battlefield more graphically than *The War of the Roses*. Oliver (Michael Douglas) and Barbara (Kathleen Turner) Rose start out as nice young lovers who, once they begin acquiring the accoutrements of the yuppie uniform, turn into violent hateful monsters who ultimately kill each other over possession of their house. *The War of the Roses* stands as the decades' most strident indictment of yuppie America's elevation of material possessions above humanness. In it, the objects have literally taken over; the uniform has consumed its wearer.

Yuppie Flight If the yuppie lifestyle waged war on the battlefield of the workplace and created materialistic monsters out for revenge, that lifestyle of competition, anxiety, and materialist obsession also provided the setting for an incredible number of comedies. Yuppies, it seemed, proved remarkably easy to poke fun at in broad slapstick ways. For example, the slapstick version of *Wall Street* was *Hot to Trot* (1988) that featured young Fred Chancy (Bob Goldthwait), a retarded version of Bud Fox in *Wall Street*, trying to get ahead in business by doing all of corporate raider and ruthless business dealer Sawyer's (Dabney Coleman) dirty work. Another mugging comedy, Michael Ritchie's *The Couch Trip* (1988), broadly satirizes yet another eighties yuppie aberration, media psychiatric counseling of the Dr. Joyce and Dr. Ruth sort. When Dr. George Maitlin (Charles Grodin), popular radio and TV sex tharapist, shows signs of having a nervous breakdown, the producer of his profitable radio show sees this media gold mine deteriorating. To give Maitlin some time off to rest and yet still maintain his popularity, they go looking for the worst psychiatrist in America and, by a series of mishaps come up with Jack Burns (Dan Aykroyd), an escaped mental patient from Chicago who comes to Beverly Hills and proves more sane and a better media shrink than Maitlin. The film's point is that these yuppies need counseling for their self-involved, superficial problems, and almost anyone is qualified. There are five psychiatrists in *The Couch Trip*. One is an escaped mental patient. Another is an incompetent boob. A third is in the midst of a manic depressive nervous breakdown. A fourth is a sleazy media hustler. The fifth is a blonde and beautiful piece of furniture present only for decorative purposes. The irony of this dissection of this yuppie profession is that the most successful psychiatrist of the lot is actually the mental patient.

Two other yuppie comedies, *Chances Are* (1989) and *A New Life* (1988), explore the tensions and anxieties of being in love and being a yuppie at the same time. Both emphasize that it is hard to be a yuppie in love because too many other competitive pressures demand one's attention. *Chances Are* is a militantly Wasp movie set in places like the Yale University library and an eighties Georgetown townhouse. Corinne (Cybill Shepherd) and her worshiping lawyer friend, Phillip (Ryan O'Neal), are not so young urban professionals as they were twenty years earlier in 1963 when they first came to Washington in company with Corinne's new husband who was immediately run over by a car. The whole film is about these burned-out yuppies trying to find their feelings for each other once again. *A New Life* is also about middle-aged yuppies, this time of the New York variety, trying to find themselves after the shocks of selfishness-triggered divorces and work-triggered heart attacks. These comedies emphasize the confusion of yuppies toward their own feelings and the necessity of stepping back from the pressures of the yuppie lifestyle to put the pieces of their emotional lives back together.

One place in which young urban professionals sought refuge when they fled the battlefield of their city jobs was envisioned (in films like *E.T.*, *Close Encounters of the Third Kind*, *Poltergeist*, *Gremlins*) through the eyes of Steven Spielberg. But his vision of suburbia was more family oriented than expressly defined as a refuge from yuppie angst. Others' visions of suburbia, however, were decidedly nightmarish and represented that supposed place of refuge of the urban job-stressed yuppie as just another battlefield. In *The 'burbs* (1989), a suburban neighborhood actually is turned into a battlefield. One of the suburb's residents, a middle-aged Vietnam Vet (Bruce Dern), actually defends his lawn and driveway with automatic weapons. Mild-mannered yuppie Ray Peterson (Tom Hanks) only wants to spend his one-week vacation from urban work hanging around his own house, working on the lawn, taking out the trash. His suburban neighbors, however, simply will not let him rest. *The 'burbs* is an unholy wedding of "Leave It to Beaver" and "The Munsters" set in a suburbia plagued by the traditional yuppie idiosyncracies (nosiness, racism, paranoia about property values, house pride) exaggerated beyond caricature into dementia. *The Money Pit* (1986) also indulges in this demented exaggeration of the pitfalls of yuppie ambition. In it, a suburban house actually becomes an active antagonist of two young married yuppies, a physical presence that attacks them like a wily guerrilla fighter setting snares.

When the refuge to which the yuppie escapes turns against him, the yuppie must flee further from the pressures of both the urban workplace battlefield and the hostility and paranoia of suburban life. That is exactly what Clark Griswold (Chevy Chase) and his family attempt in *National Lampoon's Vacation* (1983) and *National Lampoon's European Vacation* (1985). In each case, their own klutziness makes the American and European road a minefield, but in the third film of this series, *National Lampoon's Christmas Vacation* (1989), Clark and his clumsy family decide to stay at home in their safe suburban house, and as in *Poltergeist*, *The 'burbs*, and *The Money Pit*, the house turns on them.

One other set of films, perhaps best represented by *Risky Business* (1983), *Sixteen Candles* (1984), and *Ferris Bueller's Day Off* (1986), portray the rebellion of the eighties teen generation against their yuppie parents' attitudes and things. The major tragedies in these films are yuppie tragedies such as the repeated crashing of a father's expensive sports car. In *Risky Business*, the sports car goes into a lake; in *Ferris Bueller's Day Off*, it crashes through the back of its cantilevered garage and over the side of a cliff. With their yuppie parents too caught up in materialistic obsessions and job ambitions, these neglected teens get attention by trashing their parents' uniform and all its accessories.

When the flight to the suburbs or vacation flight to faraway places or the social flight of teenagers in the face of either their yuppie parents' neglect of them or ambitions for them fails to solve the problems of yuppie angst, some eighties yuppies actually set out on mythic quests. In *Romancing the Stone* (1984), Joan Wilder (Kathleen Turner), a New York City imprisoned, editor-harassed, romance fiction writer, longs to escape her urban professional life to experience some of the real romance that she only fantasizes for her readers. Given a chance to travel to Columbia, she hooks up with Jack Colton (Michael Douglas), a swashbuckling mental midget, and together they obliterate her memories of her nice safe yuppie existence.

After all their adventures, however, Jack comes to get her in the city and liberates her in a very eighties yuppie way. He shows up in front of her Park Avenue apartment in a sailboat on a trailer and they sail off into the middle of New York City traffic. *The Jewel of the Nile* (1985), the sequel, begins with Colton and Wilder living a jet set life of yuppie ease aboard their sailboat off the French Riviera. But Joan Wilder, the yuppie wall-flower, is bored. Their yuppie lifestyle has once again proven unsatisfying.

Albert Brooks's *Lost in America* (1985) and Martin Scorcese's *After Hours* (1985) come closer to meeting the specifications of the mythic journey. The central characters in each film, David (Albert Brooks), an extremely successful L.A. advertising executive, and Paul Hackett (Griffin Dunne), a New York word processor, are both the ultimate in yuppieness despite the huge differences in their salaries. In *Lost in America*, David is in full possession of both the yuppie uniform (the right house, the right car, the right boat) and the yuppie angst that goes with it. He longs to drop out and take to the road like the heroes of his favorite film, *Easy Rider* (1969). Obsessed with his career, his possessions, David is a constant worrier that things will not go the way he plans, and when they do not he cannot handle the trauma. David's wife, Linda (Julie Haggerty), is also a yuppie suffering in the boredom of her department store job in her glass-enclosed office, where she must conform to the expectations of everyone looking at her. When David quits his job, he persuades her to quit hers as well, and they sell off their whole yuppie uniform and set off to discover themselves in a huge motor home with a $145,000 parachute. They get as far as Las Vegas. On the first night of their mythic journey, Linda loses their whole nest egg in a casino, and they face the yuppie nightmare: being penniless without any parachute. *Lost in America*, however, never really rejects the yuppie lifestyle and the angst that accompanies it. After losing all the money, David actually longs sentimentally for the lifestyle. In a hilarious interview with an employment agent in a small desert town, David quotes his former yuppie salary with pride and the hick just shakes his head at the incomprehensible numbers.

If *Lost in America* is a rather lighthearted yuppie odyssey, Scorcese's *After Hours* is the ultimate yuppie descent into the underworld. Paul Hackett gets off work in his Manhattan office and stumbles into an invitation from a pretty stranger to visit her SoHo flat. For this timid, button-down yuppie, this is an invitation to adventure. His only money accidentally blows out the window of his cab, but being without even that most essential yuppie parachute does not deter him and he continues on where yuppies fear to tread. The result is a gritty black comedy about the way that big cities can chew up the unsuspecting. During his night of vicarious slumming, yuppie Paul is terrorized by an ensemble of all the people in New York who, for one reason or another (age, intelligence, race, politics), have been excluded from the yuppie dream.

What both *Lost in America* and *After Hours* are saying is that yuppies ought to be more satisfied with their superficial lot in life because reality, working without a net, tends to be much more dangerous. In fact, in the eighties, the essence of the yuppie ideal was the act of erecting so many nets around one's life, attaching so many parachutes to one's existence, that everyday reality actually could be closed out. Unfortunately what the yuppie could not exclude was the self. It is invariably the yuppie himself who challenges the values and uniform that he has spent his whole career acquiring.

The Yuppie Issues

If the yuppie uniform, the yuppie materialism, the yuppie obsession with success in the workplace, the yuppie exclusiveness all opened themselves to caricature, there were also serious issues that attached themselves to the yuppie lifestyle. A broad range of yuppie-specific issues arose out of yuppies' own existential questionings. Caught in the competitiveness, materialism, and superficiality of yuppieness, members began examining their problems. Rarely did the obvious alternative of rejecting the yuppie lifestyle arise as a viable option, rather yuppies attempted to accommo-date the specific problems that the lifestyle occassioned. Thus yuppieness was accepted, but not unequivocally. Issues that needed to be resolved were recognized and confronted both in society and in eighties films.

The major equivocative issues of the yuppie lifestyle were:

1. The loss of idealism and social consciousness in the face of materialism and selfishness
2. The fragility and superficiality of sexual relationships in the face of the pressures of the lifestyle
3. The redefinition of the family in terms of the lifestyle

Each issue had both a social and a personal side. For example, had the yuppie ideals eroded all possibility for social consciousness in a whole generation of young Americans and made it impossible to become in-volved in either social or personal relationships? Or had the yuppie lifestyle not only taken passion out of sex but once and for all destroyed the institution of the family? Yuppies were adamantly unwilling to give up their lifestyle, but they were also innovative in finding ways to accommo-date solutions to these problems to that lifestyle. The films of the eighties, most often in serious dramatic explorations, but frequently in witty social comedies, observed these yuppies facing up to these lifestyle issues.

Can Yuppies Have a Social Consciousness? Of course they can, but often they have to seek it out rather than having it thrust upon them, as was the case in the sixties. Roger Baron (Robert Downey, Jr.) is doing exactly that sort of seeking in *True Believer* (1989), which is an exploration of the lost idealism of the sixties generation in the cynical eighties. But in its subtext, centered in the character of Roger Baron, *True Believer* is a film of the eighties generation's need to rekindle the fire of the sixties idealism doused by Vietnam, Watergate, and the social austerity of the Reagan eighties. *True Believer* is about two generations, the hippies of the sixties and the yuppies of the eighties, both trying to find their social consciousness.

In the sixties, Eddie Dodd (James Woods) was right there when it all was happening. A radical lawyer a la William Kunstler, Eddie defended and won the biggest cases of the antiwar and civil rights movements. In the eighties, however, all that is left of Eddie Dodd's sixties idealism is his long hair. His practice is defending drug dealers, because they pay in cash that is never reported to the IRS. He is a classic burned-out case until young Roger Baron comes along. Roger comes off the University of Michigan Law Review with civil liberties stars in his eyes and a yuppie wardrobe of pinstriped suits and class ties. James Woods's Eddie Dodd burns up the screen in *True Believer*, but the film is also about the young yuppie Roger and his quest for idealism in the midst of the disengagement of his generation. Roger Baron, with all of his exterior yuppie trimmings, goes against the stereotype of the socially apathetic, cynical, money-possessed, and ideologically barren eighties generation. *True Believer* is two parallel generational quests. Pauline Kael argues that the real social theme of *True Believer* adresses the inadequacy of the American legal system in the eighties, "how legal trade-offs violate the system of justice."[8] That theme of trade-offs, plea bargains, deals, symbolically represents what is wrong with the yuppie lifestyle. In the age of Donald Trump, "the art of the deal" is the shortcut away from social engagement. What Roger tells Eddie is that you just cannot make deals about right and wrong. If your client is innocent, you ought to get him out of jail not deal for a shorter term. The yuppie generation has made too many material trade-offs and has ignored their social responsibility too long Roger Baron repeatedly emphasizes.

Can Yuppies Maintain Sexual Relationships?   That depends, but even when they manage to establish relationships it is a real struggle. Perhaps the single most frightening bugaboo of the yuppie lifestyle is the specter of involvement. That scary spook haunts the title characters in *When Harry Met Sally* (1989). They are yuppies to their eyebrows, and the film tracks their relationship over twelve years—1977 to 1989—in New York. In a sense, *When Harry Met Sally* is a social history of this single issue—fear of relationships—across the whole yuppie era.

Harry is a fast-talking, witty advertising man, while Sally (Meg Ryan) is an emotional, picky, highly ironic careerwoman. The film focuses upon their talk—in cars, in restaurants, in airplanes, in Central Park, on the telephone in separate beds—about the ironies of yuppie sexual insecurity.

Each generation has its own version of this film—in the fifties it was *Pillow Talk* (1959); in the sixties Audrey Hepburn and Albert Finney were *Two for the Road* (1967); for the seventies it was Barbara Steisand and Robert Redford analyzing *The Way We Were* (1973)—and *When Harry Met Sally* is the eighties decade's romantic chronicle. Laughing at the byzantine intricacies of yuppie insecurities, *When Harry Met Sally* is about the difference between friendship and relationship. Of course, the difference is sex. The film fixates on twelve years of a single couple trying to sort out the stresses of being friends or lovers or both. If they are representative of the yuppie generation, then it is a miracle that the concept of marriage still exists and celibacy is not universal. It is no coincidence that the funniest scene in the film is a faked orgasm. The film is about coitus interruptus, about sacrificing an inner life for an outer life of simulation and show.

St. Elmo's Fire (1985) and *About Last Night* (1986) were earlier, serious versions of *When Harry Met Sally*. These two films also agonized over what sex means and how much of a sacrifice love is among yuppies. Both films observe control groups of new college graduates trying to gain entry into the real world while simultaneously trying to cope with the attractions and demands of sexual relationships. What both films emphasize most strongly is the terrible fear of commitment.

St. Elmo's Fire provides a rogue's gallery of interpersonally screwed-up yuppies. How can these Georgetown graduates have been so successful in their studies and in their new jobs, yet be so terribly confused in their personal lives? Alex (Judd Nelson) is a ruthless congressional aide and Kirbo (Emilio Estevez) is a law student, but both, in the presence of women they are trying to impress, make complete fools of themselves. Billy (Rob Lowe), a talented sax player, has exactly the opposite problem. Though he is married and has a child, he still chases women and flees the commitment of his family. Kevin (Andrew McCarthy) is a would-be writer whose Byronic poutiness covers his insecurities. The women in this rogue's gallery are no less yuppie and no more stable than the men. Wendy (Mare Willingham) is a Washington, D.C., welfare worker, but she must be a rigorously sheltered one because she falls for the narcissistic self-absorption of Billy. Leslie (Ally Sheedy), an architect, is smart enough to see through the utterly dishonest Alex but falls for the moody Kevin. The most self-deceived is Jules (Demi Moore) whose cocaine habit turns her into "a sad and funny Yuppie slut."[9] Ultimately, *St. Elmo's Fire* is about the paralyzing insecurity that these otherwise decisive, intelligent, and successful young professionals feel in their private lives.

About Last Night is a more focused study of the chronic inability of yuppies to commit to each other. Adapted from David Mamet's play *Sexual Perversity in Chicago*, the dirtiest of the legions of dirty words in this film is "love." In *St. Elmo's Fire*, all the stilted couples were still holding out hope that they could actually find love. In *About Last Night*, as its title implies, one must apologize for even seeking it. One couple, Danny (Rob Lowe) and Debbie (Demi Moore), try to love each other but are too afraid of commitment. The other couple, Bernie (James Belushi) and Joan (Elizabeth Perkins), openly despise each other from the outset. Both are utterly cynical in their taunting of the two serious lovers and instrumental in dooming any of Danny and Debbie's sincere attempts at relationship. For *About Last Night*'s yuppies, the sex is good, the specter of commitment frightening, and the city's singles bars the barren, loveless refuges of the cynical and the insecure.

But if those two brat-pack films are the most serious anatomies of the yuppie fear of commitment, *Key Exchange* (1985) may be the most Mickey Mouse treatment of that theme. Somehow it seems inconceivable that anyone would consider making a film about the momentousness of boy and girl yuppies trying to decide whether or not to exchange keys to their apartments. Lisa (Brooke Adams) is similar to Debbie in *About Last Night* and Philip (Ben Masters) is a clone of Billy in *St. Elmo's Fire*. Both are card-carrying yuppies trying to fit what they think might possibly maybe somehow perhaps potentially be a relationship into their busy work lives and their self-absorbed conceptions of themselves. Lisa is a TV producer, who wants Philip to move in and pay attention to no one but her. Philip is a mystery writer with a flexible, self-employed work life that he enjoys employing for the self-gratification of casual sexual affairs with other women besides Lisa. Both characters' mobility of commitment is symbolized by the bicycles they ride through New York. Their yuppie lives are moving so fast that they just cannot slow down enough to touch each other.

But fear of commitment was not the only relationship problem that plagued the yuppies of the eighties. Two yuppie horror films, *Heartburn* (1986) and *Fatal Attraction* (1987), focus upon the ravages of commitment in a world where the cynical warning of *About Last Night* about the death of love has gone unheeded. Both films are about marriages that because of infidelity go violently awry. Their violence ranges from a Key lime pie in the face to a huge butcher knife in the bathroom, but both make the same point: that in a high-pressure yuppie world where the ego must be continually reinflated, monogamy is not a strong enough support structure.

In *Heartburn*, Rachel (Meryl Streep) is a magazine food writer and Mark (Jack Nicholson) is a Washington political columnist. These two yuppie characters are based on real-life yuppies Nora Ephron and Carl Bernstein, and the film is adapted from Ephron's revenge novel about their breakup. Rachel and Mark's nice yuppie marriage seems to be going along just fine. The only real problem is communicating with their Hungarian contractor who is renovating their Georgetown townhouse. The first half of the film seems to be an anatomy of a happy, healthy, yuppie marriage, but then Rachel finds out that Mark is having an affair with a Washington socialite, and suddenly it is as if their whole lives have caught cancer. Little attempt is made to salvage the marriage. Rachel flees back to the workplace, where she is consoled by her old editor. He promises her old job back and that seems to make everything fine again. The moral of the story seems to be that for a yuppie, as long as one has a good job there is really no personal betrayal or emotional hurt or psychological pain that can undermine one's basic position of strength. For the yuppie, the public life is all that counts and a fulfilling private life is never anything but a romantic illusion. David Ansen, reviewing *Heartburn*, hits the film dead center when he writes, "it's less a slice of life than a slice of lifestyle."[10] While *Heartburn* is a harmless gloss over the fragility of a yuppie marriage, *Fatal Attraction* is the ultimate yuppie marriage horror story. As in the old vampire and werewolf movies, the two central characters of *Fatal Attraction*, Dan Gallagher (Michael Douglas), a successful New York lawyer with a lovely wife and small daughter, and Alex Forest (Glenn Close), an unmarried publishing house executive, are easily recognizable contemporary types. He is a model yuppie family man. She is an intelligent, successful, liberated, extremely attractive career woman. Yet both, when crowded by circumstance, become monsters. Each is flawed; each is guilty. Both are victims. Happy in his marriage, loving toward his family, adept in his job, Dan is momentarily seduced by Alex's style and freedom. Given the seductive opportunity, he indulges himself in a one-night stand with Alex, which he immediately regrets and from which he flees the following morning. Alex, who has been exploited by men all her life, at first enjoys controlling the naïve Dan, but then breaks down: first, as someone once again a victim of sexual exploitation; and then, as a vengeful monster driven by her sexual obsession for possessing Dan.

The primary text of *Fatal Attraction* is similar to that of *Wall Street*. It is a film about the wages of opportunism, about the dangers of greed. Dan Gallagher has it all; he possesses the yuppie uniform with all its accessories, yet he grabs for more in the form of Alex Forest. The visual characterization of Alex focuses upon her long, wild tangle of curls that signal the film's controlling myth. Alex and the greedy, self-absorbed, instant gratification ideal that she represents is the Medusa curse of the yuppie lifestyle. It is tremendously attractive, but in order to attain and sustain it one must give up the self. Subtexted within this primary text is also an elaborate metaphor for the threat of AIDS in a one-night stand yuppie society. As a film about contemporary sexual responsibility, *Fatal Attraction* is like *Kramer vs. Kramer* (1979) gone berserk. Here, the yuppie family is threatened by something much more tangible, physical, than simply the ravages of divorce. Alex Forest descends upon the Gallaghers like a plague.

One other sociological horror film, like *Heartburn* and *Fatal Attraction*, showed sexuality as a threat to the stability of the yuppie family. *The Good*

Mother (1989) follows in the footsteps of *Kramer vs. Kramer* and *Ordinary People* (1980) in exploring the topic of family breakup. In *Kramer vs. Kramer*, the young son of a soon-to-be divorced, single-parent father goes to the bathroom in the middle of the night and meets a naked lady (Terri Garr) in the hallway. It is a curious hilarious confrontation played strictly for laughs. In the dramatic custody trial that provides *Kramer vs. Kramer*'s climax, no mention is ever made of sleepover girl friends or the psychological problems of the young boy resulting from his comic confrontation with nocturnal nudity. No one seems to care if a young boy accidentally saw a naked lady. But what if a young girl sees her divorced, single-parent mother's sleepover boy friend walking around their Harvard Square flat in the nude? No matter that the young girl has been encouraged to read books about the facts of life. No matter that sexual anatomy has been openly discussed in her day-care classes. Despite all of these circumstances, a young girl confronting a naked man is wrong, unhealthy, and, in fact, actionable in a court of law, grounds for a charge of maternal incompetence in a child custody suit. That change in gender and sexual consciousness from *Kramer vs. Kramer* is the crux of *The Good Mother* and attests to the tenacity of the sexual double standard in American life.

The Good Mother explores the insidious ways that the sexual double standard places strictures upon female independence. Anna Dunlop's (Diane Keaton) life is assaulted and emptied because she wants to live a life of powerful maternal love simultaneously with a passionate and equally fulfilling sexual awakening. She lives for her daughter, Molly, and comes alive with her lover, Leo (Liam Neeson), but the male protectiveness of society refuses to grant her both lives. In fact, her former husband, her patriarchal lawyer, and the male judge humiliate, intimidate, and frustrate her into turning her whole life into a lie. The child simply becomes another material object, a part of the yuppie uniform, that has to be divided upon divorce. Though *The War of the Roses* is savage and violent in a black comic way, *The Good Mother* is much more violent in its utter dehumanization of both Anna and her child, Molly, by a patriarchal male society. *The Good Mother* is not just a film about the breakup of a yuppie family but a direct and forceful feminist political statement as well. Anna is punished because she dares to be open about her sexuality. It represents a world in which a woman cannot be both a mother and herself, a world in which divorce (which should set one free) is actually a different sort of imprisonment, a world in which patriarchy and sexual politics overrule maternal love and personal selfhood.

Like so many other aspects of the yuppie lifestyle as portrayed in the films of the eighties, the issue of whether that fast-paced, high-pressure, materially obsessed public lifestyle allows for a private life of human relationship was plagued by self-doubts, guilts, and indecisiveness. Within both love relationships and family relationships, doubt was consistently raised as to the yuppie's ability to redirect his or her energies from the public lifestyle to the private life.

Can Yuppies Have Babies? Eventually they can, after they get the job and acquire the uniform and manage to overcome their fear of commitment. If 1987 was the year of the Vietnam War films, and 1984 was the year of the farm crisis films, then 1987–88 was certainly the year of the yuppie baby, both in American society and in films. The National Center for Health in 1988 released statistics indicating that 3.8 million babies were born in 1987, the largest number of births since 1964. "Parents are facing the biological clock," National Institute of Child Health population analyst Arthur Campbell speculated. But if there was a significant baby boom in society, there was also one in the films of the last three years of the decade. From *Raising Arizona* (1987) to *Baby Boom* (1987) to *Made in Heaven* (1987) to *Three Men and a Baby* (1987) to *She's Having a Baby* (1987) to *For Keeps* (1988) to *Big Business* (1988) to *Look Who's Talking* (1989), babies proved the most popular props available. In *Raising Arizona*, a baby strapped in a car seat gets left on the roof of a car and ends up on the center line of a highway; in *Baby Boom*, a baby gets checked in a restaurant coatroom; in *Three Men and a Baby*, a baby is backpacked up the sides of skyscrapers; in *Big Business*, two sets of twins are mixed up in the hospital; and in *Look Who's Talking*, a baby starts talking just before conception, complains all through his nine months in the womb, and comes out commenting wryly on his world. In these films, the babies are either props (as in *Raising Arizona* and *Three Men and a Baby*) or catalysts for grown-up plots (as in *She's Having a Baby*, *For Keeps*, *Made in Heaven*, and *Big Business*). Some of these films, however, actually explore the impact that a baby has upon that always vulnerable yuppie lifestyle.

In *Baby Boom*, J. C. Wiatt (Diane Keaton) is a Madison Avenue genius with a Yale business degree, a Harvard MBA, a six-figure salary, a corner office, and a Wall Street broker live-in who specializes in making love in four minutes so as not to interrupt her work schedule. J. C. thrives on sixty-hour weeks, which has earned her the title "The Tiger Lady" for her tenacity on the job. She is a yuppie career woman poster girl when suddenly she inherits baby Elizabeth. *Baby Boom* is a combination of *Mr. Mom* (1983), *9 to 5* (1980), and *The Money Pit* (1986). J. C. first has to learn to be a mother, then fight her patronizing male bosses because she is being a mother, then rebuild an old farmhouse in order to continue being a mother. But more interesting than anything else in the film is its constant parody of the yuppie lifestyle. *Baby Boom* is a comic checklist film that touches on every problem that a yuppie working mother could possibly confront. It asserts that an urban career woman cannot be a mother as well. J. C. must retreat to the country in order to have her baby and her career too.

Three Men and a Baby takes a similar approach to critiquing the yuppie lifestyle. The credits roll over a montage of three bachelors alternately decorating their Park Avenue apartment and working at their urban professions as an architect, an actor and a cartoonist. Thus even before the film begins, the focus is upon their jobs and their uniforms. In one brief moment, however, a baby in a basket is left on their doorstep, and they are changed from the swinging yuppies of the year to just three sorry mothers. Actually this is the same film as Baby Boom only tripled. Again, the major satiric target is the yuppie lifestyle that when intruded upon immediately shows itself to be vulnerable. When something human, like a baby or a love relationship, interrupts its tight scheduling, the yuppie lifestyle collapses like a house of cards.

Of all these yuppie baby films, the most serious is Lawrence Kasdan's *Immediate Family* (1989). It is a family melodrama, a weepy, made specifically for the yuppie eighties. *Kramer vs. Kramer* was really the first family melodrama directed at the yuppie population, but by 1987 the yuppies had their own TV show, "thirtysomething." *Immediate Family* could be an ongoing episode on "thirtysomething." It is about the frustrations of infertility and the agonies of adoption. Julie (Glenn Close) and Michael (James Woods) Spector cannot have a child no matter how hard they try. In desperation, they turn to a lawyer who specializes in open adoptions. This is a scenario in which the adopting parents meet and support the pregnant mother before the to-be-adopted child is born. This film slowly examines the emotions of all four of the members of this urban baby's immediate family.

One afternoon, Julie Spector gets a long-distance call from a young woman named Lucy (Mary Stuart Masterson). Julie sits in her Early American decorated, bay-windowed house overlooking the ocean in Seattle while Lucy talks from a phone booth next to the one-pump gas station on a paint-peeling crossroads of East Nowhere, Ohio, while her boyfriend Sam (Kevin Dillon), in leather jacket and boots, smokes cigarettes and nervously fingers his dog collar.

Immediate Family takes a completely different view of yuppiedom than all of these other films. Julie and Michael Spector are presented as ordinary people who, granted, have bought into a particular lifestyle, but who nevertheless have remained human, capable of relationship and commitment, able to balance their public yuppie lives with their private emotional needs. They have looked at the holes in their yuppie lifestyle and are going about doing something to fill them.

One of the final yuppie baby films of the eighties, *Look Who's Talking* (1989), in its central point of view, makes one of the funniest yet most universal comments upon not only the yuppie lifestyle but all of these other yuppie films. *Look Who's Talking* is a continuously self-reflexive film in which a single observer inside the film comments ironically, comically, upon the events and the world of the film. That observer just happens to be a baby and the self-reflexiveness of his critique of the eighties world into which he is born could serve as a metaphor for what is happening in every yuppie film of the decade. Consistently this competitive materialist lifestyle is questioned and critiqued. Every yuppie film, whether a social drama like *Wall Street*, a weepy like *Immediate Family*, a political film like *True Believer*, or one of the hundreds of yuppie comedies, turned on the idea that yuppies were finding out that though they made a lot of money and owned a lot of nice things, they were still coming up empty-handed as human beings.

9

Film in the Holograph
of New History

THE JANUARY 1990 cover of *Mother Jones* magazine scoffs at "HOLLYWOOD'S 'FRAIDY '80'S" and charges:

> American movies are still reaping the harvest of Ronald Reagan's reign of mediocrity and escapism. . . . In the Eighties, the conventional critical wisdom was that American movies no longer reflect real life, that they offer only teen comedy, derring-do, gross-out horror, and special effects—in a word, escape. And it's true that American movies are largely about escape. But that's what American public life has been all about too—form and symbol over feeling and substance.[1]

In one obvious sense, this evaluation of eighties film history is true. The films were heavily influenced by the neoconservatizing of America that Ronald Reagan's eight years of media manipulation in office masterfully accomplished. But in another sense, this evaluation is dead wrong because it overlooks both the self-reflexive nature of eighties film and the consistent subtextualization that gave movies a constant double edge, enabled them to offer the comedy, the derring-do, the special effects while at the same time allowing them to critique both their own excesses and the excesses of the society through subtexted themes and controlling metaphors, what eighties moviemakers came to call "through lines."

Oliver Stone, perhaps the most prominent anti-Reaganite, culturally critical, mainstream director of the eighties, defined his reaction to the first five years of the decade when he said: "The 1980's is the era of phony endings. It's time to cycle a change."[2] And he proved, in the last five years of the decade, in *Salvador*, in *Platoon*, in *Wall Street* and *Talk Radio* and *Born on the Fourth of July*, one of the most adamant and unrelenting cultural critics of his time. But especially in the second half of the decade, Stone was not alone in cycling change. Not only other directors but all across the film industry, moviemakers became more rigorous not only in representing sociohistorical reality truthfully but also in subtextually critiquing the cultural reactions to the major concerns of eighties society.

The films of the eighties portrayed a post–Vietnam War world attempting to disengage from its recent troubled past while at the same time attempting to overcome its own cynicism and find some hope for the future. Besides the shadow of Vietnam, two other major threats overshadowed the eighties decade: the forty-year-old threat of nuclear holocaust and the stepped-up threat of global terrorist guerrilla war. In the eighties, American films consistently explored these international issues, but they also examined indigenous social issues, such as the farm crisis, the new racism, the society's expanding gender consciousness, and the rise of the yuppie materialist ethic. Other equally important domestic and international issues, such as the old racism—as explored in *Ragtime* (1981), *A Soldier's Story* (1984), *A Passage to India* (1984), *Betrayed* (1988), *Alien Nation* (1988), *Mississippi Burning* (1989), *Who Framed Roger Rabbit?* (1989), *Do the Right Thing* (1989)—or apartheid—as in *Cry Freedom* (1987), *A Dry White Season* (1989), and even *Lethal Weapon II* (1989)—or the corruption and violence beneath the surface of small-town American life—as in *Body Heat* (1981), *Gremlins* (1984), *Blood Simple* (1984), *Witness* (1985), *At Close Range* (1986), *Blue Velvet* (1986), *Betrayed* (1988)—were also examined in clusters of eighties films. As Graeme Turner wrote: "Film is a social practice for its makers and its audience; in its narratives and meanings we can locate evidence of ways in which our culture makes sense of itself."[3] Dominick LaCapra, discussing history, whereas Turner is writing about film, iterates the same audience need: "the need for reconstructing a historical consciousness that integrates the present with the past is much more than the professional interest of the historian. It is rooted in the general need of our time."[4]

Social history is so textually complex that professional historians cannot be its sole compilers, commentators, critics. All manner of historians from the academy to the media to the pulpit to the Congress to the general store participate in the generation of this New Historicism, and the techniques of history and criticism and politics and economics and sociology and philosophy can all contribute to the creation of the holograph of social history.

In *The Last Tycoon*, F. Scott Fitzgerald's last and unfinished novel about Hollywood and the magic of making movies, Monroe Stahr, the moviemaker hero, says: "Our condition is that we have to take people's own favorite folklore and dress it up and give it back to them."[5] As early as the thirties, Fitzgerald was fully aware of the sociohistorical mission of the movies, and each period in film history since that time has faced up to that mission according to the historical dictates of the period. Hollywood is not simply responsive to the events of social history, but it has the New Historicist ability to analyze and critique that history as well as simply present it. Film is one layer in the holograph of history that contributes to the substance and motion of the overall figure. Film is one of the important subtexts that helps form the metatext of New History.

Notes   Index

Notes

Preface

1. James Greenburg, "Bringing It All Back Home," *American Film* (September 1988): 54.

2. Quoted by Jack Mathews, "Woods, European Superstar," *USA Today*, 20 May 1985.

3. Graeme Turner, *Film as Social Practice* (London and New York: Routledge, 1988), xiv.

4. Quoted by Mike Clark in "Expect Films with a Touch of Class," *USA Today*, 26 August 1984.

5. Thomas Myers, *Walking Point: American Narratives of Vietnam* (New York and Oxford: Oxford University Press, 1988), 7.

6. Edward Pechter, "The New Historicism and Its Discontents: Politicizing Renaissance Drama," *PMLA* 102, no. 3 (May 1987): 292.

7. Dominick LaCapra, *History and Criticism* (Ithaca, N.Y.: Cornell University Press, 1985), 21.

8. LaCapra, *History and Criticism*, 43.

1. The Holograph of History

1. Hayden White, *Tropics of Discourse: Essays in Cultural Criticism* (Baltimore: Johns Hopkins University Press, 1978), 48.

2. Larry Engelmann, "McHistory" (Paper delivered at the National Conference on the Teaching of the Vietnam War, Washington, D.C., April 1988).

3. McDonald's "Big Mac" television commercial, 1982–84.

4. Michael Herr, *Dispatches* (New York: Knopf, 1977), 13.

5. Todd Gitlin, "Hip Deep in Post-Modernism," *New York Times Book Review*, 4 September 1988.

6. White, *Tropics of Discourse*, 42–43.

7. White, *Tropics of Discourse*, 50.

8. White, *Tropics of Discourse*, 50.

9. Dominick LaCapra, *History and Criticism* (Ithaca, N.Y.: Cornell University Press, 1985), 9–10.

10. Dominick LaCapra, *Rethinking Intellectual History: Texts, Contexts, Language* (Ithaca, N.Y.: Cornell University Press, 1983), 15.

11. LaCapra, *History and Criticism*, 18.

12. LaCapra, *History and Criticism*, 11.

13. LaCapra, *Rethinking Intellectual History*, 14.

14. LaCapra, *History and Criticism*, 83.

15. LaCapra, *History and Criticism*, 25.

16. LaCapra, *History and Criticism*, 35.

17. White, *Tropics of Discourse*, 2.

18. White, *Tropics of Discourse*, 21.

19. White, *Tropics of Discourse*, 29.

20. White, *Tropics of Discourse*, 41.

21. White, *Tropics of Discourse*, 41.

22. LaCapra, *Rethinking Intellectual History*, 16.

23. Hayden White, *Metahistory* (Baltimore: Johns Hopkins University Press, 1973), ix.

24. White, *Metahistory*, 6–7.

25. White, *Metahistory*, 17–18.

26. White, *Metahistory*, 24.

27. LaCapra, *History and Criticism*, 19.

28. LaCapra, *History and Criticism*, 80.

29. Haskell Wexler, "Dialogue on Film," *American Film* (October 1988): 19.

30. "Interview with Richard Lester," *Los Angeles Times*, 30 October 1983, Calendar, 25.

31. Peter Boyle, "Midsection: '68/'88," *Film Comment* (August 1988): 61.

32. James Monaco, "Into the Nineties," *American Film* (January 1989): 24.

33. David Puttnam, "Puttnam's New Mission," *American Film* (October 1986): 45.

34. Terence Davies interviewed by Harlan Kennedy, "Familiar Haunts," *Film Comment* (October 1988): 18.

35. Gavin Smith, "'Mississippi' Gambler," *Film Comment* (December 1988): 30.

36. Quoted by Gavin Smith, "'Mississippi' Gambler," 30.

37. Quoted by Thulani Davis, "Civil Rights and Wrongs," *American Film* (December 1988): 36.

38. Quoted by Davis, "Civil Rights and Wrongs," 36.

39. Marc Cooper, "Up in Smoke," *American Film* (March 1987): 55.

40. William J. Palmer. *The Films of the Seventies: A Social History* (Metuchen, N.J.: Scarecrow Press, 1987), 100.

41. Ian Jarvie, *Movies and Society* (New York: Basic Books, 1970), 137–38.

2. The Vietnam War as Film Text

1. The month of April 1988 is a good example of this increased fascination with the Vietnam War in the college classroom. Three full conferences—the American Studies Symposium at Purdue University, the Wisconsin Conference on the Teaching of History at the University of Wisconsin Centers, Waukeesha, and a national Conference on the Teaching of the Vietnam War sponsored by the Indochina Institute of George Mason University in Washington, D.C.—were held that focused exclusively upon the Vietnam War.

2. In *Rethinking Intellectual History* (Ithaca, N.Y.: Cornell University Press, 1983), Dominick LaCapra writes: "To refer to social or individual life as a text (or as 'textualized') is in an obvious sense to employ a metaphor. But the metaphor is not a 'mere' metaphor. It combines the polemical vehemence of assertion with the critical distance that counteracts dogmatism. The reliance on a metaphor to provide a way of seeing problems nonetheless involves

linguistic inflation. If this risk comes with the opportunity to understand problems better than in alternative perspectives—for example, the one that takes 'reality' or 'context' as an unproblematic ground or gold standard—then the risk is well worth taking. But the metaphor of textuality is in no sense perfect, even as a medium for contesting the standard dichotomy between metaphor and its opposites (the literal, the conceptual, the serious, and so forth)" (19).

3. William Duiker, author of *The Communist Road to Power in Vietnam* (Boulder, Colo.: Westview Press, 1981) presented the keynote address at the Wisconsin Conference on the Teaching of History (April 1988) and, at the national Conference on the Teaching of the Vietnam War in Washington, D.C. (April 1988), a similar paper on the need to study the Vietnamese side of the war in order to escape America's thus far ethnocentric/Amerocentric approach to the study of the war.

4. See Al Santoli, *Everything We Had* (New York: Random House, 1981) and *To Bear Any Burden* (New York: Random House, 1986); Mark Baker, *Nam: The Vietnam War in the Words of the Soldiers Who Fought It There* (New York: Morrow, 1981); Wallace Terry, *Bloods: An Oral History of the Vietnam War by Black Veterans* (New York: Random House, 1984).

5. Samuel Popkin, "A Sample Course and Its Rationale" (Paper delivered to the Conference on the Teaching of the Vietnam War, Washington, D.C., April 1988).

6. Though none establishes such a "contextualist" film history for the Vietnam War films, three other books survey either partially or in full the films of this subgenre. Robin Wood's *Hollywood from Vietnam to Reagan* (New York: Columbia University Press, 1986) discusses the films of the first phase as does my own *Films of the Seventies: A Social History* (Metuchen, N.J.: Scarecrow Press, 1987). Paul Monaco's *Ribbons in Time: Movies and Society Since 1945* (Bloomington: Indiana University Press, 1988) deals with the kinds of theoretical relationships between movies and society that *The Films of the Seventies: A Social History* also explored. Albert Auster and Leonard Quart, *How the War Was Remembered: Hollywood and Vietnam* (New York: Praeger, 1988) most closely parallels the material in this book.

7. Greil Marcus, "Journey up the River: An Interview with Francis Coppola," *Rolling Stone*, 1 November 1979.

8. Jerrold Stahr, "Teaching the Vietnam War: Issues and Methodology" (Paper delivered to Conference on the Teaching of the Vietnam War, Washington, D.C., April 1988).

9. Larry Engelmann, "Teaching McHistory" (Paper delivered to Conference on the Teaching of the Vietnam War, Washington, D.C., April 1988).

10. Peter Blauner in *New York*, 8 December 1986, writes that in *Platoon* Oliver Stone "has gone after a lean, terrifyingly real vision of war, one that audiences will find hard to shake." Stanley Kauffman (*New Republic*, 19 January 1987) writes: "Stone has written and directed a war film so strikingly genuine that we never bother to think that it's better than most war films." Pauline Kael, whose mixed review in *New Yorker*, 12 January 1987, rightly sees the *Platoon* script as a heavy-handed morality play, also acknowledges that while the film "doesn't deal with what the war was about—it's conceived strictly in terms of what these American infantrymen go through." David Denby in *New York*, 15 December 1986, praises *Platoon* because "it captures, with an

enduring power, and from the inside, what the commonplace horror of the conflict felt like."

11. Stanley Kauffman in "An American Tragedy" in *New Republic*, 19 January 1987, makes this same point as he writes: "The action is not used as a ground for a story, conventional or otherwise. It is the experience of the war that this film wants primarily to give us, not drama" (24).

12. In Palmer, *The Films of the Seventies: A Social History*, an extended comparison of Coppola's *Apocalypse Now* with Melville's *Moby Dick* was made.

13. Pauline Kael (*New Yorker*, 12 January 1987) notes how the protagonist of *Platoon*, Chris Taylor, "arrives in the confusion of Vietnam" and suffers from "initial disorientation," but she quickly drops this theme for a more political and equally valid theme: "The film is about victimizing ourselves as well as others; it's about shame. That's the only way in which it's political." Please compare Kael's definition of this theme of shame with the discussion of the final scene of *Platoon* herein, which deals with the irony of Americans killing each other rather than the enemy. David Denby (*New York*, 15 December 1986) also notes that "Stone has told the familiar young soldier's story without copping out on the ineradicable bitterness and confusion of the Vietnam War."

14. In Palmer, *The Films of the Seventies: A Social History*, the long discussion of Roman Polanski's *Chinatown* contains a reading of that brilliant film as metaphoric Vietnam War film.

15. Philip Caputo, *A Rumor of War* (New York: Ballantine, 1978), writes: "A phosphorus grenade bursts in a cloud of thick, white smoke, and a hut begins to burn. Another goes up. In minutes, the entire hamlet is in flames, the thatch and bamboo crackling like small arms fire. . . .

"'They've gone nuts, skipper,' Tester says. 'They're shooting the whole place up. Christ, they're killing the animals.'

"He and Peterson try to stop the destruction, but it is no use. . . . The hamlet which is marked on our maps as Giao-Tri 3 no longer exists. All that remains are piles of smoldering ash and a few charred poles still standing. . . . We are learning to hate" (103–4).

16. J. Hoberman, "America Dearest," *American Film* (May 1988): 39.

17. Susan Linfield (interviewer), "The Gospel According to Matthew," *American Film* (October 1987): 22.

18. Penelope Gilliatt, "Heavy Metal," *American Film* (September 1987): 21.

19. Quoted by Gilliatt, 22.

20. Stanley Kauffman in "Blank Cartridge," *New Republic*, 27 July 1987, 29, disagrees: "Part One could be dropped completely without markedly damaging the rest. The killings in the boot camp toilet have nothing to do with what follows."

21. Caputo, *A Rumor of War*, 255.

22. Michael Herr, *Dispatches* (New York: Knopf, 1977).

23. Thomas Myers, *Walking Point: American Narratives of Vietnam* (New York: Oxford University Press, 1988).

24. Gustav Hasford, *The Short Timers* (New York: Bantam, 1980).

25. Palmer, *The Films of the Seventies: A Social History*, 34–38.

26. Gilliatt, "Heavy Metal," 22.

27. Hoberman, "America Dearest," 44.

28. Pauline Kael, "No Shelter," *New Yorker*, 7 September 1987, 97.

29. Paramount Pictures Corporation, *Hamburger Hill: Handbook of Produc-*

tion Information.

30. Kael, "No Shelter," 97.

31. This refers to the chapter title "The Forgotten Vietnam War Film," in Palmer, *The Films of the Seventies: A Social History.*

32. William Duiker, at Conference on the Teaching of the Vietnam War, Washington, D.C., April 1988.

33. Hoberman, "America Dearest," 45. In this essay Hoberman makes a number of other assertions that are only partially true. He writes that the "defusing of blame is a key aspect of the new Vietnam films." He also writes that the films make "no attempt to re-create the racial imbalance of the military." In *Platoon, Full Metal Jacket, Hamburger Hill,* and *Off Limits* as well as in *Apocalypse Now* nine years earlier, large numbers of blacks are in evidence. Hoberman is wrong in stating that there was no consciousness of the presence of blacks in Vietnam in these films, but he is correct in his assertion that black consciousness from the point of view of black soldiers is rarely offered, with the definite exception of *Hamburger Hill.*

34. F. Scott Fitzgerald, *The Great Gatsby,* the last page.

3. The "Coming Home" Films

1. In Palmer, *The Films of the Seventies: A Social History,* full discussions of all of these films and of the "coming home" theme as it took form in this first phase can be found in chap. 6, "The Vietnam War Films."

2. Charles Figley and Seymour Levantman, eds., *Strangers At Home: Vietnam Veterans since the War* (New York: Praeger, 1980). In his preface, Figley writes that "Vietnam veterans are not tolerating any more negative stereotypes and mistreatment in the press, but the press is treating the Vietnam vet differently, too" (x). When Figley wrote that in 1980, his judgment was accurate, but what he did not foresee was the manner in which in the next five years the media stereotyping of the Vietnam vet would shift to the opposite extreme, to the mythicization of a comic book supervet like Rambo.

3. Thomas Myers, *Walking Point: American Narratives of Vietnam* (New York: Oxford University Press, 1988), 57–69, and John Hellmann, *American Myth and the Legacy of Vietnam* (New York: Columbia University Press, 1986). Philip Beidler, *American Literature and the Experience of Vietnam* (Athens: University of Georgia Press, 1982) also invokes the intertextuality of *Moby Dick* in relation to the Vietnam War literature extant when his book was written.

4. In Palmer, *The Films of the Seventies: A Social History,* chap. 8, "Superimposed Realities: The Visual/Verbal Themes in *Apocalypse Now*," presents an intertextual reading of that film and *Moby Dick.*

5. See Palmer, *The Films of the Seventies: A Social History,* chap. 5, "*Chinatown*: A World of Inscrutable Reality."

6. Pauline Kael, "As Swift as the Buzzard Flies," *New Yorker,* 29 September 1980.

7. Silvio Gaggi, "Rush's *The Stunt Man*: Politics, Metaphysics, and Psychoanalysis," *Post Script: Essays in Film and the Humanities,* 4 no. 1 (Fall 1984): 18–34.

8. Michael Herr, *Dispatches* (New York: Knopf, 1977), 188.

9. See the quotation from *Full Metal Jacket* in chap. 2 of this book. The "Vietnam: The Movie" metaphor is, perhaps, first offered by Julian Smith in *Looking Away: Hollywood and Vietnam* (New York: Charles Scribner's Sons, 1975) and is also quoted in chap. 1 of this book.

10. Joseph Conrad, *Lord Jim* (New York: W. W. Norton, 1968), 130.

11. F. Scott Fitzgerald, *The Great Gatsby* (New York: Charles Scribner's Sons, 1925), 182.

12. Pete Hamill, "Vietnam, Vietnam," *Atlantic* (October 1985): 50.

13. Frank Friedel, Preface, in Figley and Levantman, *Strangers at Home*, vii.

14. Clark Smith, "Oral History and 'Therapy': Combatants Accounts of the Vietnam War," in Figley and Levantman, *Strangers at Home*, 15.

15. John P. Wilson, "Conflict, Stress, and Growth: The Effects of War on Psychosocial Development Among Vietnam Veterans," in Figley and Levantman, *Strangers at Home*, 126.

16. Hamill, "Vietnam, Vietnam," 51.

17. Hamill, "Vietnam, Vietnam," 55.

18. This concept of the "corporate villain" is fully defined in chap. 2, "Movie Villains: The Seventies Look," in Palmer, *The Films of the Seventies: A Social History*.

19. As the keynote speaker at the Wisconsin Conference on the Teaching of History at Waukesha, Wisconsin, in April 1988, George McGovern told this story of how LBJ in 1965 ran McGovern out of the Oval Office yelling "I'm sick of you historians from the hill telling me to pay attention to history. I don't give a damn about history!" McGovern smugly commented that perhaps this is exactly what LBJ should have been paying attention to.

20. Martha Bayles, "The Road to *Rambo III*: Hollywood's Visions of Vietnam," *New Republic*, 18 July 1988, presents an excellent survey of the political themes of most of the Vietnam War films since *The Green Berets*.

21. Leo Cawley, "Refighting the War: Why the Movies Are in Vietnam," *Village Voice*, 8 September 1987.

22. J. Hoberman, "The Fascist Guns in the West," *American Film* (March 1986): 44.

23. William Duiker, author of *The Communist Road to Power in Vietnam*, speaking at both the Wisconsin Conference on the Teaching of History and the national Conference on the Teaching of the Vietnam War held at Waukesha, Wisconsin, and Washington, D.C., respectively, in April of 1988, became the major proponent for changing this Amerocentric and racist media and scholarly attitude toward the Vietnam War.

24. About this scene, Jack Kroll (*Newsweek*, 5 November 1984) writes: "In one ambiguous, disturbing scene, Schanberg, safe at home in New York, puts a ravishing Puccini aria on his stereo while watching videotapes of Cambodian atrocities . . . wallowing in splendid masochism." Jack Matthews (*USA Today*, 8 November 1984) agrees as he describes the films' "excessive urge to demonstrate Schanberg's guilt, once he's comfortably home, takes it to the brink of melodrama." These negative views of this scene do not take into account the film's need to link the personal survivor guilt of Schanberg to the national guilt that is also emphasized in every major stateside scene in the film.

25. Pauline Kael prefaces her review of *Uncommon Valor* (*New Yorker*, 23 January 1984) with just this sort of meditation upon racism in the Vietnam

War films as well as other American films in which "white heroes slaughter people of color in quantity, either affectlessly or triumphantly."

26. These two other forms of eighties racism will be discussed in later chapters.

27. Tim O'Brien, "The Violent Vet," *Esquire* (December 1979), 96. O'Brien goes on to write that "these are message movies, more or less, and at least one message comes through loud and clear: Victim or villain, the Vietnam vet is a basket case. 'Talk about an image problem,' sighs Robert Muller, a former Marine Corps. officer, now a lawyer and veterans 'activist.' If you fought in Nam, you're either a weirdo or a psychopath.'" O'Brien goes on: "If the movie version is cartoonish and ill drawn, what would contribute a more accurate likeness? Who is the 'typical' Vietnam veteran? What are his problems? How is he adjusting to peacetime? Is he really suicidal?" If the movies of the eighties are any indication, this negative stereotype of the 'typical' Vietnam vet as a violent time bomb in American society has changed in only one way. Nowadays, more often than not, that time bomb is not a criminal, he is a cop.

28. O'Brien, "The Violent Vet," 100.

4. The Terrorism Film Texts

1. Palmer, *The Films of the Seventies: A Social History*, see chap. 2.

2. Monica Collins and Jack Curry, "Terrorists: Hollywood's New Heavies," *USA Today*, 7 February 1986, focuses upon the fictional made-for-TV movie *Under Siege* but briefly mentions a number of terrorist-as-villain films such as *Commando* (1985), *Iron Eagle* (1986), *Invasion U.S.A* (1986), and *Delta Force* (1986). The one useful concept that this essay defines is that of the "generic terrorists" whose anti-USA political stances are vehement and violent, but whose homeland and cause are never made clear.

3. Thomas L. Friedman, "What's behind Mideast Terrorism?" *New York Times*, 12 December 1983.

4. L. A. Jolidon, "Guerrilla Leader Survives Blast: Who Set Explosion a Mystery," *USA Today*, 1 June 1984.

5. "Terrorism," Gannett News Service, 1 January 1989.

6. "Hamadi didn't kill driver, witness says," Associated Press (28 September 1988).

7. "Report: CIA Believes Iran Hired Bombers," Gannett News Service, quoted from *Washington Post*, 15 April 1989.

8. "Iran Calls for Terror against Americans," Gannett News Service, 7 May 1989.

9. The term *spectaculars* and the Jenkins and Joyal quotes are from "Terrorism," Gannett News Service, 1 January 1989.

10. Joan Borsten, "Debate Rages in Israel over 'Drummer Girl' Filming," *Los Angeles Times*, 6 November 1983.

11. Peter Osnos, London bureau chief of the *Washington Post*, quoted by Borsten.

12. John Powers, "Alex Cox," *American Film* (November 1986), 35.

13. Michael Herr, *Dispatches* (New York: Knopf, 1977), 66.

14. Elizabeth Mehren, "All's Chic in Love and War," *Los Angeles Times*, 20 November 1983.

15. Richard Bernstein, "Controversial *Under Fire* Puts Journalistic Ethics in Limelight," *New York Times*, 4 November 1983.

16. Palmer, *The Films of the Seventies: A Social History*, 48–49.

17. Herr, *Dispatches*, 17.

18. David Puttnam, "Dialogue on Film," *American Film*, November 1984, 36.

19. My thanks to Professor S. F. D. Hughes of Purdue University for his research into the factual events portrayed in *The Year of Living Dangerously* as presented in his review of the film for the Cinema Now series.

20. Associated Press, 5 September 1989.

21. Associated Press, 10 September 1989.

22. Associated Press, 15 September 1989.

23. For this discussion of *The Formula* see *The Films of the Seventies: A Social History*, 47–49.

24. Alexander Cockburn (interviewer), "Oliver Stone Takes Stock" (December 1987), 24.

25. Kevin Thomas, "A Deluge of Movie Violence," *Los Angeles Times Calendar*, 20 January 1984.

26. *Newsweek*, 27 April 1987, as quoted in the "Production Notes" to *Colors*, Orion Pictures, 1988.

27. Michael Schiffer, screenwriter of *Colors*, quoted in "Production Notes."

5. The Nuclear War Film Texts

1. Tim O'Brien, *The Nuclear Age* (New York: Knopf, 1985), 281.

2. Don DeLillo, *End Zone* (Boston: Houghton, Mifflin, 1972), 20-21.

3. *American Film* (October 1982): 57–69.

4. Quoted in Clarke Taylor, "Freeze Heats up Hollywood," *American Film* (October 1982): 58.

5. Taylor, "Freeze Heats up Hollywood," 58.

6. Taylor, "Freeze Heats up Hollywood," 58.

7. Stephen Farber, "The End of the World, Take 1." *American Film* (October 1982): 61.

8. Quoted in Farber, "End of the World," 63.

9. Quoted in Alexander Cockburn, "The Selling of the Pentagon," *American Film* (June 1986): 32.

10. Quoted in Cockburn, "Selling of the Pentagon," 31.

11. Pauline Kael, "Fun Machines," *New Yorker*, 30 May 1983, 89.

12. Quoted by Richard Schickel in "Help! They're Back!" *Time*, 28 July 1986.

13. Quoted in Michael Burkett, "Making Silkwood," *Orange County Register*, 24 January 1984.

14. Interview with Meryl Streep, *Family Weekly*, 15 January 1984.

15. Quoted by Burkett.

16. Jim Runnels, "Government was after Silkwood, investigation says," *Orlando Sentinel*, 10 January 1984.

17. Reed Irvine, "*Silkwood*: Political Message Overrides Facts," *Washington Post*, 27 December 1983.

18. Michael Burkett, "Nichols' even-handedness enhances his triumph in "Silkwood," *Orange County Register*, 1 January 1984.

19. Deborah Caulfield, "Real People," *Los Angeles Times*, 18 December 1983, Calendar.

20. Pauline Kael, *New Yorker*, 18 December 1983: 99.

21. Sheila Benson, "On the Day after *The Day After*," *Los Angeles Times*, 20 November 1983.

22. Barry Koltnow, "The Film: Not for Children, but a Must-See for Parents," *Orange County Register*, 20 November 1983.

23. Quoted by Stephen Farber, "The End of the World, Take 1," *American Film* (October 1982): 63.

24. Marcel Ophuls, "After *The Day After*," *American Film* (November 1984): 34.

25. David Langness quoted by Mary Taugher and Cheryl Downey-Laskowitz in "Local Reaction: Watch It, Think about It, Discuss It, Urge Anti-Nuclear Groups," Orange County Register, 20 November 1983.

26. Howard Rosenberg, "Show of the Week," Los Angeles Times, 20 November 1983, TV Guide.

6. From the "Evil Empire" to *Glasnost*

1. Quoted in "Soviets Stewing about U.S. Films," Associated Press (AP), 10 February 1986.

2. Quoted in "Seeing Red," *USA Today*, 20 January 1986.

3. "Notes and Comment," *New Yorker*, 21 August 1989, 23.

4. Jack Garner, "America as seen on screen: Hollywood film festival starts today in Moscow," Gannett News Service (GNS), 19 February 1988.

5. Alexander Cockburn, "James Bond at 25," *American Film* (July/August 1987): 31.

6. J. Hoberman, "The Fascist Guns in the West," *American Film* (March 1986): 48.

7. Cameron Stauth, "Requiem for a Heavyweight," *American Film* (January 1990): 24.

8. Quoted by Peter Rainer, "Mixed Messages," *American Film* (March 1986): 48.

9. "Rocky will battle Russian in fourth of movie series," Associated Press (24 November 1986).

10. Jack Kroll, "Blood, Sweat and Cheers," *Newsweek*, 3 June 1985.

11. Jack Kroll, "Socking It to the Russians," *Newsweek*, 9 December 1985.

12. David Ansen, "Turncoats in Suburbia," *Newsweek*, 4 February 1985.

13. This reading of *Moonlighting* is heavily indebted to Donald Seybold's notes for that film's screening in the Cinema Now film series at Purdue University, 30 November 1984.

14. Pauline Kael, "Circus," *New Yorker*, 16 April 1984, 142.

15. Ivor Davis, "From Poland, Joanna Pacula stroll through 'Gorky Park,'" *New York Times*, 16 December 1983.

16. David Ansen, "Hoofing It to Freedom," *Newsweek*, 18 November 1985, 94.

17. Pauline Kael, "Straightjackets," *New Yorker*, 18 November 1985, 153.

18. Quoted by Peter Rainer in "Mixed Messages," *American Film* (March 1986): 48.

19. Mike Clark, "The fun sets quickly on 'White Nights,'" *USA Today*, 22 November 1985.

7. The Feminist Farm Crisis and Other Neoconservative Feminist Texts

1. W. P. Kinsella, *Shoeless Joe* (Boston: Houghton, Mifflin, 1982), 193.

2. Quoted by Jack Curry in "Old Glory Is Season's Hottest Star," *USA Today*, 7 December 1985.

3. Reported in *Newsweek*, 22 July 1984.

4. Reported by Lorrie Lynch, "'Reel' life plea for farmers, " *USA Today*, 7 May 1985.

5. Reported by Chuck Ruasch, "Celebrities aid problems down on farm," *USA Today*, 9 May 1985.

6. Quoted by Linda Gross, "On Golden River," Los Angeles Times, 13 November 1983.

7. Quoted by Bob McKelvey in "Men: Kings of the Box-Office," Knight-Ridder Newspapers, 22 January 1984.

8. Cf. Pat H. Broeske, "The Year of the Actress," Knight-Ridder Newspapers, 25 December 1983; William Wolf, "Women Grab Gutsy Fall Film Roles," Gannett News Service, 25 August 1985; Richard Corliss, "Calling Their Own Shots," *Time*, 24 March 1986; and Jack Kroll, "A Touch of Class," *Newsweek*, 23 June 1986.

9. Jack Curry, "For acting honors, a double standard," *USA Today*, 3 February 1986.

10. Sheila Benson, "Hollywood's New Trick Film Making," *Los Angeles Times*, 9 October 1983.

11. Pauline Kael, "The Comedy of Evil," *New Yorker*, 9 January 1989, 78.

12. Jack Mathews, "Engaging 'Mrs. Soffel': A tautly told love story," *USA Today*, 28 December 1984.

13. Jack Kroll, "Romance on the Run, *Newsweek*, 14 January 1985.

14. Linda R. Miller, "Victor of Circumstances," *American Film* (October 1988): 29.

15. Pauline Kael, "Trials," *New Yorker*, 28 November 1988, 103–8.

16. Lewis Beale, "Coming to 'Terms' and Hating It," *Los Angeles Times*, 17 December 1983.

17. Pauline Kael, "Retro Retro," *New Yorker*, 12 December 1983, 150–52.

18. David Ansen, "The Woman on the Quay," *Newsweek*, 21 September 1981.

19. See Palmer, *The Films of the Seventies: A Social History*, 144–49.

20. Pauline Kael, "The Comedy of Evil," *New Yorker*, 6 October 1986, 130.

21. Loree Rodkin, quoted by Cathleen McGuigan and Peter McAlevey, "Cher's Odyssey," *Newsweek*, 18 March 1985.

22. Pauline Kael, "Bodies," *New Yorker*, 6 October 1986, 130.

23. Pauline Kael, "Bird Thou Never Wirt," *New Yorker*, 10 October 1988, 122–23.

24. Quoted in "The Years of Living Splendidly," *Time*, 28 July 1986.

25. Pauline Kael, "Hair," *New Yorker*, 14 November 1983, 171–74.

8. The Yuppie Texts

1. Quoted by Leonard Klady in "Fiction in Advertising," *American Film* (February 1990): 10.

2. Quoted by Jefferson Graham in "Executives' moves will affect the films we see," *USA Today*, 25 September 1984.

3. "Survey: Students seek life in material world," *Associated Press*, 7 August 1986. The number of students characterizing themselves as political conservatives rose from 18 percent in 1970 to 21 percent in 1985, and those characterizing themselves as liberals dropped from 37 percent in 1970 to 22 percent in 1985. The number listing "being very well off" as a top personal goal rose from 44 percent in 1965 to 71 percent in 1985. The number interested in "developing a meaningful philosophy of life" was 80 percent in 1967 and dropped to 43 percent in 1985. In 1966 14 percent of the students planned to major in business while 25 percent did in 1985.

4. Harry F. Waters, "Yuppie versus Muggie," *Newsweek*, 14 January 1985, 53.

5. See Palmer, *The Films of the Seventies: A Social History*, viii and 78–82.

6. Pauline Kael, "Vamps," *New Yorker* 4 May 1987, 132.

7. Pauline Kael, "White and Grey," *New Yorker*, 16 January 1986, 105.

8. Pauline Kael, "Marriages," *New Yorker*, 20 February 1989, 96.

9. Jack Kroll, "Hollywood's Lost Lambkins," *Newsweek*, 1 July 1985, 55.

10. David Ansen, "Where Has All the Passion Gone?" *Newsweek*, 28 July 1986, 70.

9. Film in the Holograph of New History

1. Michael Stragow, "Gross Projections," *Mother Jones*, January 1990, 23–24.

2. Quoted by David Ansen with Joseph Harmes, "Oh What an Ugly War," *Newsweek*, 9 September 1985, 89.

3. Graeme Turner, *Film as Social Practice*, London and New York: Routledge, 1988, xiv–xv.

4. Dominick LaCapra, *History and Criticism* (Ithaca: Cornell University Press, 1985), 25.

5. F. Scott Fitzgerald, *The Last Tycoon* (New York: Charles Scribner's Sons, 1941), chap. 5.

Index

About Last Night, 301, 302
Accused, 255, 259–60, 286
Achille Lauro, 116, 121. *See also* Terrorism
After Hours, 298–99
Against All Odds, 258–59
Agnes of God, 261
"Airhawk," 64, 66
Alamo Bay, xiii, 67, 105–8, 229
Alas, Babylon, 180
Alien, 185–86, 272
Alien Nation, 309
Aliens, 185–86, 272, 275
Allen, Henry, 27
Allen, Woody, 278, 285
All the President's Men, 14, 187
Altman, Robert, 56, 71, 248, 272
Amadeus, 274
Amateur, The, 120
American Graffiti, 24, 200
Amerika, 208
Anderson Tapes, The, 227
Angel, 256
Ansen, David, 230, 267, 303, 321n, 322n, 323n
Antonioni, Michaelangelo, 133–34
Apartheid, 9, 109
Apocalypse Now, xiii, 9, 16, 18, 21–23, 25, 28, 33, 36, 37, 41, 50, 58, 61, 78, 80, 99, 103–4, 109–10, 316n. *See also* Coppola, Francis
Arafat, Yassir, 116
Armstrong, Gillian, 255, 258
At Close Range, 309
Atlantic City, xiii, 256, 272
Atomic Cafe, The, 183
Attenborough, Sir Richard, 9
Auster, Albert, 315n
Avenging Angel, 256

Baader-Meinhof Gang, 114
Babenco, Hector, 141, 144
Baby Boom, 178, 281, 305
Back to the Future, 13, 185
Baker, Mark, 315n
Barry Lyndon, 37
Bataan, 104
Batteries Not Included, 14
Bayles, Martha, 96, 318n
Beaches, 278
Beale, Lewis, 322n
Beatty, Warren, 237
Beidler, Philip, 317
Bellisario, Don, 66
Benson, Sheila, 256, 321n, 322n
Benton, Robert, 249
Bernstein, Richard, 137, 320n
Best Little Whorehouse in Texas, The, 256
Betrayed, 11, 103, 106, 109, 272, 309. *See also* Racism
Beverly Hills Cop, ix, 132, 291, 293
Beyond the Limit, 141–44, 146, 148
Bhopal, India, xiv
Biden, Joseph, 155
Big Business, 305
Big Chill, The, 283–85, 289, 293
Big Clock, The, 226
Big Red One, The, 21
Birdy, 61, 66–67, 71–75, 79, 83–84, 87, 104
Birth of a Nation, 105
Black Sunday, 63, 120
Black Widow, 255, 272
Blauner, Peter, 315n
Blaze, 274
Blood Simple, 309
Blow-Out, 134
Blow-Up, 133–34, 241
Blue Velvet, 111, 226, 309

Bodey, Donald, 16
Body Heat, 257, 309
Bogdanovich, Peter, 56, 112
Bolero, 257
Bono, Sonny, 272
Book of Daniel, The, 191
Boorman, John, 186
Border, The, 155–56
Borderline, 155
Born on the Fourth of July, viii, 22, 210, 308
Borsten, Joan, 319n
Boy and His Dog, A, 203–4
Boyle, Peter, 8, 314n
Boys in Company C, The, 21–22, 39, 50, 103
Brazil, 150, 168, 239, 240
Breakfast Club, The, 294
Brewster McCloud, 71
Brewster's Millions, 292
Bridge Too Far, A, 7
Bright Lights, Big City, 175, 282–83, 285, 289. *See also* Yuppies
Bringing Up Baby, 73
Broadcast News, 286
Broadway Danny Rose, 285
Broeske, Pat H., 322n
Bronson, Charles, 260
Brooks, Albert, 298
Brothers Karamazov, The, 234
Brown, Robert K., 62
Bull Durham, 179, 272
'*burbs, The*, 177, 296–97
Burglar, 280
Burkett, Michael, 187, 320n
Burn, 147
Bush, George, xi, 182

"Call to Glory," 64
Cameron, James, 185
Camus, Albert, 48, 262
Cano, Larry, 186
Canticle for Liebowitz, A, 180
Capricorn One, 202
Caputo, Philip, 16, 21, 31–32, 39, 43, 316n. *See also Rumor of War, A*
Carter, Jimmy, 115
Casablanca, 80
Casualties of War, 165

Catch-22, 71
Caulfield, Deborah, 321n
Cawley, Leo, 98, 104, 318n
Cease Fire, 25, 61, 66, 71, 75, 77, 104
Chances Are, 296
Chariots of Fire, xiii, xiv, 274
Chartoff, Robert, 218
Cher, 255, 272
Chernobyl, xiv, 179–80, 183, 207
"China Beach," 37, 64
China Syndrome, The, 80, 179, 188, 255
Chinatown, 31, 80–81, 85, 160, 162, 269, 316n
CIA, 120, 129, 134, 139, 140, 149, 159, 222, 225–26, 229–32, 244
Cimino, Michael, 108
Cjopra, Joyce, 255
Clark, Mike, 99, 313n, 322n
Clayburgh, Jill, 181
Close, Glenn, 255, 265
Close Encounters of the Third Kind, 296
Coal Miner's Daughter, 248, 276
Cockburn, Alexander, 209, 320n, 321n
Coelho, Tony, 248
Collins, Monica, 319n
Color of Money, The, 293–94
Color Purple, The, 11
Colors, 11, 158, 162–64, 169
Come Back to the Five & Dime, Jimmy Dean, Jimmy Dean 272
Coming Home 12, 16, 18, 20, 22, 25, 61–64, 103, 109, 254
Conan the Barbarian, 98, 210
Conrad, Joseph, 25, 32–33, 57, 78, 84, 128, 186, 318n. See also *Heart of Darkness*; *Secret Agent, The*
Conversation, The, 134
Coolidge, Martha, 255
Cooper, Marc, 12, 314n
Coppola, Francis, xiii, 23, 28, 52–55, 78, 80, 103, 111, 120, 134, 160, 185, 316n
Corliss, Richard, 322n
Corman, Roger, 203
Costa-Gavras, 11, 106, 138, 141, 187
Cotton Club, The, xiii
Couch Trip, The, 296

Country, ii, xiv, 247–54, 273
Cox, Alex, 132, 147
Crane, Stephen, 21
Crazy People, 281
Crime and Punishment 215
Crimes and Misdemeanors, 285
Criminal Law, 260
Cronauer, Adrian, 55–56
Cross Creek, 254, 277
Cruise, Tom, 182
Cry Freedom, 9, 274, 309
Cry in the Dark, A, 255, 261–62, 273
Curry, Jack, 219, 319n, 322n
Cutter's Way, 66, 75–79, 83–84, 87, 104

Dad, 281
Damnation Alley, 179
Dance with a Stranger, 262
Dangerous Liaisons, 257–58
Daniel, 191
Darby's Rangers, 21, 153
Daschle, Thomas, 248
Davies, Terence, 8, 9, 314n
Davis, Ivor, 321n
Davis, Thulani, 314n
Day After, The, 11, 180, 182, 191–205. *See also* Nuclear war
Day of the Jackal, The, 121
Deadline, 126–28
Deal of the Century, 132, 191
Dear America: Letters Home from Vietnam, 19, 54
Death Wish, 203, 260
Deer Hunter, The, 16, 18, 22, 25, 37, 50, 61–66 passim, 102–4, 108–9, 255, 273
Deitch, Donna, 255
DeLillo, Don, 180–81, 320n
Delta Force, The, 130
Del Vecchio, John, 16, 19, 20, 25, 78. *See also 13th Valley, The*
Denby, David, 29, 315n, 316n
DePalma, Brian, 134, 158–60, 162
Dernier Combat, Le, 199
Desert Bloom, 190
Desperately Seeking Susan, 273
Détente, xi, xii, xiv, 8, 12, 206, 223, 228
Devil's Brigade, The, 21, 153

Diary of a Mad Housewife, 264
Die Hard, 118, 130–32
Dirty Dozen, The, 21, 153
Dispatches 1, 16, 20, 22, 24, 28, 31, 36, 43, 45, 55, 80, 134. *See also* Herr, Michael
Diva, xiii
Doctorow, E. L., 191
Dogs of War, The, 153–54
Dog Soldiers, 63
Dollmaker, The, 252
Dostoevsky, Feodor, 215, 234, 242
Do the Right Thing, 309
Down and Out in Beverly Hills 292–93
Downey-Laskowitz, Cheryl, 321n
Dr. Jekyll and Mr. Hyde, 282
Dr. No, 191, 209
Dr. Strangelove, 37, 179, 181
Dry White Season, A, 309
Dr. Zhivago, 237
Duiker, William, 18, 50, 315n, 317n, 318n
Duke, David, 11
Dune, 184–85
Dylan, Bob, 53

Eastwood, Clint, 260
Easy Rider, 298
Educating Rita, xiii, 256
Edwards, Mickey, 155
Einstein, Albert, 198
Eisenhower, Dwight, ix
Eleni, 274
Elephant Man, The, 112
Eliot, T. S., 190
El Norte, 156
Emerald Forest, The, 186
Empire of the Sun, The, 179
End Zone, 180–81
Engelmann, Larry, 23, 313n, 315n
Escape to New York, 205
E.T.: The Extra-Terrestrial, 14, 108, 172, 192, 209, 226, 228, 232–39, 296. *See also* Spielberg, Steven
Everything We Had, 19
Evil That Men Do, The, 130
Executioner's Song, The, 272
Extreme Prejudice, 156–57, 260

Fail-Safe, 179, 181
Falcon and the Snowman, The, 228–32
Falling in Love, 264, 273
Farber, Stephen, 182, 320n, 321n
FarmAid, 246, 254
Farm crisis, xii, xiv, 8, 11, 246–54, 305
Fatal Attraction, 264–65, 302–3
Fate of the Earth, The, 181, 183
Fat Man and Little Boy, 180, 264
Fearing, Kenneth, 226
Feitshans, Buzz, 210
Fellini, Fedorico, 147
Feminism, ix, 12, 173–74, 246–79
Ferris Bueller's Day Off, 297
Field, Sally, 273
Field of Dreams, 246, 253
Fields of Fire, 16
52 Pick-Up, 111
Figley, Charles, 66, 317n
Firefox, 25, 182, 213–17, 220
First Blood, 24, 61, 64, 66, 67–71, 73–75, 83–84, 86–87, 98, 104, 106. *See also* Rambo/*Rambo*
Fitzgerald, F. Scott, 309, 317n, 318n, 323n
Five Corners, 260
Flag for Sunrise, A, 132
Flashpoint 155–56
Fletch Lives, 183–84
FNG, 16
Fonda, Jane, 255
Ford, John, 104, 105, 128, 247, 249, 253
Ford, Tennessee Ernie, 188
For Keeps, 305
Formula, The, 118, 140, 156
Forster, E. M., 258
Forsyth, Frederick, 153, 223
Fort Apache, 90
Fort Apache, The Bronx, 256
Foster, Jodie, 260
Foucault, Michel, x
Fourth Protocol, The, 191, 223–25, 228
Fowles, John, 113, 123, 266
Frances, 273
Francis the Talking Mule, 203
Frank, Pat, 180
Frantic, 120

French Lieutenant's Woman, The, xiii, 254, 266–70. *See also* Fowles, John
Freud, Sigmund, 260
Friedel, Frank, 88, 318n
Friedkin, William, 291
Friedman, Thomas, 319n
Friendly Persuasion, 206
Friday the 13th, ix
Full Metal Jacket, 20, 25, 28, 30, 36, 37–56, 60, 80. *See also* Kubrick, Stanley

Gage, Nicholas, 274
Gaggi, Silvio, 317n
Gallipoli, 117
Gardens of Stone, 25, 52–56, 61, 111. *See also* Coppola, Francis
Garsch, Jack, 321n
Gandhi, xiii, 274
Gilliam, Terry, 150, 239
Gilliatt, Penelope, 38, 47, 316n
Gitlin, Todd, 1, 313n
Glasnost, 206, 207, 210, 223–25, 230, 232, 240
Godfather, The, 52, 159, 160, 271. *See also* Coppola, Francis
Godfather, Part II, The, 52, 120. *See also* Coppola, Francis
Going After Cacciato 16, 26, 60, 73, 81, 84, 85, 109. *See also* O'Brien, Tim
Good Morning, Vietnam, 25, 55–57
Good Mother, The, 261, 303–4
Gorbachev, Mikhail, 182, 199, 206–8, 210, 224, 225, 240
Gorillas in the Mist, 174, 273, 275–76
Gorky Park, 233, 237–39
Go Tell the Spartans, 16, 22, 35, 49, 53, 55, 61
Grant, Lee, 255
Grapes of Wrath, The, 247, 249, 251, 253
Great Gatsby, The, 81, 85, 117
Green Berets, The, 18, 56, 104, 132
Greenberg, James, x, 313n
Greene, Graham, 80, 87, 132, 142
Gremlins, 296, 309
Griffith, D. W., 105
Gritz, Bo, 66

Gross, Linda, 322n
Guevara, Che, 212
Gung Ho, 108

Hackford, Taylor, 241
Haid, Charles, 62
Halberstam, David, 27, 28, 62
Half Moon Street, 118, 127, 128
Halloween, ix, 226
Hamburger Hill, 20, 25, 37–38, 47–
    52, 55–56, 60, 70
Hamill, Pete, 87, 89, 319n
Hamlet, 78
Hampton, Christopher, 142
Hannah and Her Sisters, 278, 285
Haines, Randa, 255
Harmes, Joseph, 323n
Hasford, Gustav, 16, 21, 39, 43–45,
    316n. See also *Short Timers, The*
Hawks, Howard, 73
Hawn, Goldie, 271
Heartburn, 273, 302–3
Heart Like a Wheel, 277
Heart of Darkness, 25, 28, 33, 36, 57,
    78, 141–42. *See also* Conrad,
    Joseph
Heaven's Gate, xiii
Heckerling, Amy, 255
Hellman, Lillian, 254
Hellmann, John, 78, 317n
Herbert, Frank, 184
Heroes, 21, 22, 61, 63, 109
Herr, Michael, 1, 16, 20, 22, 24, 28,
    31, 36, 43–45, 55, 80, 134, 313n,
    316n, 317n, 319n, 320n. See also
    Dispatches
Hill Street Blues, 64
Hinckley, John, Jr., 260
*History of White People in America,
    The*, 293
Hitchcock, Alfred, 215, 257
Hitler, Adolph, 212
Hoberman, J., 38, 47, 50–51, 99,
    210, 316n, 317n, 318n, 321n
Hoffman, Tony, 281
Honeysuckle Rose, 263–64
Honorary Consul, The, 132, 142
Hotel New Hampshire, The, 295
Howard, Ron, 281
Hughes, S. F. D., 320n

Hume, Edward, 182
Hunt for Red October, The, 214
Hustler, The, 294
Huston, John, 141, 146–47

Iceman, 186
If You Love the Planet, 183
Immediate Family, 262, 306–7
Invasion USA, 129–30
IRA, 114
Iran-*contra*, 114, 157, 159, 229
Iran Hostage Crisis, 114–15, 121
Iron Eagle, 130, 213
Iron Eagle II, 214, 216, 218
Ironweed, 273
Irvin, John, 52
Irvine, Reed, 187, 320n
Ishtar, 132

Jarvie, Ian, 15, 314n
Jaws, xii, 8
Jenkins, Brian, 117
Jewel of the Nile, The, 298
Joel, Billy, ix
Johnson, Lyndon, 92, 100, 318n
Jolidon, L. A., 319n
Jones, L. Q., 203
Joyal, Paul, 117
Julia, 254
Just Another Secret, 224, 225

Kael, Pauline, 28, 47–48, 71, 80, 90,
    96, 104, 183, 190, 236, 257, 261,
    263, 271, 274, 275, 277, 293,
    315n, 316n, 317n, 318n, 320n,
    321n, 322n, 323n
Kanten, Anne, 248
Karate Kid, The, 108
K-9, 158
Kasden, Lawrence, 283, 306
Kauffman, Stanley, 34, 315n, 316n
Kaufman, Philip, 240
Kennedy, Harlan, 314n
Kennedy, John F., xi, 26, 32, 38, 58,
    100, 155, 159, 196
Kerouac, Jack, 69
Key Exchange, 302
KGB, 215–16, 222–28, 230–31, 233,
    235, 238–39, 243–44
Khomeini, Ayatollah, 116

Khrushchev, Nikita, 196
Killing Fields, The, 61, 67, 99–102, 133, 150–52
King, Martin Luther, Jr., 159
King's Row, 209
Kinsella, W. P., 246, 322n
Kiss of the Spider Woman, The, 141, 144–46, 148, 151
Klady, Leonard, 324n
Klute, 256
Koltnow, Barry, 195, 321n
Kramer vs. Kramer, 273, 281, 283, 303, 304, 306
Kroll, Jack, 218, 258, 318n, 321n, 322n, 323n
Kubrick, Stanley, 23, 37–39, 42, 45, 52, 80, 200
Kunetka, James, 180

LaCapra, Dominick, x, xiv, 3–7, 309, 313n, 314n, 323n
Laclos, Choderlos de, 257
Lahti, Christine, 271–72
Landis, John, 80
Lange, Jessica, 248, 255, 273
Langness, David, 321n
Last Chase, The, 205
Last Temptation of Christ, The, 11
Last Tycoon, The, 309
Lawrence, D. H., 271
Lawrence of Arabia, 274
"Leave It to Beaver," 297
LeCarre, John, 123, 126, 209, 223
Lee, Spike, 273
Legal Eagles, 272, 286
Leone, Sergio, 160, 162
Lester, Richard, 7, 314n
Lethal Weapon, ix, 19, 58, 67, 110–11, 309
Let's Get Harry, 156
Levantman, Seymour, 317n
Lewis, Andy and Dave, 256
Liaisons Dangereuses, Les, 257
Linfield, Susan, 316n
Little Drummer Girl, The, 122–29, 159
Little Nikita, 208, 226–28
Littman, Lynn, 191, 195
Lipstick, 260
Lockerbie, Scotland, 116, 121, 126

Longest Day, The, 7
Long Walk Home, The, 273
Look Who's Talking, 306
Lord Jim, 84. *See also* Conrad, Joseph
Lost in America, 298–99
Love Canal, 180
Lowry, Malcolm, 146–47
Lucas, George, 281
Ludlum, Robert, 227
Lumet, Sidney, 191
Lynch, David, 184

McAlevey, Peter, 322n
MacArthur, Douglas, 274
McCarthy, Joseph, ix, 191
McGovern, George, 92, 318n
McGuigan, Cathleen, 322n
McGuire, Barry, 179
Machiavelli, Niccolo, 257
McInerney, Jay, 282
McKelvey, Bob, 322n
MacLaine, Shirley, 255
Made in Heaven, 305
Mad Max, ix, 180, 202, 203. *See also Road Warrior, The*
Mad Max Beyond Thunderdome, 205
Magnum, Thomas, 64
"Magnum P.I.," 66
Magus, The, 113, 123
Malamud, Bernard, xi
Malle, Louis, xiii, 105, 229
Mamet, David, 301
Manhattan, 283
Manhattan Project, The, 180, 190–91
Mann, Michael, xiv
Marcus, Greil, 315n
Marie, 273, 275
Marx, Karl, 1, 78, 79, 138
Marx Brothers, The, 149
M*A*S*H*, 56, 71
Mask, 112, 272
Mastrosimone, William, 260
Mathews, Jack, xiii, 73, 258, 313n, 318n, 322n
May, Elaine, 255
Mazursky, Paul, 149, 233, 234
Mehren, Elizabeth, 319n
Melville, Herman, 316n
Mencken, H. L., 65
Metamovies, 145, 267

Metatheater, 123–26
Meyer, Nicholas, 195–96
"Miami Vice," 19, 64, 110, 157
Mike's Murder, 255, 272
Milagro Bean Field War, The, 253, 254
Milius, John, 22, 23, 211–12
Miller, George, 202, 203, 322n
Miller, Walter, Jr., 180
MI-6, 222, 224
Missing, 132, 141–43, 145, 148–51
Missing in Action, 22, 25, 94–96, 100, 102, 104
Missing in Action series, 61, 64, 66, 89, 94, 96
Missing in Action II, 95
Missing in Action III, 95, 166
Mississippi Burning, 9, 11, 103, 106, 109, 229, 309
Moby Dick, 28–29, 31, 78–79, 316n, 317n
Modine, Matthew, 38
Monaco, James, 8, 314n
Money Pit, The, 297, 305
Monkey Business, 73
Moonlighting, 205, 233, 239
Moon Over Parador, 149, 150
Moonraker, 191
Moonstruck, 272
Monaco, Paul, 315n
More American Graffiti, 24
Morrell, David, 67
Moscow on the Hudson, 233–40
"Mr. Ed," 203
Mr. Mom, 305
Mrs. Soffel, 258
"Munsters, The," 297
Murphy's Romance, 273
Myers, Thomas, xiv, 18, 36, 44, 78, 313n, 316n, 317n
Myth of Sisyphus, The, 48, 52, 194, 251

Naked Gun, The, 116
National Enquirer, 259, 283
National Lampoon's Christmas Vacation, The, 297
National Lampoon's European Vacation, The, 297
National Lampoon's Vacation, The, 297

NATO, 223, 232
Natural, The, xi
Network, 188, 264, 287
Never Cry Wolf, 274
Never Say Never Again, 191
New Historicism, x, xi, xiv, 1, 2, 3, 4, 10, 11, 13, 15, 107, 118, 119, 148, 149, 308, 309
New life, A, 296
Nichols, Mike, 186, 187, 190, 270
Nighthawks, 118, 121–22, 126, 128–30
Night in Heaven, A, 257
Night of the Comet, 199
Night Shift, 256
Nimoy, Leonard, 185
1984, 150, 239–40
9 to 5, 270, 271
Nixon, Richard, 100, 102, 115, 210, 229
No Man's Land, 290
Noriega, Manuel, 115, 157
Norma Rae, 255, 271, 273
Norris, Chuck, 22
North, Oliver, 91, 157, 225
Nothing in Common, 281
No Way Out, 171, 225, 226
Nuclear Age, The, 180
Nuclear war, xi, xii, xiv, 8, 11, 12, 179–205, 309

O'Brien, Tim, 16, 73, 81, 109, 112, 180, 181, 319n, 320n
Officer and a Gentleman, An, 272
Official Story, The, 133, 148–49
Off Limits, 19, 20, 25, 37, 51, 57–60
Once Upon a Time in America, 158, 160–62
Once Upon a Time in the Revolution (Duck You Sucker!), 162
Once Upon a Time in the West, 162
On the Beach, 179, 181, 194
On the Road, 69
Ophuls, Marcel, 196, 321n
Ordinary People, 304
Orwell, George, 150, 239
Osnos, Peter, 319n
Osterman Weekend, The, 226–27
Outlaw Josey Wales, The, 203
Out of Africa, 277–78
Overboard, 271

Package, The, 179, 191, 224–25, 228
Pakula, Alan J., 117, 256
Palmer, William J., 314n, 315n, 316n, 317n, 318n, 320n, 322n, 323n
Parenthood, 281
Passage to India, A, 309
Parker, Alan, 8, 9, 11, 73, 106, 229
Pastora, Eden ("Commander Zero"), 115
Patton, 274
Pechter, Edward, xiv, 313n
Peckinpah, Sam, 44, 147, 226, 227
Peggy Sue Got Married, 13, 185
Perfect, 257
Perot, H. Ross, 91
Personal Best, 256
Pfeiffer, Michelle, 255
Pillow Talk, 301
Pinter, Harold, 266, 267
Places in the Heart, xiv, 11, 247, 249, 252, 253, 273
Planes, Trains and Automobiles, 281
Planet of the Apes, 205
Platoon, xiii, xiv, 9, 20, 22, 25, 26–37, 38, 42, 45, 47–51, 54–57, 60, 64, 70, 78, 98, 136, 210, 288, 308, 315n, 316n. *See also* Stone, Oliver
Plenty, 273
PLO, 114, 116, 167
Poindexter, John, 225
Polanski, Roman, 316n
Polar Star, 209
Pollock, Sydney, 277
Poltergeist, 192, 193, 226, 296, 297
Popkin, Samuel, 19, 315n
Porky's, 200
Poseidon Adventure, The, 13
Powers, John, 319n
Presidio, The, 67, 110, 111–12
Pretty Woman, 256
"Price Is Right, The," 264
Prince, The, 257
Private Benjamin, 271
Prizzi's Honor, 294
Protocol, 271
Psycho, 257
Puig, Manuel, 144
Pumping Iron II: The Women, 257

Purple Rose of Cairo, The, 285
Puttnam, David, xiii, 8, 150, 314n, 320n

Quart, Leonard, 315n
Quiet American, The, 80, 87

Racism, ix, x, xii, 9, 11, 12, 18, 50–52, 62, 67, 102, 103–9
Radio Days, 285
Rafsanjani, Hashemi, 116
Ragtime, xiii, 103, 309
Rainer, Peter, 321n
Raising Arizona, 305
Rambo/*Rambo*, ix, 22, 62, 63, 66, 67–71, 77, 91, 112, 182, 210, 218, 247, 272. *See also First Blood*
Rambo II, 18, 23, 25, 38, 50, 61, 62, 64, 65, 66, 89, 90, 93, 94, 95, 96–99, 102, 104, 108, 109, 156, 206, 208, 210
Rambo III, 23, 24, 210, 213–15
Randall, Steve, xiii, 63
Rand Corporation, 117
Reagan, Ronald, ix, x, xi, xiii, xiv, 8, 9, 10, 11, 12, 16, 21, 82, 88, 89, 90, 91, 92, 96, 99, 108, 109, 113, 115, 138, 139, 159, 181, 182, 183, 185, 206, 207, 208, 209, 210, 212, 213, 214, 215, 218, 228, 229, 241, 242, 247, 248, 249, 254, 260, 280, 308
Real Genius, 191
Red Badge of Courage, The, 21
Red Brigades, 114, 126
Red Dawn, 208, 210, 211–13, 214, 215
Redford, Robert, 253
Red Heat, 158, 208, 236–38
Reds, 237
Reich, Robert, 247
Remo Williams: The Adventure Begins, 108
Return of the Jedi, The, 183
Rhetoric, xiv, 41–46, 92, 118–19, 121, 124, 131, 132, 136, 139, 140, 141, 164, 206, 207, 208, 209, 221, 222, 232, 240, 245, 255, 289
Rice, Donna, 225
Rich and Famous, 278

Right Stuff, The, 182, 218
Risky Business, 200, 256, 297
Ritchie, Michael, 296
River, The, xiv, 11, 247, 249, 252, 253, 273
Road Warrior, The, 204, 205
Robocop, 14, 158, 170
Rocky, ix, 247
Rocky IV, 206, 208, 209, 214, 218–222, 224, 245
Rodkin, Loree, 322n
Rogers, Sharon, 116
Rolling Stones, The, 132
Rolling Thunder, 20, 22, 61, 63, 110
Rollover, 117, 118, 122, 127, 128, 129, 281
Romancing the Stone, 150, 257, 297
Room with a View, A, xiii, 258
Roosevelt, Teddy, 211, 212
Rosenberg, Howard, 321n
Rosenberg, Julius and Ethel, 191
Rossen, Robert, 294
Roxanne, 283
Ruasch, Chuck, 322n
Rudford, Michael, 239
Rumor of War, A, 16, 21, 31, 39, 43. See also Caputo, Philip
Runnels, Jim, 320n
Running on Empty, 226, 272
Rush, Richard, xiv, 80
Rushdie, Salman, 116
Russia House, The, 209
Russians Are Coming, The Russians Are Coming, The, 232, 236
Russkies, 172, 208, 233
Rust, Matthias, 214
Ruthless People, 293

St. Elmo's Fire, 301, 302
Saint Jack, 56
Salinas, Viafara, 155
Salvador, 133, 137–41, 144–46, 148–51, 288, 308. See also Stone, Oliver
Sands of Iwo Jima, The, 21, 43, 44
Santoli, Al, 19, 315n
Sarandon, Susan, 255, 272
Sarris, Andrew, 104
Satanic Verses, The, 116
Say Anything, 294

Scarface, 157–60, 161, 162
Schell, Jonathan, ix, 181, 183
Schepisi, Fred, 186, 262
Schickel, Richard, 96, 320n
Schiffer, Michael, 320n
Schlesinger, John, 228, 230
Scorcese, Martin, 11, 63, 298
Scott, Ridley, 185
Secret Agent, The, 128
Secret of My Success, The, 281, 289, 290, 291, 295
Seidleman, Susan, 255
Sequels, ix, x, xii, 218, 219, 256, 260, 297
Sergeant York, 21
Sexual Perversity in Chicago, 301
Seybold, Donald, 321n
Shakedown, 67
Sharky's Machine, 256
She-Devil, 273, 295
Shelton, Mike, 167
She's Gotta Have It, 273, 274
She's Having A Baby, 305
Shining, The, 37
Shoeless Joe, 246, 253
Short Circuit, 14
Short Timers, The, 16, 21, 39, 43. See also Hasford, Gustav
Silent Scream, The, 11
Silkwood, xiv, 114, 180, 184, 186–90, 199, 205, 254, 255, 271, 272, 273
Silver, Joan Micklin, 255
Simon and Simon, 64
Singin' in the Rain, 8
Situation, The, 150
Six Characters in Search of an Author, 125
Sixteen Candles, 297
Skolimowski, Jersey, 233
Smith, Clark, 88, 318n
Smith, Gavin, 9, 314n
Smith, Julian, 24, 318n
Smith, Martin Cruz, 209
Smokey and the Bandit, 150
Soldier's Story, A, 103, 309
Some Kind of Hero, 24, 25, 50, 61, 64, 66, 71, 73–75, 83, 84, 104, 256
Someone to Watch Over Me, 291, 293
Somewhere in Time, 184

Sons and Lovers, 271
Sophie's Choice, 255, 273
Spacek, Sissy, 252, 273
Spielberg, Steven, 14, 129, 179, 192, 193, 209, 228, 232, 233, 281, 296
Spies Like Us, 228
Splash, 273
Spottiswoode, Roger, 133, 137–38
Stahr, Jerrold, 23, 315n
Stallone, Sylvester, x, 21, 96, 206, 210, 218
Stand-up, 273
Star 80, 256
Star Trek, 121, 122, 130
Star Trek IV: The Voyage Home, 13, 184, 185, 186
Star Wars, ix, 14, 28, 183, 184
Stauth, Cameron, 321n
Steel Magnolias, 173, 278
Steinbeck, John, 251
Still of the Night, The, 255
Stone, Oliver, 11, 23, 26, 31, 35, 42, 78, 136, 137, 138, 159, 160, 288, 308, 315n, 316n
Stone, Robert, 63, 132
Stragow, Michael, 323n
Stranger, The, 241, 262
Straw Dogs, 203
Streep, Meryl, 187, 255, 272, 273, 320n
Street Smart, 256, 286
Streisand, Barbra, 255, 266
Strieber, Whitley, 180
Stunt Man, The, xiv, 24, 25, 61, 66, 67, 75, 80–87, 104
Sudden Impact, 260
Superman, ix
Suspect, 272, 286
Sweet Dreams, 273, 276, 277
Swing Shift, 271
Switching Channels, 257, 286

Talk Radio, 288, 308. *See also* Stone, Oliver
Target, 120
Tarzan the Ape Man, 257
Taugher, Mary, 321n
Taxi Driver, 20, 22, 61, 63, 65, 73, 110, 260
Taylor, Clark, 181, 320n

Taylor, William, 187
10, 257
Terminator, The, 13, 14, 184, 186
Terms of Endearment, 262, 263, 272, 278
Terrorism, xi, xii, xiv, 8, 12, 14, 114–64, 167–70, 218, 309
Terry, Wallace, 315n
Testament, xiv, 180, 188, 191–94, 197–205, 226, 254
Textuality, 3, 6, 7, 9, 10, 12, 13, 15, 16, 17–20, 21, 23, 26, 60, 67, 68, 87, 93, 100, 105, 113, 119–21, 125, 133, 146, 153, 155, 156, 160, 163, 164, 183, 184, 187, 209, 210, 228, 231, 244, 247, 265, 281–82, 291, 309
Time After Time, 184
They Died With Their Boots On, 90
Thief, xiv
13th Valley, The, 16, 19, 20, 25, 78
"thirtysomething," 306
Thomas, Kevin, 320n
Threads, 199
Three Men and a Baby, 305, 306
Three Mile Island, 179, 180
3 Women, 248
Thunderball, 191
Tocqueville, Alexis de, 105
To Hell and Back, 21
To Live and Die in L.A., 19, 111, 291
Tootsie, 149, 180, 254, 266, 277
Top Gun, 182, 184, 207, 213, 214, 216–17, 220
Tour of Duty, 37, 64
Towering Inferno, The, 14, 130
Trading Places, 256, 293
Trainor, Gen. Bernard E., 27
"Trapper John, M.D.," 64
Troop Beverly Hills, 176, 292–93
True Believer, 300, 307
Turner, Graeme, xi, 309, 313n, 323n
Turner, Kathleen, 255
Turning Point, The, 254
Tutu, Archbishop Desmond, 154
Twice in a Lifetime, 264
Twilight's Last Gleaming, 120, 179
Twilight Zone: The Movie, The, 24, 80
Two for the Road, 301

Two-Minute Warning, 120
2001: A Space Odyssey, 200

Unbearable Lightness of Being, The, 135, 240–41
Uncommon Valor, 22, 25, 61, 64, 66, 89, 90–96, 99, 102, 104, 156, 210
Under Fire, 133, 134, 138, 139, 141, 144, 145, 148, 149, 150, 153, 241
Under the Volcano, 132, 133–36, 141, 145, 146–47
Unmarried Woman, An, 254
Untouchables, The, 158
Urban Cowboy, 272, 281
USS Vincennes, 116

Vanderbilt, Cornelius, 147
Vietnam, ix, xiv, 7, 12, 114
Vietnam veterans on television, 64, 109
Vietnam War, xi, xii, xiii, 9, 10, 13, 15, 16–113, 132, 137, 138, 141, 142, 144, 147, 157, 158, 160, 162, 165, 166, 182, 186, 202, 206, 212, 214, 243, 249, 288, 297, 305, 308, 309, 314n, 316n

Wade, Kevin, 270
Walker, 147, 271, 274
Walker, John, 225
Walker, William, 132, 147
Wall Street, 114, 281, 283, 285–90, 291, 292, 294, 295, 304, 307, 308. *See also* Stone, Oliver
War Day, 180
War Game, The, 180
War Games, 14, 180, 191, 199–202, 215, 232
War of the Roses, The, 278–79, 293, 294, 295
Watergate, 12, 13, 14, 99, 114, 115, 160, 162
Waters, Harry F., 281, 323n
Wayne, John, 18, 43, 44, 57, 73, 104, 128
Way We Were, The, 301

Weaver, Sigourney, 255, 272
Webb, James, 16
Westmoreland, William, 27
West Side Story, 162
Wexler, Haskell, 7, 314n
Wheeler, John, 65
When Harry Met Sally, 281, 300–301
White, Hayden, x, 1–7, 13, 148, 313n, 314n
White Nights, 208, 209, 215, 241–45
Who Framed Roger Rabbit? 309
Who'll Stop the Rain, 20, 22, 61, 63, 109, 110
Wick, Charles Z., 208
WIFE (Women Involved in Farm Economics), 248
Wild Bunch, The, 44, 157
Wild Geese, The, 153
Wild One, The, 203
Wilson, John P., 318n
Winger, Debra, 255, 272
Winter Kills, 14
Witches of Eastwick, The, 272
Witness, 309
Wodka, Steve, 187
Wolf, William, 322n
Wood, Robin, 315n
Woods, James, x
Working Girl, 258, 270–71, 289
World, the Flesh and the Devil, The, 179, 199
World War II, ix, xiv, 7, 39, 43, 129, 151, 207, 222
World War III, 180, 198, 203, 211, 212, 229
World War IV, 198, 203
Wuthering Heights, 276
Wyler, William, 206

Year of Living Dangerously, The, 133, 151–53
Year of the Dragon, 67, 108, 109
Yentl, 66
Young, John Sacret, 191, 195
Yuppies, x, xii, xiv, 7, 8, 12, 14, 175, 176, 177, 178, 280–307

William J. Palmer is a professor of English at Purdue University, where he teaches both fiction and film. He is the author of *The Fiction of John Fowles* and *The Films of the Seventies: A Social History* as well as numerous articles on Dickens, Richardson, Fowles, Hardy, Faulkner, Stendhal, Camus, and contemporary film. He is also a novelist whose *Detective and Mr. Dickens* was a Main Selection of the Mystery Guild, and an Alternate Selection of the Literary Guild and the Doubleday Book Club, and whose *Highwayman and Mr. Dickens* was an Alternate Selection of the Book-of-the-Month Club. He is presently completing a trilogy of comic novels about midwestern life.